Shush! Growing Up Jewish under Stalin

Shush!

Growing Up Jewish under Stalin

A MEMOIR

Emil Draitser

UNIVERSITY OF CALIFORNIA PRESS

BERKELEY   LOS ANGELES   LONDON

Excerpts of this book appeared, in somewhat different form, in *Partisan Review, North American Review, Michigan Quarterly Review,* and *Midstream*

University of California Press, one of the most distinguished university presses in the United States, enriches lives around the world by advancing scholarship in the humanities, social sciences, and natural sciences. Its activities are supported by the UC Press Foundation and by philanthropic contributions from individuals and institutions. For more information, visit www.ucpress.edu.

University of California Press
Berkeley and Los Angeles, California

University of California Press, Ltd.
London, England

Library of Congress Cataloging-in-Publication Data

Draitser, Emil, 1937–.
    Shush! : Growing up Jewish under Stalin, a memoir / Emil Draitser.
        p.   cm.
    Includes bibliographical references and index.
    ISBN: 978-0-520-25446-6 (cloth : alk. paper)
    1. Draitser, Emil, 1937—Childhood and youth.
2. Jews—Ukraine—Odesa—Biography.   3. Odesa
(Ukraine)—Biography.   I. Title.

    PG3549.D7Z46   2008
    305.892'404772092—dc22   2008003979
    [B]

Manufactured in the United States of America
17 16 15 14 13 12 11 10 09 08
10 9 8 7 6 5 4 3 2 1

This book is printed on Natures Book, which contains 50% postconsumer waste and meets the minimum requirements of ANSI/NISO Z 39.48–1992 (R 1997) *(Permanence of Paper).*

To the memory of my mother and father,
Soybel Bendersky and Abram Draitser

CONTENTS

Plates follow page 144.

ACKNOWLEDGMENTS

FIRST AND FOREMOST, I WANT TO THANK (alas, posthumously) my parents, Soybel Bendersky and Abram Draitser, who, quite early in my life, through their deeply expressed emotional attachment to things of the past, unknowingly helped me understand much later in my life that the past should never be discarded from our memory. For the past not only often bears on the present but also offers us glimpses of the future. After their death, not unlike many other children, I realized that I missed them much more than you would expect when parents pass away after living a long life: my mother in 1994, at age seventy-nine, and my father in 1999, at age eighty-nine.

In hindsight, however, I wish I had been more inquisitive and learned more details about their lives and the lives of my grandparents and great-grandparents. But, alas, as a Russian proverb goes, we are all "wise after the event," *zadnim umom krepki.* My only excuse is that, in our hard-working blue-collar family, there was hardly ever time for a leisurely gathering near a fireplace, complete with father smoking a pipe and mother knitting a sweater. To begin with, my father never smoked, my mother never knitted, and, during all my formative years, we lived in a communal apartment in which a fireplace was considered a bourgeois luxury. All the bits of information that eventually found their places in this book came from snippets of verbal exchanges between my parents and their close kin and family friends. As a rule, these exchanges were made on the go, while all involved were busy with a chore at hand.

Once I decided to write this book, to revive events of years long past, to avoid losing many important details, I spent many hours talking to the members of my extended family: my brother, Vladimir; my uncle Misha and my aunt Asya; as well as my cousins, first and second, and their spouses: Eva and Efim Ingerman; Yan and Natasha Tenster; Maya Khanis and her husband, Lev; Boris and Zhanna Bendersky; and the late Fira Kagan.

Talking to my adult children, Svetlana, who grew up in Russia, and Alinka and Max, raised in America, was also illuminating. During our talks, I've learned a great deal about myself that, as many other parents discover, does not necessarily coincide with my own view of me and my life. This boosted my efforts to present myself as objectively as is humanly possible. (To what extent I succeeded in this, of course, the reader is the final judge.) To the same end, conversations with my American relatives and dear friends, Charlotte and Edith Barr, who showered me and my family with their generous attention during our first, quite painful, stages of adaptation to life in a foreign land, helped me to better understand the way in which my personal story, set in quite different times and on quite different soil, has to be told to be as fully comprehended as possible by American readers.

Berta and Yasha Sklyansky, Jane Hamer, Dr. Gregory Massel, Zhenya Turovsky, Dr. Boris Gasparov, and Dr. Tatyana Novikova read some chapters of the manuscript and offered their feedback.

Nellie Peltsman, Boris Zamikhovsky, Mila and Sergei Rakhlin, Yevsey Tseitlin, and Dr. Jolanta (Jola) Kunicka took on themselves the tedious work of reading the whole manuscript line by line. I appreciate their valuable feedback regarding the content and shape of the manuscript.

During the first stages of the manuscript development, I greatly benefited from the editorial input of Kaleria Nikolaevna Ozerova. The supportive responses of my colleagues Dr. Toby Clyman, Dr. Sarah Blacher Cohen, and Dr. Gavriel Shapiro renewed my energy and confidence in pursuing my project to its end.

The cheers of fellow writers Lara Vapnyar, Boris Fishman, Jennie Staniloff-Redling, Solomon Volkov, Semyon Reznik, Dr. Ieguda Nir, the late Mariam Yuzefovsky, and the late David Westheimer, who read either the whole work or substantial portions of it, have been most encouraging.

At various points in my writing, most of the time without realizing it, just by the sheer sincerity and spontaneity of their responses to my story, my friends Martin Weiss, Selim Karady, Dr. Anthony Saidy, Dr. Gary Kern,

Lev Mak, Si Frumkin, Lida and Michael Feinstein, Tamara Chernyak, Dr. Jeremy Azrael, and Dr. Victor Dmitriev gave me their moral support and nurtured my confidence.

I also appreciate the efforts of Rebecca Gould and Bill Bly, who helped me to fine-tune my command of idiomatic English. In this respect, Dr. Benjamin Rifkin's expertise and enthusiasm for my undertaking were both most helpful and inspirational.

At various times, Dr. Robert Rothstein, Dr. Regina Grol, and Dr. Yitzhak Berger served as my consultants in regard to the transliteration of Yiddish phrases sprinkled all through the manuscript, which I recorded as I remember hearing them in my youth. Whatever mistakes might be found in the final text are, of course, my own responsibility.

Last but not least, I am blessed with the luck of having Stan Holwitz, the University of California Press acquisitions editor, read my book proposal, get excited about it, and eagerly see my work all the way to its printing stage. I also deeply appreciate the care and respect for my work shown by my editor, Suzanne Knott, and copy editor, Robin Whitaker, and am most grateful for their vigilant reading of my manuscript and many insightful suggestions. I'm also in debt to the helping hand that Randy Heyman has given to me at various stages of book production.

For various reasons, some names of real people described in this book have been altered.

NOTES ON LANGUAGES AND TRANSLATION

ALL YIDDISH WORDS in this text are rendered the way my aural memory holds them. In my family, the language was spoken in two different versions. My mother and all the relatives on her side spoke Yiddish during their youth in Uman', Ukraine. My father and all the relatives on his side were born and raised in Minsk and, therefore, spoke Yiddish with the northwestern accent (known as the Litvak accent). Also, some Yiddish words and expressions rendered here have meanings different from the ones found in current dictionaries. In this book, I adopted the YIVO standard of Yiddish transliteration. I transliterated Russian words according to the Library of Congress system for the Cyrillic alphabet. However, for some names, I have kept their traditional rendering in British-American literature. All translations of excerpts from Russian poetry, lyrics, and prose in this book are my own. Titles of films mentioned in the text are given in Russian transliteration followed by the titles under which they were released in the United States. The names of towns that belonged to the Russian Empire at the time in the narrative are given in their rendering in Russian at that time.

Prologue

ONLY NOW DO I BEGIN to understand the numbing of memory. It's when you push something shameful so deep down in yourself that you won't stumble on it. When asked why I left Russia some thirty years ago, I usually shrug. It seems obvious to me. I couldn't have explained it clearly to anyone. Maybe I could do it just in the most general terms. Only recently, little by little, carefully, as if stripping bloodstained bandages from a half-healed wound, have I begun to retrieve those deeply hidden emotions that go back to the early years of my life.

A small incident prodded me in that direction. Some ten years ago I was invited to speak at the State University of New York at Albany. Later, at lunch, the chair of the Russian Department, Professor Toby Clyman, told me her story. She had come to America from Poland as an eight-year-old Jewish girl. I told her about my life in my native city, Odessa, then in Kiev and in Moscow. Suddenly, she stopped me: "Do you realize that each time you pronounce the word *Jewish,* you lower your voice? Why? American Jews say, 'I'm Jewish,' calmly and clearly, without looking around."

I winced. Indeed, she was right. By then I had been living in America for a long time, almost twenty years. Russia was left behind, beyond an ocean, beyond the mountains and fields of many countries. But I still spoke in half whispers about anything concerning matters Jewish.

Recently, while lecturing on twentieth-century Russian culture, I had to force myself to utter the last name of the director of outdoor theatrical shows in postrevolutionary Russia. Nikolai Nikolaevich Evreinov was an ethnic Russian, but his surname happens to be the equivalent of the English "Jewison." I was still apprehensive that I might hear chuckles following the mention of his name. Among my students were recent immigrants from Russia. Some might have chuckled. Or did it only seem to me that they might have?

My consciousness began to register that not only was I still ashamed of being Jewish, but I also simply couldn't recall a single moment in my life when the shame of it wasn't an intimate part of my existence.

Sometime later, another incident took place. I was interviewed for a project called the Oral History of East European Jews. This was a government-funded project that aimed to record the history of thousands of immigrants. One can find such tapes filed in libraries across the country—for example, in the New York public libraries. The interviewer, a young graduate student, asked me about my early life in the Soviet Union. When I began thinking, I suddenly felt a lump in my throat, and my eyes grew moist. I couldn't believe what was happening. After all, a grown man . . . But the interviewer reassured me by saying that I shouldn't feel bad about reliving the memories of bygone years. Many others who were interviewed for this program had the same reaction.

This incident made me realize that what I felt was typical for the whole generation of Russian Jews who grew up in the post-Holocaust years, during the period of late Stalinism. They also were forever affected by the era they had lived through. When and how did these experiences all begin? I felt a need to get to the very roots of that phenomenon, to return in my thoughts to the time when these feelings took root.

As a bathyscaphe submerges deeper and deeper into the ocean so that it can illuminate some ship wreckage, I began going back further and further into my past, left far behind in time and space. It seemed that I had forgotten all of it. But soon I realized that my forgetfulness was a defense mechanism, my way of resisting things buried deep inside my consciousness. I discovered that my impressions of my early years refused to disappear from my memory. They were removed from my sight only temporarily and packed away in the manner of index cards in library drawers. After one recollection, another one would come. And then another and another.

My memory turned out to be whimsical. Not for nothing is memory often compared with headlights of a car moving at night along the streets of a dimly lit town. Here and there, the beam randomly snatches objects out of the darkness—here a cat pressing itself against a fire hydrant, there a bakery shop with a dashingly twisted pretzel, there the bare shoulder of a beauty on a movie poster bubbled under the strikes of rain drops.

But soon I discovered that my recollections only seemed separate; something did connect them. While often refusing to line up chronologically, they coupled with one another in other ways. They all evoked in me the same emotional response. Sometimes, without asking my permission, an episode of my early years suddenly turned up next to another one a few decades later in order to return to a time even earlier than the initial one. Finally, I decided to give my memories free rein and follow them wherever they took me.

When I had just contemplated writing this book, I thought it would be about only what had startled me then, during that lunch at the campus of an American university. But when I began my work, I felt like expanding the main theme. I began recalling events and people who, in one way or another, influenced me. As a result, a picture of the life that had shaped my identity emerged. My book turned into a private testimony of a life in a country that had just emerged from a bloody war and was now choking on the fear and false optimism produced by its victory. I was forced to observe the rise of Russian chauvinism with the bewildered eyes of youth. Not unlike glass stressed to the limits, threatening to burst into zillions of fragments, the years during which I reached adulthood promised peril to everything alive.

Although the terrible war with Hitler was just over, preparations for a nuclear war with the West were under way. It was a time when the Soviet regime's ideological attacks became even harsher than before and were directed both outside and inside the country. A fierce Cold War between recent allies broke out. For the Soviet people, it was the time of official endorsement and cultivation of hate. Unleashed by the defeated enemy a decade earlier, the politics of hate were picked up and kept alive by one of the victors of the war against Nazi Germany, Joseph Stalin.

Soon after his victory against the world's most notorious anti-Semite, Stalin began anti-Semitic campaigns of his own. These campaigns of hate arrived in waves, as tsunamis come, threatening to destroy everything in their way. The first wave arrived under the guise of a "struggle with the Cosmopolitans," as many Soviet, primarily Jewish, intellectuals were labeled. They were accused of allegedly serving as the fifth column of the bourgeois West.

Then the Soviet Anti-Fascist Committee, composed of prominent figures of Jewish culture and created on Stalin's order during wartime to raise worldwide support for the Russian war efforts, was accused of selling out to the capitalist enemies. As a result, the most talented Russian Jewish poets, writers, and actors were arrested and shot in the basement of the KGB headquarters in Lubyanka.

Finally, the ominous frame-up of the "Doctors' Plot" was made public; the announcement paved the way for the mass persecution of Jews. Only Stalin's death saved them from another Holocaust.

Those perilous times formed the background of my suppressed existence. It was the time when, as a child and an adolescent, I used to hear the anxious whispers of my parents, who tried to protect me (and themselves) from trouble at every step in our lives. *Sha!* Shush! Be quiet! Still! Don't say your Jewish name in public. Shush! Don't speak a word of Yiddish. Shush! Don't you dare cry over your loved ones who perished during the Holocaust. The Soviet media keeps silent about it, and you should too. Shush! Don't listen to Israeli radio or the Voice of America or the BBC. Be inconspicuous. Don't express any interest in the history and culture of your people—or you'll be accused of "bourgeois nationalism" and severely punished. Shush!

In our family, there were two versions of the story of how my parents' paths crossed. According to my mother's version, it happened in Minsk, in the driveway of a building on Lenin Street; both of them ran there to hide from a sudden downpour. My mother wore a red raincoat. It attracted my father's attention; he discovered that the owner of the red raincoat was a pretty young woman.

According to my father's version, they ran into that fateful driveway when they heard a siren howl. The year was 1936, and the siren was part of an air raid drill. The country in which I had been destined to be born within a year after that meeting was preparing for war. Decades later, on the dusty shelves of my alma mater, the University of California at Los Angeles, I found posters that had hung on the streets of Soviet cities at that time. One of the posters, with a German soldier in a helmet, bears a three-line inscription in Russian:

FASCISM IS A DISASTER.
FASCISM IS TERROR.
FASCISM IS WAR.

On another one, a mustached blue-collar worker has a rifle leaning against his lathe: "IF WAR IS TOMORROW . . ."

My first recollections pick up a few years later.

PART ONE

ONE

How I Failed My Motherland

"YOU'RE MAKING TROUBLE! What's got into you?"

First barely audible, then more and more clearly, my mother's voice reaches me. I look back to my childhood, trying in that faraway fogginess to detect and, if I'm lucky, to solve the riddle of my life. After several unsuccessful attempts, gradually, like the decals of my childhood, the events of that faraway time begin to become faintly visible. We used to paste these little decals on the covers of our notebooks, their patterns half hidden under a layer of paper until we moistened them with our saliva and carefully, with our finger tips, rolled off bits of paper, one after another, until, bright as fresh paint, squirrels, hares, steamships, and crocodiles appeared.

For a long time, I can't figure out anything in these snatches of my childhood impressions. A few details flash in front of me. A round granite stand for public notices on the curbside at the corner of Gavan and Lanzheron streets is covered with scraps of old posters, left over from the Romanian and German occupation. Not too many events happen in a city that is trying to put its normal life back on track. I catch glimpses of the central City Garden, its stone lions holding balls under their paws with goalkeepers' confidence; the rotunda for small orchestra concerts, which were not yet revived; tall honeysuckle bushes in which I go to catch dragonflies. The streets give off the smell of cold ashes. The war is over, but there are many ruins. The Germans have demolished the front wing of our building.

We—Mama, Papa, and I—live in the back, in a small, two hundred-square-foot room. We are very fortunate: Mama managed to prove in court that this living space belonged to us before the war. The neighbors, those who occupied it under the Germans, had to give the room back to us. However, they secured the adjoining room, small and windowless, for themselves, the room in which Mama said I used to sleep before the war began.

We moved there from an empty grocery store, where we had slept on the floor after returning from evacuation. We moved back with our belongings—a suitcase, threadbare on one side, a bundle of old linens, a shoebox with three spoons and forks, a pocket knife, and an alarm clock—all piled on a wheelbarrow, pushed by an aging unshaved man my mama had hired. As we were walking along the street, we heard a loud cry behind our backs, "That's what we've lived to see! The reptiles have returned!"

Mama scowled. I looked back, toward the source of the cry. We were passing the driveway of some building on Richelieu Street. By the wrought-iron gate, their arms crossed, their faces heavy and unsmiling, stood two middle-aged women in kerchiefs. I couldn't understand what their words meant then. Why were they addressed to us? During the war, "reptiles" were what the boys called fascists. How could fascists have managed to return if the war had ended with Germany's unconditional and full capitulation? I had seen the victory parade on Red Square in the newsreels. The soldiers threw swastika banners on the steps of Lenin's Mausoleum, and Comrade Stalin himself reviewed the parade on the square's grandstand.

Finally, in the amateurish, poorly spliced film of my memory, a sound track produces Mama's voice: "You're making trouble! What's got into you?" Here it is. The first reproach. The first evidence of my withdrawal into myself, into my own inner life that is not given away to anyone. Gradually, frame by frame, it all comes to me—that hardest time of my life, the dread of days echoed in the nights' dreams.

The early fall of 1945. Less than a month after Japan capitulated. I am on my way to the first-grade class on the first day of the first postwar September. I am walking there with my mama, walking along the streets of my native town washed in the pale autumn sun.

The school, number 43, is located across from the main post office, on Gogol Street, overgrown with acacias. From our home on Deribas Street, 18, it's not far—four and a half blocks. Mama attempts to hold my hand. I pout and try to break away from her. Well, what's next? To hold onto

Mama's skirt? I'm already a big boy. Mama frowns. Along the roadway, raising dust, their motors roaring, trucks rush about. They carry bricks to the construction sites. They are rebuilding the ruined city. Why bother with pedestrians? Finally, Mama and I compromise. I let her hold my hand only when we cross the street. On our way to school, there are three crossings—on Lanzheron Street, at Bania Alley, and at the Sabaneev Bridge. I extend my hand reluctantly.

Children and their parents fill the schoolyard. Everybody is excited, making a racket, like seagulls on a jetty. Many first graders hold out bouquets of luxuriant red peonies, the favorite flower of Odessa. The color of the South!

They have placed me in the first-grade class "A." Mama is satisfied. *A* is the first letter of the alphabet. It means that her son is among the first, in the vanguard.

With its windows wide open onto the street, the classroom on the first floor smells of fresh black paint. The covers of all thirty-two desks are coated with it. The paint hasn't quite dried. If I keep my elbows on the same spot for a while, it sticks to my skin, leaving little archipelagos of black speckles. In secret, I attempt to dig them up with my nails, but I spread the paint over my skin even more.

We are told we should bring ink in an inkpot, in a little bag tied up with a string. (Later, a favorite prank would be to slip carbide bits into an inkpot. To find carbide wasn't difficult; welding was going on everywhere to fix the water pipes broken during the war. Ink would bubble, pour out, become pale, like bluish milk.) My briefcase is made from black oilcloth with the same design of raised diamonds that we had on our prewar portable record player.

High above the blackboard, almost at the ceiling, portraits of our leaders hang. From my desk in the first row, I raise my head to examine them. I already know some of them, the major ones, of course. Stalin, Molotov, Malenkov, Beria, and other members of the Politburo are slightly squinting, looking somewhere far above our heads. They live somewhere over there, far away, in the North, in Moscow, in the Kremlin, a thousand miles from my city. They are made of the same wonderous material as the heroes of the Russian fairy tales I've begun reading. The leaders are Russian epic heroes. Our enormous country rests on their shoulders. I believe that somewhere there, in the big world beyond the borders of my city, in the northern forests, Kashchey the Immortal lives, and Baba Yaga gallops, laughing wildly in her bronze mortar, and Vasilisa the Wise rides a gray wolf that rushes her to her Ivan Tsarevich; I see an immense country, powerful but benevolent, remarkable in every respect.

I am prepared for school. I can read, and not just by syllables. Anxious before the start of the school year, I've read many pages not only of the textbook but also of the reader *Rodnaia rech'* (Native Speech). Mama got it on the black market. For a long time, I didn't understand what "the black market" was. I know only two other markets in Odessa—the Novyi (New) and Privoz (Fresh Delivery). I also don't know yet that "to get" means "to buy with great difficulty." But I already know from *Native Speech* that I am fortunate. I happen to be born in the best country in the world—the biggest, the most beautiful, and the most just. Everybody in this country is fortunate too. Over the radio, I often hear the famous song from the film *Tsirk (Circus):*

> From Moscow to the far-off border districts,
> From the southern mountains to the northern seas,
> A man walks as the proud master
> Of his boundless native land.

And more:

> I don't know any other country,
> Where a man can breathe so freely.

I don't know about metaphors yet. I imagine the person from the song as a colossus who marches over the woods and fields and noisily inhales and exhales air from his giant lungs.

Our teacher's name is Galina Ivanovna. She speaks loudly to us, the way a commander in the movies addresses his soldiers before attacking the enemy. She's wearing a dark-blue dress with an embroidered bodice. The dress seems too tight on her. She pulls at it constantly under her arm. First, she makes us repeat her name, both the first and patronymic, syllable by syllable. Then, she takes a brand new class record in a brown paper cover from her desk. "As soon as you hear your name," she says, "you have to stand up and say clearly, 'Here.'"

Alexandrov, Burkin, Velikhov, Goriun, Doroshenko . . . I'm next in turn. Reading my last name, the teacher stumbles. She trips in the middle, raises her eyebrows in puzzlement, and makes an unhappy face. Though she is pronouncing all the names for the first time, she handles all the others easily. All the other surnames are normal. Only mine is the devil only knows what kind:

"Drrr . . . Dey . . . Drei . . . Drai . . . Drai-tser?"

I jump up and utter, "Here."

The class laughs. What kind of a last name is this? With a ferocious look, his eyes popping out, his bangs hanging down to the bridge of his nose, the boy next to me turns toward me and asks, "Your last name doesn't sound Russian. Who are you? A kike? That's who you are?"

I don't know what he is talking about, but, judging by the others' facial expressions, I understand that to be "a kike" is shameful. I freeze. I have never before heard this word. The roll call continues, but I am dumbfounded. I've waited for the beginning of my schooling—and here I am. I don't even know what to think, but I see that my classmates look back at me from time to time, their eyes mean. I can hardly wait for the class to end. Luckily, the teacher lets us go early on the first day. We sit there only till noon.

In the schoolyard, Mama waits for me. She is in the same—elated—mood as in the morning. After all, it's a milestone in her life. Her firstborn has spent his first day in school! She notices my head is low. She bends over me: "What's happened?"

I'm silent, my eyes cast down.

"Why don't you answer me?"

I'm silent.

She squats in front of me, straightens the collar of my shirt, tries to look in my eyes: "Well, what's the matter?"

I mumble something under my breath. I shift my eyes; now my nose is almost down against my chest.

"Can't you tell me what's happened?"

"No- . . . thing," with difficulty, I squeeze out of myself.

"Why are you upset?"

"I'm not."

"Why do you say you're not, when I see that you are?"

"I'm not. I'm not."

"You're making trouble!" Mama says. In punishment, she grabs my hand though we are still far from the street crossing. I groan and try to pull my palm out of her warm hand, but she restrains me. In my helplessness, no matter how hard I try to hold them back, tears roll out, stinging my eyes. Mama holds on to my hand. With all my strength, I try to break loose so that I can wipe off the tears with my fist. Mama reluctantly lets me go, again squats beside me. From her black purse with a little clicking clasp, she takes a perfumed white lace handkerchief. I turn away. That's a good one! To use a female handkerchief.

"Wait!" she says impatiently. "Let me wipe it off. Well, what's happened?"

Her face expresses concern. Her brow furrowed, she considers something, turns her head back to the school entrance.

"OK, I'll ask the teacher why you're crying."

Next to us, little twin boys are standing; they both wear the same gray pants and white shirts. They hold hands, their fingers interlocked. Their eyes are also wet. They've spent a long time today among unfamiliar adults and children, far from their mama. Craning their thin necks, they look for her in the crowd. They are frightened and hungry, and cry just because they're small.

It seems that this changes Mama's mind. She assumes that her son is simply a crybaby, though he wasn't known for this before. She is annoyed with me. I spoil her big day—the beginning of my school life.

At home a freshly cooked dinner awaits me—smelling wonderful, filling the whole apartment with all the spices of the world—borscht and sweet-and-sour meatballs with gravy. Mama knows my favorite dishes.

At first I refuse to eat. I am silent as before. I lie down on a windowsill and pretend to look down at our courtyard, where it is drizzling over the flagstones. A cat called Murka is running from one hallway entrance to another. In search of coins, lowering his head on his chest, Boska, our caretaker's son, makes his rounds over the yard, as always. I looked forward to the beginning of school so much! Now I feel bitter. Maybe I won't have to go back. I ask myself how I can manage not to go there anymore. Maybe I should get sick with something serious? But how to make it happen?

"Well, stop it! Come over and eat." Mama raps a spoon on the table. "Everything's getting cold. Stop your tricks!"

I'm somewhat afraid of Mama, especially when she talks that way. While I'm finally eating, she sits beside me.

"What a whiner I've got myself here. The only thing you want to do is to hang on to your mama's skirt. You're already a big boy! They go to the first grade at seven. And you're already eight and a half months older. You should show the little ones the way. And yet you're the same as they are." She's still disappointed with the look on my face. I haven't shared her first-day-of-school excitement.

I sleep poorly that night. I try to understand what has happened in school. Why was I laughed at for the first time in my life—almost eight years long now?

The next day it doesn't get better. I should get acquainted with my neighbors. I should let them know my name. I hear normal names from all sides—Kolya, Vanya, Petya, Seryozha. Now it's my turn.

I keep my mouth shut. My neighbor with the tousled hair nudges me. "What's your name?"

I'm silent.

"Hey, you! Are you deaf? What's your name?"

I'm silent.

"Why ask him?" A jolly voice comes from one of the desks in the last row. "If he's a Jew, it means he's little Abram."

I don't have time to understand why yesterday they called me "a kike" and today "a Jew"—another insult, I guess, somehow tied to the first. Before I can figure this out, the whole class begins to jump up and down, bang the desks with their fists, clap their hands in time to the song I've heard on the streets. I haven't understood it and, therefore, didn't pay attention to it before. (They sing all kinds of stuff on the streets!) The class hoots, mockingly dragging out vowels, distorting the *r* sounds in every line:

A little old hag with no hurry
Crossed the little street;
A cop's stopped her:
"Well, granny, you've broken the law,
You've broken the law,
You'd better pay your fine or else!"
"Oy, my God,
Please let me go home,
Today's my little Abram's day off.
I have a little bun for him,
A little piece of chicken,
A little piece of chicken,
And a little pie!"

So the old granny is funny, the very name Abram is funny. It can't be said without laughter. It's clear that you should utter this name only this way, with mockery and contempt. My last name, Draitser, has already made me a laughingstock. And now I've just learned that my patronymic, Abramovich, is no better. That is, my papa's name is Abram, nicknamed Abrasha, "little Abram." Both my uncles, my mama's brother and her sister's husband, are called Abram and Abrashe as well. From all sides I have solid

Abrams. And that nasty little song, which gives everybody so much joy, therefore, is about all of them. I'm dumbfounded by these discoveries.

"Well, so, what do they call you?" the neighbor persists.

I am wondering what to say. At home, for as long as I can remember, everybody has called me Milya. I don't quite like this nickname, because it sounds like the Russian *milyi*, "cute"; it's too delicate for a boy. Although I don't quite see what could be bad about it, I'm afraid the class won't like it as well. I keep my mouth shut.

The teacher notices my unwillingness to give the neighbor my name. She leans over the class register.

Here I suddenly recall that, on my birth certificate, when I visited the school with Mama to file my documents, I saw that my first name was somewhat unusual and terribly unattractive. Better to give him my nickname: Milya.

The neighbor wonders what kind of name this is.

For the umpteenth time, Galina Ivanovna adjusts the bodice of her dress and says, with a smirk on her face, "It's not good to deceive your classmates, Milya. What? Do they call you that at home?"

I'm silent.

She looks into the class register again.

"What? Do you want to say that the register's wrong?"

I feel myself blushing.

"Well, why don't you answer me?"

I'm silent. I feel the tears beginning.

"Andrei," Galina Ivanovna says loudly so that all the class hears, "this boy's name is Sa-mooh-eel."

"Mo-o-lya," my neighbor sustains his voice in jolly amazement. "Mo-o-lya, stop bugging me!"

Everybody laughs.

I remember—Moolya—that's what they called the funny character Samuil in the movie *Podkidysh (The Foundling)*. And the whole expression comes from that movie. But I'm not a foundling. I have a mother and a father.

"Mo-o-lya, Mo-o-lya!"

The neighbor even launches into a dance around me and begins to pinch me.

Why am I silent? Why don't I dare hit him in the face?

"Sa-mooh-eel," the neighbor says joyfully and at the same time with scorn, "What kind of a name is it? Ah, that means you *are* a kike after all?"

He stares at me. It's evident that, though he knows the word, he's never seen a living "kike," or maybe he has seen one, but that one was an adult, and he wouldn't have teased him. For all he knew, he could have got it in the neck.

"It's not good to talk that way," the teacher says. "You should say 'a Jew,' not 'a kike.' Children, in our country, according to our Stalin's Constitution, all nationalities are equal. The Russians, and the Ukrainians, and the Byelorussians, and the Georgians, and the Jews."

She is saying it, and I feel in my bones that she herself doesn't believe what she's saying. There is a stir in the class. The children at the back desks whisper to one another; the front ones are deliberating.

"Yes, yes," Galina Ivanovna goes on. "Even a member of our government, Lazar Moiseevich Kaganovich, our comrade Stalin's comrade-in-arms, is also a Jew."

"It can't be!" somebody from the last row blurts out. "All them Jews are cowards. During the war they all hid their asses in Tashkent."

My heart begins to pound. It's all true. I'm a base coward and the lowest traitor of my motherland. They're right! They're right all around.

After all, I too sat out the war in Tashkent.

Back then, in the autumn of 1945, a child, I had no idea what was behind my classmates' hallooing. The war was still giving off smoke in the hearts of those children who had grown up in it. Many of them were from the families that had chosen to stay on in Odessa, even with German troops advancing.

During the two and a half years of occupation, first by German troops, then by Romanian troops, the newspapers and lecturers—professors of Odessa institutions of higher learning—unleashed Nazi-inspired anti-Semitic propaganda. Posters proclaiming, "Destroy the Jews!" were pasted on the walls at every street corner.

Many of those who stayed behind seized the opportunity to occupy the apartments of the Jews who had been driven into the ghetto or had escaped the Nazis on foot and in horse carts, on cargo trains and boats, small and big. They looted Jewish belongings, acquired over a lifetime, on a massive scale. The authorities of the Romanian occupation opened up commission stores, and Jewish valuables left behind during the frantic escape—china sets, rare books, antique furniture—quickly filled up the store shelves and floors.

After the battle of Stalingrad, when it became clear that the Germans would lose the war, panic seized the city. Those who were hoarding any unsold loot hid it and reinforced the apartment doors with additional locks and bolts. When Jewish women and their children knocked on the doors of their prewar apartments, after having survived the internal exile, famine, illnesses, and long exhausting travel, their former neighbors, clenching their teeth and breathing heavily with unsuppressed hatred, roared from the other side, "Damn you! What dragged you here? Go back where you've come from. May you all go to hell!"

At times, determined to hold on at any cost to the seized rooms, which they had become used to during the war and now considered their own, the former neighbors reached for their axes. In despair, the refugees sought justice in the customary way of the time, by sending telegrams and letters to the Kremlin—to Comrade Stalin, to Comrade Kalinin, to General Voroshilov. Local courts had a hard time coping with the avalanche of claims from the homeless. Though, in these disputes, the Soviet law was on the side of families of front-line soldiers (and the overwhelming majority of the evacuated were from such families), it wasn't very easy to win a case in court. Ironically, the defendants bribed the local judges with the money recovered from the looting of the very same claimants.

As was the case with Mama and me, while the trial deliberations stretched for months on end, the returnees had to spend nights in empty buildings that had been shattered by the bombardments or in the attics and basements of the buildings surviving the war. Some families found refuge with their relatives, often huddling up in one room with them. There wasn't enough sleeping space for everyone. Some slept on the floors, some on stools and chairs thrown together, or on desks and tables. That was how my aunt Clara and her six-year-old daughter Eva lived in the apartment of my mother's cousin Dunya.

The wartime Nazi anti-Semitic propaganda infected the young as quickly as measles or chicken pox could. For a long time after the war ended, in the quiet corners of Odessa streets, in the remote alleys of the parks, in the secluded places among the ruins, gangs of youngsters hunted for Jewish kids, survivors of the Holocaust, and harassed and beat them up, often till they bled. My second cousin Yan Tentser was seven when he returned from Tashkent with his mother. As he approached his building, two adolescents threw chunks of dried-out clay at him, shouting, "You little kike!" They got him in his ear. He fell down and lost consciousness. Blood oozed from his ear. He became partly deaf for life. They also shot at my Jewish schoolmate Boris Zamikhovsky's brother with a slingshot, damaging his eye. So, as I realized much later, Mama insisted on escorting me to school because she knew that the reckless truck drivers were not the only ones she had to protect me from.

When Mama and I walked along the streets, I saw huge crosses drawn in chalk on the gates of many buildings.

"What's this for?" I asked.

"This is a sign that the building's been disinfected," Mama said, knowing that it was better to answer me right away. Otherwise I might wear her out with my questions: I was at the age of the incessant "whys." For me, a war child, the word *disinfecting* was familiar. Usually it meant that they steam your clothing to kill nits, the typhus carriers. I didn't ask any more questions, but Mama spoke in a muffled voice and somewhat strangely, with a bitter grin that seemed odd to me.

Only many years later did I learn the reason for Mama's strange look. The Romanian occupation powers drew the crosses on the gates of Odessa buildings. Our standard sappers' sign "CHECKED: NO MINES" still adorned the corners of every city block for a long time; in the same way, as a war memory, the chalk cross-marked the gates. It meant: the building is cleansed of Jews.

TWO

Fathers at War

"ALL JEWS ARE COWARDS. During the war, they hid in Tashkent." My schoolmates' words ring in my ears. This attack made a very lasting impression on me, probably because it was totally unexpected. There was no signal or warning sound of impending trouble. I already know of one warning sound—an air-raid siren, howling and piercing my head. Along the deserted predawn streets smelling of cooled dust, a man's monotonous voice resounds from loudspeakers on lampposts: "Citizens! Air-raid alert! Air-raid alert!" It sounds as if the announcer himself is sick of repeating the same thing several times a day.

My head rests on the sill of the window flung open to the summer, on a pillow somewhat damp with morning dew. With her bridal veil of hair let down for the night, Mama tugs at me. She takes me in her arms and presses me to herself. Her body, languid from sleep, radiates warmth. I am barely able to unglue my eyelids; according to Mama's stories, I was an awful sleepyhead in my childhood. She wraps me in a blanket, looking up again and again at the barely lit sky. From above, some loud banging reaches us.

Already on my mother's shoulder, I notice an airplane high in the sky. From below, a bunch of orange dotted lines are rushing; they crackle and catch up with one another.

Papa in his T-shirt is next to us. His face is pale. It seems that I see him then without his glasses for the first time. He squints, trying to find them on his nightstand. He finally grabs them and stretches his hand to a dish made of thin black cardboard on the wall. Inside the dish there is a flat board with two screws. Now a male voice, now a female one, and sometimes music emanates from the dish. I already know that this is a radio. Now a stern man's voice utters something, pausing after every word. I get chills up and down my spine from this voice, as if a mean fairy-tale wizard is uttering an awesome incantation. Something like *abracadabra:* "News from the Soviet Informburo!" (These were the official Soviet press releases.)

When my classmates made the accusation that all the Jews sat out the war far away from the front, especially in Tashkent, where many refugees were evacuated, I didn't respond right away that my father also fought in the war. Was it because, when the war broke out, my father put on not a soldier's uniform but overalls? And he held in his hands not the usual handgun but a special one, shooting not with bullets but with paint. Drafted into the army, a first-rate housepainter, he was immediately dispatched to the Repair Shops of the Second Air Force Army, set up at the outskirts of the city. After our fighter planes were hastily repaired, he gave them a fresh coat of paint and sent them back, ready to fly into the sky to fight the German bombers.

(As I would learn from my mother after the war, that draft into the Red Army was my father's third one. I was less than two years old when, in September 1939, a few weeks after Hitler had invaded Poland, Stalin moved his troops across its eastern border to claim the agreed part of the Polish territory. My father left his young wife and his firstborn child to guard some Polish warehouses. He returned a few months later, but soon he was drafted a second time, now to fight Finland, which Stalin decided to attack. My father had already boarded a train packed with other draftees heading north when an order came for demobilization: the Finns fought fiercely, put the Red Army to shame, and Stalin had to sign a peace treaty.)

Now my father was drafted a third time. He no longer slept at home, but, for a while, we saw each other every day. Odessa was under attack for a long time: for over two months Soviet troops defended the city. Early in the morning, Mama and I would go to Greek Square, a block away from our home, and board tram number 17. We rode for a long time, almost as long as when we had traveled to the beach before the war. We got off at some iron gates adorned with a five-pointed star. A sentry stood at the entrance. Mama went to a little glass house, the office where she was hired to work in inventory, and I headed toward two little huts of plywood fenced off with chicken wire, the daycare for the children of the many other civilian women employed at the Repair Shops.

As German troops got closer to the city, Papa's Repair Shops received orders to leave the city by railroad. First, Papa arranged tickets for Mama and me for the steamship *Lenin,* but, when that attempt at escape failed (about which, more detail later), they took Mama back as the Repair Shops' employee and allowed her and me to board the air force evacuation train. Together with the rest of the Red Army, the Repair Shops retreated first to the North Caucasus, then to Stalingrad. The train would make a leap backward in time, into the unoccupied territory. The Repair Shops hurriedly unloaded their equipment and people and quickly went back to fixing our war planes. Mama kept working at the Shops, and I stuck around her work place. Trying to occupy me with something useful, sometimes Mama handed me a rag and a piece of sandpaper to clean off bullets before they were loaded into plane machine guns. I still remember the smell of that lubricating grease on my fingers.

Mama persuaded the Repair Shops chief, a short man with the stripes of a major and a gray strand in his pitch black beard, to allow me to have lunch with my father on the assembly line. Shortly before midday, I raced out of the improvised kindergarten and headed toward the hangar where my father worked. I slipped through the heavy door covered in sheet metal and pressed myself close to the wall. I would see in front of me a MiG or a LaGG fighter, staring upward, patiently waiting to be made presentable, like a customer at a hairdresser's. As soon as its scabs of putty were covered over with turquoise paint, it was ready in an instant to throw itself against the German bombers.

I was all eyes as my father worked. Squinting (Papa's eyesight was getting worse, but he'd had neither the time nor the opportunity to get his glasses changed), he was moving sideways slowly along the fuselage, squeezing the trigger of a huge goitrous pistol. Instead of bullets, a cone of emerald paint whistled out in a fan. The nitrate paint smelled of melon pulp. In the difficult places under the taut little belly of the plane, my father knelt, wrinkling his nose with the effort to make out the gaps, and managed to fill them in with short spurts. Blue splashes settled on his eyeglasses, and he had no time to wipe them off. My father's eyes were speckled like a kitten's.

Two ladies in white robes and caps with reddish ringlets peeking out brought covered pots of borscht and pearl barley kasha. The lids had small holes in the middle, for steam. I sat down next to my father and the other assembly workers at a long narrow bench with wrenches, drills, and hammers, which were put on the floor during lunchtime. The thick smells of axle grease, machine oil, processed tin, and red-hot iron did not dampen my appetite. I would eat the borscht and barley straight out of the pot, just like a soldier, with an adult tin spoon that my father pulled out of the top of his boot. Although all I was doing was eating, for some reason I made Papa's comrades smile. From time to time, like Papa, they would manage to sneak little pieces of meat from their pots into mine.

A siren would often interrupt lunch, and someone would shout, "Frame!" Father would scoop me up under his arm, grasp the handles of his and my pots, and, together with everyone else, run to the trenches about a hundred meters from the hangar. I soon understood: "Frame" was the nickname of the reconnaissance Junkers with crossbeams on the wings and tail. It would take no more than ten minutes from their appearance in the sky to the coming of the Focke-Wulffs with bombs and machine gun fire. There in the trenches we would often finish lunch.

In Stalingrad, we parted with Papa. The war fortunes had changed, and, together with the front line, his Repair Shops moved westward. Mama and I headed for Tashkent, where Mama's sister, Clara, with her little daughter, Eva, wound up running from Odessa. I remember how Papa and I said good-bye to each other. On that night, the sky was thundering and flashing as from a distant rainstorm. I couldn't fall asleep for a long time. When I finally dozed off, Mama woke me up. Half awake, I sulked and was grumpy. My father took me in his arms. He was prickly. The cheek he pressed to me was prickly, his overcoat was prickly. He looked at me sternly and seriously through his round, horn-rimmed glasses. Finally he lowered me to the floor, headed for the door, muttered something, and crossed the threshold without looking back.

I saw my father again after the war was over, in June 1945. Together with his Repair Shops, he had reached Bucharest and Vienna. They awarded him medals "For the Defense of the Caucasus" and "For Victory over Fascist Germany." (Mama also was given these medals. Until their last day, both Papa and Mama saved these awards as mementos of the most trying times in their lives.)

Many others of my family also fought in the war. When the last grumbling of the cannons faded away, Uncle Abram, the father of my cousin Eva, came home, his arms and legs intact. He had served in the army as an artillery gun layer. Tall, with large facial features, he always looked at you inquisitively, because he saw poorly without his thick glasses. Yet he found German tanks all the same, finishing off the last of his targets in the outskirts of Berlin. With the medals on his chest tinkling, he bent down a bit when stepping into the basement where his wife, Clara, and daughter, Eva, lived after returning from evacuation.

He came in with another tall man, a Ukrainian gun loader; they had been inseparable throughout the whole war. The little girl with a huge bow in her hair huddled up against her mother and glowered at the strangers bursting into her home. For fun, the other man asked, "Well, girlie, which of us is your daddy?"

Perplexed, Eva rolled her big eyes, looking first at one giant man and then at the other. She didn't remember her father. She was only two years old when he had left for the war. From her mother's stories, she knew that her father wore glasses. That's why she approached the man with the glasses. She asked him cautiously, her nostrils inflating with excitement, "Are *you* my daddy?"

My second cousin Yan Tentser didn't remember his father, Itzchak, either. From the family stories, he knew only that, as a young man, his father had fought for the revolution in the First Cavalry Army led by the legendary General Budenny. Then he studied medicine, supporting himself as a stevedore in the Odessa port, and ultimately became a surgeon. A very good surgeon. Before the war, they wrote about his operations in the papers. In 1940, when Yan was born, his daddy was at the Finnish front. After the German attack, he immediately offered his services. They assigned him, an outstanding surgeon, to a rather quiet and well-equipped hospital for the upper-rank officers, colonels, and generals. He insisted on a frontline field hospital. Yan's mother received just a handful of his letters. He was captured when his field hospital was surrounded by German troops near the city of Sevastopol'; he was killed there.

Yan's uncle on his mother's side, Ilya Bronfman, also volunteered for the front and perished during the fierce Battle of Kursk. They handed Yan's grandmother the "killed in battle" notice on the threshold of their clay-walled hut on the outskirts of Tashkent. She collapsed, falling face down onto the dusty courtyard. She shrieked terribly, as if all her insides were yanked out at once. When her daughter, Yan's mother, came from work and found her mother prostrate on the ground, in a flash, she knew what had happened. Her face turned white so intensely that even her pupils whitened.

The husband of my mother's other cousin, Rosa, went through the whole war as an infantry private. An electrician before the war broke out, short

Naum went bald early and was never very successful in everyday life, but he was very fortunate that he returned from the war alive.

My second cousin, Froychik Greenberg, became the secretary of the Komsomol (Communist Youth League) at the age of sixteen. He took flying lessons at a training school for amateurs. In 1939, at the time of the great terror, he was imprisoned, tortured brutally, and, as was routine at that time, accused of spying for several foreign intelligence agencies. Then a miracle took place: they released him! During the war, as a military pilot, he flew deep into the occupied areas several times and dropped weaponry and foodstuffs to the Byelorussian partisans. He was recognized with awards and ultimately attended a reception in his honor at the Kremlin. I imagine that Comrade Stalin might have shaken his hand and said, "Many thanks, Comrade Froychik Greenberg." Five times Froychik flew into the German rear lines. Five times they had to change his plane after it had been riddled with German bullets. But the sixth time was his last: his plane was downed by enemy fire, and he perished.

Two other relatives of mine distinguished themselves equally well on the battlefield. In the heat of a fierce battle near the city of Velikie Luki, Abram Malyar single-handedly pulled our armored train from under heavy fire. Pinchas Rabinovich led the defense of a sector of Leningrad during the nine-hundred-day city siege. After the war, he studied at the celebrated Frunze Military Academy and wrote a book about his military experience. (Then, for the next twenty-five years, he served in the Far East Military District. Even though the military forced him to change at least his Jewish first name, Pinchas, to a Russian one, Pyotr, it helped only so much: though he carried out a general's duties until his retirement in the early 1970s, he was not promoted beyond the rank of colonel. Unlike during wartime, Jews were not to become generals anymore.)

There was also my aunt Asya's husband, "Ivan" Tabenkin. His real name was Isroel, but he became Ivan, thanks to the Germans. In the first months of the war, near the city of Gomel, in Byelorussia, he was surrounded and captured. It was getting dark; aiming their flashlights at the captured soldiers' faces, the Germans hurriedly divided the prisoners into two groups— "Ivans" and "Juden." They took the latter to a nearby ravine and shot them.

A young German über-lieutenant had glanced at Isroel's heavy chin and light-gray eyes and shouted: "Ivan!" But Isroel knew that, come the morning, they would check more thoroughly by forcing prisoners to drop their pants. That night, with the help of his buckle—in their haste, the Germans hadn't thought to take his belt away—he dug a ditch under the wire fence and slipped away to the Dnieper River. Near Gomel, where the river isn't too wide, he swam across to his own troops. A tank driver, he sloshed his machine through the mud of war till its last day. He was burned three times but survived and rolled his fourth tank onto the paving stones of a Berlin roadway. He was given awards for bravery several times.

Now, from the distance of more than half a century, recalling how the Jews were accused of cowardice during the war, I think of how much it would mean for me and other Jewish children to know how the Jews really did fight. Half a million Soviet Jews went to the battlefield; two hundred thousand of them never came home, giving up their lives in the struggle against the Nazis. The Jews fought heroically: over 170,000 of them were awarded orders and medals. About 150 Jewish fighters received the supreme military honor, Hero of the Soviet Union. Per hundred thousand in population, the total number of Jews awarded this honor was higher than that of any other nationality, including the most numerous ones—the Russians, Ukrainians, and Byelorussians.*

As children, we played air combat with models of Soviet fighters, handmade from wooden chips. We knew them all by heart, all those LaGGs and MiGs. We knew that a famous military pilot, Kozhedub, had brought down sixty-two Nazi pilots flying a LaGG plane. How much it would have meant for me, as well as other Jewish boys of my generation, if authorities had declared for all to hear that one of the designers of that LaGG, Semyon Alexeevich Lavochkin, was a Jew! How could we have known? His name sounds quite Russian. I wish we had known then that Lavochkin's patronymic (the middle name derived from a child's father's name), Alexeevich, wasn't his real patronymic. To improve his chances in life, his father, formerly a *melamed* in a *kheyder* (a teacher in a Jewish school), had changed his Jewish name to a Russian one—Alexei.

How could we children have known that the last letter of the MiG acronym honors one of its designers, Mikhail Gurevich, a Jew? The Jewish

*For a comprehensive survey of Jewish participation in the Great Patriotic War (1941–45), see Mark Shteinberg, *Evrei v voinakh tysiacheletii* (Jews in the wars through millennia) (Moscow and Jerusalem: Mosty kul'tury-Gesharim, 2005), 263–430. For an estimate of decorated Jewish fighters and war heroes, see Fedor Sverdlov, *Entsiklopediia evreiskogo geroizma* (Encyclopedia of Jewish heroism) (Moscow: Dograf, 2002), 11–12.

origins of quite a few war heroes was hushed up. Back in August 1941, less than two months after the Germans' invasion of the USSR, while the Nazis were still bragging to the whole world that they had destroyed the Soviet Air Force, a Jewish Hero of the Soviet Union, Captain Mikhail Plotkin, together with other Soviet pilots, bombed Berlin, to prove that our air force had survived and would continue to fight. Another Jewish war hero, Mark Gallai, brought down a German plane for the first time in the history of air warfare while carrying out a night fight in the Moscow skies. When the Germans were getting close to Moscow in the late autumn of 1941, the first military unit that stopped them was the Special Cavalry Corps headed by another Jew, General Lev Dovator.

Who among us, the children of the war generation, didn't know about Nikolai Gastello's exploits? He flew his burning plane right into a column of enemy tanks. Following in his footsteps, we would get all worked up as we imagined an air raid, shouting, "I'm going down, but I'm taking you with me," and then throw our whole bodies onto the empty barrels behind our neighborhood grocery stores.

Ah, if only the papers and radio had informed the whole country that the next day, still knowing nothing about Gastello's sacrifice, another pilot, Senior Lieutenant Isaac Presaizen, gave up his life the very same way. Although the front commander nominated him for the Hero of the Soviet Union award, nothing happened. It took another fifty years to acknowledge Presaizen's heroic deed and to award him—posthumously, of course, and with a lesser decoration—the Patriotic War Order.

And Zoya Kosmodemiyanskaya! One of the most celebrated names of the Great Patriotic War. Many schools and libraries, and even a steamship, were named after her. A partisan seized by the Nazis, she refused to give anyone away and faced her death with dignity. But who among us knew then that, a month earlier, in front of a huge crowd in Minsk, the Germans had hanged a similar hero, the seventeen-year-old Jewish girl Masha Bruskina? She had participated in a guerrilla operation: she had helped to arrange the escape of a big group of captured Red Army officers from a German prison. Arrested after someone had denounced her to the Nazi authorities, she was led with other prisoners through the city streets to serve as a warning to others. Around her neck, they hung a signboard in German and Russian: "A partisan who shot at the German troops." Masha was the first from the group of captives to be brought to the gallows. They threw a noose around her neck, but she gave her executioners no satisfaction. She behaved with dignity, showed her contempt to them, and didn't flinch even once.

At the last moment, she shouted in their faces words similar to those of Zoya's: "Our blood won't be spilled in vain!"*

One of the most prominent war heroes, a Russian soldier by the name of Alexandr Matrosov, rushed to block enemy machine gun fire with his own chest. Many others repeated his extraordinary deed. But one did it a whole year earlier than Matrosov. In a battle for the village of Kholmets, in the Kalinin region, Private Abram Levin sacrificed his life in the very same manner. Posthumously but with little delay, Matrosov was awarded the title of Hero of the Soviet Union, and his name became a legend of the Great Patriotic War. It took the country another twenty-five years to acknowledge Abram Levin's heroism. And he, like Presaizen, was posthumously awarded a lesser decoration—the Patriotic War Order.

The award rank doesn't matter that much. But if the whole country had learned during wartime about Levin's feat, as it did about Matrosov's a year later, then, perhaps, the boys in my class wouldn't have sung that vile ditty about Abram, sitting things out at home.

But, perhaps, I am too naive. Maybe they would have sung it anyway.

Publicizing Jewish war efforts was a complex matter. To my surprise, although real live Jewish warriors were unsung, a place was found for them in wartime Soviet feature films. Many years after the war, already living in America, watching the beloved movies of my childhood again, on videocassettes now, I made a discovery. I found in these films Jewish characters, one way or another taking part in the war effort. In *Dva boitsa (Two Soldiers),* one of the film's heroes, played by Mark Bernes, visits his wounded friend Sasha in a military hospital. On his way to Sasha's bed, he notices another wounded soldier: "Misha! Shapiro!" Bernes exclaims with com-

*Today, Bruskina's heroism is acknowledged and commemorated by the Museum Yad Vashem in Israel and the Holocaust Museum in Washington, D.C. A memorial dedicated to her and other Jewish women fighters has been erected in Tel Aviv, and a Jerusalem street was named after her. Bruskina's heroic deed inspired American writer Jennie Staniloff-Redling to write a libretto of a musical based on her life. Yet today, in Bruskina's own native land, Byelorussia, her Jewishness seems to be the only obstacle to paying homage to her. In the local museum, she's still listed as an "unknown heroine." See Mikhail Nordshtein, "Pochemu u belorusskoi geroini otniato imia?" (Why did they take away the name of a Byelorussian heroine?), http://news.tut.by/society/85685.html, posted April 5, 2007.

passion and rushes to him. In another episode in the film, before boarding a truck, a woman in charge calls the roll of women who had volunteered to dig antitank ditches. One of the first surnames on this list is a Jewish one—Meyerovich. In tightly censored Soviet films, Jewish names couldn't have appeared by chance. Such were the demands of counterpropaganda.

To undermine the fighting spirit of the Red Army, the Germans dropped leaflets urging Soviet soldiers to turn their weapons against the Jews. According to the claims of those leaflets, the Jews were sitting out the war in the rear while the Russians were spilling their blood, protecting them. In a thinly veiled form, the film *Two Soldiers* reflects the effect that such claims had on the spirit of the fighting men. When a certain gunner learns that the film's lead character, played by Mark Bernes, is a native of Odessa, the gunner says to him with contempt, "Ah, don't we know your kind, the Odessans!" His intonation makes it quite clear that, to him, an Odessan means a Jew, a euphemism still alive in Russian lore today. Thus, his words acquire a latent anti-Semitic meaning: "The Jews are cowards, not fighters."

Bernes rebuffs him: "What kind of Odessans? The marines? Women and children under the German bombs? You know that kind?"

The gunner smirks. "Oh, don't we know your Odessa well!"

Bernes defies him: "Listen, don't you touch Odessa. There, they have only grief and blood."

Thus, cultural authorities were ultimately compelled to include in Soviet wartime films Jewish characters participating in the war effort. Nonetheless, the facts of Jewish bravery were not depicted on the screen. In another wartime film, *Zhdi menia (Wait for Me),* the Jewish character Misha Weinstein has a supporting role. What other kind could a minority representative count on in the Soviet cinema? Weinstein, played by the Jewish actor Lev Sverdlin, is made a war correspondent. That is, though he doesn't fight himself, he still supports the war effort in some way. He keeps up the fighting spirit of the troops by publicizing the Red Army's heroic struggle with the enemy. Perhaps the filmmakers felt that Weinstein's contribution might not be enough for wartime audiences, so his character is wounded while carrying out an assignment of his Russian friend, the film's hero.

Weinstein is also shown as a man on the same level as all the others in the film: his hand is in bandages and he drinks as much vodka as the other men. And, on his Russian friend's request, he cheers up the buddy's wife, who is waiting for him despite all odds. "True men have a very good habit," he says to her. "When you wait for them in earnest, they always return."

The true man is Russian, of course: his name is Nikolai. But the Jewish character is also a good fellow. He doesn't let his friend down. He's a reliable pal. At the end of the movie, the Russian hero embraces Weinstein warmly, a supreme award for a Jew in real life. He's accepted. Approved of. They don't ridicule or humiliate him. He should be grateful at least for that.

It's just like in the old Russian joke: "He's a good man, even though he's a Jew."

When the war broke out, I was too small to remember all my relatives who died at the front. One of them, however, though I hadn't even been acquainted with him personally, appeared in my youthful dream several years after the war ended. Usually, no matter how colorful dreams can be, they fade in our memory as quickly as falling snow melts on the ground still warm from the autumn sun. But that dream has stayed with me for a long time. And, though it came to me a long time ago, nearly fifty years, it seems no older than last week.

Around the time in my life when my memories begin, my grandma Sarah, my father's mother, was staying with us. Her and Grandpa's apartment in Minsk had collapsed after German bombing. One day, she showed me a passport picture of a lean youth with curly fair hair. "Lazar," Grandma said biting her lip to hold back the tears. It didn't help. Her eyes grew moist. Lazar was my father's younger brother, my uncle, that is, who had perished during the war. The photo had grown gray and had little spots and fleecy little cracks all over. No other picture survived. The Germans entered Minsk rather swiftly, on the sixth day of their invasion of the USSR. The family had to run, taking along what was deemed most needed on the road—a pillow, a frying pan; there was no time for burrowing in family albums.

According to Grandma, my uncle died young, at the age of nineteen. He was an attractive and tall lad, the spitting image of his father, my grandfather Uri. Lazar was born on the very day that Lenin, the leader of the revolution, died, on January 21, 1924. Lenin passed away at 5:30 P.M. And around midnight, Lazar appeared. The country was in mourning, but there was joy at my grandparents' household. After all, a baby boy was born, a helper.

The family was working-class, and, in theory, power belonged to that class. Although the family wasn't religious, they gave the newborn baby a name according to the Jewish tradition, with the first letter signifying the name of the person in whose honor it was given—in this case, Lenin. The family wasn't overly pious. Nobody in the household read either the Old Testament or the New. They had no clue that the name Lazar was the most suitable for those who would want to see the deceased leader resurrected.

My young uncle perished as a result of an unlucky confluence of circumstances. In early July 1943, right after he had graduated from Kuybyshev Infantry School with the rank of junior lieutenant, he was thrown into action in one of the major World War II battles, the Battle of Kursk. He could easily have gone up in smoke in that furnace in many ways, but he died as the indirect result of a good deed. Eleanor Roosevelt, the American president's wife, wanted to reclothe the Red Army soldiers, who, during the first years of the war, had worn out all their uniforms. As legend from the front has it, Eleanor sent to Russia, engaged in a desperate struggle, not just any kind of material but the best kind. She selected smooth woolen cloth with a greenish tint, from Yorkshire.

Little did she know that the Red Army quartermasters would inadvertently turn the generous gift into a death sentence. To please the young officers entering the battlefield for the first time, they sewed overcoats for them from that very material. German sharpshooters might have thanked the luckless Russian quartermasters: the color of the cloth easily set the young officers apart from the privates under their command.

That's how Uncle Lazar, the only poet in the whole family line, took a bullet in his chest, the chest from which a line of a new poem had just been born. About his first battle. About the proverbial Kursk nightingale, which felt like warbling a bit but couldn't. The clanging of the tank tracks and the banging of long-range guns scared it off.

A government letter Grandma received notified her that her son had died a hero's death and expressed condolences. From that time on, whenever she remembered her Lazar, her eyes filled with tears.

Though Grandfather Uri was pleased that a son was born to him, he became disappointed while the boy was growing up. Quite early in his life, Lazar began writing poetry. And there wasn't much use for a poet in a working-class family.

But for Grandma Sarah, the most beloved of her three sons was Lazar. Perhaps because he was delicate, because he never talked back, was always reading a book or writing his verses. He attended a poetry club at the Minsk Palace of Young Pioneers. From time to time, his mother took his pad away. "Take a rest, go for a walk, you're pale," she would say. He hugged her, taking the papers she held behind her back: "I'll do some walking. I promise."

"He was defenseless," his older sister, Aunt Asya, recalled later. "Tall, thin, tender, and defenseless."

For half a year after they had fled from the Germans approaching Minsk, Asya watched over him in a motherly way in the Tatar settlement of Tlianchi-Tamak. Though frostbite injured his toes in the bitter winter of 1942, he was drafted into the army anyway.

They came for him in a cart dragged by an old horse. Asya ran after the cart for a long time, almost a mile till the road forked toward the railroad station. She ran and sobbed and knew in her heart that she had seen her brother for the last time. She wasn't even surprised later when the death certificate arrived. But from that day on, pain for her own blood, for a tender defenseless poet, lodged itself in her heart once and for all.

I recalled Uncle Lazar later, about eight years from the day I had seen his picture in Grandma's hands for the first time. I was sixteen, and, as happens with many youngsters, an urge to compose poems seized me. They wandered in me in Brownian motion. They tossed about inside my chest, groaned there like unfed doves behind the window of our apartment on the third floor of our big Odessan building. The poems flapped their little wings but couldn't take off. Indistinct words were born inside me. I muttered them. It came out something like *ta-ta, ta-ta, ta-ta, ta-ta.* I felt the melody and the rhythm of the poem that was about to be born, but, no matter how hard I tried to write down something sensible, nothing would come out.

The torture of muteness when the thirst for self-expression rends your heart and you can only mumble to the melody droning in your head became unbearable. I ran across the whole city to my second cousin Maya Khanis. She was a whole seven years older than I. She had already graduated from Odessa University and taught literature in a Poltava high school. She spent the summertime in Odessa with her family, basking in the sun and swimming in the Black Sea.

Maya lived near the railroad station, on Karl Marx Street. I couldn't wait for a streetcar. I rushed headlong along the rails, now and then looking over my shoulder in the hope that the streetcar would catch up with me. Eventually it did, but it was overloaded with clusters of people riding on its running boards. I moved and moved, murmuring under my breath some lines that stubbornly refused to acquire any articulate form. When I reached Maya's courtyard, I threw myself up the rickety wooden ladder to the second floor where the Khanises lived.

I called Maya out and demanded of her: "How do you shape a poem?"

She came out onto the balcony, hardly seeing me without her glasses, leaned heavily on the balustrade, and said, "For starters, try first to write down what you want to say. As prose."

But that was exactly what tormented me the most: I had no idea of what I wanted to say. The music of poetry was humming within me, and the beauty of that music, which only I heard, intoxicated me and dulled my senses. My attempts at its verbalization felt like pitiful blathering. I tried to write some lines and destroyed them right there and then. Only sheer nonsense would come out. It was incomprehensible to me the way in which seemingly usual words suddenly take off from paper, flit up, and hang in the air as a stable little flock. How could these words, wild geese arriving from Egypt in the spring Odessan skies, know their exact place in the flock, keep a distance from one another, and stay on course?

No matter how hard I tried to solve this problem, it remained a mystery to me. A poet shouldn't trust his intellect too much: this simple truth would open up to me years later. But back then my intellect held me hostage. In the same state of frenzy, I hurried back home, mumbling unyielding words and beating time to the unborn poems with my fist at my side. It may well be that passersby took me for an asylum patient, released prematurely.

It was then, in those intoxicated days of my struggle to unearth the mystery of poetry, that Uncle Lazar, the only poet in our family, appeared in my dream. One May night, in the confusion of dreaming, I opened my eyes. Uncle Lazar stood in front of me. He wore a smart greenish-gray military overcoat made of smooth woolen British cloth and the brand new crisp leather shoulder-belt of a junior lieutenant of infantry troops. He smiled the same tender smile that he wore in his picture in the hands of my grandma. And although he was my uncle, I suddenly realized that he was my own age then. Well, of course, the picture had been made for his first passport, the only one he ever had. He wasn't destined to renew it.

"Uncle Lazar!" I said into the darkness. "Why are you here? After all, you died in the Battle of Kursk."

"Who told you such nonsense?" he replied.

"My uncle Misha told me, your younger brother."

"He's a chatterbox, that little Misha."

In a magician's gesture—voila!—Uncle Lazar dragged something through the upper buttonhole of his overcoat. When he opened his fist, a blue-gray German bullet turned up in it. I recognized it right away. It had two rings at its end; it was a sharpshooter's rifle bullet. We, the children of the war, collected bullets and cartridges with the same passion that boys in peacetime gather seashells, stamps, and butterflies.

"Here," Uncle Lazar said smiling, "it came in and there it came out. It didn't even graze me. I didn't die at all. The only thing that did happen is that I forgot how to write poems. Nothing comes out," he said and closed his eyes.

"But Uncle Lazar, you're my last hope! There's no one else I can ask. Is it possible that I would never write a beautiful poem? How did you do it?"

"I forgot," my young uncle said and closed his eyes. "That's my only misfortune. I'm alive. The only thing that's wrong with me is that I stopped writing poetry. I try to recall how I did it before. But I can't do it no matter how hard I try. I feel like sleeping all the time." He sighed sorrowfully, without opening his eyes. His greenish overcoat began turning gray right in front of my eyes.

"Uncle Lazar, don't go away!"

"I'm here, I'm here. But I can't help but fall asleep."

I peered into his face as it grew pale till it blended with the ceiling above my head. Then I woke up. It was morning. Another morning. Another day of my mute, inexpressible, unbearable suffering.

THREE

Path to Paradise

"ALL JEWS ARE COWARDS!"—my schoolmates' words keep ringing in my ears.

They accuse me of cowardice, but I am silent. I feel guilty when boys halloo around me, jumping on the school desks. The looks they give me are those of hatred and contempt. But alas, it's true; I spent most of the war with Mama in Tashkent.

It's also true that I didn't feel happy about it. No matter what my life in Central Asia was like, as a child, I accepted it as the norm. Now, from a distance of more than six decades, my life there seems like paradise, only because time has carefully removed everything bad from my memory. The shrill cold of February nights. The pain of starvation in my stomach. The reek of the cowshed where, on an armful of hay thrown onto its floor, Mama and I slept.

And the road to Tashkent was a path to that paradise, a purgatory of a kind. The magic word *luck* served as the password through it. Luck sorted us, children with our mothers running from the German bombs and death camps, into two unequal groups: the survivors and the dead. In the lottery fate hastily organized for us, only those who picked a winning number made it to Central Asia.

Apparently, my lucky streak started with my birth. In Mama's stories, I was born in a "shirt," that is, having some pellicle around my shoulders. As a myth popular among Russian mothers has it, this is a sign that a baby's life is going to be lucky. From time immemorial, we humans long for a stroke of good luck, and that makes us think of an anomaly, true or imaginary, as a sign of blessed providence. I remember how, on the threshold of marriage, the girls of my youth—their faces serious and agitated, full of hope to meet their great love—stirred lilac clusters, in bush after bush, trying to find a little five-petaled flower among the ordinary four-petaled ones.

"You're a lucky one," Mama said from time to time, her eyes radiating happiness. "Lucky!" She smiled joyfully, proud that she had given birth to a lucky child.

Now, thinking back to the time when the war broke out, I feel that Mama was right after all. I was fortunate indeed. Decades later, living in the West, I would learn about a myth circulating in America both during and after World War II. According to this myth, right after the German invasion, Stalin made special arrangements to save Soviet Jews. As soon as German troops began advancing, he evacuated the Jews to the eastern parts of the country, making sure that they wouldn't get in harm's way.

However, over two millions Jews exterminated in Riga, Minsk, Kiev, Vilnius, Odessa, and many other cities and towns in the European part of the USSR testify to the opposite. A relatively small portion of Russian Jews survived. Shocked by the betrayal of his recent friend Adolf Hitler, who tricked him with a sudden attack, Stalin had better things to worry about than taking care of civilians in general and of Jewish ones in particular. Amid total chaos and government collapse, shocked and paralyzed by the news of Hitler's invasion for about two weeks, Stalin eventually managed to pull himself together. Among other things, he ordered the evacuation of war-industry factories and specialists from the areas of imminent German occupation. And Jewish women with their children rushed to join these evacuation trains.

My winning lottery ticket took the form of a ticket for travel on the steamship *Lenin,* the last evacuation ship departing from the Odessa port. The steamship was loaded with the equipment and workforce of the war industry. Thousands wanted to board it. Perhaps people unconsciously believed that a vessel bearing the name of the prominent Soviet leader was safe in God's bosom.

To be exact, Papa arranged two tickets for us, one for Mama and one for me.

Night bombings of the city have become more and more frequent, and we spend more and more time in the basement of our building. In a month, I have learned to guess the model of an enemy plane by its sound: the evil roaring of the Focke-Wulff; the fierce howl of the Messerschmitt; the tinkling of the Junkers spinning through the sky. I know it's time to run to the shelter.

Then comes the day of departure. The Germans are already speeding along the southern steppes toward Odessa, their motorcycle wheels blowing up dust. On the floor of our apartment on Deribas Street, Mama hastily collects clothing into a small suitcase. We are heading for the port. Mama pulls my hand: faster, sonny, faster! The port is not too far from our home. A half block along Deribas Street, two blocks along Gavan Street, down Matros Slope, and we will reach the port area. From there, the pier is just a stone's throw away.

Mama rushes me. I'm three and a half years old. No matter how I try to keep up with her, I lag behind. From time to time, she is forced to take me in her arms.

I press my favorite toy, a small stuffed elephant, to my chest. As we hurry down Matros Slope to the port, time and again we run into other women with children. I look askance at them. I press my elephant closer to myself so that they won't eye it with envy. Just in case.

At last we reach the pier. A huge crowd sways and rumbles there. A hundred meters from the gangway of an enormous white steamship with a huge black smokestack, Mama realizes that it's not going to be easy to make our way to it. She's afraid to lose me in the crowd. And she's worried about the purse under her arm.

She decides to regroup her efforts. To ease her movements, she gives me her purse. "Hold it as tight as you can!" she says, and plants me on her shoulders.

I hold the purse in one hand, my elephant in the other. Mama tries to take it from me: "Let it go, sonny. It's no time for toys. I'll buy you another one, a bigger one."

My eyes well up with tears. I iron-grip the elephant. I don't want to let it go for anything in the world!

"What a stubborn boy!" Mama says in despair. "Hold the purse tighter!"

I press both the purse and the toy to myself with all my might.

Mama holds me with one hand and drags our suitcase with the other.

I like my new position. I am a head taller than everyone in the crowd. Around me, the pier is packed with a multitude of heads. The crowd's swaying from side to side. We move slowly. Somewhere in the midst of the crowd, some babies cry. The sun's scorching already, and I'm thirsty.

The closer we are to the ship's gangway, the more difficult is every step for Mama. People press in on her from left and right and from behind as well. From time to time, she cries out: "People! What are you doing! For God's sake! You'll throw my baby down!"

Nobody listens to her. The steamship signals in a rich and fat bass voice. People become frantic. They press in on us from all sides with double force.

"Purse!" Mama shouts to me. "Hold on to the purse, Milya!"

"Stop pushing! For God's sake, do you want to be crushed?"

A sweaty elderly serviceman, with a rolled-up field cap about to jump out of his chest pocket, has a hard time controlling the crowd at the gangway.

"Only the next in line are going through!" he shouts. "Only the next in line! Get your tickets ready, ladies. No one without a ticket gets aboard. I, Sergeant Prikhodko, am telling you that. And you better believe me!"

Nearby, a boy like me, also sitting on his mother's shoulders, holds an airplane in his hands, one with red stars on its wings. I try to examine the remarkable toy more closely.

We are only a few steps away from the gangway, when Mama gets pushed from behind. The purse slips out of my hands and falls down, under the crowd's feet.

"Mama, Mama!" I shout, "Your purse!"

But it's too late. We are pushed again, now away from the gangway. It's impossible for Mama to look for her purse.

"People, please stop!" She cries out. "My purse! My tickets! My passport!"

To make things worse, the steamship gives another signal, deep and sad. A curly little cloud of milky-gray steam emerges from the smokestack. Everyone around yells at Mama to hurry up. But without tickets, it makes no sense to keep moving toward the gangway. The guards try to control the crowd. Furious at the disobedient and sweaty, Sergeant Prikhodko will not let us on the steamship anyway.

Mama pulls me to the side, out of the crowd, sits down on our suitcase, and, putting me on her lap, she cries.

We sit that way for a long time till the steamship departs, hooting, the oily water boiling up around its sides. From the city, the smell of burning wafts in.

We are not alone at the pier. There are still many others as desperate as Mama. It turns out that the number of tickets issued for the steamship far exceeded its capacity. Mama lifts me to my feet and pulls me along, walking around the pier.

"Look around," she urges me. "Let's try to find it. You know what my purse looks like, don't you? Let's look for it."

We go around the pier. We look at the ground and examine garbage cans. There is no sign of Mama's purse anywhere. It has vanished into thin air.

"My passport," Mama keeps saying. "Passport! If only I could get back my passport!"

I'm too young to understand what it means for a Soviet citizen to lose his or her passport, especially in wartime. If the police or a military patrol stops you, it could spell deep trouble.

After a while, there is nothing else for us to do but return home.

As we enter our apartment, I feel dead tired. As soon as my head hits my pillow, I dive into a deep sleep.

Two days later, there is a terrible banging at our apartment door. It's early morning. Outside the window, the dawn gleams faintly.

"*Vey'z mir!*" Mama jumps to her feet. "Woe is me! My God! It's Germans!"

She rushes to the window and looks down. We live on the third floor. Jumping from that height is out of the question. What to do, what to do? Mama wrings her hands. She starts hastily dressing, now herself, now me.

The banging resumes with a renewed force.

Mama covers my mouth with her hand. With her other hand, she tries to pull my trousers up.

"*Vey'z mir!*" I hear her faltering whisper near my very ear. "*Vey'z mir.*"

"May your father go to hell!" The muffled voice of a man shouting in Ukrainian comes from behind the front door.

My one leg in my pants, Mama freezes.

"Uncle Fedya?" Mama shouts.

She rushes into the corridor. "Coming, Uncle Fedya, coming!" her voice is joyful now. "Just a moment! Ah!"

Clinking and din resound in the corridor. It's Mama's stumbling on a bucket of water as she rushes to the door. The last few days before leaving for the port, in case of a fire caused by German bombing, she had filled it with water, along with all our other household vessels—all our pots and even a washtub.

Mama clanks the locks, hooks, and latches. For a long time, she jingles the door chain.

At last, she opens the door. There stands our middle-aged neighbor, whom we call Uncle Fedya. He lives in the second of our two-room apartment. I like the old man. He's big but kind. Though, for some reason, every time he sees me he's tempted to pinch my cheek, he does it gently, without hurting me. He usually smells of old tobacco smoke. But sometimes he reeks of some other smell, sharp and unpleasant. It happens when he comes from the streets, his eyes red and watery, his legs shaking, his tongue babbling something incomprehensible. Mama begins worrying when he comes home in this condition. But he smiles, trying to calm her down: "Little Sonya, don't worry. Everything will be all right. Just fine. I'll go to bed right now."

This time, though, Uncle Fedya is just cheerful. And a bit surprised.

"Why are you here, little Sonya?" he asks. "Weren't you supposed to leave?"

"I lost my tickets for the *Lenin*. But why are *you* here, Uncle Fedya? Weren't you supposed to leave with the *Lenin* too? As a stoker?"

"What a lucky girl you are, little Sonya!" Uncle Fedya suddenly roars with laughter. "What luck! Losing those tickets was a blessing!"

And he tells Mama that the morning after departing from Odessa, near the Crimean port of Yevpatoriya, the steamship *Lenin* ran into a German mine. Only a few managed to save themselves. He, Uncle Fedya, did as all experienced sailors do when their ship is about to sink. He put his passport inside his cap, secured it on his head, and jumped into the water. He hitch-hiked back to Odessa.

"To hell with it!" Uncle Fedya says. "I'm not going anywhere anymore. I'll stay put right here, at home. What would the Germans do to me? I'm not a Commie. And not a Jew. I've had enough of running. I'm tired of it. How much worse could it be for me?"

The next day, Mama finds out that, as luck had it, Papa's Repair Shops haven't left town yet. We are allowed to board the evacuation train in a car wagon designated for other employees' families who were unable to run away from the Germans by other means. In three days, we turn up in a freight car crammed with many women and their children. "8 persons, 40 horses," I read, syllable by syllable, from an inscription on its wall. Curious, I peer into the depths of the car, hoping to see at least one horse. Far from it! So many people are packed into the car that a horse would hardly find space for itself. According to Mama's postwartime stories, at this time I come down with croup. It's stuffy in the car; I need fresh air. She tries to bring me closer to the only small window near the ceiling. But there is no place to step. There was no time to knock some plank beds together, and everyone's lying on the floor. There is no way she can reach the window.

That's how Mama's and my flight by rail began: now in a freight car permeated with the smell of horse manure; now on a flatcar, under a canvas, next to our tanks and guns heading to the rear for repair. Sometimes, if we get a break, we get to ride in a normal car—that is, a passenger car. In the daytime, the train hides in the woods. It makes up for lost time at night, when, with its whole might, it rushes eastward. Sometimes, after a stop, the train starts moving backward. Then everyone in the car gets nervous. What's happening? Is the road ahead cut off? Do we go back to Odessa, where death awaits everyone?

Still, long after the war, our flight from Odessa comes to me in a recurring dream, which wanders freely and unpredictably somewhere near my basic dream, provoked by the intense daytime events of a boy's life. In this other dream, I am not an eight-, ten-, twelve-year-old boy, a Young Pioneer, even a chairman of a Young Pioneer group with stripes, in the form of an equals sign, on the sleeve of my little jacket. I am another I, a child not quite four years old. That child is awakened in the middle of the night by the jerking of the long-distance train that is taking him away from the bombs of the rumbling war. And it is not I but that little boy who lies in the middle of the night, eyes open, on a hard freight-car floor, his head bobbing on someone's backpack, his ears straining to hear the knocking of the wheels on rail joints.

Even today, traveling by rail, I involuntarily listen for this knocking, though I keep reminding myself that I listen in vain. Much time has passed. Now, they weld rails together, making a smooth seam. But then, in the late fall of 1941, the knocking of the car wheels against the rail joints is the only night sound that calms me. If the wheels keep knocking, it means we aren't standing still, we are moving. That knocking also serves as entertainment. If desired, it can be put to music of any kind. If you want a cheerful tune, then count one knock for one measure. So-so, so-so, and only so. Bang-bang, bang-bang, once again bang. If you want melancholy music, then skip one measure or even two. You don't need an orchestra for this.

Sometimes the sharp knocking gives way to a booming echo from below. I hold my breath: the echo tells me that the train is rushing across a bridge over a river or a mountain gorge, a bridge that has so far escaped bombardments. At night with the accompaniment of that knocking, it's easy to dream. I imagine that the wheel knocking is the beating of Earth's giant heart and that I'm rushing toward an unknown, fantastic, dangerous, and beautiful life, a life full of adventures.

This ability to perceive an unusual event in life as an adventure is an enviable quality of a child's mind. My second cousin Eva, the daughter of my mother's cousin Rosa and her husband, Naum, who lived near Privoz, the big Odessa farmer's market, saw from her window a huge fiery ball from one of the first German demolition bombs that fell. It broke an awning over the open-air counters and shot a flame up to the sky. Eva was three years old then. Excited, she rushed to her grandmother, shouting, "Have you seen it, Grandma, have you seen it? A piece of the sun fell on the market! A piece of the sun!"

When the war began, her sister Maya was eleven. Their family had to run from Odessa, not by train or steamship, but in a cart harnessed to a pair of horses with the funny names Masha and Hero. Their uncle drove the horses, which belonged to the Lvov Drama Theater, from which he was running when the Germans advanced. The theater manager, he had been rejected by the army because he limped. The family loaded its haphazardly gathered belongings into a cart and headed east, as far away as possible from the Germans, who were already bombing the city.

Maya rejoiced that, though she had been staying home since school was over for summer, now she was going to travel in such an unusual manner. It would be something to make her girlfriends envy, when in the fall she returned to school and told about it. She would not manage to return for four years, however. The majority of her girlfriends would no longer be among the living. She herself would no longer have any desire to tell about anything that happened to her. And those girlfriends who survived while she was away would be difficult to surprise with anything.

I don't really know what's going on around me. I compensate for the lack of information with imagination. Where am I? Where does this train take me? Mama's sleeping near me, on the floor, having let down her magnificent chestnut braids for nighttime. She is young and beautiful. And though she is my mama, I think of her as a character from a Russian fairy tale—little sister Alyonushka, who protects her little brother Ivanushka from the iron geese-swans attacking us from the sky. It's dark behind the window. Pulsing in time with my heart, a small circle of light around my eyes looking into the darkness is all that is my night world. Time and again, the locomotive blows its whistle, now prolonged and alarming, now dying out halfway. Somehow, it makes me identify with the locomotive pulling the train for all it is worth. I see it as a child lost in the night and looking for his mother, in whose arms he could finally rest.

End of October. The first snow has just fallen. My throat chokes me. I cannot breathe. From a crack in the wall, cold air streams into the freight car. I'm running a high fever. I try turning my hot forehead toward the air stream to cool it. Mama notices my maneuver and stops up the crack with an old stocking. She is afraid I'll get worse.

In the middle of the car, a round pig-iron stove, nicknamed *burzhuika,* a "bourgeois woman," is blazing. Quite often forced to balance on one leg, Mama steps over the bodies on the floor, making her way to the stove with an aluminum cup. She wants to brew some tea for me. "You should drink a lot," she says. "Drink, drink, and drink." I don't feel like drinking anything hot. High fever makes me want to suck on ice.

Mama is already next to the "bourgeois woman." The train suddenly brakes. Mama loses her balance and falls onto the burning stove. I hear her scream, but I have no strength even for crying. Women bustle around Mama. They lay her down near the wall and, cautiously, ignoring her screaming, remove the stocking on her legs, exposing the skin of her hip, which is covered with blisters.

"Urine," says one of the women. "It'll take care of your burn right away. It's a reliable remedy. Lady, tell your boy to urinate."

They tug at me. I am bewildered. What do they want from me?

"Turn away from him, citizens," the same woman says. "Don't confuse him. After all, he's a little man. Give him a chance to concentrate."

They lift me to my feet and put me in a corner of the car. After long urging, blushing from the presence of girls around me, I finally fill somebody's jar with my urine, as watery and translucent as my tears.

We speed along the empty cold steppes. Time and again, down from the sky, a Focke-Wulff plunges on us. When this happens, the train stops, and everyone pours out of the car and runs, sliding down the railway embankment into the ditches along the side of the road. I can still smell the fuel oil saturating those railroad ties when I think about those days.

New York, 1999. On a wet December midday, I am sitting in an auditorium of the New School for Social Research, on 12th Street in Manhattan, viewing a documentary about an exhibition at the Hamburg Institute of Social Research titled "Wermacht on the Eastern Front." The exhibition consists of thousands of pictures that raze the myth that regular German soldiers had nothing to do with the atrocities committed against the civilian population in the East during World War II. Until now, Germany has consoled itself with the notion that only the monsters of Einsatzkommandos SS, special formations charged with killing the Jews, were capable of such things. Young German journalists interview on camera some visitors of this scandalous exhibition. They ask them what they think about the exposition. Among the visitors are quite a few former German soldiers who fought in Russia.

I feel not quite myself. For the first time, I see up close the faces of those—perhaps exactly those—who threatened my young life then, decades ago, in the southern steppes of Ukraine. I look at the screen and shudder from old memory. What could be more terrifying and more disgusting for me, then, than the faces of German soldiers! Only recently have I learned to see them as just human beings whom Hitler sent to the war, and to forgive them, at least intellectually. But now, in the darkness of a screening room, my memory still tightens the skin on my back from the old and, it appears, not completely overcome fear.

A journalist places her microphone in front of an elderly German, his hair neatly combed and waxed but his eyes restless. He sighs time and again as he glances at the photos on the walls. He shifts his hat from one hand to another. Creases it now one way, now another. Sniffles. Fidgeting on his chair, he tries to turn his face away from the lens. He says finally, "I didn't see any of this. The whole wartime, I was in the Luftwaffe. I didn't take part in all these affairs," he nods toward the pictures.

I catch myself laughing involuntarily. Then I whisper to my neighbors in the auditorium, apologizing. "An innocent Luftwaffe pilot" is still an oxymoron for me. An ominous oxymoron! I peer into the face of the former Luftwaffe ace on the screen as if I could see and remember his face then, nearly sixty years ago, when I was a boy on the railway embankment, lightly strewn with the first snow, in the chilly steppe near Odessa. He was in the sky, in his Focke-Wulff cockpit. So, that is what he might have looked like, this one, perhaps, the very same one who jumped from the sky down on me, my twenty-six-year-old mother, and other women and children on that ominous day, flooded with blood, in my memory!

"They bombed us good at the Razdelnaia Station," Mama recalls more than once in the first postwar years. I feel her irony. How can any bombing be "good"? Every time Mama tells me about this episode, she glances at me, and a complex expression flashes across her face. There is both the horror of recollecting this episode of the recent past and—like the flash of magnesium in an antiquated camera—an instant, satisfied, even joyful, smile. It will take me years to decipher it.

"You were so frightened for me," she says when retelling the story.

And I discover that it is not only that children need their mother's love; mothers need to feel love from their children as well.

And now I see that day at the Razdelnaia Station.

"Not a good place to stand still," says a tall thin woman in a black dress with a man's jacket thrown around her shoulders. Using both hands, she pulls herself up to the little window in the boxcar. We cannot open the door of the car; it is the end of October, and it's cold already.

"A lousy place to stand still," she says. "Does it make any sense to keep a train with refugees standing at a strategic station? The Germans will pounce on it for sure."

We do not stand for long, no more than half an hour. The Germans would certainly want to blow this station to bits by all means. It has a range of rails, wide as a good-sized river. Here, trains leaving for the front are put together. Flatcars with guns and tanks under canvases. Cisterns with engine fuel. On adjacent tracks, freight cars like ours are packed with soldiers with rolled-up overcoats strapped to their shoulders. The station dispatcher shuffles cars as if they are a pack of cards for fortune-telling. What's in store for those who travel in them? Will their long journey end in a safe place or in a grave?

I lie on the floor, my head still on someone's backpack. Through badly puttied cracks and the little window near the ceiling, the sickening smell of the fuel oil penetrates the car. Sharp smoke from the engines stings our throats. A "cuckoo," a small maneuvering locomotive with a huge pipe, whistles alarmingly time and again.

The whole car population freezes in horror. Everyone's silent. (Many years later, recollecting that ominous morning, I will understand: the most frightful fear is the fear of the unknown.) With their faces wrinkled and gray, like poorly washed bedsheets after many sleepless nights, some women sit on the floor; others squat. Still others stand, leaning against the car wall, tilting their heads, their ears like radars aimed toward the ceiling. The general tension passes on to me. I also tilt my head toward the sky.

An old woman with a checkered scarf around her head breaks the silence: "How long are we going to stand still?"

The old woman's question is not an idle one. If you know the time of departure, you can run to the station building to get some water. If you are very fortunate, you might even find some boiling water, the elixir of a refugee's existence. Where there is boiling water, there is life. You can warm yourself up, brewing tea directly in your cup. You can pour some flour into it to prepare a stir-up soup for children.

Sometimes during such stops, a soldier runs along the freight cars. He knocks at the car walls with his rifle butt, shouting, "Twenty minute stop!" However, more often than not, uncertainty reigns. Sometimes, when mothers take their children outside to attend to their private needs, seemingly from nowhere a Messerschmitt dives right onto the train's spine. Like a lizard saving itself from an eagle's beak, the train tears forward from its place, its wheels shooting orange sparks. To stand still means to perish immediately. The last desperate hope is in running. The mothers' screams are dreadful. How many children were left behind to die in the cold lonely steppes on such casual stops! How many of them were crushed under the wheels! How many mothers, looking for their children, leaned out too far and, blinded by fear for them, didn't spot oncoming trains and telephone posts in time and were knocked off to the ground! How many of them threw themselves out of the cars in a desperate attempt to reunite with their children! Who will count the number of wasted human lives on the dreadful roads of war!

Everyone hushes the old woman. Nobody wants to miss the very first faint drone coming from the sky. I already know what is going to happen as soon as they hear that sound. They will lean on the heavy door of the car, roll it away, and jump off, grabbing their children under their arms and pulling them along to the ground.

Now, amid the buffer clanging, the car couplers' shouting, the dispatcher's hoarse barking over the station radio (these cars to uncouple, those to couple), the locomotive whistling—sometimes heartrending, high and sharp like a shriek of despair; sometimes a low, calm bass, unfitting for the moment—everybody fails to notice the planes roaring until a bomb explodes nearby. Pushing one another—faster, faster, little ladies, why are you relaxing?—everyone rushes to get out of the car as quickly as possible.

Where to run? Of course, not along the tracks but across them. And not toward the station building but in the opposite direction, toward the steppe. The Germans would rather bomb the station than hunt for people scattered all over a field.

I am in Mama's arms, but she sets me down on my feet. Otherwise, there is no way we can pass under the cars. She dives under one of them and pulls me after herself. Go, go, quickly. I step over the first rail, then the second. Faster! Faster! We rush under another car. Nearby, one more bomb explodes. A sudden wave of air jolts the train we are clambering under. Its wheels start rolling, but we manage to jump clear and dive under a flatcar on the adjoining tracks.

I move even faster than Mama: I don't have to bend over so far. Afraid to lose sight of her, I look out of the corner of my eye. Mama pushes me lightly: Run, sonny, run. I run with all my might. I step over the rails. Sharp edges of gravel between cross ties stick into the thin soles of my sandals, worn smooth over the summer: I lost my regular shoes somewhere along the way.

We are ready to make our way under the last flatcar, heading for a cornfield, not reaped yet. If we reach it, we are safe. Over there we will be as hard to capture as the wind.

Here Mama screams, shortly but loudly, "Ah!"

I look back. Horror seizes my whole being. At this moment, I am not afraid of the hallooing whistle of the falling bombs anymore. What I see is a million times more terrifying. Mama holds on to her head. Blood is spurting through her fingers and flooding her face. My breath stops. I also grab my head. I shout right after Mama. I am sure that it is *my* head that is punctured and *my* blood that is gushing. I scream with all my might. I am afraid to look at my hands. It seems to me that they, too, are covered with blood. Through my wet eyelids, semiclosed in crying, I see a wet solar ball slowly rolling over the wing of a low-flying Messerschmitt, turning in my direction. Then I see only the glass dome of the plane cabin and a German pilot in big glasses behind the steering wheel. The giant steel machine is rushing toward me.

I squint in horror. I cannot move from my place. Someone among the women running by picks me up and runs with me to the cornfield. The moisture from the corn leaves sprinkles onto my face and brings me back from the shock. I shudder and shout as loud as I can, "Mama!"

"I'm here, I'm here." She's already next to me. She presses me to herself with her hands, pink from blood. Everything has worked out. Mama has lost a lot of blood, but she has survived. She is just dizzy for a long time. She holds my hand firmly, and this calms me. Even now I recall how stricken I was at the sight of Mama's blood. Then, for the first time, I realize what I have not understood before. Mama is mortal. She has blood. She can die.

It takes me a few days, from Mama's conversation with our travel companions, to understand what has happened. She made her way under a flatcar and, thinking she had cleared it already, she lifted her head too soon. An iron wedge of the flatcar frame, which served as a fastener for the ropes and cables securing tanks, pierced the top of her head.

But she has survived. I have been lucky again. Perhaps, my mother has been right all along: I'm indeed born fortunate.

FOUR

What's in a Name!

"THEY ALWAYS WORM THEIR WAY in front of others. They're not used to staying in line like everybody else!"

Now, recalling the events of my first school days, I realize that they weren't completely unexpected for me. Something in my classmates' voices was distantly familiar.

Back in Tashkent, where my mother took me to escape the Nazis, and after returning to Odessa, Mama pulled me into countless lines, despite my resistance. They were an integral part of our everyday life. Just as the atmospheric pressure could be higher or lower, the lines could be longer or shorter. But both existed always. I was angry with Mama, dug my heels in and whimpered. But you couldn't argue with Mama. I had to do it, and that's all there was to it. She needed me to cooperate not so that I could entertain her while she was standing in line but for other reasons. First, provisions were often rationed, say, one package of flour or ten matchboxes per person. Second, she needed somebody to keep her place in one line so that she could run off to another one a few blocks away.

Short lines were relatively peaceful. But the long ones, which meant several hours of standing, ignited as easily as a smoldering piece of coal from a drop of gasoline. The reason was always the same. As soon as some unscrupulous woman (standing in line was primarily a female responsibility) attempted to insinuate herself into the line, those already waiting jumped on her from all sides. They would spew curses: *nakhalka,* "insolent woman"; *naglaia baba,* "impudent hag"; *chuchelo besstyzhee,* "shameless scarecrow"; *vydra,* "otter"; *Chtob ot tebia muzh sbezhal!* "May your husband run away from you!" (To tell the truth, I didn't quite understand where someone's husband could run away to. What about his residence permit? Everyone had a passport stamp marking a place of residence. But I took it on faith that it was possible for one's husband to run away and that such punishment fitted the crime of cutting in line.)

I was entirely on the side of the shouting people. My sense of justice was offended as well. I, too, was angry at those who tried sneak in without standing in line. How could anyone bear to wait longer in this monstrous boredom? I had already developed a love for reading, but Mama forbade me to read while standing in line. With a book in hand, I forgot myself. As a result, I turned up at the end of the line no matter how long it was.

To taunt the woman who violated the order of the line, people would address her rudely, for example, not merely using the familiar second-person pronoun *ty,* "you," instead of the formal pronoun *vy* (as in "you, ma'am"), or yelling things like, "Just where do you think you're cutting in, you and that impudent mug of yours?" but in the third-person singular pronoun: "Just look at her! How she blathers, the scarecrow!"

But sometimes, instead of *you* or *she,* suddenly *they* appeared: "*They* always try to get it without standing in line!" "*They're* not used to standing as everyone else has to!" "*Their* kind never has enough of anything!"

Listening to such cursing, I wondered, Who are the mysterious "they"? Why did the accusers address that woman in a brown wool-knit jacket with the third-person plural? To my inexperienced eyes, she looked not much different from the one who was scolding her. I already knew that *pronoun* means "instead of a noun." So, instead of what noun in plural is *they* used?

I didn't dare to ask Mama, and she wasn't in the mood to answer me anyway. I didn't understand why, though, she became gloomy just witnessing such an attack, even if she wasn't the one they were scolding. She would purse her lips and lower her eyes. For some reason, she would grab my shoulders and press me to herself. I looked at her in perplexity; where did she see danger? These people were scorning some "them," some mysterious, anonymous people. What did I have to do with them?

Mama was very sociable. Often people who were total strangers to me stopped her in the street and chatted with her. One time when Mama was standing in line, a woman approached her. Everybody around me began to grumble:

"Lady, move away, move away. Don't worm your way in!"

"I just want to say a word to this woman. Are you beasts or what?"

"Here she's found a place for chatter! Get lost! *They* have already struck up an agreement between themselves. No conscience whatsoever. Well, of course, *they* only think about their own."

The very same hostile and cold note resounded in the voices of my schoolmates when they attacked me on my first day of school. Now, I didn't have to guess anymore whom they had in mind. Being the object of their hate had by this point become a familiar part of my existence.

My first days of school mark the beginning of my secret emotional torture. At this time a burden descends onto my shoulders, a burden I'll carry almost all my life. Probably it is at those times that I begin to be secretive. When for the first time I, a schoolboy, read the famous lines "Be silent, conceal and harbor / your feelings and dreams," I felt that the great Russian poet Tyutchev was addressing me personally in "Silentium."

While our teacher, Galina Ivanovna, drums into our heads the alphabet and teaches, first on our fingers and then in our minds, how to add two apples to one pear, I live intensely, trying to comprehend the world around me. It acquires optical depth. When I was even younger, someone showed me a stereoscopic device, which I couldn't appreciate right away. I was instructed to look through special glasses in a cardboard frame at two adjacent pictures. On both there was an ancient building with porticoes, columns, and little steps. At first, I didn't understand why the device had to have the two identical pictures. Only after peering deep into the images could I see that the columns on the building's portal were rounder and more massive than they were when I wasn't looking through the glasses. One of them cast a shadow that lay upon the steps like a strip of carpet. A boy sat with a cat in his lap at the bottom of one of the columns. I remember trembling at the sight of that lonely boy who looked at the square deserted at high noon. Now I understand why I shuddered. I felt a prophetic premonition that I was soon to become this boy, looking for warmth even from a cat whose little belly was nestled against my palm.

I begin to comprehend complexities of the world in which I live, continually running into inexplicable things and phenomena. "What is that? What is that?" Unable to fall asleep, I grow restless at night under my blanket. I feel surrounded from all sides. There's no place to run. How can I protect myself from the misfortune that's stricken me?

For the first time, with amazement, I discover that I'm not like others but worse, much worse. Immeasurably worse! Everything, everything about me is abnormal, beginning with my disgusting name and my surname, equally bad. They're horrifically indecent. They cause laughter and contempt. (Years later, coming upon the Shakespearean line "What's in a name?" I grinned to myself at the naïveté of the Brit: "You don't know the first thing about my life, William! Yes, everything's in a name. Everything!")

But I'm still a first grader. I passionately dream that my surname will change by some miracle. It seems to me that its ending is especially awful. Why can't it end, not in -er, identifying it as Jewish, but in -ev, as many ethnic Russian names end? That would be a normal surname, that is, a good one, like that of such people as the film director Ivan Pyriev and the actress Yulia Solntseva. Let me have, if not an ethnic Russian surname, at least a Ukrainian one, with the characteristic -enko ending. If I were not Draitser but Draitserenko, my stomach wouldn't ache every time I wait for my name to be pronounced during the roll call. What should I do then? And who's guilty of putting me in this predicament?

I come to the conclusion that it's all my parents' fault. I secretly hate them for not giving me a normal first name at least. I would have far fewer problems had they done so. Was it really impossible to come up with a decent name—Yura, Seryozha, Petya, Vasya, names for normal boys, that is, Russian boys? There are enough normal names to choose from.

I'm especially vexed by the letter u (pronounced as "oo"), the second vowel of my name in Russian—Samuil. All my misfortune is in that letter! It gives me away. Kolya, Stëpa, Sasha, Dima, Vanya—I can list the names of my classmates indefinitely. Not one of them has a name with that disgusting, menacing sound. Oo, I'll give you grief! Oo, you get yourself into trouble with me! Oo! Oo-oo-oo.

I make more unpleasant discoveries. It turns out that, in my own family, I'm surrounded with people who pose as not who they actually are. At home, Mama calls Papa "Abrasha" (a nickname for Abram), but in the streets, if she hails him, she shouts, "Arkady" or "Arkasha." How come? What is his real name then?

Once, on our dinner table, I come across the passport of my uncle Misha, Papa's brother. He's just been discharged from the army and has no place to live. He and Papa are both housepainters. They work together, and my uncle sleeps on a folding bed in our only room. He's left the passport for Mama to take to the police precinct for his residence registration. Next to my uncle's photo, I read, "Draitser Samuil Urovich." His patronymic is strange. Obviously, a typing error. It should be Yurievich. (I don't yet know that Uri is a legitimate Jewish name and that Urovich is his patronymic in Russian.) But the name Samuil? Another Samuil? But everybody around (and he himself) calls him nothing other than Misha! Therefore, in his passport his full name should be Mikhail. What does Samuil have to do with it?

Why on earth was I born into a family like this? No matter who you turn to, I have a relative who has one name on his or her passport but quite a different one in real life. My papa is Abrasha; that means he's Jewish. But Mama introduces herself to everybody with her first name and patronymic; both of them Russian—Sofia Vladimirovna. Her looks aren't much different from those of the mothers of my Russian and Ukrainian classmates. She has a small nose and light brown hair, a slightly darker shade than theirs. I was very sure that she was a normal woman, that is, a Russian woman. One of our neighbors even told me once that Mama reminded her of a Russian silent-movie star, Vera Kholodnaya. What a surprise I'm in for when, full of doubts after the episode with my uncle Misha's passport, I seize the moment to get into the top drawer of our sideboard, where Mama keeps our documents, and peep at her passport. My heart rolls downward. My worst fears are justified. It turns out that she is Soybel Wolfovna! And in the "nationality" category, "a Jew" is written, in black and white. I didn't expect this treachery from her!

But there's more to come. Everyone calls my mother's sister Clara, a Russian name, but her name is actually the Jewish Khaya. My mother's cousin Dunya is sometimes called by the affectionate variant of the Russian name Dariya, but, in fact, her true name, that is, her Jewish name, is Dvoira. This means that I'm not the only one who's ashamed of his name! It means that all of them—Papa, Mama, my uncle and aunts—are quite aware that their true names are repugnant. They use better-sounding Russian variants of them. Deep hopelessness settles in me once and for all. I belong from all sides to a people who admit their own inferiority. I'm a Jew. It looks like I'm stuck with being a Jew forever.

(I had the good sense to remove a splinter from the name, the ill-fated letter *u*, only ten years later. I chose for myself the name Emil. Having kept three letters of my true name, *m, i,* and *l,* I managed to get rid of the disgusting letter *u,* which oppressed me the most. No more Samuils! I'm Emil and that's it. I was eighteen or nineteen when I changed it. It was too late to change my passport. My true name, a name that I so often dreamed of getting rid of, stuck out in my passport like a bone lodged in my throat. But, introducing myself to girls, I already began to use my new name.)

That happened later, in my adult life. But meanwhile the damned Russian letter *u*, which looks like the English *y*, sticks out as if an ugly growth. It sticks out in the middle of my name, just as the other source of my despair, my nose, sticks out in the middle of my face. I avoid looking at myself in a mirror. Though I'm not a Quasimodo—I have neither a hump nor any other obvious disfigurements—it seems to me that I'm a monster. I have an abnormal nose, nothing like the nose of the overwhelming majority of my peers, short and snubbed, but a long one that is somewhat aquiline. When they take pictures of me, I avoid being photographed in profile or even in three-quarters' view. They can do it only *en face* or, even better, from a bit below. That way I look tolerable, though my face with my head thrown back acquires a haughty expression, uncharacteristic for me.

"*Sr-r-rool',* turn your rudder!" they shout to me in the class.

Apparently, for those who shout it, the phrase has the advantage of having several harsh-sounding Russian *r* sounds, which they purposely pronounce as gutturally as they can. When it happened for the first time, I even thought that they were not addressing me, that they had confused me with someone else. I don't have difficulty pronouncing this sound, as some Jews do. (As I will learn many years later, because the Russian *r* sound is very different from the Yiddish *r* sound, Soviet Jews who grew up speaking Yiddish tended to speak Russian with an accent that highlighted a Yiddish *r* sound.)

The association of the Yiddish *r* with Jews caused a queer thought to occur to me when, for the first time, I saw a play featuring Lenin as a character. Lenin had a speech defect and couldn't pronounce his *r*'s properly, making him sound as though he had a Jewish accent. Trying to resemble the real Lenin, the actor playing him enunciated his *r*'s just as Lenin had, and a bewildering thought flashed through my mind: really—can it be that Vladimir Ilyich Lenin was also a Jew?

Now, no matter how I strain my sight looking at pictures of me of that time, I cannot find any rhinoceros. My face is like any other face. And my nose is not so terrible. Clearly the horn did not sprout from between my eyes at that time; it sprouted inward, into my head, which was squeezed by fear. My classmates hounded me for no reason. During class breaks, my nose evoked all the other nicknames that existed in Russian: Rubil'nik (Knife Switch), Paial'nik (Soldering Iron), Rumpel' (Tiller). They even included a degrading-sounding made-up name, Shnobel. (Later, when in America, at the age of forty, I inwardly shuddered at how calmly a broadcaster introduced himself when opening the music program *Morning Becomes Eclectic* at the NPR station in Santa Monica: "At the microphone is Tom Shnobel.")

I take part in my class field trip to a theater. The teachers lead us in pairs to Paster Street, where the Theater of the Young Audience was located before relocating to Theater Lane. The play's title is *Cyrano de Bergerac.* I don't suspect anything bad. Before settling down in a soft armchair, fitted with red plush, I try furtively to rock a bit on its collapsible seat. At last, the lights dim, triumphant music resounds, and from the wings, a sword in hand, a man in a raincoat darts out in a few huge steps onto the middle of the stage. The spotlight projected from the ceiling hits his face. It's him, Cyrano de Bergerac. And suddenly the hall begins giggling in perplexity, and then the laughter turns into a roar. At first I don't understand what the matter is. But as soon as I peer into the actor's face, a hot wave of fear and shame rolls over my body. De Bergerac has a huge nose!

My ears are burning. It seems to me that everyone knows that the play is about me. Not daring to look around, I slip gradually from the seat of the armchair. I cover my nose with my palm. Why have they brought me to this performance? Have they really done this so that they can all laugh at me together? I should have a pretext not to take part in this collective outing. To get ill or to think up something else. How could I have known what awaited me? I told Mama the day before that after school we were going on a field trip to the Theater of the Young Audience. But she didn't warn me about Cyrano's looks.

Holding my breath, with one eye, I follow Cyrano as the action develops. I'm surprised that the hero of the play doesn't lose heart because of his defect. He composes poetry. He engages in sword fights. He courts a young beauty. I suddenly begin to understand that the play was written to console freaks like me. The beauty eventually falls in love with Cyrano. I force myself to believe that true beauty is spiritual, not physical, until my heart hurts. Therefore, there's hope for people like me. Talent, noble behavior, and kindness can make miracles happen; they can make the world forget that you're an ugly creature. And a female heart, the highest prize that one can win in life, is possible to captivate by eloquence alone.

I'm not the only Jewish boy in our class. There's also Yura Lerner, a lean muscular boy, his forehead bulging, his nose so thin that the blood capillaries shine through it under the light of the sun; indeed, the shape of his nose resembles a lifeboat rudder.

There's tall Edik Barmash, who looks to be a year or two older than the others, in a dark blue tunic like an old tsarist-era high school uniform.

There's fat Vova Braslavsky. They often place pens on his desk seat when he stands up to answer a question in class. We don't feel any solidarity with one another. We don't try to protect one another. Each of us is on his own. Each of us is only mildly consoled when, from time to time, they forget about one of us and switch to another. The shame of belonging to a despised tribe paralyzes and weakens our spirit. We do not cover for one other, as the Jews are often accused of. With the rash cruelty of raw youths, we, the Jewish boys, sometimes even sting one another.

My neighbor lives in the building around the corner, on Gavan Street. He attends the same school as I, in another class. His name is Boris, and his surname is Leyechkis. Once he distinguished himself. Coming home from school, he noticed that smoke was oozing out from the ground-floor window in one of the buildings. He also saw a flash of flame. Boris was frightened at first. But, brought up in the spirit of the Young Pioneers, whose duty is always to be civic-minded, he rushed to a payphone and called the firefighters. They put out the fire in time to save the old woman who lived there.

Some days later, the next general meeting at school was held, conducted by our principal, Vasily Petrovich. Boris was absent the day of the meeting; he was sick with the flu. On the way home, I stopped by at his place to bring him homework assignments. I told him about the meeting. Then I surprised myself by saying, "You know what Vasily Petrovich said? He said, 'Boys and girls! There's a hero in our school. His name's Boris Leyechkis. He did a noble thing. He rescued an old woman from fire. Let him be an example for all of you. Boris Leyechkis is a hero, even though he's a Jew.'" But the principal hadn't said anything like that. Far from revealing the hideous fact of Boris's origins, he had just given the usual boring report on the world political events. Probably Vasily Petrovich wanted to tell about Boris's heroic feat as an example of how true Young Pioneers have to act. But he couldn't present the hero personally to the audience of other schoolchildren.

As he listened to my report, Boris rose halfway on his bed. The muscles of his face, every single one of them, began to twitch. He fixed his gaze on me. It seemed that he was about to cry. But he only turned pale and cried out in a thin, girlish little voice, "He *really* said so?" Then Boris huddled up in horror. He seized his pillow in his arms and pressed it to his chest as if he were being shot at and was trying, in this pitiful way, to save himself from the bullet.

Boris hid his ethnicity. Since his surname ended in *-is,* he pretended to be Lithuanian. A fragile and undersized Jewish boy, he knew that not only his classmates' sneering mockery and malicious insults were in store for him now but beatings as well. He was afraid that he wouldn't be able to stand up for himself.

"Did he really say *that*?" Boris uttered with a deep, almost an adult, groan. Tears appeared in his eyes. At this minute I recalled the ancient Greek custom of killing messengers who brought bad news. Could it be that, after all, the ancient Greeks were right to do so? After all, with my foolish prank, I had nearly finished him off. What had I invented all this for? Mischief making wasn't in my character. Though for the most part reticent and gloomy, I wasn't pernicious. Why had I scared him by saying that his Jewishness had been exposed? Because I didn't have any opportunity to disguise myself? Could I not handle my own feelings of guilt in being born Jewish?

I recall another shameful episode. I was already in the fifth or sixth grade. Once, during class break, I was beaten up. I came home with a bruised lip. Next day, Mama egged Papa on to come to school. ("Are you a father or not? They're beating up your son, and you couldn't care less!") He asked me who my offender was. After balking for a long time ("nobody, nobody"), I pointed to my classmate Kolya. (Later, though we didn't become friends, we established a mutual peace. As an honor student, I was assigned to be his tutor. I began visiting him at his home and helped him to catch up with the rest of the class in mathematics.)

Papa called to Kolya and asked him, "What have you beaten him up for?"

"For nothing!" he said.

"Why beat on someone who's weaker than you? Is that worthy of a man? Especially when there's no reason for it."

"No, I have a reason. He's strong but afraid of being hit."

It was true, and he was right. I wasn't a sickly boy. Perhaps not brawny, but I stood strong on my legs. Not many succeeded in pulling me down to the floor. Why was I afraid of getting hit? Why didn't I even try to fight back? It was all for the very same reason. It was a secret I kept even from myself: I assumed that it was *proper* to beat up boys like me. I carry an indelible mark of natural misfortune. I'm the worst thing of all: I'm a Jew. It's like an ugly birthmark across your face. You can't be blamed for being born that way, but, all the same, you can't help but feel that it serves you right if they look back and laugh at you. Just like Boris, I also felt like disappearing, dissolving among the others. But neither my first name, nor my patronymic, nor my surname, nor my appearance provided me with the opportunity. My situation was hopeless. I still avoided looking into the mirror. If by chance I glanced into it, I turned away at once, spotting my face out of the corner of my eye, glum, frowning, and tight-lipped.

The episode when I was beaten up was humiliating. My own powerlessness, the absence of the spirit of resistance, disgusted me. I found small consolation only in the fact that I wasn't the only one like that.

In the other class, the "B" class, there was another boy whose first and last names, as well as his appearance, were unmistakably Jewish—Monya Bortman. One of the tallest boys in school, during physical education classes, he easily lifted a dumbbell with the heaviest weights, "pancakes," as we called them. One day, walking across our schoolyard, I saw how three boys from the streets attacked Monya. In the early postwar years, little groups of adolescents roamed the streets of Odessa aimlessly, in search of a scuffle. Not knowing what to do with themselves, they often visited schoolyards. This trio of orphans, their growth stunted by wartime malnutrition, were almost a head shorter than Monya. They encircled him like sparrows around a raven; they swung their fists in the air, vainly trying to get at Monya's face. It was enough for him to raise his chin slightly, and the fists of his attackers couldn't even touch him. And here, after some vain attempts to reach his face, one of them, with a fierce, barely washed face, shouted out, menacingly and contemptuously, "Hey you, kike's mug, bend over!" And Monya obediently bent. His weak-willed hands hanging beside his long body, they beat up his face until dark red streamlets of blood began running down from his nose. Then the attackers dispersed.

Certainly, there were also Jewish boys who were able to stand up for themselves. Lënya Mak, in another class, was annoyed that the others constantly poked fun at him, calling him not only a "kike" but also, because of his corpulence, *zhir-trest-kombinat* (Fat-Trust-Corporation) and *kolbasa* (sausage). He joined a weightlifting training circle at the local sports center. In time, he became the Ukrainian teenage weightlifting champion. His persecutors not only ceased to accost him; they began to force their friendship on him.

But recalling the strong boy Monya Bortman and the expression of confusion and impotence on his face, I understood why he didn't resist, why he voluntary submitted to the blows. Apparently the deepest guilt resided in him, just as it did in me. This feeling had appeared in his and my early subconscious as though it were part of our genetic inheritance—*I'm a Jew; beating me is the right thing to do.*

FIVE

Black Shawl

When I was young and gullible,
I passionately loved a young Greek girl.

The beauty was tender with me;
But soon I came to live a day of darkness.

FROM "THE BLACK SHAWL,"
ALEXANDER PUSHKIN

I MEMORIZED THESE PUSHKIN LINES right way. And I never forgot them. Perhaps they stayed imprinted on my memory because they reminded me of that day of darkness that I lived through.

Early September 1949. I'm almost twelve. It's still warm during the day, but in the mornings there's already an autumn chill. I shiver a bit as I rush along the sandy trails of Primorsky Boulevard, little pebbles crunching under my feet. I am heading to the Young Pioneers Palace at the other end of the boulevard. No one in Odessa calls this palace by any other name, except by the name of its former nineteenth-century owner, Count Vorontsov, Pushkin's contemporary.

In the back of the palace, overlooking the seaport from a cliff, there is a semicircular colonnade. Behind this majestic structure of Corinthian columns sit two rusty six-barreled German mortars, smeared with dirty yellow paint for camouflage. I inch toward them with curiosity and apprehension. The vile, short-nosed barrels are turned toward the port. It is there, down below; you can see it as clearly as if it were in the palm of your hand. You have to admit, they're positioned conveniently. Mortars are another reminder of the recent war.

I don't linger at the colonnade for too long. I am hurrying to the palace. In its halls, groups of Young Pioneers, girls for sewing and whittling, boys for making model airplanes, now gather where hussars used to curl their mustaches at the mirrors.

Young chess players also have a club here. Our instructor, a chess expert, is Arnold Aronovich, a tall man who has black eyebrows and usually looks sullen. He leans on the edge of the table with his long hands, curly black hair peeking out from the cuffs of his shirt. He looks at our chessboards. In the frenzy of attack, we bang the pieces down on the boards and, unlike serious adult players, try to scare our opponents by yelling "CHECK!" as loudly as possible when attacking the king and "GARDE!" when threatening the queen. Our primitive chess skills almost make Arnold Aronovich sick. I, too, am not a great player, but I quickly discover that half of the kids in the group play worse than I, and I win my first chess rating: fifth category, the lowest. Then I get to the fourth category. Within a year, I am solidly in category three.

Chess teaches me something important—to think not only about how to respond to my opponent's thrust but also about what can happen next. If you can see at least one move beyond what your opponent can see, you win. It turns out that the only things required in chess are thinking and keeping your emotions in check. And also perseverance. Even while losing, if at least some pieces are still on the board, there is always hope.

But the main reason for my visits to the palace is its remarkable library. From my earliest childhood, I am enchanted with the printed word. I read everything in sight. Whenever Mama sends me somewhere, be it to get sour cream or cooking oil or mineral water, no matter how urgent the chore, once I get to the streets, I can't help but dash to the nearest newsstand. I know where to find pages of *Pravda, Izvestiya (News), Sovetskii sport (Soviet Sports),* and *Literaturnaia gazeta (Literary Gazette)* posted under glass for everybody to read. I can tell them apart from afar. Each newspaper has its own typographical look. The letter *A* in *Pravda*'s title has two cross-strokes, the top one thicker and the lower one thinner. The heavy bars of *Trud* (Labor) newspaper look as if they've been flattened on an anvil. The swirls of the *Soviet Sports* title remind me of a figure skater's pattern on the ice.

I walk around the little wooden huts of the newsstands. I examine the covers of brochures behind the window glass. On the corner of Deribas and Karl Marx streets, I watch the newsstand attendant at work. He places a stack of the freshly printed papers on the counter. A long line already stretches out, waiting to buy them. Any time of the year, even in ninety-degree heat, his long-peaked cap over his eyes, the newsman works with the dexterity of a magician. With one hand he whisks a customer's coin off the counter into his apron pocket; licking the fingers of the other hand, he picks up the paper and, managing to fold it in midair, shoves it under the arm of the customer who is himself overloaded with shopping bags. He even has time to pat the customer's back in farewell: "Move it, move it, dear man. Don't hold up traffic. Next!"

I steal up to the seller and sniff out the air. The very smell of the typographic ink excites me. Soaking into the pores of the paper, turning from ink into a printed word, the word now takes on a magical power. A manuscript carries a sign of individuality and is automatically deprived of legitimacy in the world in which I live. Being printed in a newspaper, typed text carries a sign of the supreme power of approval. I am completely aware that, through a newspaper, a certain higher power, to which I and each and every other person are subordinate, expresses its will.

"*Gotenyu,*" my mother says in Yiddish when I return home. "Dear God! You're slower than molasses in January. Well, where were you for so long? How much time, I ask you, does it take to get a half a pound of sour cream?"

"There was a line," I mutter.

This excuse always works. In those days, lines were the permanent fixture of our daily lives.

Once I have developed a passion for reading, I cannot shake it off. I've read everything that is the least bit interesting in our scant postwar school library. The edges of my library card have been frayed for a long time. There is also a neighborhood children's library on Karl Marx Street; it's cramped, poorly lit, with low ceilings. The librarian is stern. If you're a day late returning a book, she can take away your borrowing privileges. A red flag appears on your library record, marking you forever as untrustworthy. And to allow anyone to step over the barrier, to come close to the shelves themselves, is out of the question here and in any other library at this time.

The Young Pioneers Palace is a totally different matter. The reading hall has high ceilings and shiny parquet floors. The light hits the huge windows, through which you can see our gentle sea all the way to the horizon. The walls are decorated with frescoes on the subjects of *The Thousand and One Nights.* And immeasurably more books are located here than in any other children's library. But the most important thing is that here I enjoy the rarest and sweetest of privileges—I can pick books from the shelves myself.

I am the only person with access to the restricted shelves. I earned this privilege accidentally. I was once nearby when the librarian, Maria Vasilievna, cried out at the sight of a dead mouse under one of the book stands. Suppressing my disgust, I picked it up by the tail, took it out of the building, and tossed it over the banister and off the cliff. (I did this not without secret pride. At that moment I felt myself a man, a protector of a woman who, although an adult, couldn't manage a tiny mouse without my help.)

Slowly, in awe, I move along the shelves brimming with books. At the very sight of the gold-stamped covers of the Library of World Adventures set, my heart stops. Mayne Reid's *The Headless Horseman.* My throat dry, I read it right there, my forehead pressed against the library shelf. Here, too, the children of Jules Verne's Captain Grant wander under the scorching sun of Patagonia. The place-name itself sounds incredibly romantic. At the Young Pioneers Palace, the usual Soviet odors linger: the staircases reek with cat urine, the poorly swept corridors smell of dust, and the large halls smell of rotting parquet and dead mice. But for me the air is infused with the aroma of the mind-altering grass of the pampas, herds of wild mustangs galloping across them.

But because of Kaverin's *Two Captains,* the North lures me the most. The farther to the north, the better. In the North, the heroes of this book battle with hurricane winds and giant icebergs. I want their motto to become the directive of my future life as well: "To search against all odds and not give up till you find it."

But, as my spirits lift, I plunge into despondency there and then. As much as I try to imagine myself in the place of these fearless captains, something is not quite complete. I lack a common thread with the lives of the heroes in *Two Captains.* How can I even hope to ever be like them? Do I belong to the big Russian nation living in the North, kind and strong, noble and magnanimous? Odessa is the melting pot of the southerners—of Ukrainians, Armenians, Greeks, Bulgarians, and . . . Jews. I will never stand on a captain's bridge. I will never guide my ship through storms to some mysterious shores.

Only poetry invokes in me an unspoiled delight. I worship Pushkin. I already know that he is the greatest poet on earth. The 110th anniversary of his death has just recently been celebrated. I listened to the radio broadcast about the anniversary celebrations in Moscow and read about them in the papers. I am already aware that Pushkin was Lenin's favorite poet and that Comrade Stalin has called him the pride and glory of the Russian nation. "Pushkin," the articles said, "was the echo of the Russian people, its great son. He embodies all the best traits of Russian genius—simplicity, breadth of soul, love of people, sharp mind, and extraordinary sense of beauty." Our teacher, Galina Ivanovna, speaks of him as nothing less than a luminary: "The sun of Russian poetry rose on May 26, 1799, when a boy named Alexander was born to an ancient gentry family of Pushkins."

Our assignment is to learn his poems by heart and then recite them in class:

> Frost and sunshine, a wonderful day!
> . . . .
> Under the blue skies,
> A splendid rug,
> The snow glistens in the sun.
> *"Zimnee utro" (Winter Morning)*

My heart aches even from the beauty of Pushkin's lines. I close my eyes and imagine the fluffy snow as far as the eye can see, the branches of the huge fir trees covered with it, and the blue-gray ice of the river. We get snow here in Odessa too. But it doesn't last long, sometimes for an hour or two or, if we are fortunate, for a day or even two. Then it melts. It gets wet outside, and Mama makes me put on galoshes. It's totally another matter there, in the North, where Pushkin lived—"frost and sunshine!"

I've read each and every one of his poems in our class reader *Native Speech.* And now here, in the library of the Young Pioneers Palace, I see a neat edition of Pushkin's *Selected Verses and Narrative Poems,* in a hard burgundy cover with a gray inset. First, I leaf through the volume. A picture of a young aristocrat, A. P. Kern, is stuck inside it. Pushkin was in love with her; she is the one to whom he dedicated his famous poem "I Remember the Marvelous Moment." From just one glance at her deep cleavage, I steam up. The topic of love is already tormenting me. My ears burn from reading Pushkin's lines dedicated to his beautiful contemporaries. I barely understand the meaning of the fancy words of love poetry of that time, words such as *persi, lanity,* and *lobzanie* (old-fashioned variants of *bosom, cheeks,* and *kissing*). They sound magnificent. And I am already starting to guess their meanings, so I blush reading them. To make sure that Maria Vasilievna won't accidentally notice how my ears glow, I squat between the shelves with the book in my hands.

I eat up one Pushkin poem after another until I get to "The Black Shawl."
I begin reading. As always, I revel in Pushkin's language.

When I was young and gullible,
I passionately loved a young Greek girl.

The beauty was tender with me;
But soon I came to live a day of darkness.

Suddenly and sharp as a nail piercing my chest, one line transfixes me:

Once when I gathered jolly guests,
A despicable Jew knocked on my door.

I stop. My face gets hot and flushed. Tears involuntarily well up in my eyes.
I am totally floored. If the great Pushkin, the sun of Russian poetry, is saying such a thing . . . Holding my breath, I read the poem again. Why is the
Jew despicable? Maybe I missed something, some line where the Jew's fault
is explained? I move from stanza to stanza—no longer tasting the enjoyment of poetry, but with caution, carefully fumbling as if I am in the dark
hallway of our communal apartment, where you need to stick your hands
out in front of yourself to avoid stumbling against the wash-bin hanging
on the wall:

"While your friends are feasting with you," he whispered,
"Your Greek girl is cheating on you."

I gave him some gold coins, damned him,
And I called my faithful serf.

I don't understand a thing. Why is Pushkin angry with this Jew? What happened? "A despicable Jew knocked on my door." Let's dissect the sentence
according to the rules of grammar. *Jew* is the sentence's subject. *Knocked* is
the predicate. *Despicable* is a modifier. Since the man happens to be Jewish, does that mean that he is automatically despicable? Does that modifier
go hand in hand with *Jew*?

Still, why does the greatest Russian poet hate this Jew so much? What
kind of evil thing did he do? After all, he didn't hammer on the door. He
delicately knocked so as not to disturb the neighbors. (It didn't occur to me
at the time that Pushkin's hero didn't know what a communal apartment

was, the kind of apartment in which I spent my childhood and adolescence.) This means that the poet knew in advance that only an antisocial person, specifically a "despicable Jew," would knock at the door and upset the host at the moment when a sumptuous feast reaches its highest point.

Then again, the real culprit is the unfaithful woman. But at this moment, she doesn't count. Otherwise, why would Pushkin say, "I gave him some gold coins and damned him?" He damned not the Greek girl who cheated on him, but the Jew. Why? It was obvious why. So that he wouldn't ruin the festivities.

Again, as in the incident with my neighbor Boris Leyechkis, I remember the ancient Greek custom of killing those who bring bad news. I read about this in my favorite book, *Mify drevnei Ellady (The Myths of Ancient Greece)*. Back then it seemed terribly unfair. The messenger didn't do anything bad. He just informed about a mishap. And for that they killed him.

But the great Pushkin couldn't have been so unfair. Why, though, why did he pick the Jew to play the thankless part? I try to find some technical reason. Maybe the rhyme pattern let him down? He wrote, "Once when I gathered jolly guests / a despicable —— knocked on my door." He started to think about whom he should cast in the role of the messenger with the bad news. He needed a two-syllable word that ends with *-ei* (guests, *gostei*), and the rhyming Russian word for Jew is *evrei*. "Ah!" Pushkin said and slapped himself on the forehead. "But, of course, *evrei*!"

My cheeks are burning as if they were just horsewhipped. Why underscore the nationality of the person who happened to knock at the wrong time? Instead of the word *evrei,* couldn't he have used the word *lakei* (lackey)? "A despicable lackey knocked on my door." How great that would be! And historically justified. Pushkin's time was the time of serfdom, the feudal times, the times of man exploiting man. Servants were contemptuously called "lackeys." There are no longer any lackeys in our time, but the word appears sometimes in newspaper articles on international topics. Just recently this heading appeared in *Pravda:* "The American Secretary of State Dean Acheson Is an Imperialists' Lackey."

With a sunken heart, I reread the poem again:

I enter the distant bedroom alone . . .
An Armenian man is kissing the unfaithful girl.

And suddenly it dawns on me why the boys tease my dark-eyed classmate sitting two desks to the left of me, Ashotik Grigoryants, calling him *armiashka,* "little Armenian." In Pushkin's poem, both bad people are non-Russians—a Jew and an Armenian. And the unfaithful woman is Greek. (I'm only twelve, and I don't know yet that Pushkin's hero in this poem isn't necessarily Russian, that the whole plot is just a romantic convention of the poetry of the time. And the poem itself is not an original composition but a rearrangement of a Moldavian song. The volume was published in a series for schoolchildren; although it had plenty of footnotes, the information about the poem's origin was absent. It's clear that the publishers didn't want the young readers to doubt that Pushkin expressed his own attitude toward the Jews here.)*

Finally, I decide that this was just one of Pushkin's artistic devices: a non-Russian person means "the bad one." That's the kind of synonym it is. The story of a poet who feasted carefree with his friends once and for all clarifies the distinction between him and the people that I belong to. I still can't clearly explain this to myself, but I already feel that the poet and his friends, on one hand, and the Jew who came with the bad news, on the other, are made of different human fiber. They have nothing in common. I am overtaken with disgust for myself. It was *I, I* who knocked on the door of the great poet while he was feasting with his friends. It was *I* who brought him bad news. *I* whispered in his ear that he's being betrayed and upset him. What on earth caused me to be born a Jew? How horrible! Absolutely horrible!

I have hardly lived through the events in "The Black Shawl" when, at school, we are assigned Gogol's novel *Taras Bulba* to read. I want to be strong and brave like its heroes, the Zaporozhian Cossacks. I read the great Gogol, and my heart aches from the oppressive feeling that I will never be like the Cossacks. Here he writes: "Intoxicated and insensate Cossacks gathered in the square." In my mind, I try to substitute the Cossacks with my closest relatives—my father, my uncle Abram, my uncle Misha, but no matter how I strain, I just can't do it. I have never seen them "intoxicated and insensate." My father is a housepainter, a workman. At a holiday dinner, he may have one or two shots of vodka. But he cannot drink a whole glass of vodka in one gulp and without having a snack right after it. No one in our family can do it. Alas, no matter how hard we try, we can't be Cossacks.

*A. S. Pushkin, *Izbrannye stikhotvoreniia i poemy* (Selected verses and narrative poems), Biblioteka shkol'nika (School Student Library Series) (Leningrad: Leningradskoe gazetno-zhurnal'noe i knizhnoe izdatel'stvo, 1949), 67–68.

I get to chapter four. The Cossacks, in "torn knit sweaters," are arriving by ferryboat. They have drunk away everything they had, including their fancy clothes. Their commander is speaking angrily in the square. But he's chastising not the Cossacks for knowing no limit to revelry. He is outraged that many Zaporozhians "are so deep in debt to kikes and their fellow Zaporozhians that they have stopped observing the rites of their [Christian] faith." Therefore, it's not the Cossacks who have to be blamed but again the Jews. It's all their fault. I feel stupid that I have a hard time grasping such logic.

In another place, Gogol calls the Jews *zhidki,* "little kikes." I cringe inwardly. I'm a boy. This means that I am not even a full "kike" but just a speck of one, a "little kike." The commander announces that, where the Cossacks have come from, the Jews have taken over everything: "The churches are rented from kikes. If a kike isn't paid in advance, the Mass can't be held." And the commander suggests revenge for the desecrated religion by "drowning all the rascals in the river." Not those Jews who took over the churches—they are too far away—but those who are nearby, in the settlement on the other side of the river.

I reread this scene over and over and am still puzzled. The Cossacks exclaim, "We are prepared to lay down our lives for our faith!" They are laying down not their own lives, however, but those of unarmed people whose only fault is that they are also Jews. What lesson do I learn from the work of the great Gogol, whose sympathies lay totally with the heroic Cossacks? It's all the same which Jews to beat up—the ones that are at fault or any other. They're all the same.

Then, with ecstasy, Gogol describes how, "roaring with laughter," the Cossacks "drowned the little kikes in the Dnieper." The Jews ask the thugs for mercy, "We are like blood brothers with the Zaporozhians." Their pleas are answered with, "The devil is your blood brother!" The Jews try to save themselves, "losing every little bit of their spirit, no matter how petty it was to begin with."

I shudder. Just like my classmates, Gogol thinks that the Jews are nothing but cowards. (I still don't know anything—and won't know anything for a long time—about the history of the people I belong to. I don't even suspect that the Cossacks would slit their own throats from shame if they were to learn that their assurances of readiness to give their lives for their faith is childish bragging compared with the selflessness of the defenders of the ancient town of Masada. About them, as about many other Jewish heroes—Judah the Maccabee, Bar-Kokhba, the Warsaw ghetto fighters, the units of Jewish guerrilla fighters during the Great Patriotic War [1941–45], the Jewish members of the French resistance, and many others—I will learn only twenty-five years later in Rome, in the Library of the Jewish Fund, when I leave the Soviet Union forever.)

Reading *Taras Bulba* plunges me into deep bewilderment. I try to reconcile the greatness of Gogol on one hand and the moral lessons taught at school on the other. At the time we discuss the story titled "A Murdered Small Bird," from our reader *Native Speech.* Imagining himself a hunter, a young boy thoughtlessly kills a small bird with a rock. He begins to feel sorry for it and to feel that he's a criminal. "Poor creature. What have I done?" he asks, tormented. "Maybe she has small children? They will be waiting for their mother." Taking turns reading the story aloud sentence by sentence, we then answer the questions printed at the story end for our teacher Galina Ivanovna: "Why did the boy kill the bird? How do you relate to the pointless killings of living things?"

The story says that the boy ran over to the dead bird and saw that it was "sweet and gentle." Maybe this is the answer? If a living thing is "sweet and gentle," then it is shameful to kill it, but if it is ugly . . . Therefore, the Jews are hideous creatures not worthy of pity. In Gogol's work, people, not birds, are mercilessly drowned in the river, without even a thought that they might have small children. I can't find any explanation for this, except one: a Jew is worth less than a small bird. Jews are like annoying insects. I have never seen anyone kill a fly or a mosquito and experience any pity for it.

Reading Gogol chokes me with a horrible discovery: I belong to an exclusive breed of people who can be killed without remorse. I retreat into myself more and more. I feel there is no way out. It turns out that even great Russian literature—as we are taught, the fairest, most humane, which defends the weak and the deserted more powerfully than any other literature of the world—is against me.

A few years will pass. Already a high school student, I will get to Pushkin's little play in verse, *Skupoi rytsar' (The Covetous Knight).* Compared with this play, "The Black Shawl" will seem like a eulogy to the Jewish people. What will pain me the most will be not that a Jewish character in *Knight* suggests to the hero that he poison his own father so that he can get hold of his inheritance earlier. And not even that he offers to commit the crime with the help of another Jew, his pharmacist friend. (What other nationality could an evildoer, secretly trading in poison, possibly belong to? A Jew as a character is indispensable when a scoundrel or murderer has to be portrayed.) The most unbearable aspect for me will be that, no matter how much he thirsts to borrow money, the Gentile hero addresses the Jew whose favors he seeks in no other way than with contempt, calling him a "damned kike." And the Jew doesn't even get upset, as if such insults were merely a form of endearment.

I have yet to come to Nikolai Nekrasov's vilest anti-Semitic verses and Dostoevsky's malicious spittle directed at Jewry. Out of habit, I'll still rejoice when I read a kind word thrown in passing, like alms, by the literary idol of my youth, Anton Chekhov. In his story "Moia zhizn'" ("My Life"), the narrator notices that the libraries in his provincial town are frequented by Jewish teenagers only. This compliment is needed for pejorative contrast. Here, he says, how low we, the Russian people, have sunk in our laziness and indifference to everything: in our towns, nowadays only Jewish youth strive for culture.

I'll find little consolation in the fact that the great Russian literature stores up no less enmity toward other minorities—the Poles, Armenians, Chechens:

The Terek [River] streams over the rocks,
The muddy waves splash about.
A mean Chechen's crawling on the shore,
And sharpening his dagger.
            Kazach'ia kolybel'naia pesnia
            (A Cossack Lullaby)

The author of these lines, another great Russian poet, Lermontov, can't even fathom that a Chechen has more than enough reason to be angry and sharpen his dagger. After all, he's crawling not on someone else's, some Russian's, Lermontov's shore, but on his own Chechen shore, which he's trying, selflessly and hopelessly, to protect from invading enslavers.

I'll still feel a lump in my throat and tears of emotion involuntarily well up in my eyes when I encounter sympathy and respect toward the Jews in the works of Leo Tolstoy, Maxim Gorky, Vladimir Korolenko, and Alexander Kuprin. Apparently, some Russian writers are capable of sympathizing with the woes and sorrows not just of their own people.

Many years will pass before I learn that Gogol's Cossacks are not just the fruit of the writer's imagination. A pogrom described with good-natured humor in *Taras Bulba,* the Cossacks laughing at the pitiful Jews trying to save themselves, will seem like an idyllic scene compared with the pogroms of Bogdan Khmelnitsky, the seventeenth-century Ukrainian Cossack commander. Unaware of the bloody part he played in the fate of my people, I will make dates with delicate young girls at his monument in the center of Kiev in the days of my youth. (It is still there.) My body will grow cold, I will be ready to cry, filled with helpless terror, four decades later, when in America, I will read an eyewitness account of a Khmelnitsky pogrom:

> Some of them [the Jews] had their skins flayed off them and their flesh flung to the dogs. The hands and feet of others were cut off and they were flung onto the roadway where carts ran over them and they were trod under foot by horses. . . . Many were buried alive. Children were slaughtered [at] their mother's bosoms and many children were torn apart like fish. They ripped up the bellies of pregnant women, took out unborn children, and flung them in their faces. They tore open the bellies of some of them and placed a living cat within the belly and left them alive thus, first cutting off their hands so that they should not be able to take the living cat out of the belly . . . and there was never an unnatural death in the world that they did not inflict upon them.*

And still, no matter how sad my later discoveries will be, they won't shock me as much as the first slap in the face that great Russian literature gives me, an unsuspecting youth, beside myself in love with it, on this chilly September day in the elegant library of the former Count Vorontsov's palace.

*The description of a Khmelnitsky massacre is excerpted from a Hebrew chronicle translated into English; see Rabbi Nathan Hanover, *Abyss of Despair (Yeven Metzulah): The Famous 17th Century Chronicle Depicting Jewish Life in Russia and Poland during the Chmielnicki Massacres of 1648–1649,* trans. Rabbi Abraham J. Mesch (New York: Bloch Publishing Company, 1950), 31–32.

SIX

Us against Them

MY FORCED RETREAT INTO MYSELF, my frantic division of the world into "us against them," coincides with the time when the world around me is divided into black and white, friends and foes. I grow up when the psychology of confrontation ("Who will do whom in—will they destroy us or we them?") weighs upon my chest. "If the enemy doesn't surrender, he has to be crushed." Though this slogan is old, in the early postwar years this intolerance is an echo of the giant battle that has just rumbled away. Fear and hatred are still alive in our hearts, like the ruins of the past war that still reek with burned gunpowder and smoke, filling the basements of the surviving buildings with fumes.

We, the children of the war, don't understand neutrality. We consider it a form of treachery. "You're either with us or against us." Noninterference boggles our minds. How could one not fight the Nazis? How could Switzerland have declared neutrality in World War II? We know how neutral they are! We bet they helped the Nazis secretly. (Our boyish intuition proved close to the truth. Now, some sixty years after the war it is well known that some Swiss banks financed the Nazis' military machine and assisted them in smuggling their looted valuables of Holocaust victims.)

The war has ended, but for many more years the Party and government teach me to hate. It seems that, little by little, they prepare me during all my school years to earn a high school diploma whose main subject is hatred.

The list of those whom I have to hate is long. They teach me to hate in the past, the present, and the future. Tsarist autocracy in general and each of the tsars separately (except for the progressive Peter the Great and the liberator from the Tatars, Ivan the Terrible). Exploiters of all shapes and colors—slaveholders, feudal lords, landowners, capitalists, all rich people in general. A rich man is the equivalent of a villain; a poor one is by definition a good person: "Poverty is no vice," as the Russian saying goes. "We, the Soviets, have our own pride," we learn by heart the Mayakovsky poem *"Brodvei"* ("Broadway"). "We look down on the bourgeois."

We are taught to laugh at religion in general and at all believers in particular. Special hatred and contempt are reserved for the priests. They are the target for acerbic Russian proverbs and sayings, caricature posters, and the heavy artillery of Russian literature. Pushkin himself is drafted for this purpose with his "Fairy Tale about a Priest and His Blockhead Servant." All priests are presented as invariably of the same kind—greedy and licentious, fat and silly.

The list of those whom we are urged to hate seems infinite. It grows from day to day. Hatred is a strong feeling; it demands a large supply of emotional energy. I feel that I don't have enough of it. Most of the time, I remain indifferent to the calls to hate. No matter how hard I try to understand who is scolded and why, all the targets of government attacks merge into one endless stream of people who are given the denigrating epithets, all those "turncoats," "enemies of the people," "idlers," "parasites," "relics of capitalism and birthmarks in people's consciousness," "embezzlers of socialist property," "revisionists of Communist ideology," "transmitters of bourgeois morality," "lovers of easy money," *letuny* ("grasshoppers," persons continually changing jobs), "Talmudists and pedants of Marxism." (At the mention of Talmudists, I huddle up internally. I already know from Papa that the Talmud is one of the sacred books of Judaism, and it seems to me that *Talmudists* means all Jews.)

The list of what I am expected to love is much shorter: Russian nature, the Russian language, our socialist motherland, our Communist Party, our dear Soviet government, and, of course, Comrade Stalin, Iosif Vissarionovich himself.

No matter how extensive the list of domestic objects the true Soviet citizens are called on to hate with all their heart, the list is negligible in comparison with the list of those whom Soviet citizens have to despise *beyond the borders* of the country. Here are the "Chiang Kai-shek clique," and "South Korean puppets acting on Washington's orders," and "the Japanese toadies of American capital," and "reactionary English trade unions," and the "German revanchists," and the head of the Yugoslavian Communist Party, Iosip Broz Tito. In the satirical magazine *Krokodil (Crocodile),* Tito is depicted as a midget with a woman's high bottom and a blood-stained axe in his hands. I haven't managed to figure out whose heads he cut and why he is drawn almost the same way as the Spanish dictator, General Franco, only that Franco wears a funny hat with a pompon dangling at his eye, and Tito wears a general's cap with a high crown, like the type Hitler's officers wore.

Warmongers are the main object of hate at the end of the 1940s and the beginning of the 1950s. They are imperialists and capitalists of all countries, but are mainly from England and America. In the newspaper caricatures, they are either undersized with hairy hands, thick stomachs, and cigars in their mouths or, on the contrary, long-legged and thin as macaroni, their grins exposing horselike teeth. The United States—led by the "inspirer of the Cold War," Harry Truman; the "lackeys of American capital," Secretaries of State Dean Acheson and John Foster Dulles; and the American Congress, "swinging about with a bugaboo of Communist aggression"—especially catches hell. It is joined by the "Trojan horse of American capital in Europe," known as the Marshall Plan, the American army in general, the military-industrial complex in particular, the "venal" Western press, the city of the "Yellow Devil," New York, and "decadent" Hollywood. In fact, our newspapers and magazines brand everything American as inherently evil, with the exception of simple folks, whom the capitalists of the United States hold in fear of the future.

Half of the back covers of our school notebooks depict the figure of an insect with little horns. A slogan is printed above it: DESTROY THE COLORADO BEETLE! This insect attacks potatoes, the main food staple you could buy in Soviet shops in the first years after the war. The papers hint that the "transatlantic warmongers" have sent this bug down into our fields. Frustrated that they cannot conquer us militarily—our Soviet army is the strongest in the world!—the warmongers have decided to starve us to death. Everywhere I see the appeal "Everyone Off to Fight the Colorado Beetle!" (Sadly enough, thirty years later, this nonsense about the Colorado bug will be repeated by writer Victor Astafiev in his notorious sketch "Catching Gudgeons in Georgia.")

Since the time when I saw *Cyrano de Bergerac,* I've become a theater buff. I want to believe that, besides the life around me, there is another one, a better, kinder, and more forgiving life, in which being a citizen of your country doesn't necessarily entail having to hate someone. I try not to miss any good plays. I see productions in both Russian and Ukrainian. Luckily, Odessa is not an out-of-the-way place. Besides the Theater of the Young Audience, there are five others. Three of them are dramatic theaters: the Soviet Army Theater, the Ivan Franko Ukrainian Dramatic Theater, and the Ivanov Russian Dramatic Theater. This last one, just a few blocks from my home, on Greek Street, is the best of them. Odessa also has the Opera and Ballet Theater, famous for its beautiful building, the second in Europe after the Viennese one, as any Odessan will proudly inform every out-of-town visitor. But I'm bored there. Both opera and ballet are of little help when it comes to interpreting the life around me. There, as a rule, all the productions are placed in other historical epochs. (Finally, the most popular theater in Odessa is the Operetta Theater, but it's not for me. I go to the theater looking for answers to serious questions about life, not just to be entertained with dancing and singing about love lost and regained.)

Dramatic theaters are a totally different matter. There I see everything, one play after another. I frequently go alone. At school, the teachers organize "culture trips" to selected performances. On one such trip, they bring us to see Konstantin Simonov's play *Russkii vopros (The Russian Question)*, devoted to life in America. Ruffled up, sitting sidewise in an armchair, I press my side against its back and glower at the stage. All the events in the play take place in semidarkness. This artistic device evinces the hopelessness of life in America. Life there is vile and awful. What else can you expect from the country of the chief warmongers?

But the play is concerned with the good and honest Americans who try to resist the capitalists. The hero of the play is a journalist. He has visited our country and seen how remarkable our life here is, but he is not allowed to write truthfully about it. His employer demands that he tell lies. When he refuses, he is threatened. Everyone abandons him, both his friends and his beloved woman.

One scene takes place in a darkened bar. The hero of the play comes to such a decadent place unwillingly. His enemies have invited him here for an important talk. As befits all immoral people, they speak in low and mean voices with impudent howling. The hero feels uncomfortable in the bar, this typically bourgeois place of vice and debauchery. Offstage, a saxophone drones on and on, overly familiar, with a nasal twang. A woman approaches the hero. A cigarette in the corner of her mouth, her face brightly painted, she walks up to him, swaying her huge hips. She is a *prodazhnaia zhenshchina,* a "woman for sale," as the Soviet newspapers call this type of female who belongs exclusively to the tsarist past and the present Western world. What this term means, I sort of know already. She is not a saleswoman in a department store, as I thought initially when I heard this expression for the first time, but a woman who sells what cannot be sold—love. I'm only twelve, and the details of her trade are still vague for me. It seems she kisses men for dollars or something of that kind.

And at this point the journalist's enemies step up onto the stage. They walk in pairs, hiding their faces with the lifted collars of their mackintoshes. They have good reason to hide them. When, for a short time, spotlights catch them, I see crooked physiognomies complete with thin and mean short mustaches under their hooked noses. The enemies, as well as the "woman for sale," talk without taking the cigarette out of the corner of their twisted mouths.

A half-liter jar in hand, I drag myself along to the vegetable store on Karl Marx Street. My mother has sent me to buy some sauerkraut. As always, I begin reading newspapers spread open under glass at the stands, one after another. In *Pravda,* I run into a poem by the same author, Konstantin Simonov, about his recent trip to America. The title is perfectly in the spirit of the time—"Friends and Enemies." Lifting up my head and blocking the sun with the hand free of the jar, I read:

> I stepped up onto a speaker's rostrum.
> The hall reminded me of war,
> And its silence echoed the silence
> That breaks off the first volley.
> I entered and I saw them,
> Them, taking all three rows,
> Them, a stone's throw away,
> Them, spiteful, satiated, young,
> In raincoats, chewing gum in their teeth,
> Hands in their pockets, teeth bared,
> Legs crossed and soles exposed.
> So, that's what our enemy looks like!

I am already well-grounded in politics. I understand all the semantic nuances of the poem. I already know that a satiated person is a bad person; the one who hasn't eaten enough is morally superior to the one who has. A hungry person is closer to us in spirit; he's *our* person. "Arise, you prisoners of starvation!" as the very first line of the "Internationale," the anthem of world socialism, has it. And, as a Russian proverb says, "A satiated man is not a comrade to a hungry one." Satiated people are our enemies; they don't understand us. In the language of the time, to be satiated means to be self-satisfied, haughty, and spiteful.

Another attribute of the people addressed in this poem is that they are young. Apparently, it's a reference to a Russian phrase: *"iz molodykh, da rannii"* (a brash young fellow). The papers report frequently about those kinds of people: "Revelry of Young Fascist Thugs in USA"; "Failed Attempt of Young British Louts to Break Up Performance of Soviet Actors."

Good clothes are additional proof that the young men in the poem are good-for-nothings. Their affluence speaks of their boorishness. To wear raincoats in a concert hall is a sign of their lack of culture. This isn't surprising at all. It's well known that culture in the USSR is much more developed than in the bourgeois countries. I pretty much know already what kind of raincoats the young thugs in the poem wear. They are most likely the same kind sported by foreign tourists who appear from time to time on Odessa streets. Those raincoats aren't of our Soviet make, that is, dark blue, with a rubberized and fine-checkered lining; instead, they are light in color— beige, light blue, the color of coffee with milk, the colors of a moth. Such raincoats emanate the smugness of those who, lacking things to worry about, intentionally pick their clothes of light, that is, impractical, colors on which even a small stain is visible. Of course, the dry-cleaning expense is a trifle for those who have money to burn.

Hands in their pockets, teeth bared,
Legs crossed and soles exposed.

Some pose they assume! It's known why they keep their hands in their pockets: they are hiding something. Agitated by the everyday reports from the Cold War fronts, I imagine it's a pistol. Maybe even a grenade. They bare their teeth not just to show a smile; they show as well that, if needed, they can bite you. And sitting with their soles exposed is another example of an all-too-well-known American lack of culture. Our teacher, Galina Ivanovna, tells us this every time when, during recess, one of us puts his leg up on his desk. How could one raise legs so high up? The streets are either dusty or covered with puddles after rain. On those days, when I come home I scrape the soles of my shoes on a metal bracket located outside our front entry, to remove the dirt. And, on entering our apartment, I change immediately into slippers.

So, I share our poet's indignation at the very sight of his American audience. Only the mention of the chewing gum makes me feel awkward. The truth of the matter is that I have already tasted American chewing gum many times. Perhaps, if I were living in some inland Soviet city—Kursk, for example, or Kaluga—most likely I would have no inkling what it is all about. But Odessa has that one advantage over many other Soviet cities: it's open to the external world, at least to some extent. The sea is just a few blocks from my home. Frequently, on my way along Primorsky Boulevard, while walking from home to the library at the Young Pioneers Palace, I see how the sun slowly falls over the horizon, dipping into the sea's depths. I guess that Turkey is over there, and Greece is over there. Farther away, Egypt and Morocco lie. Our port is always full of ships flying the strangest of flags. From time to time, on our central Deribas Street, little flocks of men appear dressed in snow-white bell-bottom trousers and shirts worn loosely. Rigidly starched little round caps, resembling toddlers' Panama hats, hold on miraculously to the top of their heads. Others wear some funny berets with pompons. As with all seamen, these sailors from foreign ships moored in our port waddle along the street, placing their legs widely, as if testing the sidewalk's stability. Some of them are wobbling, as if walking not on steady basalt slabs of Odessa sidewalks but on wooden deck flooring that, time and again, reels from under their feet.

Our home is in building number 18, smack in the middle of Deribas Street. Frequently, these sailors step into our courtyard. As a rule, they are good-natured and smiling. After many continuous days on the water, at last they are walking on firm ground. Even in twilight, we discern foreigners by the special, relaxed way they carry their heads. They smoke fragrant cigarettes, and, when they bend down to talk to us, we smell the fresh menthol scent on their breath.

Stepping into the driveway, they ask us boys playing soccer in the courtyard where the lavatory is. Our Soviet sailors also often stop by for the same reason. However, they seldom ask any questions. The lavatory is easy to locate by the sharp odor of bleaching powder, an odor that pinches your eyes. It smells that way because the courtyard caretaker, Vassilisa Petrovna, frequently pours bleaching powder around that place.

In exchange for our small favor, the foreigners offer us cigarettes. They pull them from little crinkling cellophane packs; with a cigarette in its mouth, a camel, squinting with pleasure, looks at you with one eye from their cover. (There are still other brands—Lucky Strikes and Chesterfields.) The sailors open these packs in a way that borders on magic. They don't pinch out a corner of the pack, as our seamen do when also offering the Soviet-made cigarettes Priboi (Surf) and Sever (North). Foreign sailors hook up a red thin ribbon with their little fingernail—and the cellophane wrapping rips open, instantly and smoothly, as if cut by a penknife. Though very few of us adolescents are smoking in earnest, we all take American cigarettes. A real honey smell emanates from them. They smell so sweet and spicy that you feel like, if not smoking, at least chewing them.

The foreign sailors don't have to offer the cigarettes and chewing gum twice. Hook-nosed Uncle Sam frequently appears on the pages of Soviet papers, depicted not only with his traditional top hat on his head but also with a nuclear bomb in his hand. But here the artifacts of the country, faraway and mysterious yet incredibly attractive, land in our hands. Before we put chewing gum in our mouths, we carefully remove its white, orange, green, or red wrapping and examine each detail of this small treasure. We marvel at how much attention they give to unimportant details: at the softness of the foil, the silky smoothness of the paper lining, its edges sawtoothed, at the embossed pattern of the little gum tile itself, the elegant tile, as if made of porcelain.

Admiring all these little things, first, with the tip of our tongues, we taste the powdered sugar the gum sticks are coated with, as fine as the pollen on a cabbage butterfly's wings. We, the children of war and ruin, inhale the strange and wonderful aromas of a distant country across the oceans, so far away that even its smells are unlike any other smells.

To chew everything that promises a gustatory sensation is an old habit of my half-starving childhood. In kindergarten in Tashkent, where we had run to from Odessa, I plucked translucent resin from cherry tree bark. The resin tasted bitter, and soon I spat it out. Imitating my peers and suppressing disgust, I also chewed tar smelling of turpentine. The boys used it for an occasional prank. They plastered a masticated lump of it on an absent-minded boy's head. You could get rid of it only after moistening the affected tuft of hair with kerosene.

American chewing gum smells of orange and lemon peels, of apples and pears, and of other fruit unknown to us in the first years after the war—of peaches, pomegranates, and bananas. Our tongues turn over the delightful elastic lumps in our mouths again and again. We try to prolong the pleasure; we are drained of enjoyment.

Sometimes, one of us gets a break; that is, he gets a whole five-pack. At once, he becomes an owner of small riches. American chewing gum is our convertible currency. For one such pack, you can get a slingshot made of thick rubber, cut from the inner lining of a soccer ball; a tennis ball, a bit worn on one side but still fleecy and jumping; a stamp with the coat of arms of the Republic of South Africa; a toy revolver that is cast of lead and shoots special fuses. All in all, there is nothing that my peers won't offer for that delicious American stuff.

"How many times do I have to tell you that chewing gum is not becoming to a Soviet schoolboy!" Galina Ivanovna says, waving a pack of it in the air. She has just snatched it from the hands of Yura Lerner, and he almost cries from the offensive loss.

Looking at our careless faces, which show no signs of understanding the gravity of the moment, she increases the volume of her voice. The veins on her neck swell. "Chewing gum isn't as harmless as you imagine in your naïveté. Yes, yes! Don't give me that blank stare. Don't pretend to be well-behaved children. You must understand that chewing gum is an instrument of ideological sabotage. With its help, our enemies are trying to undermine the morals of our society. Chewing gum today. A cigarette tomorrow. And then, you'll be drinking alcohol!"

Galina falters for an instant, apparently, looking for another substance whose abuse will make our moral degradation even worse. Evidently, when this attempt has failed, she decides to sum things up: "Seducing us with this doubtful sort of pleasure is an attempt to weaken us. They want us to a have good time and forget about what should be the center of our lives— struggling for a better life for all humanity."

We are silent. We all know, just like Yura Lerner, that we can get into big trouble for bringing chewing gum to school, but parting with it, even for a half day, is mighty hard for all of us.

According to our teacher, by chewing some gum I betray my native land, although I don't quite get how. Why worry so much about the harmful effect of the chewing gum when the sailors walking our city streets have packs of this gum in each pocket, but, judging from our newspaper articles, they and other simple people in capitalist countries still burn with envy for us, because we live in our socialist country, the most advanced, the freest, and the strongest country in the whole world?

It is enough to watch any release of the *Inostrannaia kinokhronika* (Foreign Newsreel) to become convinced that those who live on the other side of the ocean are a luckless lot. This newsreel usually starts with something predictable and boring. An opening of a new blast furnace in Prague, Czechoslovakia. The launching of a new oil tanker in Gdansk, Poland. The first postwar soccer match in a rebuilt stadium in Bucharest, Romania.

Flanked by children holding bouquets of flowers, solid men in double-breasted suits taking part in a ribbon-cutting celebration at the opening a new factory in Leipzig, East Germany.

"The industrial power of the socialist countries is growing from day to day!" the off-screen narrator utters with constrained pride.

I sigh. I endure. Blast furnaces and oil tankers bore me to death. They don't appeal to my imagination. If the narrator hadn't informed me that the action takes place in Prague, Gdansk, or Bucharest, I would think that the footage was shot in our country, in the USSR. You can't distinguish the ribbon-cutting officials in their suits in these newsreels from the ribbon-cutting officials in their suits in other newsreels from the series "Around Our Native Land." There they also smile with great effort. And you can't tell the Romanian miners from ours: they have the same helmet with a flashlight above the forehead, the same faces covered with coal dust. A blast furnace emits its first puff of carbon dioxide; an oil tanker slides off the pier into the water and produces a fountain of spray; sprinters take off along the cinder-covered stadium paths—but I don't care. Boredom is torture at any age, but it is especially unbearable in adolescence, when the brain craves newer and newer impressions.

I come to life only when the part of the newsreels titled "In the Capitalist Countries" begins. Actually, I run to the Chronicle Movie Theater on Deribas Street time and again for the sake of this very part. In the musty, poorly ventilated cinema hall, I am fidgeting in the armchair. Two opposing feelings seize me: horror and curiosity. It turns out that America is the most dangerous place on earth. Tornadoes smash wooden houses into pieces in Oklahoma. An earthquake pulls a chain of automobiles right down into the depths of the Pacific. A hurricane sweeps along the streets of Miami. Immense forests of Montana are ablaze. The Mississippi River floods all the dwellings for miles around; blankets over their heads, the homeless climb the roofs of their houses, pressing cages with birdies and framed pictures of their loved ones to their chests.

I have hardly any time to catch my breath when a Pennsylvania mine explodes right in front of my eyes. Right after that, an American Airlines jet crashes into pieces. Willy-nilly, you come to the conclusion that all these disasters and accidents are the lot of the people who have the misfortune to live in the capitalist countries. No such disgrace—neither earthquakes, nor hurricanes, nor forest fires—has ever happened before or could possibly take place in our country in the future.

But the most interesting segment of the *Foreign Newsreel* is the last one.

"The intellectual poverty of their existence, satiation with life in capitalist countries," the narrator's voice shivers in contempt, "pushes these young people to search for sharp sensations, which frequently end in tragedy." Several surfers rush at breakneck speed into stormy waves off the Hawaiian Islands. Accompanied by saxophone howling, half-naked girls and boys wriggle on the dance floor of a New York nightclub. Their wheels separating midair, racing cars jump into the spectators' stands, maiming people left and right. Fatally wounded giant bugs, the cars shiver in agony before bursting into flames at once, like matchboxes. For some reason, the burned and mutilated racers are rushed to the hospital, not straight to a cemetery.

"That's how they exist in the world of capital, with no trust in the future, no confidence in tomorrow's day," the narrator sums up with satisfaction.

I leave the cinema and squint at the sun, feeling uneasy. The newsreels teach me to despise America. But it occupies a special place in my heart. A child of the war, I remember nimble jeeps and powerful Studebakers on our roads. When a half-starved child, I adored sandwiches with American Spam and canned stew, which came to us in big yellow tin cans. (Apparently, I'll never get used to the condescending attitude toward Spam in today's American popular culture, just as I will never be able to comprehend the pleasure that American schoolchildren derive from throwing hamburgers and sausages at one another in a so-called food fight.)

And still, I take for granted that our enemies try to do us harm. The government appeal to vigilance comes from all sides. The radio stations often broadcast the famous sports march:

Hey, goalkeeper, prepare for the fight,
You're put at the gate as a sentry.
Imagine that behind you is our country's border.
Be strong—hurrah, hurrah!
Be ready for the time
To beat up our enemies!
The right-field forward,
The left-field back, don't miss
The opportunity to strike!

The march is from the prewar film *Vratar' (The Goalkeeper),* and it's still relevant. This film is shown again and again, because our enemies still dream of violating our country's borders. Our neighborhood Utochkin Movie Theater shows, one after another, such films as *Granitsa v ogne (The Border on*

Fire), Na granitse (At the Border), and *Dzhul'bars;* this last one is about a dog helping our frontier guards catch foreign saboteurs. These films reinforce the news reports about the failed attempts of those who try to penetrate our territory, to steal all our military secrets and harm us. The headline of every article about the next spy caught at the border serves as a warning: "Our Sacred Soviet Borders Are Sealed!"

Once I read in *Pravda* an epigram by Sergei Mikhalkov directed at an American archaeologist, a certain Aaron Smith. Smith informed all Western reporters that he has searched for the remains of Noah's ark on Mount Ararat in Turkey, located near our Soviet border. Though during his first trip, he didn't find anything there, he intends to fly over the site in a helicopter. But our poet knows the real reason for the American man's interest in Ararat:

> But our frontier guards aren't asleep,
> Take note of this, "archaeologist" Smith!

So, Smith is an archaeologist in quotation marks. I feel the terrible power of these punctuation marks. Put these marks around the word *person,* and right away you've got not a human being but a humanoid. An orangutan or some other animal of that kind.

In these first postwar years, numerous booklets from the *Biblioteka voennykh prikliuchenii* (Library of Military Adventures), a wide strip across their covers, circulate among us schoolboys. I devour these booklets swarming with enemy spies and saboteurs. Reading them, I realize for the first time that around me life rages, intense, full of danger and adventures, but I fail to notice anything special. Everything seems quite ordinary, as always. Each day I go to school, afterward do my homework, eat, read my books, sleep. Early in the morning, Papa leaves for work, comes back in the evening, and washes himself. Then he sits down with the rest of us to eat dinner. Before going to bed, he and Mama go for a walk around our block.

In the streets, everything is the same as well. Trams ring, their brakes grating when the trams turn. As always, jumping onto tram running boards, clinging to one another, men and women hang at the sides like heavy shopping bags. Along the streets, with their motors roaring, trucks buzz, all of them dark green, the color of pond scum. Their backboards always carry the same inscriptions in big letters: "Don't Stand in the Body, Don't Sit on the Boards" and "If You're Not Sure You Can Do It, Don't Try to Pass This Car."

Wearing her white apron and a tin badge on her chest, our courtyard caretaker, Vassilisa Petrovna, swipes the sidewalk with a broom made of rigid rods, lifting little clouds of dust. Passersby cough and sneeze. "Why don't you sprinkle some water, Petrovna!" they shout.

Boring!

Meanwhile, our history of the USSR textbook states clearly: "While the USSR is still surrounded by countries in which capitalists dominate, spies and wreckers will not cease trying to penetrate our country and harm us. The blue-collar worker and the peasant should be ever sharp-eyed. All inhabitants of the Soviet state, both children and grownups, should be vigilant in protecting its borders. Spies make their way to our factories and plants, to our big cities and villages. It is necessary to watch carefully all suspicious people and fish out the fascist agents."* Though the war is over and Fascists and Nazis are defeated, *fascist* becomes a general term for any sworn enemy of ours.

Certainly, with one's ordinary sight you won't see anything interesting. In the papers, advice frequently reads—"to look *attentively* around." The key to seeing something unusual is to concentrate, to sharpen one's sight.

One day I am walking back home with an armful of books from the library. I am already close to our building, passing the post office on the corner of Lanzheron and Karl Marx streets, when suddenly a middle-aged man overtakes me. He looks somewhat suspicious: he's unshaven, nervous, and he glances to the sides. He doesn't look like a foreign tourist; they are always well groomed. But it's a windy autumn day, and, just like many foreign tourists visiting Odessa, he's not wearing a hat and is dressed in a light-colored raincoat, not a Soviet raincoat. Its collar is raised. From books and films, I already know that a person who walks around with a raised collar is someone who must have something to hide.

Meanwhile, the man keeps moving along with the same nervous gait. Suddenly, for no apparent reason, he crosses the street. I gather up my courage and decide to pursue him. Brave Young Pioneers whose heroic exploits have frequently been featured in the booklets of military adventures always do that. As always when nervous, I get the creeps. The suspicious man suddenly dives into the driveway of building number 26 on Lastochkin Street.

*A. V. Shestakov, ed., *Istoriia SSSR: Kratkii kurs* (History of the USSR: An abridged course), *Uchebnik dlia chetvertogo klassa* (A textbook for fourth grade) (Moscow: Gosudarstvennoe uchebno-pedagogicheskoe izdatel'stvo Narkomprosa RSFSR, 1945), 252–53.

Overloaded with books, my whole body instantly breaking into a sweat, I can barely keep up with him. Holding my breath, I'm running behind him. Before turning into the driveway, I recall from the movies that spies usually wait for their pursuers around the corner, in order to knock them down.

I close my eyes. My heart pounding, I take one step. Then another. Nothing happens to me. The man is already standing in the middle of the courtyard and looking around. I freeze. He glances over my face, apparently searching for something more interesting. Then he approaches one of the entrances to the basement and disappears into darkness. I stand for a long time, not daring to follow him. I know that this courtyard, like many other Odessa courtyards, has an entrance to the catacombs. There, during the last war, partisans fought with the Germans. Most likely the saboteur has a portable radio set there, I guess feverishly. He uses it to communicate with his espionage command center, informing his superiors about the arrangement of oil tankers in the Odessa port. Or something of that sort.

I'm frightened and ashamed that I am. Young Pioneers should be fearless. On shaky legs, I descend into the basement. I allow my eyes to get used to the darkness, and I listen for a long time. In what direction has the stranger gone? Suddenly, some weak sound reaches me. It doesn't resemble the Morse code that spies usually use. The sound is too monotonous and unclear. It reminds me . . . It reminds me of something. But what? No, it can't be!

The conjecture makes me ill at ease. I jump out of the basement and look across the courtyard at its distant corner. Certainly! The public lavatory is boarded up. It's under repair. The man had an emergency, so he had no choice but to dive into the basement.

My ears are burning. How could I get myself involved in such a foolish thing? I run over to the other side of the street and fly home, turning my face away from the man, who, adjusting his raincoat, already leaves the gates. It seems to me that he has understood why I followed him, and he is about to laugh loudly at the top of his lungs.

SEVEN

I Don't Want to Have Relatives!

On a golden porch they sat:
A tsar and a tsarevitch,
A king and a prince,
A shoemaker, and a tailor.
Which one will you be?

RUSSIAN CHILDREN'S RHYME

WE STAND AROUND KOTYA LIUBARSKY, my friend from the courtyard. He pokes each of our stomachs in turn with his paw of a hand. Kotya resembles the young revolutionary poet Mayakovsky; his forelock hanging diagonally across his forehead, his gaze piercing right through us. We play hide-and-seek. Kotya counts, reciting the rhymes, and each of us has to pick one of the characters mentioned. Then, he counts again, and the one who guesses the right person goes off to hide, relieved of the duty of having to seek.

The finger that Kotya sticks into us looks ugly. He was seven when he came to the editorial offices of the *Chernomors'ka komuna (Black Sea Commune)* newspaper, located on Pushkin Street. He safely passed the guard, who was reading a fresh issue, and stamped his feet all the way through the printing shop, where his father worked. There, he wasted no time before he put his hand into a mimeograph, rotating at full speed. He wanted the text designated for the paper to print out on his palm. They stopped the machine at once, but it had already smashed his fingertips. Stitched up hastily, his hand has wound up looking like a cat's paw. Kotya is strong and courageous. He can beat up any boy in our courtyard. Nobody dares make a joke at the expense of his deformed fingers.

"On a golden porch they sat. . . ."

When Kotya stops counting and his finger stops at me, I can't bring myself to call myself "Tsarevitch" or "Prince."

"A shoemaker," I mumble. "A tailor."

Even here, when it's just for fun. . . .

I grumble when Mama and Papa are getting ready to pay a visit to any of my uncles or aunts. I want to stay home. Mama correctly guesses the reason for my obstinacy. She says sternly, "Stop balking. They're your relatives. You have to love them."

I don't dare squabble with Mama, for I hardly have any good excuse. (Several decades will pass before I'll be able to appreciate my mother's simple wisdom: no one but a relative would love you without needing a reason to, merely because you exist.)

Nevertheless, now, in my childhood I avoid my relatives. Not children, my peers—I'm friendly with all of them—but the adults. The ones who are actually Jews. I try to distance myself from any people of a nationality to which I formally belong. I'm ashamed of them. With few exceptions, all of them walk the streets of Odessa, their backs bent, their gait nervous, their heads buried in their shoulders.

(Apparently, this was the bearing I had as well during all the years of my life in my native land. Arriving in America fifteen years after I did, my daughter from my first marriage, Svetlana, brought me a gift from Russia. It was a wooden figurine of an elderly Jew, complete with side curls and a long beard. His eyes downcast, his narrow shoulders lowered, his head bent to his shoulder, he played a violin. Though I've never held a violin in my hands, my little daughter remembered me like that—sad, my head bent. She was nine when I left the Soviet Union forever. This stereotype of a poor creature that brightens up his life by scraping on a little fiddle was, apparently, the symbolic image that my daughter consciously identified with me.

"Daddy, why do you bury your head in your shoulders like an old Jew?" she asked me once in her childhood.

She was only five years old then. She said it without any spite; she loved me. And she didn't invent this phrase. Like many children of her age, she reproduced the speech of adults. In her Moscow kindergarten, someone's mother picking up her son reacted to his sullen look that way. The phrase is part of Russian folklore. It captures our Jewish bearing in Russia—our heads buried in our shoulders.

But now, in Odessa, in me, a ten-year-old boy trying to understand what the Jews are all about, this posture produces nothing but contempt. I don't realize yet that you are forced to bury your head in your shoulders when you expect a blow to your head at any moment.)

I am especially annoyed by the awful language my relatives use to communicate with one another, Yiddish. I know that they know Russian well but, still, out of incomprehensible obstinacy, keep using Yiddish time and again. Especially when they try to conceal something from me. *"Sha!"* suddenly one adult would remember, and motioning in my direction, tell the other adult, *"Red zu mir yidish."* I already understand: "Shush! Speak in Yiddish with me."

I don't like that language. It's ugly. It's clumsy and unmelodious. It's full of consonants that are either voiceless or spoken with whistling, clanking, and hissing sounds—*ts, s, k, kh, sh: tsores* (trouble), *bekitser* (in short), *shmates* (rags), *khaloymes* (worthless things). Though in time I learn these words, on principle I don't use them. Yiddish seems to me an awful parody of Russian. Instead of the Russian *mama,* it's *mame.* Instead of the Russian *dushno* (stuffy), it's *dushne.* Not *kot* (a cat), but *kats.* What a horror of a language!

Well, one day I decide, it may well be that my parents and other relatives are them—those Jews. But what do *I* have to do with it? I'm Russian, Russian. No matter what side you look at it, I'm Russian. My native language is Russian, as it is for everyone in my school. Our reading primer's even titled that way—*Native Speech.* I'm a straight-A student. In our class, we learn by heart verses composed exclusively by *Russian* poets—by Pushkin, by Lermontov, by Nekrasov. We sing *Russian* songs in unison. On cue from our teacher, we retell stories about famous *Russian* military commanders—about Alexander Nevsky, Dmitry Donskoy, Suvorov, and Kutuzov. I love Russian fairy tales, the only ones I know. About Vasilisa the Wise. About the gray wolf. About Kashchey the Immortal. I adore Russian proverbs and sayings. *Ne lykom shit,* "He isn't sewn with bast" (He's no slouch). *Sam chërt ne brat,* "The devil himself is no match for him." *Ne v svoi sani ne sadis',* "Don't get in someone else's sledge" (meaning, "Don't try to do things you're not fit for"). What a colorful language!

According to the Russian grammar textbook, proper interjections are *ookh, akh,* and *okh* (*oh, ah,* and *ouch*). But in our house, nobody ever says, *"ookh."* Nobody shouts, *"akh!"* or *"okh!"* If something goes wrong, they say, *"Oy-oy-oy"* or *"Vey'z mir!"* I already know what the last expression means: "Woe is me!" I'm irritated that a small and despised people speak in such a lofty, Shakespearean manner.

I don't even suspect that there's a language even loftier than Shakespeare's. And that it is the language of my ancestors—the language of the Old Testament, the language of the Hebrew Bible. As to Yiddish, well, how could I, an adolescent, know that it doesn't have to resemble the "great and mighty Russian language," as the classical Russian writer Ivan Turgenev called it? That Yiddish is a language in its own right? In its ability to express warmth and humor, intimacy and tenderness, it is no less beautiful than Russian. It will take me many years to learn that what seems to me an imitation of the Russian is a result of the mutual influence of cultures residing side by side. Words from one language have penetrated into the other. *Borsht* (beet soup) and *paskudinik* (a disgusting person) are Yiddish borrowings from Russian; and *khokhme* (joke) and *shabes* (Sabbath) have found their way from Yiddish into Russian (*khokhma, shabash* [end of work]).

But meanwhile, in my adolescence, my brain just splits from this confusion. In school, the word *Khaim* (Chaim) is used as a curse; it's a nickname for a Jew. The children utter this word with such contempt that there shouldn't be any doubt; nothing could be worse than being branded this way. But at home, the family, at big gatherings for a holiday meal, lift their glasses of wine and utter without blinking—*Lekhaim!* I cringe. Why do they insult themselves? I have no idea yet that there's nothing wrong with this toast. That the word simply means "To life!"

Later, as a high school senior, I'll learn by chance that, despite my shying away from Yiddish, at times I slide into it myself. I learn it from the lips of my brother, Vladimir, whom we all call Vova, ten years younger than I. As a boy he has a bent for comedic acting. (It won't be a big surprise for me that, in due course, while studying at the Odessa Polytechnical Institute, as part of its Student Variety Theater, he will become the winner of the All-Union Competition.)

He likes to make people laugh at every opportunity. When he is barely six, he gives an impromptu performance on the steps of our living room. (It also serves as our dining room and our parent's bedroom.) With the door portieres as his improvised theatrical wings, he does impressions of all the members of our family. First, he shows how Papa rides a streetcar, hanging on to the running board and holding his long brush on a long stick. Then, he grabs a shopping bag and imitates Mama standing in line for some groceries.

"You, grandma in the kerchief!" the bag pressed to his chest, he shouts, "Don't squeeze yourself into this line! Get lost! You don't belong here."

Finally, Vova shows how I, his older brother, behave when coming home from school. I rush into the room, throw my briefcase onto the sofa, and shout to Mama in the kitchen, *"Epes esn?"* (Anything to eat?)

Everyone roars. I also laugh. And blush. I am angry at the little stand-up comedian for revealing the unpleasant truth about me. It turns out that, despite my efforts to avoid it by all means possible, Yiddish has managed to worm its way into me: *Epes esn!*

Later, when I peer back into the past, into the years of my adolescence, no matter how much I'll try, I will not understand how my relatives, my uncles and my aunts, displeased me. I will wonder, what was the reason for my attempts to estrange myself from them in my youth? I'll realize, if there was something unpleasant in our interactions, it wasn't their fault at all.

In the winter, I catch cold frequently. Mama's remedy consists of making me drink *gogol'-mogol'* (a concoction of butter, sugar, egg yolk, and milk) together with putting mustard plasters on my chest. If that remedy doesn't work, Mama summons the heavy artillery of our family medicine—Uncle Abram, Aunt Clara's husband. Back in his youth, he studied veterinary medicine for four years, but had to abandon his studies because of illness. In our family, he's the closest thing we have to a medical expert.

Tall, broad-shouldered, his manly face distinguished by steel-framed glasses gleaming on his large gristly nose, my uncle appears on the threshold of our apartment with a shoebox under his arm. A dozen cupping glasses jingle inside, instilling horror in me. These special glasses are used as a remedy to create suction on the back; the glasses are heated and placed (rims down) on the back to draw illness out of the patient. At that time, we're reading about the Middle Ages in my history class. And for me, my uncle's treatment of a cold with the help of these glasses resembles the tortures to which the Spanish Inquisition subjected heretics.

First, Uncle Abram greases my back with baked goose fat; its disgusting smell makes me nauseous. Then he moistens a twisted strand of cotton on a wire skewer with stinking denatured alcohol. He sets the cotton on fire and, for a fleeting moment, adroitly slips the flame into a cupping glass. He sticks the glass onto my back, which is already flinching in mere anticipation of the impending pain, each glass producing a lip-smacking sound.

When the whole stock of his glasses are suctioned onto my skin, my uncle covers me with a blanket, sits down next to my bed, and waits patiently. From time to time, he raises the blanket edge and examines my back, bloody black blots all over them, and informs Mama, "He's caught quite a cold, I tell you! But that's all right. Now, we'll cure him at once."

My soccer memories are tied in with another of my uncles, one of Mama's brothers. In our conversations, the family calls him "Abrasha" (little Abram) so as not to confuse him with Uncle Abram. The less formal name suits him. Unlike Uncle Abram, who is somewhat brusque and rather averse to compromise, Uncle Abrasha is soft mannered and smiling. (According to his passport, his full name isn't Abram anyway; it's Avner.)

I'm a passionate soccer fan. But summertime is the busiest working time in my father's housepainting business. He and Uncle Misha often work without days off, even on Sundays. On the day of a soccer match, at least an hour before the game starts, Uncle Abrasha and his son, Boris, my cousin who is roughly my age, always pick me up on their way to the stadium.

In these years, the main Odessan soccer team wears the name of its sponsor, which is not quite appropriate for this vigorous sport—Pishchevik, "Food-Industry Worker." The team plays unevenly. Sometimes it makes it into the higher League A; at other times, it rolls back into League B. But this does not affect in the least the Odessan fans' enthusiasm and love. Thus one cares for a handicapped child even more intensely than a healthy one; all spectra of emotions, from compassion to pride for even its small successes, come in to play. When the Moscow soccer teams Spartak, Dynamo, and Locomotive visit Odessa, they seem like awesome northern knights— Vikings—at whose hands, or, more to the point, legs, our Pishchevik is destined to perish. But up there, in the stands, we don't lose heart. We never surrender before the game is over. Until the very last second, until the referee's final whistle, we live in hope for good luck, for a miracle. We rejoice over every dexterous catch of our goalkeeper and every successful feint of our forwards. And when it happens that a ball, like a caught bird, thrashes about in the goal net of the opposing team, both of us, Boris and I, as well as the whole stadium, shoot up from our seats; it seems we even levitate from happiness.

The general excitement causes only a good-natured smile in Uncle Abrasha. He's hardly a true fan; he attends the soccer games not so much for his own pleasure but to please his son and me, his nephew. Dear Uncle Abrasha remains forever in my memory with a light smile on his lips, with his quiet kindness.

My parents' close friends treat me as well as my relatives do. My first teacher of photography is Sasha Beskin, the husband of Mama's old girlfriend Tanya. A lathe operator at the KINAP factory, which produces equipment for cinematography, he's a war veteran with a disability. Shot through his knee, he limps on his right leg; another German bullet scarred his cheek. When I get my first camera, Komsomolets, Sasha opens up the secrets of shooting and film development for me. Following his instructions, I search shops for the necessary chemicals. In the closet of the couple's communal apartment on Paster Street, in plastic dishes and the weak reddish light of a bulb, trees, the facades of houses, and our seacoast begin to come to life for the first time in the magic of my photo development process.

To think of it, among my numerous harmless relatives, there was one whom I had a good reason to dislike. He was that proverbial black sheep that no extended family is spared. I met him later on in my life, when I was about to graduate from high school, that is, when I was about sixteen years old.

His name was also Sasha. He was some distant relative on my father's side, so distant that I didn't know his surname exactly. It was either Schneider or Schuster. A round fat face. Black short mustache, thin and thread like. Shaggy little brows from under which the little muzzles of his unblinking eyes looked at you. He dressed like senior Soviet officials at that time: chrome boots, a dark khaki military service jacket of a modest cut, like Stalin's, with big patch breast pockets, and a wide army belt. He was either a retired major or a colonel. Sasha was born in Minsk, where the rest of my father's family comes from, but he flew in from Vorkuta to visit us.

I met him before Khrushchev's famous "secret" speech that made Stalin's crimes against humanity public for the first time. Among my relatives, there were no political prisoners that I knew of. Perhaps adults spoke about the Gulag camps of Magadan and Vorkuta, but in the haze of a teenager's consciousness struggling with the many secrets of adult life, the sense of this information hardly reached me.

Unlike our other out-of-town relatives coming to Odessa in the summer, to the sea, he stayed not with us but in the Krasnaia (Red) Hotel. This at once set him apart from the rest of my kin. He stayed there not so much because he empathized with our situation and didn't want to constrain us in our tiny apartment, cramped as it was, but because he could afford to stay in one of the best hotels in the city. Only Western tourists or high-ranking people—movie stars, directors of large factories, and prominent party officials—had access to such hotels. He mentioned in passing that he was eligible to check into the very best of our hotels—the Londonskaia

(London)—but people who had reservation privileges greater than his had already filled it to capacity.

He was far from stupid. But, as a result of his high opinion of himself, his face always assumed the somewhat bloated expression of a person who has just stuffed himself with dinner. He made considerable efforts to seem modest, though. He spoke about himself with difficulty, as if turning pebbles in his mouth, in short little phrases, considering what his listener was capable of digesting in his speech and what not.

"I owe everything to Soviet power," he would say, burring and lisping. It seemed that he was lisping, shamelessly sticking out the tip of his tongue on purpose, just to tease me.

I understood fully who Sasha was and what he was all about a few years later, after Khrushchev had made his famous speech. I recall my conversations with Sasha on the way to a grocery store. Mama used to send me to buy some things for dinner, and he accompanied me to help me carry the provisions. He also generously pitched in his own money to buy expensive cognac.

"I owe everything to Soviet power," he repeated, sighing with satisfaction.

A military pilot, he had been shot down during the war, his leg wounded. From a comment thrown out in passing: "Many people wronged the Soviet authorities, and the Party sent me to guard them," I understood that he served as the head of a guard detachment in a prison camp in Vorkuta.

The northern city of Vorkuta was one of the notorious locations of hard-labor camps for the "people's enemies." Assuming that I knew this already and, apparently, trying to soften his image in my eyes, he spoke of Vorkuta as if it were a city like any other. Nothing special. And not a bad place to live. The stores were well supplied. There was even a theater. After serving their term, many prisoners stayed there, settled down, and started families.

To my question regarding whether he had a wife, he answered somewhat evasively. Yes, there was a woman in his life. When his eyes momentarily shied away from mine (though, most often, for some reason, he looked downward, at his always-polished boots), I understood that she was one of the prisoners. He said rapidly, "She's like a wife to me." At sixteen years, I still didn't quite understand what "like a wife" meant. I still blushed at any hint of the physical aspect of relations between a man and a woman.

In another conversation, he told me that twice a year he went to Moscow to have a good time and to rest. There he stayed not in a hotel—there was always a shortage of space for business travelers from all around the country—but at a special apartment; his superiors maintained it for their own people. The tone of his voice conveyed a conviction that this was the way it should be for those who deserved it.

"Upon your arrival, everything's ready for you," he told me. "A woman lives there, too. She cooks. There's a refrigerator packed with snacks of all kinds—wine, Armenian cognac, vodka of the best sort. The woman helps you to rest. That's her job—to help the visitors rest."

In a word, that was an apartment with all the comforts for those who got tired while guarding the "enemies of the people." He said in a tone of deep satisfaction that he had reached the level of service to the government to be worthy of such special treatment, of services that a mere mortal could hardly even imagine. (Later, I realized why he told me all this when we were on our way to the grocery store, rather than when at home. My parents would hardly have been happy to hear about the way he entertained himself in the capital. They would certainly not have approved of it.)

Apparently, my teenage lethargy irritated Sasha quite a bit, though I felt that he restrained himself from taking any action. Had I not been his relative, he would have quickly set me on the right path. "May God send luck your way!" he said glowering at me disapprovingly, his face tense enough to reveal the lumps on his cheekbones. "If you won't take hold of yourself, nothing good will come of you."

His words didn't surprise me much. I didn't expect anything good from myself either. I was constantly depressed by how I was carried along in life like a log in a river. Who knew where I would wind up and what would become of me?

And so I see that Sasha slowly pacing in front of a formation of his guards. A short man with a well-earned potbelly, infinitely sure in the rightness of his duties. Here he bends down, picks up some wooden chip in the snow, examines it. Without lifting his eyes, lisping and sticking out his tongue from time to time, scolding his security guards for some blunder.

At the same time, he didn't idealize the Soviet system. Once he told me how he operated in an unfamiliar city in which, apparently, no apartment was prepared for him with a woman to serve him, and it was necessary to board at his own discretion. "First of all, I try to find out which diner in that city is newly opened. And I go there. Why? Since the diner's new, its manager and its chef might not have had enough time yet to come to an agreement as to how much food and drink each of them would steal. They're still afraid of each other. They need some time together before they learn how to help each other cheat. And I go to that place. The meals are more or less edible. I have gastritis. You don't go to the first eatery you see in a town."

Truly, Sasha "Schneider-Schuster" was an exception among my relatives. However, a few years after Khrushchev's secret speech, he stopped visiting us. Apparently, the change of the spirit of the times was not in his favor.

With Mama, Papa, and my little brother, I frequently visit my mother's cousin, Aunt Dunya. She lives near the main Odessa farmer's market, Privoz, with her family: her son, Yan, who is my age, and her father, Ruvim Bronfman. Their apartment consists of two rooms. One of them is a connecting one, without windows. Frequently, the old man, who has a long gray beard, sits there in a black threadbare suit. His eyes covered, his head bowed, he sits in the semidarkness on an ottoman, pressing to his chest some thick book with a black shabby binding. He mutters something barely audibly and slowly rocks back and forth. He wears a black hat with a black ribbon. *Shouldn't you always remove your hat when entering a house?* When she spots bewilderment on my face, Mama whispers in my ear, "He's a pious man." A Young Pioneer, I translate this as "backward and little bit touched in the head."

At the same time, I am curious at least to flip through the book that the old man presses to his chest so lovingly. I hang around him in anticipation. I seize a moment when no one is paying attention to the book and take a peak in it. But I am disappointed: in place of letters, the book has some mysterious marks. I thumb through the book, and Mama hisses, "Put it down immediately."

I leave the table. I feel my Young Pioneer superiority over the old man. I attend school, and he sits in a dark connecting room and, seemingly, knows absolutely nothing about what's going on beyond the walls of the house. In my books, for the first time in the history of aviation, the world-famous pilot Valeri Chkalov flies from the Soviet Union to America over the North Pole. Attempting a nonstop cruise along the Great Northern Sea Route, explorers from the ship *Chelyuskin,* which was crushed by icebergs, hold onto the ice floes and battle fierce winds. The fact that Yan's grandfather reads his strange book not in the light but in semidarkness seems just right to me. He tries to sort out some abracadabra that is interesting to him alone.

(Many years later, I'll learn that that man sitting in the dark room was one of the most educated people in the city. During their days off, Odessa University professors visited him for one purpose only—to have a talk with him. To avoid any suspicion of the authorities, they came one by one. They said before leaving, "You know, Reb Bronfman, I'm so grateful to you. After talking to you, I feel as if I've washed myself in cold water. My head's brightened up."

I also didn't know that Yan's grandfather served as treasurer of the synagogue. The only Odessa synagogue had been closed even before the war with Germany broke out. In September 1944, a few months after the city was freed from German and Romanian occupation, Rabbi Yosif Diment returned to Odessa and convinced the Soviet authorities to reopen the downtown synagogue, on the corner of Kirov and Pushkin streets. A trickle of Jews began making their way there during high holidays. My cousin Yan even managed to have his bar mitzvah there. Nobody was allowed to attend except the immediate family members. In 1952, in the wake of a new "anti-Zionist" campaign, the authorities shut down the temple again. Rabbi Diment relocated it to the outskirts, to the industrial area called Peresyp. He raised private funds to fix two dilapidated buildings, one to house his synagogue and the other to serve as a matzo bakery.

But his troubles were far from over. In the spring of 1953, the rabbi was arrested and accused of counterrevolutionary activities. A couple of months later, he was sentenced to ten years of hard labor with an additional five years of exile. Soon, in the spirit of the Thaw that came for a short time after the death of Stalin, the rabbi was granted amnesty. But, for decades to come, the Odessa synagogue was stripped of its only rabbi.

Yan's grandfather was also under KGB surveillance. And indeed, there was a reason for them to watch him. As with almost all the people whom I knew in my childhood and adolescence, Ruvim Bronfman played a cat-and-mouse game with the authorities. In the synagogue, his bookkeeping was creative: he kept not one ledger but two. In one of them, debit met credit, ruble to ruble, for the sake of the city auditor. The second ledger was the genuine one, the one kept for reporting to the Jewish community. This book had an extra column of expenses that went for helping the community's poor. Under the cover of night, on the creaking porch on the second floor, before the entrance to Aunt Dunya's apartment, an act of charity unforeseen under socialism by Herr Marx quite often took place. Notified by the Synagogue Council, some poor man looked around to make sure the coast was clear and knocked quietly on the door. Squinting from the light into darkness, peering into the night visitor's face, Reb Bronfman extended an envelope with money to him.)

Only two decades later did I realize the true reason why I disliked my adult relatives in my early years. An outsider helped me achieve this epiphany.

In the beginning of the 1970s, I was undergoing some medical tests at a Moscow hospital, and an old man, a certain Greenstein, occupied the bed next to mine. During the breaks between procedures, we strolled together through the park that surrounded our building. Greenstein was no more than seventy, but he was rather fragile; he wasn't holding up too well. His health had been affected by his life in earlier years. With a Ph.D. in biology, at the end of the 1940s he had persistently adhered to the "bourgeois" theory of heredity, to the teachings of such Western theoreticians of genetics as August Weismann and Thomas Hunt Morgan, which resulted in his forced study of the northeast Siberian flora and fauna for some eight years.

The lesson that Greenstein taught me during one of our strolls in the park forever cured me of any enmity that I harbored toward people of my own ethnicity. Among the many patients in our hospital wing was a middle-aged Jew with wisps of gray hair on both sides of his freckled bald spot. If he had not been so fussy and talkative, he would have resembled King Lear (of course, the Jewish Lear, played by the great Yiddish actor Mikhoels). He gesticulated when he spoke, howling, pronouncing his *r*'s not in the Russian way but in the Yiddish style, with a Jewish accent, and exhibiting all the other classical attributes of stereotypical Jewish speech. He was a manager of a tobacco warehouse, and, in my conversations with Greenstein, I nicknamed him the Tobacco Captain, after the lead character of an operetta by the Russian composer Vladimir Shcherbachev, which was popular in Odessa at the time.

More than once, while walking near us in the hospital park, the man tried to strike up a conversation. I drove him off in every possible way, but it wasn't easy to get rid of him. He didn't take offense at my coldness and kept trying. Once, Doctor Greenstein spotted a disdainful expression on my face and shook his head. The next moment, he sighed deeply, looked over his shoulder to see whether anyone was watching us, and pulled me aside by my elbow. Then he talked to me quietly, squeezing my elbow for emphasis when making a point: "Why do you brush off your Tobacco Captain? He's as good a man as any other. It's your fear playing tricks on you."

"Fear?" I hemmed. "What fear?"

"An ordinary one. A biological kind. You avoid this man because you're afraid that, thanks to him, they'll find out you're also a Jew. Otherwise, they could be misled. Though you don't look Russian, because you have fair hair, you could pass for some Baltic man—a Latvian, a Lithuanian. Mimicry's a phenomenon well known in nature. It's a means of survival. One quite intelligent man has said that only when the Jews are granted the right to have their own bastards will they be truly equal with other people. But take a close look at your Tobacco Captain: By any measure, he's totally harmless. And he reaches for you, since you've managed to become a man he's failed to become; you managed to get a higher education. But it wasn't his fault. Such were the times in which he grew up."

Then Greenstein told me the Tobacco Captain's story; he and the Tobacco Captain had met before he and I had. At the end of the 1920s, the authorities registered him, then a seven-year-old boy, as the son of a "nonworking element." His half-destitute father was neither a blue-collar worker, nor a peasant, nor an office worker, but a ragman. With this work, he fitted the definition of a "private entrepreneur," grudgingly tolerated in the Soviet state under the New Economic Policy (NEP). In a small Byelorussian town, they declared people like him *lishentsy,* that is, individuals deprived of full civil rights. Children of these people couldn't receive a high school education. His parents found that the only way to beat the system was to make him an orphan. Soviet newspapers of that time reported, with deep pride in the new regime, that in the glorious city of Leningrad homeless children were picked up from the streets and sent to boarding schools set up especially for them. To scrape together enough money for a railroad ticket to Leningrad, the young Tobacco Captain's father walked all over the courtyards in his vicinity in search of rags. He gave his son some grub for a day or two and ordered him, as soon as he arrived in Leningrad, to spend the night on some railroad-station bench. The police would pick him up, and he had to say that his parents had died from typhus. It wasn't hard to believe this legend. At that time, thousands were dying from that disease.

The Tobacco Captain followed his father's instructions to the letter and got into the boarding school for orphans. Twice a year, a woman who called herself his aunt visited him there. As soon as she embraced the boy, she rushed to plug his mouth with a pie she brought along so that he wouldn't scream "Mama" by accident. She took him away for an outing to the city. She kissed his closely cropped hair, muttering some prayer under hear breath. That's how he got his high school education. But he couldn't make it to college; the war broke out.

Eavesdropping on my cautious conversations with Greenstein, the Tobacco Captain somehow figured out that I had been thinking of emigration. (What else could two Jews whisper about between themselves in the beginning of the 1970s?) When the three of us happened to be the only ones in the hospital park, he came up to me and whispered with fervor, "Go, go! Don't hesitate! I'd also leave if I were your age. It's too late for me already. I'm in charge of tobacco, and people will smoke for some time. Go! Don't deliberate for too long. You're still young. Everything will work out for you, *mazdlik kind,* lucky kid."

And I thought then with hope that the Tobacco Captain might be right. After all, Mama had frequently told me that I had been born under a lucky star. Perhaps my fortune would smile on me after all.

EIGHT

Friends and Enemies

"*ZI IS A KRISTLEKHE,*" Mama addresses Aunt Clara in that terrible language, Yiddish. "*Ikh vil nisht oysbeytn zi oyf a idishke.*"

I understand already: even though some lady is a Christian, Mama wouldn't swap her for any Jew. My mother switches to Yiddish every time she wants to express emotions she thinks are too complex for me to comprehend. Her statement surprises me indeed. As a rule, in moments of anger, Mama casts ethnic Russians in one of only two roles: either as *khazeyrim,* "pigs," or as *shikerim,* "drunks." But here all of a sudden, she would "never swap" this Christian for any Jew.

Mama's talking about Anna Ivanovna. She met her at a PTA meeting. They became friends instantly—thus once and for all discrediting in my eyes the notion that all people in the world are divided into Jews and non-Jews, as my relatives proclaim from time to time when enflamed by some Gentiles' offenses.

I think that my mother and Anna Ivanovna were attracted to each other on account of their opposite personalities. Anna Ivanovna is quiet and shy. At first, in the noisy and passionate world of my Odessan childhood and adolescence, she seemed withdrawn and cold. My lively and brave mother, capable of confronting even an on-duty policeman, appreciated Anna Ivanovna's soft nature. This woman's heart was ready to sympathize with anyone and anything in the world—people, pets, and trees. On the street, she stopped to comfort a crying girl whose ribbon had just been yanked from her braid by a bunch of boys. She fed a hungry stray cat when it poked its little snout into a salami wrapper already licked clean by the dogs. She picked up a baby sparrow that had fallen out of its nest. She used her handkerchief to tie up a branch broken by strong wind.

In summer, my mother wears bright flowery sundresses. Anna Ivanovna's dresses are mostly gray, and so are the combed wool sweaters she wears in chilly weather. Although she isn't much older than Mama, no more than forty, her hair is already gray. And she seems to wear gray out of inborn shyness; she always wishes to retire to the background, to escape the spotlight.

One day, my mother gave her a splendid silk dress with floral print pattern. "You're still a young and attractive woman, Anna Ivanovna," my mother insisted. "You look good in bright colors." Anna Ivanovna turned red from the compliment and thanked my mother profusely, even though the gaudy print of the dress clearly didn't fit her compliant and quiet personality. She accepted the gift but wore the dress only when coming to our house for dinner, just to please my mother.

Thanks to Anna Ivanovna, my life in school gradually starts to sort itself out. I wouldn't say that it becomes normal, but I find my niche in which, holding my breath, I can live. I've made a friend. His name is Zhenya, short for Eugene. He's Anna Ivanovna's son. For an ethnic Russian, his last name is strange—Henriksen. I avoid him at first. I've had enough trouble with my own surname. Then our mothers introduce us to each other and promote our friendship.

Later, I learn the origin of my friend's surname. Henriksen was the surname of an engineer from Norway who had come to Soviet Russia in the 1920s to help build socialism. He adopted Zhenya's father, orphaned during the civil war. Whether the surname is Norwegian or not doesn't make any difference to my schoolmates. It also doesn't matter that Zhenya's facial features, like his father's, are unmistakably ethnic Russian: he has a normal, short Russian nose, light gray eyes, and high cheekbones. All the same, his foreign-sounding surname is enough to make the boys suspect him of being Jewish. His friendship with me confirms their suspicion. When some boys call him *zhid*, "kike," Zhenya just brushes it off with a good-natured laugh: "Some idiots!" The insult doesn't sting him. I try to act the same way, but I fail. The difference between us is that Zhenya knows he is not Jewish.

Often after classes, Zhenya takes me to his home. The Henriksens live a block away from our school, also on Gogol Street but closer to the sea, in a building with two huge statues of Atlas at the entrance; on their backs, they each hold a stone globe with raised stars. The building is old but still holds up. The Henriksens' apartment is always tidy; it emanates a stable and orderly way of life. "It even smells of cleanliness," Mama says in admiration. She tries to keep our place tidy as well. But ours is the dwelling of a tradesman's family, not that of an engineering expert of the State Black Sea Shipping Management.

The Henriksens' home doesn't look like either our home or our relatives' homes, where both adults and children slam the doors, run around, and speak loudly, even shouting from time to time. Here silence reigns. Polished floors shine. Zhenya and his family place their books not on a shaky bookshelf purchased in a store, like the kind I have, but in huge mahogany bookcases made to order and sealed up with thick glass.

I saunter along in front of the bookcases in awe. I examine books with leather bindings made by some old-time craftsmen. Here, behind the glass, are treasures that even the library at the Young Pioneers Palace can't match. The entire *History of Wars* series. And *Ships of the Russian Imperial Fleet.* And *Outstanding Sea Battles.* And Brokhaus and Efron's multivolume *Encyclopedia.* I open these books at random. They turn out to be difficult to read. Published before the revolution, they use old spelling, with several obsolete letters.

A wide desk covered with green cloth is neat and tidy; a precise stack of papers is placed on one corner, several technical reference books on another.

Models of ships—including a three-masted brig, a steamship with a black smokestack, a fishing schooner—are everywhere. On wardrobes, on cupboards, on cabinets, and on the piano. Also a shining bronze barometer hangs on the wall. Its marks read: Dry, Changing Weather, Storm. Most often, the light-colored barometer arrow points to Dry: in Odessa, there are 250 sunny days a year.

Even at home, Nikolai Petrovich Henriksen, Zhenya's dad, often wears a marine engineer's dark blue tunic; his sewn-on white collarets are always fresh. From Mama's conversations, I learn that Anna Ivanovna and her husband have some relationship problem. Out of solidarity, Mama sides with her girlfriend. She feels for her deeply.

"He's a cold person," Mama says with indignation. Nikolai Petrovich's coldness to his wife offends my mama personally. "He doesn't know what a woman needs," she adds mysteriously.

The allusion to some women's needs is so vague that, for a long time, I remain ignorant about what exactly Mama means. Moreover, I'm puzzled.

Zhenya's dad doesn't seem like a cold person to me. Each time I visit the Henriksens, he welcomes me warmly: "Greetings, greetings, young man! I'm glad that Zhenya finally befriended such a serious person. No more of those good-for-nothings."

Visiting the Henriksens, I don't sense any tension between the spouses. They address each other politely and speak in a low voice. True, Nikolai Petrovich always speaks that way. With Anna Ivanovna, with Zhenya, with me. With everybody else too, as a matter of fact. This is not only because he treats everyone with equal respect but also because he is unable to speak louder, even if he'd like to. As I learned from Mama, in childhood, during the civil war, Nikolai Petrovich fell ill with a severe case of diphtheria. He probably would have died of suffocation if his doctors hadn't urgently made an incision in his throat to let air in. Now, before talking, in order to pass air through his mouth so that his lips and palate make his hissing articulation, he has to press an aperture valve hidden under the bandages on his throat.

Like his dad, Zhenya also always wears a marine-blue tunic with sewn-on white collarets. He dresses like that even when attending school. I wear an ugly, Soviet-made, jacket and pants altered from Papa's military riding breeches. But I don't envy Zhenya's outfit. The real object of my hopeless envy is his big, almost adult-size, strong and dexterous hands. Our joint games are hard to consider either games or joint. I just stand next to Zhenya and watch as he makes all kinds of little working devices.

When it comes to doing something with my hands, I'm totally inept. As Papa puts it, I have "two left hands." He waves in my direction, as if he has given up hope that I'll ever amount to anything good. Once, as part of our homework in a manual labor class, we had to make a spirit level, a device masons use to run the next row of bricks evenly. It isn't difficult to make a spirit level. You take a glass tubule, hold it over a spirit-lamp flame, bend it a bit in the middle, and then fill it with water, leaving a little air bubble inside. Then you fit the tubule into a smooth little bar—and the spirit level is finished. But making that item took me so long, it was as if I were constructing not a single spirit-level but the whole spirit-level factory. I earned a miserable C for that homework. No matter how hard I tried, my spirit level refused to sit steady, wobbling at the slightest touch.

That episode depresses me for a long time. The lack of manual skills makes me feel even more superfluous in a society where a blue-collar worker is considered the salt of the earth. From ubiquitous posters, a multitude of workmen in caps and overalls frown at me as if repeating after Papa: "Nothing good will come out of you, Two-Left-Hands Boy!"

Zhenya is a completely different story. I venerate the sacrament of the birth of an object under his hands. I watch him working and get chills of excitement up and down my spine. Zhenya even has his own small workbench with lots of metalworking tools. His clever hands deal with each of them deftly—the emery bar, the pliers, the wire cutters, or the little hammer. There's even a small red-painted lathe. I cannot tear my eyes off a tiny model of a steam engine he's making, complete with little pistons, cylinders, and rods.

Occasionally, Zhenya brings me into the action. He entrusts me with holding some wooden plank while he saws it off. Proud to be part of my friend's creativity at least to some extent, I take up the task zealously. "Easy, easy," Zhenya cautions me.

Technical terms sneak into his everyday conversation. When he estimates what benefit some regular action could bring, he says, "Let's think, what efficiency ratio can we expect here?" He employs technical metaphors even when speaking of something useless. "Ah, that," he waves his hand. "It's a fruitless undertaking. It's coal burned in air."

While still an adolescent, Zhenya also makes noise-producing gadgets as well as functioning little models for both of us. He grips a copper tubule in the workbench vice and, with a few blows of his wooden hammer, flattens one edge of it and bends the tubule. Then he shapes a big dulled nail the same way. After that, he fits together the nail and the tubule and snaps on a thick rubber band. And the gadget is ready. With our pocket knives, we scrape sulfur off matches and pour it down the tubule. Now, to make the gadget work, it's enough to press down on the rubber coupler. The nail rams inside the tubule, hits sulfur crumbs, and a pistol shot hits the air.

Though our gadgets produce lots of noise, they're harmless. They're a means not so much of aggression as of defense. Their crackling is symbolic muscle flexing—you'd better not pick on us! These gadgets come in especially handy when there's a "window," that is, when one of our teachers falls ill and there's no one to replace him or her. As soon as the bald head of Director of Studies Kirill Grigorievich appears in the doorway instead of our teacher, our class jumps up in sweet anticipation. Brief though it be, it's freedom all the same. We all shout "hurrah," push each other, and break loose onto the street. We race to the end of Gogol Street, to the cliff facing the port.

At the cliff edge, in the place of a recent city dump, a platform has been leveled by a bulldozer. My classmates rush about it, intoxicated with fresh air. The port below rumbles. Entering the harbor, steamships from all ends of the earth blow their whistles. Huge cranes ring, turning their openwork booms. Maneuvering locomotives shout, pulling freight cars up to the pier.

I also feel like running around outdoors together with the rest. I squint at the sun and eagerly inhale the remarkable sea air. The music of the port disturbs my soul with a dream of distant countries. But I feel isolated from the rest of the class. Though I am chairman of a Young Pioneer group, this doesn't endow me with authority—at the very least, because nobody voted for me. Our class supervisor, Galina Ivanovna, decided to appoint me to that position just because I'm an A student and therefore should serve as an example to everyone. As chairman, I don't do anything special. Only during the lineup of our class in the school yard, I repeat commands that the Young Pioneer leader, a high school student, passes on to me.

On the platform at the cliff, at some distance from the others, I stand next to Zhenya, who doesn't like jumping and running. Despite my secret desire to be like everybody else, this estrangement will persist in me for a long time and last my whole school life. No matter how hard I try, I cannot overcome the invisible wall separating me from the majority of my schoolmates.

When sitting at my front-row desk in the classroom, I always expect an attack from behind. The moment our teacher gets distracted, something wet and disgusting plops onto my neck. I already know what is it and who has done it. It comes from the back of the classroom, habitually occupied by a bunch of F students. Usually older than the rest of the class, they are Gentile boys who didn't run from the Germans. Together with their parents, they stayed in Odessa for the duration of the occupation, and now they have to make up for time lost in schooling. They use the tin tubules of their pens as blowguns, spitting chewed pieces of blotter through them. They also make primitive slings out of thin elastic bands yanked from their underwear to shoot tightly twisted pieces of paper; frequently, they also shoot paper clips this way. The clip shots hurt and leave bruises on my neck. To deprive the attackers of pleasure, I grit my teeth and keep silent. But sometimes tears well up in my eyes involuntarily, and I hate myself for being unable to stop them at will. Certainly, these are usual school pranks. Sitting next to me, Zhenya also gets it sometimes. But it seems that they shoot at me much more frequently than at my Russian friend. (The persecution complex doesn't let go of me for a long time.)

Now here too, running about the platform for a while, some of the older classmates decide to entertain themselves by throwing stones at our legs: "Hey, you little Yids," they shout, "dance!"

Against my will, I jump up, thus willy-nilly obeying their command.

But this is the moment when our homemade gadgets come in handy. Though our shooters can't really hurt anybody, the loud cracking sound they produce resembles a pistol shot and discourages our persecutors.

From my early years, the courtyard of our building serves as the place where I both try to bond with children of my age who are oblivious to my ethnicity and am confronted by my enemies. On Sundays and during vacation time, lots of youngsters run around our courtyard. Who wants to stay in small and stuffy rooms all day long? Quite often, group games take place.

"Hey you, over there!" Hands linked, one team shouts to another. "Whose soul do you wish to get?"

The goal of the game is to break through the opponents' chain of hands and, as a reward, take one of them onto your side. If you don't break through, you're kicked out of the game. When they cry out my name, I grow cold from the impending test. I run across the courtyard. I wear my favorite dark gray, formerly black, thin-leather pilot's helmet, a boyish memento of the recent war. I run as fast as I can, slicing the air with my teeth clenched. I run with all my might so that my body will have the biggest possible impact. The little tin buckle of the helmet fastener whips my cheeks. They shout behind me, "Go, go!" I myself don't want to let my team down for anything in the world. I use my whole willpower to concentrate on one goal only—to break through the linked hands of the opposite team. Alas, this doesn't happen all the time. But each time I do break through, a hot wave of joy rolls over my whole body. I've won. At least in something. At least in fun. Even if only on one round, I'm not worse than others.

But in the courtyard, I also have a foe, a youngster called Pashka, who lives in one of the third-floor apartments. He is almost a head taller than I. The pinkish skin of his skull shows through his scanty fair hair. The moment I appear in the courtyard, he shouts, contorting his mouth mockingly: "*Shlyoma, mama doma?* [Shlyoma, is your mommy home?]" or "Shlyoma, say '*kukur-r-ruza*,' [corn]. Well, well, go ahead, say it—*kukur-r-ruza! Na go-r-re Ar-r-ar-rat r-rastet kr-rupnyi kr-r-rasnyi vinog-r-rad.* [On the Ararat Mountain, large red grapes grow. Well?]"

At first his jeers amazed me with their utter lack of logic. Why does he prompt me to pronounce some nonsense words with *r* sounds? What do I have to do with all this? To begin with, my name isn't Shlyoma. Furthermore, I don't have difficulty pronouncing the letter *r*.

But Pashka's intonations, so unnatural for the Russian speech—with howling at the end of each phrase—leave no doubt about *what* the target of his attacks is. He's irritated by the very fact of my belonging to a strange and despised tribe that dares to live next to him. He makes fun of pronunciation peculiarities ascribed to the Jews. Frequently Pashka's attacks are straightforward: *"Zhid, zhid, po verëvochke bezhit,"* he yells at the top of his lungs. (A kike, a kike's running along a little rope.) As if a Jew were some kind of bug.

It doesn't always stop with verbal attacks. Sometimes, a sling appears in Pashka's hands. Not its weak imitation, as some use in school, but a real, durable sling, made of thick rubber, with a leather pocket for little stones. Taller and stronger than I, Pashka can beat me up easily, but he prefers to prolong his pleasure by firing his sling, trying to put out my eye.

I thought I knew all his tricks by now. But one day Pashka comes up with an unusual way to vex me. In our building courtyard, German POWs, in dirty and tattered greenish overcoats, dig trenches for water pipes. A sentry with a rifle paces along the trenches, spitting into them out of boredom. Sometimes, on Sundays, when all our family has breakfast together, Papa tells us that at nights he hears screaming coming from the courtyard. He says that it's the German POWs who scream. They spend their nights in the basement of our building, and the guards beat them with thick soldier belts with heavy metal buckles. It's unclear what they have done to deserve the flogging. I understand that the guards whip them for no particular reason, as preventive maintenance of sorts. It could also be that in this way the prisoners pay for their past trespasses. Papa doesn't state his opinion about this corporal punishment. I see that he is confused. He's unable to reconcile his contradictory feelings—compassion and hatred.

I reflect over this courtyard affair. It is strange to me: how is it possible to beat adults with belts as if they were mischievous children? The war, and everything that is connected with it, still burns me. But I have a hard time imagining that these pitiful men, some almost gray, their cheeks hollow and backs bent, dressed in worn-out uniforms, are indeed those same Krauts (we call them Fritzes) of whom, during the war, I was so afraid and whom I hated so much. In the Soviet war films, all Germans are invariably haughty and cruel, like jackals estranged from a world that has compassion and mercy. In the newsreels, Hitler's soldiers stamp their goose step, flutes squealing and drums beating. Stuck-up chins. Protruding chests. It seems they put all their mercilessness into each slap of their boots against the ground. Death, death, death! The very sight of their uniforms, with shiny buttons and sewn-on pockets, the eagle wings spread on their jacket fronts, the lifted-up cockades of the officer's caps, made me cringe in fear.

But now, in the courtyard of our building, no matter how long I peer into these POWs' miserable faces, I can't find even a remote hint that these former world conquerors were ever arrogant. They dig trenches all winter long. They hollow out the frozen ground with picks. Their work goes slowly, but, it seems, nobody is in a hurry—neither the overseers nor the workers. Once in the early spring, with snowflakes melting almost as soon as they reached the ground, I come out to the courtyard. Not seeing Pashka anywhere around, I sigh in relief. I stroll around the yard and, looking down into one of the trenches, notice that one of the prisoners is staring at me. With his back nestled against the trench wall, the handle of his shovel clasped in his hands, his dirty forehead sweating, he catches his breath and looks at me with curiosity. He is short, almost a boy's height, and the stripe indicating his rank as a private has been torn off the shoulder of his overcoat.

The German catches my gaze and comes to life. His gloomy face, frozen into a sad mask, expresses a mixture of amazement and shy joy. He mutters something. Unexpectedly, I recognize some Yiddish words in his speech. What's going on? A German man speaking as a Jew?

"*Schule?*" he asks, pointing his dirty finger in my direction. Wrinkles of dried-up skin around his mouth attempt to stretch into something that resembles a smile.

I guess that he is asking whether I go to school. I nod.

The German glances from time to time at the bored guard and gesticulates. I watch his nodding toward something outside the courtyard, his sticking his finger toward me, and his pitiful smile, and I piece together *what* he is trying to tell me. That at home, in Germany, he also has a boy like me, his little son. Probably, now he's big enough to attend school too.

No matter how he tries, the prisoner is unable to produce anything more that makes sense to me. His lips begin quivering. His faded gray eyes, almost white, and dirty eyelashes grow moist. The German makes another attempt at talking to me. As he mumbles and gesticulates, out of the blue, Pashka appears next to me. I have no time to assume a defensive stance before he grabs me by the half-mangy rabbit-fur collar of my winter coat. Threatening to push me down into the trench, he shouts, "Ha, Fritz! Look—it's *Jude! Jude!*"

In surprise, the prisoner throws aside his shovel in horror and, as if it were not a cocky teenager in front of him but some horrible ghost, blocks his face with his palms. *"Nein!"* he shouts in his thin little voice. *"Nein! Ich liebe Juden! Ich bin kein Nazi! Hitler kaputt! Nazi kaputt!"*

All this lasts no longer than a few seconds. Cursing, the guard tears the rifle from his shoulder and rushes to us: "Hey you, dummies, get lost before I knock your heads!"

Pashka lets go of my collar. He's been pulling it up so hard that the hook has stuck into my throat, blocking my breath. I fly up to the third floor, clearing my throat on the run, and rush into our apartment.

"What happened?" Mama asks.

"Nothing," I say, catching my breath with difficulty.

Everything has happened so suddenly that it takes me some time to come to my senses.

Mama looks at me with suspicion. How is it that I have returned from the courtyard of my own free will, moreover, in a hurry, not in the usual way—that is, after her many cries from the open window: "Time to come home!" ("Can I stay a little bit longer?" I usually beg.)

"How secretive you are after all!" Mama says. "You shouldn't be so secretive. It'll make your life difficult." Her words are prophetic.

NINE

The Girl of My Dreams

LIKE ALL MY PEERS, I adore the cinema. Nearby, a half block from our house, on Deribas Street, at an entrance to the City Garden, the Utochkin Movie Theater is located. To get in the screening hall, you have to scale the steep ladder to the second floor. The theater is narrow and small. On both sides of the screen, a quotation from Lenin's work is displayed in huge letters: "Of all the arts, the most important one for us is cinema." I am too little to know any subtleties of Marxist-Leninism. I don't know yet that "for us" means for Lenin's party, for the authorities, for the Bolsheviks. I understand it as *for all of us*. I agree with Lenin. For me, cinema is the most important of all the arts too.

Once in a movie, I forget about everything in the world: my school troubles, my homework assignments, my Jewishness. The lights die away; then in the emerging darkness, silver rain drizzles, and, at the sounds of a trumpet, the shivering credits appear on the screen; before reaching our movie theater, the film is already fairly worn.

As soon as darkness retreats to the corners of the hall, I stop feeling my body. I fly forward onto the sparkling canvas; springy, time and again changing their force and direction, mote-filled columns of light beam. I fly there, where another life, exciting, full of adventures, blazes. My favorite movie of that time is *Chapaev (Chapayev)*, about a legendary civil war hero. I've seen it many times. Twisted on my shaky armchair, I gallop on a horse next to a machine-gun cart. I press myself to a trench wall during the psychological attack of the White Guards, under drumbeat, their bayonets moving directly at me. I swim next to the wounded commander, offering him my shoulder.

The films about war are also about love. *Serdtsa chetyrëkh (Four Hearts), Nebesnyi tikhokhod (The Sky Slow-Mover), Bespokoinoe khoziaistvo (A Noisy Household), V shest' chasov vechera posle voiny (Six P.M.).* I don't know much about love besides what I have understood from these pictures and song lyrics on the radio. One thing is clear: love is a source of anxiety, strange behavior, and, on occasion, temporary speech paralysis.

In the secluded corners of our central Deribas Street, leaning on a granite parapet adjacent to the stairs leading downward to the Port Club, high school students gather in a circle. They pluck guitar strings and sing strange songs, utterly unlike those in radio broadcasts and the movies. In these songs, a woman is not a "friend, comrade, and brother," as conscientious Soviet people must treat one another, but a special creature, capricious and tender. In her presence, even thieves and rogues behave like some counts and princes: "Raya, my dear! I ask you—no, I simply beg of you—to grant me that salon tango!"

In these songs, the ordinary "Masha" becomes the exotic English "Mary." For the right to dance with her, men draw their knives: "Steel sparkled. The sailors clenched in a fight. A young cabin boy fought like a lion. They fought for ashy braids, for baby Mary's dreamy image."

On birthdays, in addition to giving gifts, adults write on greetings cards: "Wishing you success in work and happiness in private life." At home, at dinnertime, Mama tells the latest city news: on Malaya Arnautskaya Street, in a fit of jealousy, a husband killed his wife. Why? If success in work comes first, why risk going to prison for murdering your own wife?

When ironing, Mama sings some prewar cabaret song. In the last stanza, a father who abandoned his family for a nightclub singer responds to his son's pleas to leave "that awful woman" and come home:

You're right, my little boy! Your father made a mistake.
The woman is a drug.
I lost my marbles when I fell in love with her.
She deceived me with her promises.

The question of whether I got it right torments my bookish soul. Has Mama sung, "*The* woman is a drug" or "Woman is a drug"? That is, is mind numbing the effect of a nightclub singer, or do all women have such an effect? I don't dare ask Mama.

The mystery about the place of woman in the life of man keeps plaguing me for a long time. But in the same summer, in the Young Pioneer camp near Arcadia, on the outskirts of the city, at night (and even in the daytime, after a midday snack, during the "rest hour"), as soon as I close my eyes, an image of a girl flickers before me, a red-haired girl with long red eyelashes and sun-baked lips. I don't even know her name, but at the line-up when I see her face, whether in full view or just in profile, I'm ready to swear my allegiance to her instead of to our Soviet flag.

I never venture to begin to speak to her. I'm unattractive—that I know for sure. My nose alone is a nuisance. With such a nose, even to approach such a beauty is only to disgrace oneself.

Already in seventh grade, among notebooks and textbooks in backpacks and briefcases, some books appear, their covers carefully wrapped in dense journal paper. We read them under the school desks, during class time, as if engrossed in our thoughts, shielding our eyes with our palms. These books are about subjects that our textbooks don't cover. A few phrases about the pollination of flower stamens with butterfly wings or bee paws don't count.

Russian literature is as chaste as the Virgin Mary. In the classical works, when an affair reaches the most interesting moment, you run up against a whole line of dots as if against a barbed-wire fence. A brisk exchange goes on in our class. Someone finds a scene in Sholokhov's novel *Tikhii Don (And Quiet Flows the Don)* in which its heroes, Aksinya and Grigory, cannot constrain their passion. In Nikolai Ostrovsky's *Kak zakalialas' stal' (How the Steel Was Tempered)*, Pavel Korchagin cannot tear his sight from the bouncy breasts of Rita, his comrade-in-arms.

But we value Guy de Maupassant the most. To get him even for an hour is great luck. Once, my ear tips flaring, I forget myself while reading his novel *Milyi drug (Bel-Ami)*. And here, our teacher Vera Vasilievna's hand snatches the volume from me. "And you too, Draitser!" she exclaims in the same tone that, perhaps, Julius Caesar used when he uttered, "And you too, Brutus!" "Quiet deep waters teem with devils. Ah, ah, ah! And you're the honor student! To read this muck! This dissolute writer! Well, well! I didn't expect this from you."

She is convinced that an all-around A student can't have any interest in the physical aspect of love. Such an interest is incompatible with his high status. An F student is the kind that gets distracted during a class with such disgraceful things. But an honor student! She shakes her head in disbelief for a long time.

Soon after the war, foreign films taken as trophies from German storage start to appear in Odessan movie theaters. Along with Hollywood films starring Greta Garbo, Marlene Dietrich, Deanna Durbin, and Jeanette MacDonald, there is also one German movie, *The Girl of My Dreams*, starring the singer and dancer Marika Rökk. Neither films about Tarzan, nor *Treasure Island*, nor *Espionage Networks*, nor even *The Roaring Twenties* (retitled *A Soldier's Fate in America* for propagandistic purposes), with Jimmy Cagney, in which, for the first time, the famous song "Come to Me, My Melancholy Baby" reaches us, enjoy as much success as Marika Rökk's film. Throughout our city, with the speed of a steppe fire fanned by the strong lower wind, the gossip spreads that Marika is the dream girl of none other than Hitler, that she is his former mistress. No lack of people wish to take a look at the woman whom the Führer himself held in his embrace. At the local party censor's instructions, above the box office of the Utochkin Movie Theater, where they show *The Girl* to packed houses, including the additional midnight showtime, an announcement is posted: children under sixteen are not allowed to see this film.

You are forced to wait until the film plays at the open-air theater on Deribas Street, arranged where a building was destroyed by German bombs. Then, through the attic, covered with a thick layer of dust, you have to make your way to an adjacent roof. There, you can watch the movie as much as you wish. Until policemen spot you.

The film is a musical, in color, made on the first-class German film stock "Agfa." But I'm disappointed. I don't find anything to warrant the prohibition against children younger than sixteen watching it. Marika sings, dances, and flirts, making eyes at men. And that's probably all. I discover that, as it turns out, after the first days of the film screening, on the instructions of the regional party committee, the only suggestive scene was cut—Marika bathing in a barrel.

Nevertheless I eventually manage to admire Marika in the barrel. We boys entertain ourselves collecting dumped film scraps. They serve as currency of sorts in our street "casino." You clamp a clipping of a few frames in your fist and ask, "Even or odd?" The one who guesses correctly takes the clipping into his possession. The one who guesses incorrectly has to give away one of his film scraps.

Somewhere, my courtyard friend Kotya Liubarsky has wangled a clipping of four frames with Marika in the barrel. I ask him to let me get at least a quick look at Hitler's mistress in the nude. For a long time, Kotya turns me down. Then, saying, "For display you have to pay," he takes payment from me in the amount of twenty frames with Tarzan.

"In my hands only!" he says.

I raise his elbow up to the light. He grabs hold of the film with his stumped fingers. He is afraid that I'll deprive him of his treasure.

In a huge wooden barrel, like the one our courtyard caretaker puts under a drainpipe during a downpour, the red-haired beauty splashes. Only her bared shoulders are visible. There is a crafty smile on her face that lets everybody know she doesn't doubt her power over men's imaginations whatsoever.

The girl of my dreams. Who was she in my adolescence? Long before we will be excited by the movie with the rumored mistress of the Führer, a huge log lies in a corner of our courtyard, in the same place that it once grew as a tree trunk. The tree was cut down at the request of tenants who wanted more sun. In the evening, after dinnertime, one by one, like sparrows to a birdhouse perch, we boys and girls of our courtyard come flying in here. The boys exchange stamps, ancient coins, and the American chewing gum while girls exchange postcards with pictures of movie stars.

Here, under the windows of tenants who threaten time and again to pour a bucket of water on us if we don't cease making a racket, I vent film impressions that overwhelm me. At the log edge, I impersonate the hero of the film *Admiral Nakhimov*. Like him, I stand on the captain's bridge of his frigate and point a spyglass at the flagship of the Turkish fleet. "Ah, the first bullet's wounded me," I sing, circling on imaginary crutches and twisting my face like a bandit. I try vainly to give my thin little voice the hoarseness of the anarchist Ataman Makhno, "And the second bullet's wounded my horse."

Then I show how, in the film *Dva boitsa (Two Soldiers)*, their legs shaking with fear, Fritzes attack our pillbox, but, cut down with a burst of our machine-gun fire—*tra-ta-ta-ta-ta!*—they fly head over heels.

I seem to have only one spectator, my friend Kotya. Girls don't care about action films. But I have overcome my habitual shyness for the sake of others there. I look stealthily at our neighbors' girls, Susanna, Raya, and Paullina, lined up on the log. They whisper something in one another's ears, giggling and secretly glancing at me and Kotya. I blush, for I already guess the content of that whisper. They are discussing us boys and determining who is in love with whom. I am jealous of Kotya. He is a strong, dexterous boy, and handsome. Our girls all like him.

I also want somebody to like me, but none of these girls captures my imagination. It is entirely occupied with the one who isn't there among them—with Liza Lyaskovsky. She lives on the second floor of the front-wing building of our courtyard. In the first days of war, a bomb hit that building. They've restored it recently, and some distinguished people occupy it now. We live in the city center, and Liza's dad is a writer. But this fact isn't overly important to me. His little booklet about the whaling flotilla, *Slava (Glory)*, was issued by our Odessa publishing house Maiak (the Lighthouse). I'm partial to authors whose work appears in Moscow or at least in Leningrad. The genuine life is happening over there. And here, in Odessa, one thousand kilometers from Moscow, in my opinion, everything, including authors, is second-rate.

Once on Sunday, I sit on the log, waiting for Kotya and pensively sharpening a stick with my pocketknife. It is spring. When I close my eyes and turn my face toward the sun, I suddenly feel that somebody's eclipsed the sun for me. I open one eye slightly. Within a solar aura, a golden nimbus of maiden hair appears. With my face distorted because of the squinted eye, I probably look like a fool. To make matters worse, I'm dressed in trousers that I'm rapidly outgrowing. Mama barely manages to extend them with wedges cut from Papa's old military trousers, which are riding breeches. I suddenly figure out that I'm sitting in such a way that the inserts are visible. Liza smiles. It seems to me that her smile is indulgent because she's noticed the patches on my pants.

Suddenly she sits down next to me. I even feel the warmth of her maiden body. A hot lump forms in my throat. I swallow hastily; it tumbles down to my stomach and, for some time, rolls there in a spiral, the way a motorcyclist rolls at the country-fair attraction "the Vertical Wall." We speak about something. I'm still sharpening the foolish stick. Then Liza rises and goes on with her affairs.

Now she doesn't approach me anymore. Sometimes, I catch sight of her from afar, always with a stack of books under her arm. She waves at me with her free hand. I never dare to come close to her.

The log episode frequently appears in my dreams in quite different versions. In one of them, she sits next to me and kisses me. Me! She, such a beauty! I am so used to the idea of being ugly that, out of surprise, I wake up. Already awake, I suddenly decide that she likes me. But I drive the idea away from myself right on the spot. How can a Russian girl like a person with the name Samuil? Moreover, with the patronymic Abramovich. And the surname Draitser. Impossible! She likes me! If she were merely well-disposed toward me, that would still be good. That would still be a joy to my heart, constantly compressed by stress. "Even a cat would be pleased by a kind word." This saying, once heard (it seems, from the lips of the Russian movie star Tatyana Doronina in the film *Starshaia sestra [The Older Sister]),* will become my philosophy of personal happiness.

This early-established self-denigration, this habit of being content with a tiny bit of goodwill instead of true love, soon comes to dominate my life. This early choice of the subject of my intimate excitement predetermines my love life. My choice is unconscious but not accidental. Certainly, Liza is a beautiful girl. She is blond with blue eyes and curls down to her shoulders. But both Susanna and Raya are beautiful in their own ways. The first one has a graceful figure, long braids, and big gray eyes. The second one has eyes the color of melted chocolate, bushy dark eyebrows, redness in her cheeks. And Raya's younger sister, Paullina, is also pretty. But these girls are Jewish, and Liza is Russian. And that is the main thing.

How so? Between Liza and me lies a wall of sanctioned hostility. Now, at the end of the 1940s and the beginning of the 1950s, under the pretense of struggle against cosmopolitans and Zionists, the persecution of Jewish culture is in full swing. On the newspaper pages, in radio programs and film reels, animosity toward the Jews is being aroused.

My choice of a dream girl, rather characteristic of my generation, is paradoxical only at first sight. For Jewish men painfully reacting to anti-Semitism, a Russian woman is forbidden fruit. This makes her more attractive by tenfold. I grow up hearing snippets of phrases in Yiddish, whisperings of my relatives and my father's friends: "You've already seen that new secretary Natasha in the City Constructing Trust? *Davke a goyke ober a mule tam*" (She's a Gentile but a charming one); "That cashier Anya in the department store on Deribas Street is a *shtikl skhoyre,* a good little thing, after all."

"What's so special about that *goyke,* that Gentile woman?" Mama exclaims once when she tells of the scandalous marriage of a Jew to a Russian. "Nothing to look at. Phooey!" That is, she doesn't approve of the interest a Jewish man might have in a beautiful Russian woman, but she understands it. However, she is not always true to her views.

We visit the Tentsers, Aunt Dunya and her son, Yan. We climb shaky wooden stairs to the second floor. A neighbor of the Tentsers descends the stairs toward us. She is a tall young Ukrainian woman with a thick braid of fair hair and protruding full breasts. Out of surprise, Papa freezes for an instant. He follows the beauty with his eyes.

"Abram!" Mama says. "Don't linger! We're already late as it is. Don't stare!"

Papa needs more than a minute to come to his senses. He even opens his mouth but is unable to utter so much as a word. He tries to take glasses from his jacket breast pocket. He follows the neighbor with his squinted eyes and shakes his head grievously, and then he obediently follows Mama.

Even though Papa's interest in the neighbor lasted for only a fleeting moment, Mama hisses at him all evening long: "He needed his glasses! Well, tell me, please, what did you want to see that was so special? Why are you silent? After all, I see that you can't wait. Please go, if you feel like having another look. There, go to the balcony. Perhaps, you'll see that indecent broad one more time. Both of you have no shame or conscience! Neither she, nor you."

An adolescent, I'm amazed. Why does Mama reproach that woman? How was she to blame? She just passed by us.

An interest in a Russian woman is frequently the result not so much of an attraction as an attempt to escape the Jewish environment. The Jewish girl is frequently too well-known. She is too close. She is almost a sister. She is deprived of the mystery so necessary for amorous imagination. The Russian girl is freer in the display of her feelings, less held down by fears and by her mother's interdictions than the Jewish girl. A romance with a shikse seems more exciting. In our school, pupils in their senior year gather in smoke-filled restrooms and brag of sexual conquests with Russian female sea bathers from Moscow and Leningrad. These victories become part of the school folklore.

Though I live in a multinational country, the female ideal here is a Slavic blue-eyed and light-haired beauty. A bookish boy, I fall in love with the heroines of Russian literature, one after another—Tolstoy's Natasha Rostov, Pushkin's Tatyana Larina ("Tatyana, with her Russian soul"), and his Maria Dubrovsky. As a rule, all movie stars of this time are also Russian: Lyubov Orlova, Lyudmila Tselikovskaia, and Marina Ladynina.

Even when it happens that an actress is Jewish, this identity is carefully hidden. In 1957, the film *And Quiet Flows the Don* comes out, with Elina Bystritskaia in the lead role of the young Cossack girl Aksinya. You can't tell her nationality by either her first or last name. Newspaper interviews with her avoid addressing her in the customary Russian way, which includes the first name and the patronymic. Many years will pass before I learn that this is not by chance; her patronymic is Avraamovna.

I don't know the Bible. I don't know the names of the heroines of my people—Esther, Bathsheba, Dalila, and Shulamith, whose beauty not only changed the course of ancient history but also inspired poets to create supreme examples of love poetry. (Only a decade and a half later, in the early 1970s, when, eventually, they publish the complete works of Alexander Kuprin, forgiven for his flight from the revolution, will I read his retelling of the Song of Songs.)

No matter how paradoxical it may seem, the primary factor in choosing a Russian as the "girl of my dreams" was anti-Semitism. It was in the air of that time. Ubiquitous, caustic, it suffocated us like the vapor of a poisonous gas. In conversations among Jewish adults, oft-repeated phrases such as "our children should marry only our own" served as a kind of spell.

I internally resisted these talks. I was an internationalist, raised on school, radio, newspapers, and cinema. I couldn't stand other people's habit of judging on the basis of nationality alone. Once, Papa said that Jews are the chosen people of God. He said it in such a tone that I felt he himself was surprised at this divine calling. By no means does Jewish exclusiveness match the reality of the time in which we lived. How could we reconcile being the chosen ones with our life made of half whispers? I perceived Papa's statement as irony only—the Jews are chosen by God to serve as a target for sneers and jeers.

Choosing a Russian girl as the object of my adoration was an unconscious form of my protest against dividing people according to the principle of nationality. To act that way myself meant to liken myself to my persecutors, to justify what can't be justified.

But the matter wasn't only that. Tired of asking myself the immemorial Jewish question "For what?" and persecuted by the fact of my ethnic belonging, I internally pushed myself away from Jewish girls just as I avoided my Jewish relatives. I pushed myself away from the Jewish world. But I tried to escape from my destiny in vain.

TEN

How They Laugh in Odessa

"YOU'VE CERTAINLY HEARD ABOUT the famous writer Marshak?" my father's colleague, a housepainter and wallpaper hanger himself, whose surname is also Marshak, asks when introduced to new people.

"Well, certainly!"

"So then, you should know that I am no relation to him."

Papa frequently invites Marshak to birthday parties and other holidays in our family. His first name is Adolf. It goes without saying that, because of the recent war, the name is hardly pleasant to pronounce. Everybody calls him by his surname. The moment they cross the threshold, the dinner guests invited to our home ask Mama, "Is Marshak coming? Will Marshak show up?"

It seems that nature created him strictly for the sake of laughter. Short, with an extensive stomach on short bowed legs, he is a walking comic mask. His curly black hair, with streaks of gray, sticks out from his head like a tall fur hat. His burning black eyes sparkle like bits of anthracite. The nose is flattened and wide. His hands are twisted from birth in such a manner that they resemble a kangaroo's front limbs. When walking, he waddles from side to side and holds his hands in front of him as if in a boxer's stance. He is able to cross a threshold only sideways. He does it in two moves. First, he shifts his weight onto one leg. Then, he turns his torso and pulls the other leg across.

After him comes his son Marik; a boy of my age. He walks the same way; his hands and legs are twisted in the same manner as his father's.

But first, the father and his son gallantly usher in their wife and mother—the gray-eyed beauty Lia Isaakovna. She enters our apartment ahead of them and quietly greets everybody, slightly burring. The fine features of her face emanate the calm of a well-brought-up woman from a good family. (That is how Mama speaks of her.) Lia Isaakovna's braids are stacked on her head like a crown. Unlike her husband, she is thin. In her small ears, ancient silver earrings dangle like little icicles.

Then Marshak steps into our home and greets Mama and the other ladies. He kisses their hands and murmurs compliments. He does it with such theatrical affectedness, courtier foot-scraping, and musketeer bows that everyone bursts out laughing right away. Really, when this big-bellied shortie imitates a high-society dandy, you can't help but smile. Now Marshak turns toward me. He looks for a while at my gloomy physiognomy, that of an adolescent apprehensive of life's complexities. He doesn't resort to platitudes like "How're you doing in school?" and other adult rubbish, which usually makes me nauseous. He only peers silently at my face for a long time and begins smiling, more and more widely exposing both rows of his crooked teeth, gold crowns sparkling here and there. After some internal resistance—I'm not used to communicating with adults yet—I involuntarily respond with a smile of my own.

From conversations between Mama and Papa, I already know that Marshak used to be an actor at the Odessa Jewish theater. During the war, the authorities evacuated his theater to Central Asia but, after the victory, as happened with many other Jewish theaters around the country, disbanded it. Marshak, along with his wife and their small son, faced starvation. Urgently, he mastered the wallpaper-hanging trade. He attracted his customers not so much with the quality of his work as with the charm of his extravagant personality.

Now, in my adolescence, I don't yet know how hard it was for him to lose his theater. I have no idea of the pain he carries in his soul. He has been deprived of the joy an actor experiences in perceiving the breathing of the audience when he steps onstage and feels on his face, his hands, on his whole body, the inquisitive look of the spectator. Well, tell us what we don't know about ourselves! Surprise us, make us laugh, move us deeply. Act!

(I will understand Marshak's torment and feel an audience's infernal attractiveness a decade later when trying my own hand at acting. First, at the theatrical circle of my Odessa Polytechnic Institute, then at the city student theater, Parnassus-2, together with the future variety show stars Mikhail Zhvanetsky, Victor Ilchenko, and Roman Kartsev.)

Marshak brings a delightful ease and poetic playfulness into the home of a hard-working blue-collar laborer. He slowly rolls from the corridor into the kitchen, where Mama hastily puts the last touches on her signature napoleon pastry. He rubs his enormous stomach and feigns torments of a person whom destiny has punished by endowing him with a fat body.

"Soybele! Little Soybel! Precious!" he exclaims, rolling his eyes up as if in the throes of death. "I know *what* you have in your hands. It's my poison! My life isn't dear to me anymore. Give it to me!"

His wife, Lia, doesn't appreciate her husband's humor. She admonishes him: "Adolf, how can you! Where's your shame?"

Marshak twists his head in grief and recedes. Together with everyone else, he enters our living room and sits down at the table. The dinner starts, but he waits for his time. When the main course is over, Mama serves dessert. Along with candies and nuts and small dishes with jam, she brings the pastry that has survived Marshak's attack. Half a sigh, half a groan escapes from everyone's chest. After a sumptuous dinner, there is no space for sweets. But who has the strength to reject Mama's napoleon?

At last, the dinner is over. Though the guests know from experience what to expect if Marshak is sitting at the table, the former actor does not rush. He knows that to capture the attention of the spectators completely, he must first wait for them to show signs of impatience.

Gradually everyone stops talking. Marshak still sits, his head lowered onto his hands, his eyes closed as if praying before entering the stage. Then, he slowly raises his head. Instead of the theater curtain that's been taken away from him, it's his chubby cheeks that slowly move apart, in a smile. His eyes begin to flicker like spotlights.

The women around the table burst into laughter. Marshak directs at them the terrible gaze of a theatrical fireman who's noticed a cigarette in a forgetful spectator's hand. Instead of abating, the laughter resounds with renewed force. Now Marshak is sure that the public is warmed up and ready for the show.

He grabs his jacket from the back of his chair and, in one move, throws it over his head. Now he is the spitting image of a shtetl photographer behind his ancient camera. Then, he emerges from under the jacket and portrays the photographer's customer, an old Jew. He straightens his invisible beard and stares with much apprehension. He has come to have his picture taken for the first time in his life, hasn't seen a camera before, and is scared.

"It won't hurt?" he asks in a constricted voice.

"If you won't do what I say," the photographer howls from under the jacket, "it will! Your nose is too long, Reb Gopnik. You don't fit the frame. Pull your nose in. More! Still more! Do what I tell you; otherwise you can kiss your money good-bye."

Marshak emerges from under the jacket. He is already the customer again. Frightened at the prospect of losing money, the old Jew tries to pull his nose in with all his might.

Laughter explodes around the table. Uncle Misha's wife, Tina, a thin, big-eyed former ballerina (before marriage, she danced in the corps de ballet of the Odessa Operetta Theater), becomes numb from laughter. She can't stop giggling. It is enough for her to take one look at Marshak's face, and she begins laughing loudly again. Sometimes she can't restrain herself; she jumps up from the table and moves into the farthest corner of the room, to my couch at a window. She watches the show from over there, catches her breath, and, time and again, in a desperate attempt to contain her laughter, turns her head away from Marshak.

She mustn't laugh so hard. It is her last month of pregnancy. For all she knows, such laughter may bring on early labor. But to restrain herself is not so simple. From time to time, we hear the next explosion of Tina's laughter.

"Pull your nose in!" the photographer howls again from under the jacket. "I'm talking to you!"

"I feel that I can't do it anymore," the customer gasps for air.

"And I'm telling you that you can, Reb Gopnik. Pull your nose in a bit more!"

The customer's face assumes a frightful expression; he inhales as deeply as he can.

"Aha!" the photographer shouts. "And what do you feel now?"

"I feel that your wife's borsht's boiled away."

And in a flash, I see a shtetl photo parlor, a half room in the photographer's house, partitioned with a bed sheet. From behind it, time and again, licking their lips in anticipation of the dinner, his poorly washed children look out.

While I watch these scenes from the past life of the people to whom I belong by sheer misunderstanding, I smile with the indulgence of a native speaker of the Great Russian language, a learned person with seven years of school behind me. I know that I should be above this shtetl humor, I who read Swift, Dickens, and Cervantes. But, to my shame, I can't help it, and, together with everybody else, I laugh at the characters of Marshak's show. Neither I nor anyone else doubts that the former actor is talented. But I take for granted that there is no Jewish theater. Why should the Jews have their own theater to begin with? People of many other nationalities live in Odessa—Armenians, Moldavians, Greeks, and Bulgarians. They don't have their own theaters either. Only those in the majority—the Russians and the Ukrainians—have theaters in their languages.

At the time, I don't even question why any people who want to have a theater in their native language aren't entitled to have one. I ignore the existence of Romen, the Gypsy theater in Moscow, though even on the streets of Odessa, a more multinational city than Moscow, the Gypsies—their women in long flowery skirts with bands of curly-haired children whirling around them—appear only occasionally.

(In my Young Pioneer's eye, for a long time yet, the naked emperor of Soviet power will sport the magnificent attire of his own manufacturing. Many years will pass before what wasn't a secret for any adult of my extensive family will finally occur to me too: that that emperor isn't only shamelessly bare but nauseatingly ugly as well.)

Though amused, I resist Marshak's humor. Big deal! One group of Jews, Odessa city folks, laughs at others of their kin, the provincial ones. It seems to me that such Jews are no longer around anymore. They belong to pre-revolutionary Russia. One day, Papa sits down next to me, bends toward me, and, as if letting me know that our conversation isn't for somebody else's ears, says, "Do you know that in the 1930s there was a movie titled *Iskateli schast'ia [A Greater Promise]*? In it, a group of Jews travels to Birobidzhan on a steamship."

Now, in the beginning of the 1950s, it seems improbable to me that once, in our country, films were made in which the main protagonists were Jewish.

"Poor people," Papa shakes his head. "*Kabtsonem.* And one of them asks the captain"—Papa shivers with laughter— "'Tell me please: how much—roughly, of course!—does such a steamship cost?'"

The movie laughed at the penniless sellers of air, smooth operators only in their dreams. In dreams, they were tycoons who sold and bought steamships, bridges, and tunnels. In my adolescence, I can barely stand Jewish jokes aimed at Jewish shortcomings. I don't know yet that the ability to laugh at oneself is a sign not of weakness but of strength, of undying spirit. One may endlessly grieve over one's own poverty and blame it for one's own sins, as that Dostoevsky character does while drinking away his last kopecks in a tavern: "The damned poverty's nibbled me to death!" But it is also possible to poke fun at one's own destitution, like a classic Jewish joke I heard in my youth:

> Known to his neighbors for serving the tastiest tea in the shtetl, old Solomon is dying. His loved ones gather around his deathbed.
> "Solomon, you're passing away. Please leave us with a good memory of yourself. Tell us the secret of your wonderful tea!"
> Solomon gathers his last bit of strength, raises himself slightly on his elbows, and whispers, "Jews, here's my secret. Don't spare tea the leaves!"

One evening, at dinner time, Mama tells Papa, "Can you imagine, this morning Tsilya from apartment 5 knocks at our door. We aren't friends with her, nothing of that sort. We just say hello and good-bye to each other. She holds up some package that spreads such an odor that I have to hold my nose. And she says, 'Sonya, my dear, you know, it looks like recently my chicken began to smell slightly. Would you find some space in your refrigerator? Mine's packed to capacity.'"

Mama and Papa laugh, but I'm ashamed. Not because the neighbor is senseless in her avarice, but because her name is Tsilya; that is, she is Jewish.

> *Sëmochka, moi tsypochka,*
> (Little Syoma, my little spring chicken,)
> *Sygrai mene na skripochka.*
> (Play your little violin for me.)
> *Kakoi zhe ty khoroshii muzykant!*
> (What a good musician you are!)
> *U tebia, navernoe, talent.*
> (You probably even have some talent.)

With comic anguish, Marshak sings this semiliterate ditty to everybody's delight. But I'm secretly perplexed: *Why does he, a Jew himself, mock a Jewish musician?*

I find it strange when I hear my parents' light-hearted teasing of other Jews, all those *shnorers* (freeloaders), *shmoks* (dummies), *shvytsers* (boasters), and big *makhers* (smart operators). Why treat them so good-naturedly? How could my parents be unaware that the behavior of all these *shnorers* and *makhers* plays into the hands of anti-Semites! In my youthful inclination to perceive the world in black-and-white terms, I can't accept that the Jewish people cannot consist entirely of angels any more than any other people can. I don't give them the right to be flawed. In my adolescent naïveté, I assume that blameless behavior is capable of calming down senseless hatred. I secretly dream that, without exception, all morally imperfect Jews will find a way to stop being a nuisance to their ill-wishers.

Still for a long time, I will not understand that to be ashamed of other Jews' behavior is not only silly but shameful in its own right. Many years will pass before I will realize that, in my young years, unable to overcome anti-Semitic ideology, I absorbed it into myself little by little and became contaminated with it. Fearing reprisals against all people in my adolescence, not only did I not give the Jews the right to their theater, their newspaper, their books, music, and songs; I did not even imagine that they had a right to their imperfections. They didn't dare to have what any other people always have—their rascals, their villains, and their renegades. I regarded Jewish humor as a way of public self-flagellation, and I was irked when a Jew evoked laughter instead of respect.

A decade later, while a college student when I read Dostoevsky's *Memoirs from the House of the Dead,* I became hot from shame that seized me when I encountered the character Isai Fomich Boomstein, the only Jewish convict that the author had ever met. He is pathetic and disgusting. "The spitting image of a plucked chicken," Dostoevsky writes, "he isn't young, about fifty, short and feeble, sly and decidedly silly at the same time." Boomstein is as harmless as a ladybug, and at the same time—could a Jew be absolutely innocuous?—he takes up usury in the prison. He takes something from other convicts as security, and, charging interest, he lends a few kopecks to them. How does he earn the author's and other convicts' sympathies? It turns out that he does it by nothing other than his good-natured response to the convicts' taunting. They shout at him, "Lousy kike!" but he couldn't care less. He just bursts into giggling.

In my adolescent eyes, Jewish humor is bad for the Jews for another reason as well: if it doesn't always humiliate them, at the very least it degrades them. Judging by Jewish jokes, the Jews are small-minded little people, incapable of deep passions. I don't know a single Jewish opera, nor can I imagine such a thing. It seems to me the very concepts of Jews and opera are incompatible. Sometimes they broadcast Mark Osipovich Reizen's concerts over the radio. "A Jew a basso?" I'm puzzled. A Jewish tenor is more or less all right. But a basso? He is way out of line. Admittedly, Reizen sings the arias of Ivan Susanin, Boris Godunov, and Mephistopheles. Operetta is a different matter. (I will not be surprised at all when, in due course, I find out that both Jacques Offenbach and Imre Kalman, whose operettas were eagerly staged in Odessa, are my fellow tribesmen.)

Now, in my adolescence, I take it for granted that the feelings the Jewish characters express are shallow and laughable. Tragedy and drama are for solid people, for the Russians. I cannot even imagine a Jewish character as noble and deep as Pushkin's Onegin or Tatyana. If you're a Jew, you belong to humor. It serves you right. We'll laugh at you in a friendly way. Aren't you laughing at yourself in your little shtetl jokes?

The most popular actor of the Odessa Operetta Theater is comedian Mikhail Vodyanoi (Water Sprite); at home they joke that, most likely, his real name is Moishe Wasserman. Short in height, he has a voice that is just enough for half singing, half whispering some satirical ditties. On top of that, he lisps noticeably. But the moment he enters the stage and shrugs in a typically Jewish gesture before beginning his little songs, the public is overcome with delight.

(As I understand now in my adulthood, Vodyanoi's image impressed the Odessa spectator. It was an image of a harmless Jew who laughed at himself and didn't take himself seriously. It was Charlie Chaplin's hero, the only difference being that Charlie had an acute sense of self-worth. He didn't let anyone humiliate him, even if it meant that he had to take to his heels after stealthily giving his offender a box on the ear.)

Watching Soviet movies of the time confirms that Jews are insignificant people, at best worthy of a good-natured jibe. In the thriller *Oshibka inzhenera Kochina (Engineer Kochin's Error),* both of the Jewish roles, an old tailor and his wife, are minor. I take it in stride. Since you don't belong to an indigenous nationality, why should you be a major character? Be thankful that you appear on the silver screen at all. As expected of them, the Jews provide comic relief in this film. The tailor's name is Abram. Which is already funny.

Not only do I take for granted that a Jewish name by itself is perceived comically in the movies, I also follow the same course in real life. When the first Sholom Aleichem book comes out, my brother and I entertain ourselves by searching for and laughing at clearly identifiable Jewish names in his works. I still remember one of them: Chaim Shlyoma Rabinovich— ha-ha-ha! Now, a half century later, our laughter, the laughter of Jewish adolescents at the sound of Jewish names, seems not only deeply shameful but sad as well. When, instead of the name Moisei (Moses), somebody said Moishe, it evoked a pejorative sneer. Moishe! In such a form, the name of

Moses was perceived as its shtetl variant, a synonym for backwardness and a narrow outlook on life. Denying our own roots, violently torn off from the history, culture, and language of the people to which we genetically belonged, how could we have known that our laughter was the laughter of the biblical Ham at his own father? That the true name of the person who had given precepts that formed the basis of Western civilization was precisely Moshe, Moishe being its Yiddish equivalent?

Thus, in *Engineer Kochin's Error,* both Abram and his wife are rendered comically. In fact, the tailor accomplishes a heroic feat: not only does he inform the secret police about an enemy plot, but, despite his frailty, he even tries to stop the spy caught in the act. Nonetheless, he becomes a laughingstock. Undersized, round-shouldered, bald, glasses on the tip of his nose, he's also absent-minded. When he leaves his home in the rain to alert our state security organs of his suspicions, his wife (played by the charming actress Ranevskaya) shouts to him with a hilarious Jewish intonation—simultaneously interrogative and exclamatory: "Abram?! You've forgotten your galoshes?!"

The phrase becomes famous. In many homes, whether Jewish or not, people repeat it, imitating Ranevskaya: "Abram?! You've forgotten your galoshes?!" Apparently, everyone likes the phrase because, in a compressed form, it expresses the Jewish stereotype. In his old age, Abram is not only forgetful; he also lags behind the times. Nobody wears galoshes anymore. For a long time, the shoes with microporous rubber soles have been in vogue.

Long before the first Sholom Aleichem book appears in our house, Papa asks me, his learned son, time and again, "Have you read Sholom Aleichem?" He lifts his finger. "Oh! What a writer! There haven't been many like him."

Because Sholom Aleichem is the only Jewish writer whom I hear about in my adolescence, I expect much from him. I expect him to be the Jewish Leo Tolstoy. Or, if worse came to worst, Maxim Gorky. I place high hopes in him. I dream that Sholom Aleichem heroes will be on equal standing with Pierre Bezukhov or Andrei Bolkonsky, that is, strong, thoughtful, and deeply passionate. When I throw myself into his books, my disappointment has no limits. All over his works, the same miserable Jews wander in search of pitiful fortune—a piece of bread—the same kind of people I've already met in Jewish jokes, in Marshak's shows, the kind I see around me in real life. The same heads pulled down on their shoulders. The same unfortunate people as Sholom Aleichem's Motl. The same shameful humor of people laughing at themselves. Sentimentality. Bitterness. I've had more than enough of that in everyday life.

As I will understand later on, the decision to publish Sholom Aleichem, a writer ideologically acceptable to the Soviet authorities because he depicts the sufferings of the Jewish poor in prerevolutionary times, is primarily a counterpropaganda measure designed to repudiate Western accusations of the suppression of Jewish culture in the USSR. But, at the time when his books first appear, it seems to me that Sholom Aleichem is published for a single purpose—to explain the existence of such an anomaly as the Jews in our Soviet life. As if to say that they are nothing but a vestige of tsarism. Generally speaking, they are an unnecessary nationality in our advanced time. After all, even the human body, nature's crowning achievement, has such useless things as the appendix, which nobody cares to know about till it begins to bother them. As if the Soviet authorities are saying that, yes, there were once ridiculous, downtrodden Jews, belittled by the tsarist policies. And here is what is left of them: pitiful ditties accompanied with a crying little violin and a flute, screaming from grief. Their little jokes about their own cheapskates and little fools. Their little tales about their own losers. Russian literature begins to shine for me with an even brighter light.

Unaware of the Bible, the greatest book ever written, I cannot even imagine that there were heroes, titans, and prophets in the ancient history of my people. I don't even suspect that in the country in which I live and which I call my native land, they hide the history and culture of my people from me. If I see Michelangelo's *David* in a museum, I huddle internally, wondering: how did a character with a Jewish name manage to get into a museum? Moreover, he has been placed in the center of the hall instead of somewhere in a blacked-out corner.

How should I know that this sculptural *David* is an ancient tsar and hero of my people? If his name does come up from time to time in newspaper articles, it is there for rhetorical purposes only—in connection with the defeated Goliath. The name David is always modified by the adjective *biblical,* which, in the Soviet lingo, means mythological, unreal, given birth by the imagination of people poisoned with religious intoxication.

My adolescent resentment toward Jewish jokes is especially incongruous, for I live in a city in which humor is as widespread as the Milky Way. Here, the usual, even course of life turns to joyful rope skipping. Laughter splashes about in Odessans' throats like a young wine in the throats of inhabitants of a Provençal village. For many years, French aristocrats planned, erected, and decorated Odessa—the duke de Richelieu, Alexandre-Louis de Langeron, Frantz de Volan, and many others. French city rulers, military leaders, architects, engineers, and other masters of trades lived here with their servants and retinues for long stretches of time. Full of love, they filled the city with many descendants. The Gallic light attitude toward life, Gallic wittiness and cheerful nature have poured from their blood into Odessa itself.

Odessans are the French of Russia. And they are the Ukrainians, simple-hearted and a bit sly at the same time. And the industrious Bulgarians. And the business-like Armenians. And the stately Greeks. Pushkin Street, the most beautiful of all, shaded with plane tree and chestnut tree crowns, was paved by the Italians, who lived on it for a long time. (Formerly, it was called Italian Street.) And, certainly, the Odessans are Jews, with their mistrust-ful, ironic, and down-to-earth attitude toward life. What other attitude can people afford when they don't dare presume that every knock on the door is just a neighbor who wants to borrow a pinch of salt for his soup?

There are no taboos when it comes to laughter. Anything goes as long as it's funny. The Russian proverb "For the sake of a witty word, he won't spare even his father" fits nobody better than the Odessans. In Odessa, the attitude toward laughter is that of rapt rivalry and one-upsmanship. No Odessans are without a sense of humor. In some, it's a bit coarser; in others, a bit finer. But they all have it. It's not by accident that Isaac Babel and Ilf and Petrov, as well as scores of other comic writers, cabaret singer Leonid Utyosov, and comedian Mikhail Zhvanetsky all came out of this city. An unsmiling Odessan is an anomaly, unless he's a recent transplant from Leningrad or from some horrible provincial town, like Ovidiopol. If you make jokes, it means you are one of us. Laughter defines whether you're alive or not; all other proofs of your existence are secondary. In my ado-lescence and youth, I attend performances of all famous comic masters of ceremonies—Garkavi, Mirov and Novitsky, Shurov and Rykunin, Timo-shenko and Berezin.

Odessans speak funny. But, for the most part, it is unintentional. Often they don't even suspect that something is wrong with their speech. The only people who roar with laughter over Odessan speech are those to whom the Russian language is native. This is the laughter of children at their fathers, caused by the generation gap. For the generation that created this unin-tentional slang, Russian was an acquired language, not inherited. The newly formed language was forged from the Russian lexicon, spiced up with

Ukrainian prepositions, inserted out of place ("I won't tell you *for* [instead of *about*] all Odessa"), and thoroughly saturated with the intonations, rhetoric, and phraseology of Yiddish. The Jews have lived here since the date the city was founded at the end of the eighteenth century. Yiddish was their native language *(mame-loshn)*. Because of the influx of people who arrived from the dying shtetlach of Ukraine and Byelorussia after the revolution and up to the mid-1930s, Yiddish was the language of class instruction in many Odessan schools. Newspapers, magazines, and books were also published in Yiddish. In many areas of the city, judicial proceedings were even conducted in the language of Sholom Aleichem. A policeman on duty could shout to an absent-minded pedestrian jaywalking across Deribas Street, "*Meshugener,* lunatic! What is it with you? Do you want those cars *tsykvetch,* to crush, you to death?"

The parodies of the rules of public behavior can be traced to that time. For instance, a warning sign above a streetcar window, "Avoid leaning out," turned into "Go ahead, stick yourself out! We'll see what's left of you!" "No riding without a ticket" became "May you reach that destination for which you bought your ticket!"

For the first generation of Jewish settlers, the Odessan language became the language of displaced persons, the language of migrants compelled to master the new, difficult Russian in a hurry. In the following generations, this language reproduced itself and became the normative language not only of those who didn't know their parents' language, Yiddish, but also of many non-Jews who grew up in this city. Expressions such as "May you be healthy for me!" "Listen over here!" "Do you hold me for [instead of *take me for* or *consider me*] an idiot?" and "Have [instead of *keep*] me in your mind" are nothing but word-for-word translations from Yiddish.

Expressive phrases used in moments of anger, frustration, and other strong emotions that saturate Odessan speech—"He dies after her" (that is, he loves her to death)—are of the same origin. Many Odessan curses and oaths also derive from Yiddish: "May my mama give birth to me in reverse order!" "You're a piece of an idiot!" "May you live on your salary alone!"

As was the custom in shtetlach, in Odessa the word *parents* is avoided. To refer to one's parents with a collective word is to show disrespect, a big sin in a Jewish family. Even an orphan in Odessa says, "I've lost my papa and mama." The Odessan language is full of tender little words that were once interspersed in conversations in the shtetl milieu: *Mummy, birdie, my little precious.* Odessans use these words not only when addressing relatives and dear ones but also when flooded with feelings not necessarily warm. "I'll bowl you out, Mummy, in such a way, no hospital will take you!" is a standard threat of an Odessan hooligan.

The language of Odessans owes its comic effect to their first attempts to construct a phrase analogously with the Russian, a strategy to which immigrants all over the world hastily resort in order to root themselves in a new language. An Odessan isn't even trying to crack a joke when he pays this compliment to a lady: "Mrs. Kantselson, today you look out wonderful!" Or when he says to his neighbors, "Please tell my wife that I've gone to take away our child from the kindergarten." Simply, "to look" and "look out," "to take" and "to take away," are the same for him.

When stumped for words, an Odessan resorts to those that he knows in the new language. Thus, instead of "She's an attractive woman," he may say, "She's not an ugly woman." For the same reason, an Odessan mother might alter a typical admonishment while feeding her juvenile son; instead of "Misha, chew and swallow," she may say, "Well, chew and make your mouth empty!"

In an Odessan's version of Russian, the simple and easily remembered words for "yes" and "no" work to their full capacity, handling all complexities. Instead of "This is an exception to the rule," in Odessa they say, "Generally, yes. But in this case—no!" Odessans turn the question, "Can you answer me definitely, yes or no?" into "Now tell me already: 'yes' is 'yes' or 'yes' is 'no'?"

These lexical simplifications often bring unexpected results. Odessan speech becomes sparkling, unusual, and funny. Thus, when a Russian says, "Don't stuff my head with all kinds of nonsense! My head's bursting," an Odessan expresses himself more succinctly, "Don't make my head pregnant!" An Odessan transforms the typical parental admonition "Why don't you listen to your papa?" this way: "Am I your papa or what?"

All this humor is unintentional, initially given birth by linguistic constraint. Another quality related to the migrants' mentality is captured in Odessan speech. It is the subconscious resistance of people who have escaped from a small secluded world and revolted against the regulations of a new system that contradicts their natural expectation of full and unbridled freedom. For those who migrated from the shtetlach, Odessa was the same as legendary America, the Promised Land. As the New World appeared to some of its immigrants, Odessa's streets seemed paved with gold and sprinkled with diamonds to the poor who inhabited the Pale of Settlement.

Odessan humor is the humor of the impatient. It is a commonsense gibe at rigid rules, a mockery of formalities. As the following classic joke testifies, the subsequent generations of Odessans have also adopted this attitude toward life in a big city:

> At the Odessa railroad station square, a woman who has just arrived from Moscow tries vainly to catch a taxi. Jingling his ignition key, an Odessan moonlighting in a private taxi service approaches her. Without saying a word, he picks up the Moscow lady's suitcases and takes them to his own car.
>
> "Wait a minute, wait a minute!" the newly arrived lady shouts after him. "This is not a taxi! I need a taxi."
>
> "Lady!" With the suitcases in his hands, the Odessan man stops. He lifts up his chin, addressing not the newcomer but the heavens, as if inviting them to witness the infinity of human stupidity. "I don't understand you! What do you need? A ride or checkers?"

This is one of the cases when the joke is born from life itself and secures its existence in folklore. In general, humor in Odessa is rarely invented. It is organic, as it is in any place where different cultures come into contact.

> An elderly Odessan woman sells ice cream on the beach. A cultured couple from Leningrad wants to buy some of it. (In Odessa, if you are from Leningrad, you are considered cultured even if you are a furniture mover.) It's hot. The saleswoman wants to get rid of the last briquettes of ice cream by any means possible. She wants to leave for home and retire to her room with shaded windows, cold mineral water, and cold borsht in her refrigerator.
>
> "Give us the ones that aren't melted yet, please," the Leningraders ask.
>
> "What, you want hard ones?" the saleswoman says. "So that they'll make you shiver?" She hands them two briquettes drooping under their own weight.
>
> "But they're absolutely soft!" exclaim the Leningraders, astonished.
>
> "Well, you're holding them with your hot hands!"

Humor is born from a mistrust of reality. One may utter an innocent phrase, but it gets reinterpreted on the spot. Its basis is pulled out, it hangs in the air, makes a somersault, and already lands as a springy, bubbly joke. The very spirit of Odessan life is sated with irony, just as the air in the aftermath of a thunderstorm is saturated with ozone. "She is as beautiful as my life," one Odessan woman may comment about another.

In Odessa, the word for "right now" quite often means "after it sprinkles on Thursday."

"Marik, ah Marik!" a woman shouts from an apartment window opening into a courtyard. "How much chess can you play? If you have so much free time, why won't you give your beloved wife a hand? Why won't you run an errand for me? Go to the manicurist Dinah on Richelieu Street and make an appointment for me."

"I'll take a running start from Deribas Street right this moment!" Marik shouts in response, without tearing himself from the chessboard for even a split second.

I will realize all this decades later. But now, in my adolescent years, I don't understand the reason for my relatives' love of Jewish jokes. I don't understand that not only do they serve as an amusing supplement at a time when entertainment is scarce, but they are also the only accessible form of a national Jewish life. Deprived of books, newspapers, and theater in their native language, Yiddish, they cling to Jewish jokes, which reflect the soul of the people—its recent history, its psychology and everyday life. Karl Marx's observation, "When laughing, mankind parts with its own past" couldn't better describe my relatives. Consider, for instance, this well-known Russian Jewish joke: "Little Fima and little Borya, stop swinging on your daddy. Your daddy didn't hang himself for you to have something to swing on. He did it so that there will be some quiet in our home at last."

These three sentences give the whole picture of life, its gloomy hopelessness, its silent despair. My family laughed in order to part forever from the cramped and wretched world of the Jewish shtetlach, from which they had escaped about two decades earlier.

PART TWO

ELEVEN

Papa and the Soviets

MY BELONGING TO AN UNPOPULAR tribe is not the only reason I am always tense.

"Abram," Mama says to my father one morning, "would you finally go to the Savings Bank? How many times do I have to ask you?"

"Oy, Sonya," my father waves his hand. "There's still plenty of time."

"Tomorrow's the last day. It's Saturday. The bank will be packed. You always put everything off until the last day."

"Sonya, stop nagging me. There are no more than thirty rubles in our account."

I already know what they're talking about. It's the last week of 1947. I've just turned ten. The radio's informed us recently that, beginning with the New Year, "devaluation" will take place. That means they'll introduce new money. And the goods in the stores will be discounted. Everything will cost ten times less. Isn't that great! One new ruble will buy the same stuff ten old rubles bought. Samples of the new bills have already been printed in the papers—they are going to be small, like play money.

"Thirty rubles?" Mama says. "So, you want to leave it all to *them*?"

First time I heard this, I didn't quite understand who "they" were. Later I got it—the Soviet authorities.

"You feel like giving *them* a present?" Mama says. "You think they'll thank you for this? Whatever is there, it'd be a pity to lose. Thirty rubles aren't money? Look at this millionaire! You don't get it, do you? If you don't take out whatever's left in the bank, it'll be zilch afterward. Haven't you heard the announcement: it's ten to one!"

Saturday comes. Papa leaves for the bank. He doesn't have to go far. It's located in the front wing of our building, right next to the entrance to our courtyard. A poster hangs in the bank window: A young, round-faced, blue-collar worker joyfully clutches a checkbook, the Soviet state emblem on its cover. Over his head, a plane is flying and, somewhat below his stomach, a train's rushing somewhere, leaving behind beautiful rings of smoke from which the slogan emerges: *He Saved His Money in the State Bank and Now He's Heading for a Resort!*

Papa left home soon after breakfast, around ten. He comes back around 3 P.M., tired and joyless. He puts everything he managed to buy with our savings in the middle of our table: a small can of crushed sardines in tomato sauce, a set of tiny forks touched with rust, and a cardboard box—bent, turned yellow from lying in the stationery store window—containing a set of wooden checkers. Puzzled, I look at Papa: neither of us plays checkers. For me, already infatuated with chess, checkers is a primitive game.

Mama leaves her cooking, comes up to the table, and glances at Papa's spoils. Then, without saying a word, she turns back to the kerosene stove. A bad silence hangs in the air for a while. But not for long. Mama is not one to keep her feelings to herself.

"That's all?" she says. "*Gotenyu!* My dearest God! And for this garbage, this *drek mit koshere fodem* [literally: crap with kosher threads], you've wasted a whole Saturday? Instead of spending the day with your family? I don't understand you!"

"Sonya, please," Papa says. "What are you saying? As if it's my fault that the store shelves are empty! This is big news to you?"

"*A melukhe!*" Mama says. "Some government!"

"Milya," Papa turns toward me, as if suddenly thinking of something with a faint smile. "Go and read a book."

"I've read enough for today already."

"Well then, read some more."

I'm familiar with this maneuver. All three of us—my father, my mother, and I—live in one and the same room. (My little brother, Vova, is to be born a few months later.) Every time my parents want to talk privately they send me off to read a book or do my homework. I walk to the window, sit on the windowsill, and stare at a randomly opened page of *Native Speech,* my fifth-grade reader. I pretend to read, but I'm all ears.

Papa says in a half whisper: "Have you heard this one already? I met Naum, your cousin Roza's husband, at the grocery store. He told me this: Two men meet. One says, 'So, have you exchanged your old money for some good stuff already?' 'Oh, yes!' the other says, 'I've bought myself a suit. And you?' 'And I've got just a table. You're a lucky dog!' 'Me? What's to be envious about! The only suit I could buy was for scuba diving. But look at you! You've got yourself a useful thing—a table.' 'Yeah, but it's an obstetrician's table.'"

"Sh-sh-sh," says Mama, choking with laughter. "Shush! *A melukhe.*" After she finishes giggling, she sighs and whispers in Yiddish, glancing in my direction: *"Zoln zey ale faln in drerd!"* I already know what that means—"May they all go to the devil" (literally: fall into/through the earth).

I understand why sometimes Mama and Papa don't talk aloud but whisper. I'm a Young Pioneer. Every morning before I go to school, Mama gives me a freshly ironed white shirt and ties my silky new tie, the color of fire, around my neck. Every morning, at the school lineup, when Ivan Fedorovich, our school provost, shouts, "Young Pioneers! Are you ready to fight for the cause of Lenin and Stalin?" we, the pupils, ages seven to thirteen, squeak in unison, "Always ready!"

We chant a poem learned by heart in class: "As you've tied up your Young Pioneer tie, guard it. After all, it's the color of our country's banner."

We also sing, repeating after our teacher:

It doesn't matter that I'm younger!
So what!
Nothing will stand in our way.
I'll also join the Young Communist League,
As my older brother did.

However, Papa and Mama don't care much about Soviet power. Even a newspaper they pick up only to look at the weather forecast. I'm convinced of their backwardness. What else can you expect from the older generation? This is how it should be. At our school, a red slogan hangs across the entrance hall: "Communism Is the Youth of the World, and the Young Will Build It." I'm a future builder of communism. My parents are doomed by history, with vestiges of capitalism still lodged in their consciousness.

Mama is a housewife. Not much is expected of her in terms of building communism. But Papa is a working-class man. The Soviet power was created for him and in his name. However, not only does he fail to go to holiday demonstrations—of the First of May, or any other—but also he doesn't express even a tiny bit of interest in them. How do you like that! The whole country's celebrating. The radio broadcasts report about holiday parades—those that take place in Moscow and those in Odessa, on Kulik Field. The radio announcer tells us, his voice trembling with excitement, "There marches the blossom of our working class. Here comes a column of representatives of the Lenin District. Now it is approaching the grandstands, where the local party and government leaders greet them. The demonstrators joyfully report their early fulfillment and overfulfillment of the five-year plan."

But Papa is oblivious to all things Soviet. I don't understand for a long time why he dislikes the Soviet power so much. As the song goes, "We, Young Pioneers, are workers' children!" I'm a Young Pioneer. Papa is a working man. And the working class is the basis of Soviet power. True, he is not the ideal blue-collar worker portrayed on street posters—a machine operator wearing blue overalls with a wrench sticking out of his chest pocket. Papa's a housepainter. And a good one. People always call him a master. "Is the master at home?" they ask when I answer the doorbell.

For a long time, I don't understand why Mama constantly reminds me to ask any stranger at our door the same question: "Who sent you?" I'll discover the reason for this later. One thing I know for sure—Papa is a master of his trade, respected for his work. What else does a son need to be proud of his father?

Gradually I realize that Papa works neither in a plant nor at a construction site, where the advanced working class is supposed to labor, according to books and posters, but in private apartments all over the city. He and Uncle Misha whiten ceilings and paint door and window frames. In some apartments, they hang wallpaper; in others they do stenciling. That is, instead of putting up wallpaper, they spray-paint circles at equal distances from one another; little cherry branches, strewn with white flowers and green leaves, will stretch out from them. To achieve that, Papa goes all around the walls, pressing on a sheet of thick paper treated with drying oil. This is the stencil itself, with cutouts in the shape of little leaves and flowers that he daubs with white, brown, and green paint.

From time to time, the stencils get worn out. Mama is too busy homemaking, so I'm called on to help. I sit at our dinner table, where I place two stacks of books and rest a thick piece of glass on top of them. On this piece of glass I place the old stencil, which is about to come apart. To see the patterns better, I position my table lamp beneath the glass. To prevent the glass from overheating and breaking, I switch on our table-top electric fan, which I put on the floor nearby. First I trace the cutouts with an indelible pencil, and then I cut them out using a scalpel, which Papa has acquired from a medical supply store by pulling strings—the way almost everything is bought in the shops at the time.

Sometimes, when Papa's work is not too far from home and I have no school, Mama sends me with his lunch. Coming to the street address Mama has given me, I locate the apartment where Papa works, not so much by its number, but by the smell of oil paint, Uncle Misha's loud voice, and white tracks on the staircase steps. As a rule, the door isn't locked, and I step into the apartment.

Often I carry a shopping bag that holds an iron pot full of buckwheat kasha with bits of lamb in it. To keep it warm, Mama has wrapped one of Papa's old flannel shirts around the pot in several layers. I bring also a peeled cucumber, fresh, still smelling of the garden bed. With one move of a sharp knife, she has cut and salted it and rubbed the grainy halves, oozing with moisture, against each other. There are also two pieces of wheat bread and a narrow half-liter jar with Papa's favorite compote, made from fresh cherries and pears.

(Now, recalling the contents of that lunch bag as an adult, I'm puzzled. How could I ever have doubted my mama's feelings for my father when I was a youngster? True, they argued a lot, and my father was often edgy around my beautiful mother. At times, they even stopped talking to each other. And for me, who grew up reading romantic literature, for a long—very long—time, love existed primarily in popular songs and sentimental movies. Years of my own life have made me understand that high-flown words are only the result of airwaves passing through vocal cords and that the language of love is much more sophisticated than I realized. Take that food that I brought to my father. It said so much more than any words could. My father wasn't a demanding man. He was always satisfied with little. Growing up in a big working-class family, in constant need, he was never fussy, was thankful for any meal. What then compelled my mother to search our squalid postwar shops for whole [without fail, whole] buckwheat grain? Why did she make many rounds of the markets, trying to find not just any pear for Papa's compote but the kind that Papa loved—the duchess pear?)

I enter Papa's workplace and immerse myself in the smell of fresh-washed floors and oil paint. To my surprise and delight, I find my father high in the air, almost up against the ceiling. With a brush in his hand and a jar of paint suspended from his neck, resting against his chest, he's standing on top of a folding ladder. With a stilt-walker's agility, he's moving along the wall, making the ladder's legs jump over the hoses and ropes on the floor. I've seen such skill only in the circus.

Papa doesn't notice me for a while, and I don't dare tear him away from his business. He's working swiftly and happily. I'm drawn into this climate of happy work—a true intoxication for a working man who makes a chore a holiday. I stand at the threshold, shifting from foot to foot and waiting for him to notice me.

"Oh!" Uncle Misha shouts from the door to another room, a couple of chairs under each arm. He's preparing a new workspace. "Abram! *Er zinele hot gekumen!* Your little son has shown up! Come in, come in. Don't be shy!"

Every time I bring lunch to my father, I'm surprised by how different he is from the way I see him at home. There, as a rule, I see him in the evenings, after a long working day—tired, hungry, and, for some reason, somewhat unsure of himself. But here, in somebody else's apartment, he's not just calm and self-confident. His face is inspired. He's absorbed and joyfully alert.

(Years later, living in Moscow, I befriended some underground Soviet artists. In the daytime, they made their living by painting Lenin and other Soviet leaders in all possible poses. In the evenings, they worked on their own, sketching out the surrealistic fantasies forbidden by the authorities. It was at such moments when, observing their faces, I encountered the same expression of joy and happy concentration that I saw on my father's face when he was working. This expression appeared on the artists' faces every time their work was going well. They suddenly saw what else could be done with something that they hadn't a clue about just a moment before.)

Papa stops. He turns toward me, smiling, and raises his little brush to greet me. He descends from his heaven and goes to the bathroom to wash his hands.

"Have you eaten already?" he asks, as always, sitting down in his stained overalls on a chair that he has carefully covered with a piece of wallpaper.

"I've eaten, I've eaten," I say, surprised that he asks me this every time I come. As if Mama would ever let me out of the house without feeding me first.

Papa eats, the iron pot between his knees; the table is cluttered with wallpaper rolls and paint cans. From time to time, in an interval between chewing, wrinkling his nose and lightly clicking with his tongue, *"ks, ks, ks,"* as he does when he is thinking, my father looks up, now at the ceiling, now at the windows. I follow his gaze. I fail to see anything but the ceiling's sparkling whiteness and the smoothness of the light blue enamel on the window frames. With the perfectionism of an artist whose painting anyone else would find flawless, he notices that, here and there, the whitewash is bleeding or the paint on the windowsill is uneven. I'm sure that, if I weren't there, if my father didn't feel uncomfortable about keeping me too long (I have to take the pot and jar back home), he'd put aside his kasha right away, grab a brush, and rush to correct whatever imperfection he's found.

Sometimes I try to paint a bit—out of cheer curiosity. What's so special about the painting business? Big deal! As if it's some art! I slather some paint on the wall.

"No, no, no," Papa stops me, smiling in embarrassment, as if *I* hadn't just smeared paint on the wall, *he* had. "You take too much paint on the brush. Dip the tip only. Don't press it, don't press! Lighter, lighter. Look." He covers my hand with his palm and moves my brush along the wall. In a minute, the shameful stains disappear.

(My father's advice on how to paint a wall—don't overdo it, work easily, as if playing—has proved equally helpful not only for that skill but also for many other things I've tried in my life. Only now, half a century later, do I see how happy I was then, back in my hometown, visiting my father at work. Alas, with the shortsightedness of raw youth, I took everything in life for granted then. What wouldn't I give now to relive those moments— those minutes of bliss in seeing my father healthy, happy with his work, and feeling his unspoken love for me. Like many fathers of his generation, he considered the open expression of love for his son unmanly. Only now do I understand what his quiet half smile was all about—that smile with which he looked at me, a ten-year-old in short summer pants altered from his old uniform. That smile was his way of experiencing love for me, his shy, gloomy son, caught up in Soviet schooling. The world of that schooling, a world of topsy-turvy values, was banished during the time spent in the company of my father at work.)

Sometimes, when my visit happens on the first day of work, Papa treats me to pleasure of a special kind. He gives me an opportunity to vent the destructive urges of boyhood. Before hanging new wallpaper in an apartment, you had to take off the old strips, torn and discolored by rays of the southern sun. With Papa's sharpened trowel in hand, I move along the wall in search of places where I can stick it in to make the paper come off in sheets. With joyful fierceness, I tear them off, one after another.

"*Sha, sha!*" Papa says, chasing away the dust I've raised. "Don't get all worked up. Take it easy, easy." But he must have enjoyed watching me, or he'd never have given me the job.

The day he finishes somebody's apartment, Papa comes home tired but happy—and a bit tipsy. What Odessa housewife would let the master leave without a hearty dinner and a shot of vodka! It's such a delight—to have the apartment repair ended. (Now, so many years later, I understand Papa's happiness on such a day—his pleasure in bringing joy to people. When, in the beginning of summer, they moved to their rented dachas, the families left behind their shabby, neglected rooms. Now, on their return, they've found that the nightmarish odor of the old apartment— of mold, dust, and dried-up wallpaper glue—has vanished. Now the air is fresh and carries the smell of oil paint, resembling that of May lilacs. Out of violet and beige circles on the walls, as if from the horn of plenty, handfuls of the milk-white cherry blossoms with wine-colored stamens pour down from all sides. "Hey, Master! You're a miracle worker, that's who you are! Oh, no, put down your brushes. Take off your jacket. Don't even dream of going away without having a feast with us in your honor!")

Coming home, Papa forces himself to sit down at the table. To refuse to eat Mama's cooking is to offend her mortally. Making believe that he's hungry, he pushes a cutlet around.

"Why didn't you tell me that they would feed you?" Mama asks angrily. "I wouldn't work all day long. Here I am—bustling around the stove, cooking, stewing, and frying. And, here you are—Count Potocki has already had his dinner!"

(Mama has brought the count's name up for as long as I can remember. Who is this mysterious aristocrat? I'll learn in time. Count Potocki played an important part in the history of Uman', Mama's Ukrainian hometown. In the stormy eighteenth century, this Polish magnate rebuilt the town burned by the Haydamaks, angry peasant rebels. Among other useful projects, he built Sofievka, an estate for Sofia, his lover. On the shore of a lake, he created a luxurious park with hanging bridges and other miracles of artful landscaping. Not surprisingly, the count's name was on everybody's lips. Mama resorts to it every time somebody in our household behaves extravagantly or defiantly. "Move over," Mama orders me if I leave too little room on the couch for my younger brother, Vova. "You lounge like Count Potocki.")

"Sonya, get off my case, ple-e-e-ase," Papa says. "I'm full." To make amends for such behavior isn't simple. "How could I know they would make me sit down at their table?"

"Ah, they forced him, the little one, to eat! Couldn't you let them know that your family's waiting for you with dinner?"

"Sonya!" my Papa says, moaning.

It has taken me a while to make a horrible discovery: my papa isn't a regular Soviet blue-collar worker but rather an outlawed private craftsman. A *private* craftsman! I don't know what to think of it. To begin with, it is such backwardness—to be a self-employed craftsman, to work for himself, not for a state enterprise, as everybody else does. Working in a collective has so many advantages! We have often read about it in class, and it's been demonstrated in the movies so often that Galina Ivanovna, our teacher, frequently cites an old Russian folk proverb, *"Odin v pole ne voin"* (One man can't win a war). When you work in a collective you're assured of mutual help. You develop a high degree of political awareness.

I already know that a private self-employed craftsman is a vestige of capitalism—that is, of the epoch, now past, of man's exploitation of man. True, Papa doesn't exploit anyone. He works with his brother, my uncle Misha, who does the work my papa can't do. Seventeen years younger than Papa, he recently retired from the army, where he was a field sergeant in a tank regiment. He is a strong man. Uncle Misha pushes the handle of a big pump up and down while Papa spray paints the stencils, producing those wonderful intricate patterns on the wall.

I'm forced to reconcile myself to Papa's way of making a living. But secretly, I'm sorry that he has no chance of becoming famous. He'll never be honored in a public place. Since he's not part of any collective, he won't have his portrait hanging in the Board of Honor on the wall near our Opera and Ballet Theater, along with the portraits of outstanding workers of the Port of Odessa, the Marti Ship-Repair Plant, the Odessa Mill Center, the Rosa Luxemburg Candy Factory.

It's a pity, of course, but one can live with it. Another matter is much more troublesome. For a long time I can't see why Papa's work produces so much agitation and anxiety at home. My parents always hide his occupation from strangers, as if he were not a worker but some crook. What crime does he commit by spraying some people's walls with paint? He isn't some underground black marketer or a speculator, people we all despise. Papa neither buys nor sells anything. He works with his own hands, and he works long hard hours. He often comes home when it's already dark outside— so tired sometimes that, once inside our door, he walks not to the dinner table, but to the sofa, where he lies down on his stomach, his face in the crook of his arm.

"Abram," my mama says carefully, "dinner's ready. We've been waiting for you. And the children are hungry."

Papa has trouble responding. Finally, unable to raise his head, he mumbles, "Don't wait for me. Go ahead, I'll eat later."

"What kind of man are you!" Mama exclaims. "I don't understand you. How many times have I told you—you're wearing yourself out!" Mama's voice betrays her ambivalence. She's angry with Papa and at the same time she's sorry for him. "I don't know! Other women have their husbands working hard. But they know when to stop. I don't understand. Why do you have to work till you collapse?"

"Oy, Sonya, stop it already, stop!" Papa gathers his strength. Slowly, in three moves, he gets up from the sofa. On his way to wash his hands, to prevent another wave of Mama's scolding if she learns that his backache has recurred, he tries to distract her in order to hide his back-rubbing. "Sonya, you should try to understand. I had to finish their bathroom today. The family is returning to the city tomorrow morning. It's the last day before their kids go back to school. They have to clean up after roughing it all summer."

"You worry about your customers more than about your own family," Mama grumbles while bustling around the table and pouring the borsht from the pot; to keep it warm, she has kept it in the stove.

Papa washes himself for a long time, as usual. First he cleans his hands with paint thinner; then he soaps them and rubs his fingertips with pumice. So much paint has eaten itself into the skin around his nails that he can't get it out no matter how hard he tries. Then, he undresses himself to the waist, bends over a basin of warmed-up water, and washes his chest and his back, puffing. (There won't be a bathroom or a shower in our apartment for a long time.)

Sometimes when Papa comes home he's not just tired. His face has turned gray and is covered with fine beads of sweat. Mama already knows why. It means that, working with a paint called zinc white, he forgot to cover his nose with gauze and has been poisoned for the umpteenth time. Now he'll be nauseous all evening long and keep throwing up all night.

"Well, what kind of creature are you?" Mama says. "Where are your brains? Please tell me!"

"Ah, it's nothing." Papa waves his hand. "It'll go away soon. I had half an hour of work left. I didn't have time to stop and look for gauze."

(In his final days, he will pay for this carelessness about his own health with many months of suffering. Having once entered his blood, zinc white will never leave it. In his eighties, skin cancer will torment him till his last breath.)

Still, for a long time I wonder why my father is forced to hide his trade. He works hard, and his customers respect him, because he's both skillful and conscientious. If some underground dealer (quite a few black marketers operate in Odessa during my adolescence) wants to hire him to do his apartment, Papa charges him full price. But if some schoolteacher asks him to freshen up her place, it's another matter altogether. While she sits in front of Papa at our dinner table, tugging nervously at her handkerchief (she isn't sure she can afford this master), Papa blushes, as he always does in a delicate situation, and says, "Let's do it this way, lady. I'll do your apartment. If you like it, you pay me as much as you can afford. Agreed?"

The teacher doesn't know how to thank him. She spots me in the room and asks what grade I'm attending. She offers free math tutoring for me.

"Thank you, ma'am," Mama says. She doesn't like Papa's delicacy when it comes to the cost of his work. "Our son's a straight-A student. We'll manage without tutors."

That said, Mama gets up, her lips pursed, and stalks into the kitchen. There she starts washing the dishes and clattering the cutlery louder than usual. Of course, she wants us to live better. Sometimes, however, I hear her telling my aunts, "My Abram isn't a chiseler. His friend Marshak is another matter. He knows no shame. He paints a hundred times worse, but he charges his customers an arm and a leg."

It takes me a long while to figure out that, like many other craftsmen, my father has no choice financially but to engage in private business, which Soviet law prohibits. Of course, he could work for one of Odessa's government-organized Centers for Household Service, but the pay is so miserable that no family can survive. People wanting work done on their apartments prefer expert painters recommended by their friends and acquaintances over the poorly skilled and undisciplined housepainters working for the centers. More often than not, those painters demand an advance for buying paints and then disappear for a long time. Most of them are heavy drinkers and stretch what would be a few days' work in the hands of a self-employed craftsman into weeks of delay and frustration.

Painters and paperhangers aren't the only ones who shy away from state enterprises. Every skillful worker looks for an opportunity to circumvent the cumbersome and obtuse state system. One of my relatives tailors men's suits behind the closed shades of his first-floor apartment. Another one fashions ladies' boots in his back room. In his backyard shed, a third one makes kitchen tables and knocks together bookshelves for his private customers.

Like other underground workers, Papa must be officially employed in order to avoid trouble with the authorities. Without a proper stamp in his passport and his work-record book, he could be arrested for "parasitism" under the very same criminal code article that will later be used as an excuse to arrest poet Josef Brodsky.

Fima Roitburt, the husband of one of my mother's friends, works as the head of a construction crew in one of the City Food Trade Trusts. He often comes to us—with his wife, round-faced Katya, and their equally round-faced daughters, Lilya and Tsylya—for birthdays and other family holidays. Fima is a small cheeky man who wears a cap with a long visor—good-natured, with a crafty smile on his face, and often fortunate. He has put Papa on the payroll of his trust, listing him as a painter of the sixth rank (the highest). Twice a month, on paydays, often in the middle of a job, Papa sticks his brush into a can of paint thinner and jumps onto the running board of a tram. Silently cursing the authorities, he crosses the city, heading toward Marazli Street. There, in the semibasement of building number 12, the adding machines of Fima's trust payroll office buzz and ring. And there, shifting from foot to foot, Papa stands in a long line leading to the cashier's office. He's pale with fear. Thanks to idiotic government rules, he must commit a crime—pocketing unearned money. To get this dirty stuff out of his hands right away, he heads straight from the payroll office to Fima's home and passes his "salary" to Fima's wife. Luckily, the Roitburts live not far from the trust. Thus, Papa frees himself from the danger of being accused of parasitism, and Fima puts extra money in his pocket. Both are satisfied with the arrangement.

Uncle Misha's cover is the Odessa Operetta Theater. His friend Ostrovsky, the theater's chief artistic director, has registered him on the payroll as stage decorator. (Almost half a century has passed since then. Looking back at those times, my uncle admits now that pretending to be somebody else, standing in line to receive somebody else's money, was the worst memory of his Soviet life. He's convinced that his weak heart is due to the stress

PLATE 1. My parents, c. 1950.

PLATE 2. My parents at a rented dacha near Odessa, c. 1954.

PLATE 3. My mother with my year-old brother, Vladimir, c. 1949.

PLATE 4. My father, c. 1960.

PLATE 5. Grandmother Sarah, 1950.

PLATE 6. Me as a Young Pioneer, c. 1948.

PLATE 7. Uncle Misha shortly before his discharge from army service, 1949.

PLATE 8. Abram Greenberg (Uncle Abram), Aunt Clara's husband, 1950.

PLATE 9. Itzchak Tentser, my second cousin Yan's father, shortly after enlisting in the army, 1941.

PLATE 10. Froychik Greenberg, with his aunt Maria, shortly before the outbreak of the war, c. 1940.

PLATE 11. Pinchas Rabinovich with his wife, Tamara, shortly after the end of the war, c. 1947.

PLATE 12. Ivan (Isroel) Tabenkin, 1971.

PLATE 13. Ruvim Bronfman, treasurer of the Odessa synagogue, my second cousin Yan's grandfather.

PLATE 14. Uncle Abrasha (Avner Bendersky) with his wife, Lida, and daughter, Zhanna, 1950.

PLATE 15. My mother's close friend Tanya Beskina with her husband, Sasha, and son, Senya, 1951.

PLATE 16. My mother *(to the left)* with her friend Anna Ivanovna Henriksen, c. 1970.

PLATE 17. My eighteenth birthday party with friends and family, 1955. Standing *(to the left of me in the center):* my cousin Boris Bendersky (Uncle Avner's son) and my friend Konstantin (Kotya, Kotka) Liubarsky; *(to the right):* my friend Zhenya Henriksen and my cousin Eva Greenberg. Sitting *(left to right):* my cousin Zhanna Bendersky, second cousins Yan Tentser and Eva Khanis, and neighbors Susanna and Raya.

PLATE 18. Actor Adolf Marshak, his wife, Lia, my grandmother Sarah, my brother, Vladimir, and Senya (the son of my mother's friend Tanya), c. 1955.

PLATE 19. Esther Bendersky, my mother's older sister, 1919. Picture taken on the eve of the Petliura pogroms in Uman', during which she met her untimely death.

PLATE 20. Aunt Judith, my father's older sister, with her husband, Yakov. The picture was taken shortly before the war. With all three of their children, they perished in the Minsk ghetto.

PLATE 21. At one of the family gatherings in the 1950s. Standing *(left to right):* Uncle Misha, an unidentified guest, Misha's wife, Tina, and my mother *(at the center).* Sitting *(left to right):* Aunt Lida (Uncle Avner Bendersky's wife), Dunya (Dvoira) Bronfman (my mother's cousin), Vladimir (my brother), Aunt Clara (Khaya Bendersky, my mother's sister), and Rosa (my mother's cousin).

PLATE 22. Me with my younger brother, Vladimir, and my parents on my college graduation day, June 1960.

of those days when he stood side by side with the theater lighting director and the operetta stock characters—the ingenue and the comic old woman—in the crowded little corridor backstage.)

To avoid wasting his precious working time standing in line, my uncle comes not on the first crowded payday but on the second or even the third. Once, however, even though it's the third payday, he finds himself at the end of a huge line. Because of some bank trouble, they have delayed the payment. This happens in August, during the big painting season. My uncle and Papa work from morning till night, without days off. Odessans are starting to return from their rented dachas, and having their apartment freshened up in their absence is everyone's dream. Standing in line is unbearable. My uncle wants to leave as soon as possible. But how can he do that without raising suspicion? Once, under similar circumstances, when he tried to do so, he was given dirty looks. "Look at the aristocrat!" people in line said of him. "Everyone else must wait to get his damned pay. But this Rothschild doesn't need money!"

He feels he has no choice now but to stand with everyone to the very end. In desperation, he decides to resort to acting himself, deceiving the professionals around him; he is amid all the leading operetta stars—the hero-lover Dynnov, the incomparable Dembskaya, who plays the heroine of the most popular operetta in the theater's repertory, Imre Kalman's "Silva," and the lisping favorite of the Odessa public, the comedian Misha Vodyanoi. With no room for retreat, my uncle grabs his stomach and bends over.

"What's with you?" they ask him.

"It's that lousy cafeteria!" my uncle whispers. "I had that awful cutlet there, and . . ."

"It's true, comrades," somebody from the line says. "Recently, I was poisoned in a diner. They barely nursed me back to life in the hospital. Maybe we should call the paramedics for you?"

"No, no!" Uncle Misha worries that he might be exposed. "I'd better get home. My neighbor's a registered nurse. If only I could get a taxi!"

Somebody runs to the street and stops a cab, and soon my uncle is on his way back to the apartment where Papa is waiting for him to resume the interrupted work. My uncle doesn't know whether he should laugh or cry in the face of life's stupidity. He, a housepainter, must hide his profession in a country hailed as a workers' paradise.

Whatever the cover, the danger of being exposed hovers over my parents' heads and poisons every waking hour. Long before I know what the words *tax inspector* and the acronym OBKHSS (Department Investigating Theft of Socialist Property) mean, I notice that my parents pronounce them with trepidation and animosity. Later, Mama will explain to me that, if some tax inspector or OBKHSS agent catches Papa working privately, not only might a huge fine be imposed on him, but he could also be imprisoned. He could get five years behind bars. "What would we do then?" Mama asked in horror.

Although those working privately are much better off, you can't call us rich. Even when our family consists of four, after the birth of my younger brother, we still occupy our same prewar dwelling, the same small, two-hundred-square-foot room. In 1953, shortly after Stalin's death, Papa will manage to exchange our sunny room on the third floor for two damp first-floor rooms around the block. We will never have a domestic helper or a car. We eat well, dress adequately. Once a year, usually in February, in the slow season of his work, Papa uses his pull to buy special passes, and my parents leave for a health resort in Yalta or Sochi. This is about all the luxury we can afford.

Of course, from the point of view of those of our relatives who live on the miserly salary paid to Soviet office workers, we are rich. When my time comes for a bicycle, Papa brings home a used one, I suspect, as part of the payment for his work. I can't even find its trademark. The paint on its frame is peeled off. The saddle wobbles under me; the bolt that holds it in place is loose. It takes me a long time to take the whole thing apart, wash its parts in kerosene, and reassemble it.

One day two women appear in the courtyard of our building. They ask us kids running around in the yard where the "master" lives. You can't hide anything from neighbors. The kids point at me, "Here's his son."

"Well, so where's your papa?" one woman asks.

Somehow I feel that she's not on private business, that she's an official. Such people speak louder than Papa's customers, who ask about him quietly and respectfully, sometimes even trying to ingratiate themselves with me. They hope to get him working for them as soon as possible. But this woman is different. She seems arrogant. I'm too young to be able to read faces, but somehow her expression puts me on my guard. She has the same air of importance that I've seen in our leaders in the portraits that hang in our classroom, appear in newspapers.

I lower my head and mumble something about my father's whereabouts. The women realize that I've guessed the purpose of their visit. They exchange glances and laugh at my awkward attempt to divert their scrutiny of my father. They leave our courtyard.

In the evening, I tell my parents about the strange visit. Papa pales. Crying out, *"Vey'z mir!"* Mama throws herself at our wardrobe, pulls out a sealskin fur coat—black, gleaming under the electric light, with a collar clasp in the shape of a fox head with two sets of small sharp teeth. It seems it is laughing at our panic. Mama motions me to help her. She also takes her sealskin muff and her little astrakhan hat, wraps them all up in a sheet, and, when it gets dark outside, with much trepidation, wincing even at the sight of traffic cops at the intersections, she and I rush the bundle to Aunt Clara's room in the basement of building number 9, two blocks down the street.

Eventually, in the summer of 1950, Papa gets in trouble with the authorities. While he is working in a first-floor apartment on Zhukovsky Street, his unlucky rival, a housepainter named Zadolnikov, passes by on the sidewalk. Through a window carelessly flung open on a hot day, he spots Papa's trademark—a futuristic, fanciful pattern of circles, arrows, and horns of plenty on the walls. A fit of envy seizes him. His heart skips a beat. He doesn't even realize that he's trotting in the direction of the local Department of Taxation. As misfortune has it, it happens to be located in Greek Square, not too far from the place of Papa's work. The police catch Papa and Uncle Misha in the act. Still in their paint-stained clothes, with brushes on their shoulders still wet with paint, they are escorted by two policemen into the office of Comrade Gorbis, chief of the Department of Taxation. On this sultry day, Gorbis, a stout bald man, is sweating in his fashionable beige linen jacket. Papa is afraid of a jail sentence, but, luckily for him, Gorbis, like all the others in his department, is on the take. The case is settled by making Papa pay a gigantic fine, half of which goes straight into Comrade Gorbis's pocket.

While interrogating Papa, Gorbis asks quietly, as if making some offhand remark, "Do you remember me?"

Papa can't see anything no matter how he stares at the taxation boss, since his glasses are sprinkled with paint. Feeling very anxious, he doesn't dare to stop the interrogation in order to wipe them off. "N-no, I have no idea. I'm here for the first time," he responds, secretly hoping for leniency as a first-time offender.

As Papa will understand later, Gorbis isn't trying to frighten him at all. There is no need to do so. Papa takes even small doses of the Soviet system poorly. And such a huge portion of it is more than he can handle for a long time to come. What is really happening is that, by talking about himself, Gorbis is trying to hint that there is a way to hush up the case. A few days later, Papa realizes where he has seen Gorbis before. In hindsight, he laughs at his own denseness and the irony of the situation. He recalls that, a few years before the fateful day of Zadolnikov's denunciation, he had an unusual job. That is, the job was usual, the pay was usual; what was unusual was the payer. One of Papa's acquaintances, a shoemaker named Izzi Morgulis, gave him the address of somebody's apartment to be fixed and paid Papa for the job himself, in advance. The apartment belonged to the very same Comrade Gorbis, who was quite pleased with Papa's work. The agents of the Department of Taxation had caught Morgulis in illegal shoemaking. To avoid punishment, Morgulis hired Papa, thus bribing Gorbis with the work of another illegal craftsman—a housepainter.

Since that fateful day when Zadolnikov spotted Papa's work through the open window, no matter how hot it is, now Papa works only behind closed shutters.

TWELVE

A Dependent

ONE DAY, SOME LITTLE OLD MAN—a dried-up boletus mushroom of a man—visits us. An emery-colored greasy little jacket. A pair of steel-frame glasses perched on the bridge of his nose. The old man is of that breed of retirees whose generation is devoted to the Soviet power; they still blaze with revolutionary ideals. He comes with a pack of some papers under his arm. The reason for his visit is either a population census or some other campaign of filling out uncountable forms. To get rid of this old man under some specious excuse is impossible.

The man opens his ledger, snatches a pencil from his pocket, clears his throat, and asks Mama, "Your social status?"

Mama has to choose one of four possible responses: a blue-collar worker, an office worker, a collective farmer, or a dependent. Mama frowns and mumbles something.

"What, what?" the old man asks her again, his palm placed to his ear.

Mama mutters something again.

"I don't hear you, ma'am," the old man bellows.

Mama can't stand it anymore and shouts almost directly into his ear; it even makes him cringe: "A dependent!"

She purses her lips in resentment. Her pride injured, she reveals her status with great reluctance. She's incensed at being labeled a dependent. In the Soviet lexicon, *dependent* means almost the same as *parasite*.

Mama works all day long, indeed. At this time, in the early postwar years, she has to stand in countless lines for every essential item; every one of them is in short supply for a long time. Her domestic chores are time-consuming as well. Appliances for domestic work have yet to be manufactured. Not only are no vacuum cleaners or dishwashers available; even refrigerators are still at a premium. Cooking gas is not available either. To prepare every meal, she has to kindle our kerosene stove. On her knees, she scrubs our apartment floor.

She especially goes through hell when doing our laundry. Besides gas, hot water in the building is also still unavailable. Even cold water reaches our third floor only sporadically. Mama does her laundry in the old washtub, which survived the war. (It still hangs on the wall of our dark little corridor.) She rests her chest against the butt end of a washboard and, fiercely, as if fighting an enemy, rubs our linens, blankets, pillowcases, and shirts against it. Sometimes in her frenzied work, she strips enough skin off her knuckles to draw blood.

She also has to boil her washing. Before taking it down from our third floor to the basement—to the laundry room—she has to wring it out. Mama calls our neighbor, Grandma Manya, to help. (When I grow up, they will bring me into the act as well. I'm hardly useful, however. I've never developed any serious muscles. All three of us—Mama, Grandma Manya, and I—grab the linens and duvet covers and twist them till the last drop of water is gone. Every time we do it, the ancient Greek sculpture *Laocoon* flashes before my eyes. The Trojan high priest of Poseidon and his sons wrestle with the snakes sent down by the goddess Athena Pallada. A copy of this sculpture is in our Archaeological Museum. And I've also seen it many times when passing by a shady corner of the Preobrazhensky Square, where another copy sits encircled by bushes.)

Then, in the semidark laundry room, its plaster walls peeling, Mama kindles a spacious stove with two built-in boilers. The firewood, like the basement, is always damp. Time and again, Mama strikes matches, then sneezes and coughs from smoke. Detergent powder has not yet been invented; the best minds of the country are busy inventing fuel for long-range missiles. A knife in her hands, Mama planes a big bar of laundry soap.

With her washing boiled, she hooks up the linens with a wooden stick, lifts them out of the hot water, risking burns, and drops them into a washtub with cold water. She rinses them first, then she blues them with bluing powder. Then she starches them. Then she has to wring them out again.

After the laundry is finally done, she drags basin after basin of it out to the courtyard for drying. To lift the linens above the heads of passersby, she props the ropes with huge poles. The sun and frost, which is rare in Odessa, are Mama's allies; rain and dust are her enemies. When I read for the first time a line from Lermontov's romantic poem "A Sail"—"and the mast bends and creaks"—I see Mama's face concerned with a not-so-romantic problem: if the wind is too strong, it will throw the linens onto the ground, wasting all her work.

When the laundry is dry, she covers our dinner table with a blanket and begins ironing, getting dizzy from steam and heat in the process. She heats her heavy iron on our kerosene stove. Quite often, red stripes and even whitish blisters cover her palms. She inflates her cheeks with a mouthful of water and sprays the bed sheets. My favorite book in these years is *The Myths of Ancient Greece*. With her cheeks puffed up, Mama surprisingly resembles Boreas, the ancient Greek god of the northern wind; his portrait's drawn in the book.

To buy produce in the market is another difficult chore of Mama's. I am about ten years old when she begins recruiting me as an assistant. She tries to come to the market as early as possible. The choice is wider and buying is quicker. And in the summer, it's easier to carry heavy shopping bags back home before the unmerciful Odessa sun starts scorching.

"Get up!" I hear Mama's voice, then half awaken. "Milya, get up! How many times should I tell you to get up?"

I'm unable either to respond or to tear my head from the pillow. Mama's voice is monotonous. But it's not because she doesn't care about me. Monotony is the result of two incompatible emotions; they collide and fall out as neutral sediment. On the one hand, she feels sorry for me, but on the other hand, she can't manage without me. We need a week's worth of produce.

At last, I get up, groaning and snuffling. For me, an early reveille is the harshest torture. And the trip seems very tedious to me; though, in reality, quite a few interesting things worth learning about happen around me.

We leave our home early, about six in the morning. The caretakers are just beginning to sweep the sidewalk with their brooms. We go past the City Garden. Sometimes, at Preobrazhensky Street, we board a streetcar that takes us to Privoz, the biggest Odessa bazaar. More often, though, we go on foot to the Novyi, on Torgovaya Street. It takes us no more than fifteen minutes to get there.

We appear at the market just at that moment when, flowery kerchiefs wrapped around their heads, young peasant women unpack their bundles and lay out parsley, celery, dill, bunches of scallions, crimson radishes, and emerald lettuce on the wooden trays. They scoop water with their palms from a bucket and sprinkle their green wares with ritual concentration, as if blessing them to be sold quickly in the name of the Father and the Son and the Holy Spirit of Commerce.

The sun already shines tenderly through latticed awnings. The early-morning marketplace smells reach my nostrils. In the violent bouquet of these smells, I catch the delicate aroma of incomparable Odessan tomatoes, warmed in the sun and tinged a shade of lilac. Firm cucumbers, pimples all over them, smell of their recent bed of freshly dug black earth. One more step, and a trail of an even thinner and gentler smell—a refined one, re-sembling a woman's perfume—the smell of freshly whipped butter catches up with me. To give Mama a taste of it, carefully—as if it's the tushy of a newborn baby—they unswaddle a yellowish lump of the butter from bur-dock leaves, still covered with dew and rough, like a cow's tongue.

Next to them on the counters are piles of plums nicknamed *tsyganka,* a "Gypsy woman." Bluish violet with a thin smoky coating, they apparently owe their name to their resemblance to the ox-eyes of the southern beauties. Right next to them are little pyramids of firm and red Jonathan apples. They are delivered to the market in huge wicker baskets sewn over with sacking. The peasant men rip up the sacking with crooked knives hand-made from scythe bits.

You can tell the unusually juicy and sweet duchess pears at once, not only by their special fragrance, but also by the swarm of bees and wasps flying onto their little pinkish bellies from all over the bazaar. Rolled newspapers in their hands, saleswomen drive them away, screaming, "Oh, oh!"

Loaded with fruit, we go to the roofed meat department. Here it's cooler, but the smell is less pleasant: that of raw meat. Their aprons sprinkled with blood, the butchers sharpen their long knives against steels. Their chins, double and replete, shake in time to the sharpening. The butchers set the tone of business over here. With good meat always in short supply, they alone decide what piece of it to make available to the customer and how many bones to slip into the package. Unlike in the vegetable and fruit rows, only men sell meat. They admire Mama; she is a beautiful woman. She re-sponds to their compliments with restraint and uses her appeal only so far as it helps in bargaining.

Then we again visit the open rows and buy young potatoes—small, smooth, and pinkish, just like year-old babies' heels. I especially approve of this purchase. The way Mama cooks these potatoes—in their skin, swimming in butter, flavored with grated young garlic, and sprinkled with dill—leaves me incapable of tearing myself away from them.

Nearby, vendors trade in regular potatoes. From the bed of a truck, its boards cast away, some unshaven peasants, with their shirts flung open on their chests, shout, "Potatoes! Potatoes! Potatoes! Potatoes!" From time to time, they jump off the trucks and, puffing and making faces from the strain, drag tightly packed sacks to the counters. They cut them open, and potatoes roll out onto the trays with a roar.

"They're the American brand," Mama notices at once. "They're crumbly."

In our home, love of potatoes is longstanding and stable. During the hard postwar years, when my father's housepainting business was just building steam, potatoes were just about the sole food in our household. We had them fried, we had them boiled, and we had them baked. With onions and pickles, they made a salad. We also had mashed potatoes, and thick potato pancakes, and baked potato pudding. (Papa called it by its Yiddish name, *kugel.*) You couldn't have counted all the potato dishes.

I recall all this now and see it with today's eyes. In my youthful years, this orgy of a generous southern bazaar didn't inspire me much. I trudge along after Mama all over the market in a half-conscious state, in the melancholy of a sleepy person. I'm angry at her—why doesn't she buy the very first foodstuffs we come upon? They look quite decent. So why not buy them and leave for home as soon as possible? I'm bored with dragging along behind Mama around the bazaar. Having nothing better to do, I flap my knees with the empty shopping bag.

"Stop it!" Mama gets irritated. She looks at me with disapproval. "To make a bazaar," as they say in Odessa, isn't easy. She has to concentrate, and here she's forced to drag a depressed teenager the way a convict has to drag his heavy irons. From time to time, my gloomy physiognomy outrages Mama. She tries in vain to appeal to my conscience. At the moment, it does the same thing that my whole being does; that is, it sleeps. "As if I need all this just for myself!" she says. "You think that doing this gives me pleasure?"

Bazaar bargaining has its own ritual, its own unwritten rules and laws. If Mama's face assumes an approving expression, she makes sure that only I see it. She doesn't want the seller to know it.

"How much do you want for this spring chicken?" Mama asks and sticks her finger into the side of a big corpulent hen, which sits on the counter and glances guardedly left and right.

"Why, ma'am! Don't you fear God?" the Ukrainian woman is outraged. "What kind of a spring chicken is it, my dear God, when it's a fully grown hen?"

"Ah!" Mama brushes it off. "For you, it's a hen, and for me it's a spring chicken." Her face expressing pessimism, Mama feels the hen all over, looking as if she's feeling a pillow in which she expects to find nothing except feathers. Grandma's stories about family jewelry, ostensibly hidden in the pillow, as expected, turn out to be just fancies of her failing mind.

Then, Mama turns the hen, its tail toward her, splits its feathers and blows through them as strongly as she can, exposing the hen's behind. If the skin shows bluish, it means that the hen suffers from dystrophy, and the broth won't be good enough. But now the skin is golden yellow. Mama seizes the right moment and whispers joyfully into my ear, "It's fat!" But she remains outwardly skeptical. The saleswoman should know that she's not quite pleased with the hen.

"Lady," Mama addresses a woman next to her at the counter and extends the hen to her. "What do you think, how much does it weigh?"

"I know?" the arbitration lady says. She takes the hen in her hands. Bewildered, time and again, the bird is blinking its whitish webbed eyelids. "I'd say, about four pounds. Well, maximum five."

"Four, five," Mama says mistrustfully and weighs the hen in her hand again. "If it weighs five pounds, then I'm a Politburo member." In the same indifferent tone, she asks the seller, "So, how much did you say you want for your hen?"

The saleswoman unties the motley scarf wrapped around her head, straightens it on her shoulders, and smiles, all steel crowns glaring in her mouth.

"Five rubles," she says and spreads her fingers wide to ensure Mama understands her rightly.

Mama's eyes get big and round. "Didn't you tell me 'four'?"

I don't believe my ears. I'm angry at Mama. I'm ready to testify that the saleswoman has never said "four." But I worry in vain. You don't fool a Ukrainian peasant that easily. She herself is capable of fooling anyone else.

"No-o-ah?" the peasant stretches it in a singsong voice. "Such a beautiful hen! Five rubles!"

"Okay, that's for talking," Mama waves it off. "And for buying?"

The peasant woman laughs. "Well, four fifty."

Mama turns away and, from somewhere, gets the money, wrapped up in a handkerchief. I already know where she gets it from: I've seen how other women do it at the bazaar. She gets it from her bra. In a bazaar, it's a more reliable place to safeguard money than a purse is. Mama has already unfolded her handkerchief and begun counting out the bills when she suddenly remembers: "How about for your first sale's sake?"

Now I understand why Mama tries to come to the market as early as possible. The peasant believes in the omen of the first deal of the day. If it fails, she won't be lucky all day long. She nods and shears some more off the price. (In those rare instances when the seller doesn't give a discount for the first sale's sake, Mama leaves the counter immediately. Her whole appearance shows that she's offended by the seller's poor manners.)

But Mama still doesn't rush with her money. She decides to buy something else from the same saleswoman, thus saving some more. "How much are your eggs, Mistress?" she asks. "Why are they looking like that of a child?" she adds. One by one, she twirls the eggs in her fingers. The eggs seem giant to me; they look like almost those of a goose.

"Of a child!" the peasant woman's beside herself, outraged. "It's unheard of! Of a child! What are you talking about, ma'am? Your boy's balls," she nods in my direction, "may look like small eggs. But a hen's eggs are always adult size. No, just look at her—a child's eggs!"

I blush immediately, but Mama doesn't pay much attention to the explosion of emotions. One by one, she brings the eggs to her eyes, turning the eggs toward the sun and examining them.

I'm angry at Mama. A Young Pioneer, I find that Mama behaves dishonestly: she's trying to deceive a hard-working Soviet peasant. I don't understand yet that Mama hasn't done anything blameworthy. She just follows the traditional southern ritual of bargaining at the bazaars. Both biting retorts and dissatisfied facial expressions are part of that ritual. (In Soviet times, a farmers' bazaar was the sole free-market spot. Prices there were controlled by demand only. Sometimes, Mama would leave for home without "making a bazaar," because the sellers charged too high a price as a result of poor delivery. Only some underground Odessan millionaires' wives could afford it.)

After money changes hands, the peasant woman thanks Mama, and Mama leaves also pleased. She's fulfilled her family duty—she saved money. I don't know the value of money yet. Only years later, recalling my trips with Mama to the market, did I begin to understand in hindsight: overpaid rubles led to Papa lying face down on our sofa, pale from nausea after inhaling too much of the poisonous zinc white paint while working long hours.

Sometimes, when Mama buys a live hen for a holiday feast, she waits a day or two before slaughtering it so that its meat is fresh. Its foot tied to a table leg, the hen wanders around our dark little corridor-cum-kitchenette with its claws clicking against the floor. It shakes its head, trying to understand what's happening and where, damn it, destiny has taken it. On the holiday's eve, Mama takes it back to the bazaar, to a flimsy shack near the exit. She says, *"Gut yontev"* ("Happy holiday!" in Yiddish) and hands the bird over to an old man sitting in semidarkness, a huge leather apron on him. He's a *shoykhet,* Mama says, that is, a "kosher butcher." The old man wears a skullcap, and I'm puzzled and secretly irritated: why declare to everybody that you're a Jew?

In some way, the old man resembles my second cousin Yan's grandfather. The same gray-haired wide beard. The same tired round eyes. Only this man's fingers aren't white and soft but dark and hardened. A safety razor blade, the kind I use to sharpen my pencils, flashes in them.

"A gut yontev, a gut yontev," the old man's voice is hardly audible.

He takes the hen from Mama's hands, closes his whitish eyelids, resembling a bird's, and mutters some prayer. I don't understand a word of it. I discern only *"Barukh attah Adonai."* Then, easily, as if it were a child's inflatable balloon, the old man stretches out the hen's neck. Indignant about such impudence, the bird doesn't produce even a cackle as the butcher runs the razor's splinter across its neck.

I don't have time yet to figure out what's going on in front of my eyes. The ritual of death bewitches me with its terrible simplicity. One movement of the razor and the bird's life is over, as if it has never been. Its throat cut, suspended by its feet, its head over a bucket filled with feathers of its equally unlucky predecessors, the chicken still desperately claps its wings, raising fluff from the floor. A terrible panic overcomes me when, from the bird's throat, bubbly blood, as rich and red as a human's, gushes out in pulses.

Over summertime, to make jam, Mama brings several pounds of fruit and berries from the bazaar, now strawberries and cherries, now apricots, plums, and quince. Our kitchenette doesn't have much space, so after borrowing a huge copper basin from Grandma Manya, Mama brings everything out to the courtyard. She puts the basin on two kerosene stoves and puts me in charge of starting them up. It's a dreary business. You have to warm up the stove head with dry spirits and then pump kerosene. If you don't guess whether the stove head has warmed up enough, kerosene spurts outside in a thin trickle and bursts into frightening bluish-yellow flames. But that's not all. The tiny hole feeding kerosene gets clogged up often, and it's my job to clean it with a special needle. Of poor quality, it bends often, driving me crazy.

Meanwhile, Mama manages to take care of many other domestic chores. She checks on me from time to time until, covered with granulated sugar, the berries turn an amber-claret color. When the mixture begins simmering, Mama uses a straining spoon to remove the white skin from its surface, cautiously and lovingly, as if removing a cloth cover from a sleeping beauty. She has to do it many times. But, eventually, she's pleased. When the jam's ready, patiently, spoonful after spoonful, she transfers it into jars. In the evening, back home from work, Papa seals the covers on the jars with a special tool and takes the jam into our little shed. In the winter, we drink tea, spooning up boiled berries from small jam dishes. Drinking tea becomes sheer pleasure.

There are still plenty of other things to do around the house.

"It's backbreaking," Mama says from time to time. "Instead, I wish I worked some factory machine for eight hours. I get no gratitude whatsoever."

In response to her speeches of that kind, Papa usually says nothing. But sometimes he can't stand it any longer. He blurts out, "What do you want? That I stop working and do laundry with you?"

And I'm lost deciding who's right in this situation. Papa has a point, and I side with him. Mama still sighs for some time, walking around and frowning.

"What a fool I am!" she says loudly enough for everybody to hear. "Why didn't I graduate from medical school? Tanya," Mama names her girlfriend of prewar years, who often visits us with her husband, Sasha, and her son, Senya, "Tanya did the right thing. Good for her! She finished school, despite everything. And, silly me, I listened to you. You said, 'It's necessary to look after the baby.'"

I know already that Mama stopped attending medical school in Odessa because she was pregnant with me, her firstborn.

"So, what of it?" Papa says. "All her diplomas in hand, doesn't she do her laundry? Does her Sasha ask for leave from work so that he can wash linens with her? Does he?"

Mama still grumbles for a while, but then she gives up. What can she do? That's her fate, and reluctantly she accepts it. In school, we learn by heart Sergei Mikhalkov's poem "A chto u vas?" ("What's Up at Your Home?"). In this poem, children talk about their mothers' professions:

" . . . Our mama
Sets out for her next flight,
Because our mama
Is called a pilot."
"Mama's a pilot, . . ."
. . . .
So what of it?
Here, Kolya's mama, for example,
Is a police woman.
And Tolya's and Vera's
Mothers are engineers.

Though the poem ends with "Mamas of all kinds are needed, / And mamas of all sorts are important," it's clear that its focus is mothers with professions. Yet, for a long time, I'll remain puzzled by the "dependent" status written in Mama's passport. A dependent is one who lives at somebody else's expense. What has Mama to do with people like that?

THIRTEEN

Without Declarations

"AUNTIE SONYA, WHAT SHOULD I DO? I've gotten caught."

"What have you gotten caught for, my dear?" Mama asks.

"Well, it's just an expression. Got pregnant by accident. And, when I ask him what I should do, my bastard sits on the fence. To do an abortion or not, ah? I'd like to have a little one very much. But I'm scared. Will I manage all by myself? Ah, Auntie Sonya?"

I'm angry at Mama. She always whispers with saleswomen. I notice with astonishment how different her face becomes from her domestic face—often tense and overpowering. It brightens up from inside with an incomprehensible light.

The true head of our family, its spirit, its energy generator was Mama. Papa was the stoker, throwing enough coal into the furnace to keep the steam pressure in the engine up. But it was Mama who was the harbor pilot, boatswain, navigator, and captain of our family ship. Her power over all of us was full and unreserved. Only when I became a college student was I able to gain some autonomy regarding my free time. In family matters I had a voice but no vote. Strong-willed, Mama kept the family matters on her shoulders. She radiated so much energy that it was enough for many, and some of it was still left unclaimed. Her energy and assertiveness would have been enough if she had been charged with running two ministries. She could have managed them without abandoning her family duties—as before, cooking first-rate borsht and baking incomparable strudels.

I don't think she had enemies. Even if there were some, they tried to steer clear of her. They were wary not only of Mama's displeasure; compared to her in moments of anger, Jupiter hurling thunder and lightning was just a snotty toddler playing with matches. No less dangerous was Mama's enormous charm. With just the touch of a hand, Christ turned water into wine, and Mama transformed an enemy into a friend. She had an uncommon ability to win over very different people—from neighbors, to salespeople in the nearby stores, to Soviet officials who were indifferent, it seemed, to everything in the world. She loved people, and I think she loved even that which I hated with all my heart—the countless Soviet lines.

Of course, she loved lines not because she was forced to stand for hours to buy flour, groats, sugar, soap, matches, and other basic necessities. (These lines, usually pushed inside the courtyards by police, farther from the eyes of foreign cruise-liner passengers, who wandered Odessan streets during a stop in our port, were especially long during the first postwar years.) The lines brought Mama in contact with humanity. The secret of her magnetism was simple. Mama was sincerely interested in everybody with whom life brought her in contact. She lavished her care on the world around her, the world that included our courtyard with all its inhabitants—young and old, healthy and sick, teetotalers and drunkards. Store managers and cashiers, superintendents and caretakers couldn't resist her cordiality and warmth. She heard all of them out—their complaints about alcoholic husbands, ungrateful children, insidious lovers, fussy bosses, about the utter stupidity of life, its injustice, its dullness and joylessness. She heard them out with such unfeigned compassion that, instantaneously, she turned from being a mere neighbor, a dweller, a customer into a close friend, a confidant, a guardian of family secrets, of matters of the heart, of somebody else's sighs and tears.

They all thanked her in any way they could. They did it so generously that, for the uninitiated, it may have seemed that Mama pretended to be sympathetic out of self-interest. But such suspicions would have been groundless. No one can fool the human heart for very long. Cordiality toward people and sincere interest in them were innately part of her nature. Mama didn't need to ask anybody for anything. Risking getting into trouble from sneaking attacks of the ubiquitous trade inspectors, young volunteer police assistants, and raids of the party-control organs, salespeople stashed away for Mama's sake the goods for which she would have had to stand in several hour-long lines: Ceylon tea, Czech shoes, Polish kerchiefs, French bras. It was just a small token of gratitude for the presence of at least one soul in the whole world—the soul of this sunny, smiling woman—who cared about their grief, their sorrows and misfortunes, small and big.

"Auntie Sonya," the saleswomen would run to her home, "in the afternoon, they're going to bring buckwheat, the kind you like—the whole-grained one. Come over later on. I'll put away a couple of kilograms for you."

These weren't mere generosities of those women's hearts. They ran home to the one they could turn to with their problems and worries, the kind you wouldn't share with your own mother and, even less so, with your father.

If, for some reason, Mama didn't go to the neighborhood stores for a while, the saleswomen, alarmed, would come knocking on our door. I'd open it and, seeing, instead of Mama's cordial face, the sullen physiognomy of an adolescent tormented by the countless riddles of life, they would fade and ask where she was, when she'd come back, if she had fallen sick, God forbid. Peering over my head into the darkness of the corridor that led to the doors of our room, they called for her in thin, mournful voices: "Auntie Sonya? Sofia Vladimirovna?"

One time, in our crammed one-room apartment, Mama even managed to give shelter to one of her charges, Nadya, a young Ukrainian saleswoman from a produce store on Deribas Street. But giving her a sleeping space under our roof wasn't enough. To live in the city, to work, Nadya needed to be registered at a city dwelling. To allow her to do it at our apartment was an act of not only extraordinary magnanimity but also unheard-of trust. In quite a few instances when a person had been registered out of compassion, the beneficiary did his or her benefactor a bad turn; he or she sued the latter for division of living space, no matter how small it was.

Mama decided to help Nadya because she took the saleswoman's circumstances to heart. Nadya had told Mama that her mother had died from tuberculosis when she, Nadya, was still a baby. In her village near Kherson, her drunkard of a father had beaten her up often and, at nights, had made indecent advances toward her. At the last moment, however, Nadya canceled the registration process because of a marriage proposal from one of her produce store customers.

In the sad tradition of many children, I became truly interested in Mama's life, tried to understand the one who meant so much to me, especially in my younger years, when she was gone. Only recently have I managed to get to the source of Mama's ability to take to heart somebody else's misfortunes and squabbles. Incomprehensible in my childhood and adolescence, even in my adult life, many things in her behavior have now become clear.

I knew little about Mama besides the fact that she was born and grew up in Uman', Ukraine. She was either eighteen or nineteen when she moved to Odessa with her family—father, mother, a brother and a sister. First she worked as a lab assistant at a creamery. Then she married my father. That's about all.

Now, having become acquainted with the ways of life in small eastern European towns (shtetlach) with a Jewish population, I've understood that the world of her Uman' never left Mama. Precisely where we grow up, we absorb once and for all those paradigms of world perception and comprehension, notions of good and evil, that we unconsciously follow all our lives. In this sense, we are like turtles: throughout all our life we carry with us the world of our childhood and adolescence—family, neighborhood, and school.

The world Mama grew up in consisted of the little streets of her native town, lost in the endless steppes, on the banks of the Umanka River. The town was inhabited by Ukrainians, Poles, and Jews. The lives of the last group ran within the triangle of home, synagogue, and marketplace. Uman' was a known center of Jewish life. It was a community of both Hasidic scholars (tsadeks) and enlightened Jews. But to the end of her days, the world of the shtetl lived in her heart.

I don't think Mama, who wasn't especially notable for her religiosity, consciously wanted to please God with her deeds, doing mitzvah. Such behavior during her years of living in the united Jewish community simply became her second nature. From misfortunes—poverty, lawlessness, and harassment—the Jews there saved themselves through unity and mutual assistance. The latter was a postulate of Jewish life in Uman'. It was the spirit of community, the spirit of *yidishkeyt* (Jewishness), the spirit of life for the benefit of a fellow human being. Members of a big family helped one another without being asked, just as Mama did during the shortage of firewood in Odessa in the cold winter of 1947. She used her shopping bag to smuggle, in secret from Papa, little logs from our own short supply of fuel down snow-covered Deribas Street to the semibasement of the building where her sister Clara's family lived. Several years later, when Clara died, following her husband, Mama, with the resolve of a person who's convinced there's no other way, immediately took on the care of her niece, treating her as if she were her own daughter.

Mama maintained the Uman' way of life, in which a woman was a mother to everybody in the family, including her husband, in our home as well. Every day, she took care of even the smallest needs of all members of our family. Central among them and considered her utmost duty was feeding all of us, which she didn't forget for a minute. The extraordinary attention she devoted to food, which was puzzling for me in my younger years, has become clear only now. Of course, in poor families, survival was the main concern in regard to food, but it was not the only concern. Food also served as a nonverbal expression of love, a symbol of a mother's devotion. It was important not only to feed everybody but also to make it tasty. As if preparing a declaration of love, Mama cooked in a state of joyful alarm: How will it come out? Will everything be good? She cooked not hastily but with the utmost care. Everybody spoke of her culinary talent. But talent *is* love. No matter what she was occupied with—whether she shredded cabbage, stuffed chicken necks, rolled dough, or carefully took out a round tin pot with a hole in the middle (the nickname of the pot was "a miracle")—her face took on a look of concentration and inspiration. Her eyes became lighter. That is why refusal to eat by anyone in the family created a sharp anxiety in her. To refuse to eat meant to reject her love, to mortally offend her.

(To my surprise, in time Mama's treatment of food was passed on to me. When my children, who grew up in America and are now adults, refuse to eat when visiting me—because it's not time yet, because they are not hungry—I catch myself unconsciously perceiving their response in the same way that Mama once did: as a sign of estrangement.)

Mama herself often ate on the run. Though we weren't too confined in means, unlike the situation in her childhood home, where food was habitually in short supply, she behaved as her mother, my grandmother, did, as I understand now. She picked up only remnants of food, or sometimes, sitting down to the table with everybody, she didn't eat at all. "I have no appetite," she would say. "While cooking, I've tasted enough."

Many things became clear to me when I learned, as an adult, that the custom in shtetlach is what influenced my parents and others to avoid expressing their love of children older than four or five with hugs and kisses. Praising children to their faces and declarations of love were not acceptable. I don't recall either of my parents telling me "I love you," as American fathers and mothers often end their telephone conversations. However, it went without saying that they, especially Mama, would love their offspring always and unconditionally, no matter what happened. It was precisely there, in shtetlach, that the notorious image of an ever-willing, always devoted, and selfless "Yiddishe mama" was born.

At the outbreak of war and the advance of German troops, when I fled eastward with Mama from Odessa by way of railroad, I was ill almost the whole time. I would be removed from the train, placed in an army hospital, where, exhausted by malnutrition, I poorly resisted diseases. My cheeks burned from fever. Pain pulsed in my temples. The hospital bed under me turned now to the left, now to the right, now soaring to the ceiling so rapidly that I would become slightly nauseous, as if I were flying in an airplane. Mama put a wet piece of cloth on my forehead, which soon became warm.

"Mother, prepare yourself that you'll lose him," the doctors told Mama, patting her shoulder. "It's just a matter of time. Give in, dear."

Give in! They didn't realize whom they advised of such a thing—my mama! She always resisted giving in. If, during her short absence, they would move me into the wards for those who were dying, rooms that reeked of carbolic acid, Mama would break into them through all cordons. She would throw aside medical orderlies who hung on to her hands, grab me as I was— in short-sleeved hospital undershirts with torn-off ties—wrap me in gray army sheets and biting army comforters, and hurry away to catch up with the next train of refugees, which had already begun rolling out of the station. To give in! It was the lowest, the most despised, the sickliest thing for my mama. Then and after. Her whole life.

Her love expressed itself in constant worry. Its intensity pointed to how intimately she not only bound herself to her children but also identified with them, not to mention her grandchildren. Before our departure to America, my year-and-half-old son, Max, spent the last summer with his grandmother in Odessa, in a rented summer house. One day, while preparing to wash the wooden floors, she left for a minute. In her absence, her grandson, in his young curiosity, sneaked up to a bucket of boiling water containing lye and stuck his hand into it. At his cry, Mama ran in, beside herself with grief. On the way to the hospital, clutching her grandson to her chest, she immediately began a dialogue with higher forces, trying to reason with them, to offer a sensible alternative to this misfortune. She appealed to Fate, the idiot, "What's that? Why such suffering to a little one? Why not to me? It's I who am guilty. It's *I* who have to be punished."

Apparently, she believed that, by catching the fate in an illogical act, she would shame it, force it, in hindsight, to change its damaging course. There was no doubt that if her pain could have taken away her grandson's pain, she would have stuck her hand into the same boiling solution without hesitating for a second. Now she could only wring her hands in impotence, tormented in being unable to take over her grandson's suffering.

She brought Max to the hospital's emergency room and waited there until the medical staff had bandaged him. Because of the late hour, they kept him in the hospital overnight. Needless to say, Mama didn't leave the reception room till dawn, despite pressure from the hospital personnel. Without closing her eyes, she turned from side to side on her chair. After they changed the bandage on her grandson the next morning, she was about to take him home, but it turned out that it was not possible to do so until after the doctor's rounds the next day—a formality that none of the nurses could take upon herself to violate.

Mama bore it for as long as she could. But when she saw how carelessly the wards had been cleaned and what tasteless, unpleasant-looking food had been brought to her grandson for breakfast, she couldn't contain herself anymore. Taking advantage of the nurse's distraction while conversing with her friend on the phone, Mama rushed headlong into the ward, grabbed Max in her embrace, and moved toward the exit.

Flabbergasted, the duty nurse blocked her path, "Where do you think you're going, ma'am? Well, put the patient back where he belongs. He's going nowhere till tomorrow. It's not allowed." But the nurse didn't know with whom she was in conflict.

"What!" Mama cried out threateningly, pressing her grandson to her chest. "The baby still has to suffer in your pigsty till tomorrow? When was the last time you scrubbed the floors here? On New Year's Eve? Or on the International Women's Day? Do you want the city sanitary inspection's visit on your heads? So why don't you say so? I can arrange it for you. My wartime female friend is the head doctor there."

"But your child's registered in our book, after all," the duty nurse implored. "Only the duty doctor can release him. They could put me in jail for negligence."

"If they put you there, I'll bring you parcels," Mama promised. "I wish to know absolutely nothing. As you checked him in, check him out of here. To hell with it, get out of my way! Otherwise it's going to be worse for you!" Shaken by Mama's pressure, the nurse retreated.

Mama's concern about everything in my younger years seemed to me incomprehensible, strange, excessive. It often irritated me: "Have you got your fill? Take some more. Soup isn't food. It's good for you. Where are you going? Be careful. Beware of hooligans in the streets. Aren't you cold (hot)?

Aren't you suffocating? Aren't these pants too tight on you? Put on gloves, you'll get your fingers frostbitten. Button up, you'll catch cold. Unbutton yourself, you'll sweat, it's cold outside, you'll go out and catch cold."

As I understand now, such was the unwritten precept of the culture into which she was born. Such constant mother's worrying supposedly served as a talisman, to protect loved ones. That is, once she expressed her worry, a misfortune, small or big, would blow over.

At times, she was angry at us. But her anger and love didn't contradict each other. Rather, her anger was a manifestation of love.

Now I understand that the main carrier of Jewish values in our family was Mama. She was the one who insisted on gathering as many relatives as possible around a holiday table. Such was the custom of the community, the custom of the shtetl. If my father, a tradesman, attempted to drink an extra shot of vodka, Mama grumbled, looked at him sternly, "*Genug is genug.* Enough is enough. We aren't *khazeyrim.*" That is, we Jews aren't swine.

Sometimes, sure of the rightness of her actions, she would take the shot glass from under Papa's nose. At first, Papa would grow pale, offended that she made a laughingstock of him in front of friends and relatives, that she bossed him around. But his resistance was futile. Mama knew her power over Papa, his unconditional devotion to her. But it wasn't a desire to show off this power of hers that led her; such a desire, inherent in petty people, never arose in her. Her reason for such decisive action was a much sounder one: "That's all what we need, to turn into *shikerim!*" I understood the meaning of her words as, "It's more than enough of God's punishment to be a Jew. A drunk Jew—that is completely the end of ends."

Mama didn't change in her old age. She considered it her duty to help everybody to whom she was related. Having come to America, she was concerned with the fate of everybody who stayed behind in the Soviet Union, without exception. And when it came to especially close ones, she made it her business to free them without any delay, without thinking whether she had enough energy or means for such an undertaking.

During one of my visits to Los Angeles, where she and my father had settled after emigrating from the Soviet Union in 1975, she asked me to take her to a notary—to witness her signature on an official invitation to one of her nieces. Without it, the niece and her family wouldn't be able to get to America. The stationery shop, where there was a notary, was located just three blocks from her house, on Fairfax Street, but Mama could no longer walk without the help of a walker. I drove up to the shop as close as possible. Mama had to take a few steps to enter the shop and approach the counter. First, rolling her eyes from the pain in her knees, hunching her back on the sticks her hands clutched, and clenching her teeth so that she wouldn't cry out in public, she got out of the car. Then, resting a bit, she took her walker in her hands and, throwing it in front of herself, put her feet cautiously on the sidewalk; groaning quietly with every step, she moved forward.

The temperature was ninety degrees. Sweat covered her face. The heels of her shoes and the walker legs were getting stuck in melted asphalt. She needed almost a quarter of an hour to make her way no more than ten yards. Finally reaching the counter, her head shaking (her nervous tic had begun recently), with difficulty she gripped the pen between her thumb and index finger, twisted with arthritis, and signed the paper. Returning home was no less tormenting.

When she died, in April 1994, falling short of her seventy-ninth birthday by a month and a half, over a hundred people—only a few of whom were relatives—came to the cemetery to bid her farewell. More wanted to say a parting word to her than there was time for in the ceremony. People mostly unknown to me, who had visited my parents from New York only from time to time, kept coming up to the microphone. One aged woman in a black kerchief said, overcoming her sobbing, "She was my closest friend. In difficult times, I'd always come to her. Sonya, my dear, whom would I come to now? Well, tell me, give me your farewell advice. To whom?"

Looking over a crowd of familiar and unfamiliar people, I thought that Mama would approve. "I want you all to be always together," I remembered her saying the last time I saw her, no more than a month before her death. Now, these words sounded in my memory as her parting words, as the only instruction to her children and grandchildren.

That Passover evening in 1994 remains in my memory. A long time ago, still in our past Odessan life, Mama had begun to insist on this rule: on the first evening of each of the big Jewish holidays, all close kin had to gather in her home. Before, I considered it a whim, an inveterate notion of the old generation, which, alas, one is forced to indulge. Now, preparing for the evening with incredible effort, trying not to groan, putting the walker in front of her, Mama reached the kitchen and, bending over the sink with difficulty, cleaned fish, stuffed it. I tried to help her. She brushed me off, "I'll do it myself. To explain every move, it's easier to do it myself."

To my attempts to persuade her not to overtire herself, to order food in a Russian deli store, she responded with a scornful countenance. She couldn't stand somebody else's cuisine.

As I understand now, both of her arguments, though sincere, expressed only half of the actual point. Already gravely ill, she could not have failed to sense that she hadn't much time left to live, that it was her last opportunity to express her love in the same way love had been expressed in her Uman', as she had expressed it all her life—without words: "I love you all. For the sake of me, be happy." "For the sake of me," superfluous in Russian (as well as in English), was completely necessary in the equivalent phrase in Yiddish: *"Zay mir gliklekh."*

FOURTEEN

Who's Who

"WELL, HOW'S BOTVINNIK doing over there?"

In the evening, just home from work, Papa washes himself, as usual. It takes a while to get all the paint off his hands. He motions to me to talk to him, "So tell me, how's Botvinnik?"

Spring 1948. In the evenings, on the wall of a building adjacent to the City Garden and facing our Deribas Street, an illuminated screen blazes up. Crowds of strolling Odessans stop to look up at it. I also stop and lift my head. On the screen is a table with scores of the participants in the match tournament for the World Chess Championship. Our three grandmasters— Mikhail Botvinnik, Vassily Smyslov, and Paul Keres—and two foreigners, the Dutchman Max Euwe and the American Samuel Reshevsky, duel one another. They play a round-robin of five games each, first in The Hague, then in Moscow.

Though Papa knows next to nothing about chess, he keeps track of the tournament with the passion of a soccer fan. He roots for Botvinnik. But he does it not because Botvinnik is our (i.e., the Soviet) grandmaster. Smyslov and Keres are also ours, but Papa doesn't want to even hear about them. Big deal, Smyslov. Keres-Shmeres. Botvinnik, now he's something. A genius! A virtuoso!

I am also Botvinnik's fan. He plays better than anybody else. After the first rounds, he has a three-point lead. But for Papa, Botvinnik's chess skills are of secondary importance. I already know what the point is for Papa: Botvinnik is *Jewish*. Smyslov is Vassily; that is, his unmistakably Russian name makes him a goy, a Gentile. And Keres is an Estonian altogether.

Right after Papa finds out about Botvinnik's performance, he asks, "And what about Reshevsky?"

Papa roots for him as well, even though he is not a Soviet grandmaster but an American one. I have nothing against Reshevsky personally, but it goes without saying that my sympathies are not on the side of a man who represents the country of warmongers. When any of our grandmasters play him or Euwe, the whole country holds its breath. Who will beat whom? Will we defeat these representatives of the capitalist countries, or will they beat us? The style of *Sovetskii sport* reports on these chess games resembles that of the news reports of the Soviet Informburo during the war. "Botvinnik exerts slow and methodic pressure on his opponent's position." "Despite heavy losses, Smyslov mounted a counterattack."

The reason for Papa's interest in Reshevsky is the same as for Botvinnik. Papa separates all chess grandmasters into two groups on a different basis from that of the rest of the country, including my own, which is ours (Soviet) against not ours (non-Soviet). For Papa, "ours versus not ours" means "Jewish versus non-Jewish." When Papa informs me that Reshevsky is a Jew, I ask him with a smirk how he knows that. His surname ends in -*sky*. Maybe he is a Pole, like the hero of the war with Germany, Marshal Rokossovsky.

"Of course Reshevsky's a Jew!" Papa says confidently and waves his hand. "Pss! And you can say that again, what a Jew he is! He doesn't play on Saturdays."

I already know where Papa gets this information about Reshevsky, which at the time you can't find in any Soviet newspaper. A year or two after the war, Papa brought home a strange-looking radio. He had bought it in one of the numerous commission stores that opened up in Odessa during the Romanian occupation. Since the war, Jewish valuables that were looted during wartime have been replaced with expensive items coming from a different source. Ours is a port city, and plenty of seamen live here. From their trips abroad, they bring amazing things for sale. Sometimes, out of curiosity, I stop by a commission store, in the same manner as you might visit a museum of natural history to gawk at dinosaurs and saber-toothed tigers. What you can't find here! Gilded American pens produced by the Parker firm. Italian concertinas gleaming with inlaid mother-of-pearl. Low-necked French dresses trimmed with ostrich feathers. Colonial British walking sticks with elaborate engravings. The cork helmets of African desert explorers. Fancifully shaped bottles filled with a greenish, alchemical liquid. (It doesn't occur to me that this is just women's perfume, though the aroma of these stores leaves me in a daze: apparently, for young saleswomen, the temptation to dip their little fingers into the magic liquid is too strong.)

Recent war trophy items also appear in these stores: knickknacks made of Dresden china, German-made Zeiss field glasses, gold and silver cigarette cases adorned with their former owners' monograms. And shelf after shelf of strange-looking radios—graceful, trimmed with polished wood, and gleaming with chrome.

One of them, its little chest draped in yellowish cloth, makes it to our home. Papa places it on his nightstand and forbids anyone to touch it. Like everything else in the commission stores, the radio is of excellent workmanship. (Even long after the war is over, I perceive all graceful things as being not of our manufacture but foreign-made—that is, in light of the most important recent confrontation, formerly belonging to the fascists. This relates to well-groomed and elegant people as well. Once when I saw the Estonian chess grandmaster Paul Keres in a newsreel, with his strict Nordic features, his fine suit tailored to his figure, his shiny greased hair meticulously styled, I grew tense inside: he's a fascist! And, for a while, I was perplexed; how could a recent sworn enemy worm his way onto our country's all-star chess team?)

In the center of the radio, across a chrome-plated ring, its brand name logo *Grundig* is written in steel Gothic letters. From films about the recent war, I associate the Gothic style with Nazis, and my stomach contracts in short spurts of fear. But the German origin of the radio doesn't bother Papa. Purchasing it excites him. Since all four of us live in a small room, late at night, when I'm already in bed, Papa moves his chair up to the nightstand and waves his hand at me, "Ah well, *makh nakht!* Good night! Sleep!"

Curiosity pesters me like a mosquito. I mutter, "I'm in bed already."

"No, no! Turn to the wall. Cover yourself with the blanket and close your eyes! It's late! You have school tomorrow!"

"It's stuffy under the blanket," I groan.

"Sleep, sleep."

I grumble, turning to the wall. But suspense is killing me. Why does Papa need an extra radio? After all, we already have a government cable radio, that "dish" on the wall made of hard black cardboard. It broadcasts the latest news, soccer reports, and musical concerts.

Papa switches off the lights and, the moment I hear ether whistling, I take advantage of the darkness. Wary of my mattress squeaking, I carefully turn back toward the radio. Stooped next to it, his breath bated, Papa touches the tuner knob. A napping cat's eye, the poisonous-green light of the tuner winks at me.

"Abram!" Mama's voice comes from the dark. "Have you lost your mind? Close the shutters at least! Do you really want all of us in jail?"

The radio's hum subsides a bit. Papa presses his ear to the speaker and becomes still.

"You've gone absolutely mad," Mama whispers. She gets up from her bed, her slippers shuffling, passes to the windows, and closes the shutters. She even places a small pillow in the crack between them. "You've gone absolutely mad," she repeats on her way to the bed.

Meanwhile, alternately with lilting, whistling, and hallooing, the radio produces an annoying buzz, as if someone is cranking up a stalled car. But, for some reason, Papa doesn't change the station. I wonder in darkness: why does he bother to listen to some stupid humming? Then, through the noise, comes the beating of a huge drum. Three short bangs and a long one. Boom, boom, boom—bo-o-o-m. Boom, boom, boom—bo-o-o-m. With small pauses, they repeat many times, endlessly, it seems. But Papa is glued to the radio. Why does he care for some foolish drumming?

At last the banging stops, and suddenly a baritone utters in the purest Russian, though with a slight foreign accent, "This is London. Here is the latest news. According to our Moscow correspondent . . ." This is the voice that informs us one night that because the next round of the match tournament for the World Chess Championship is scheduled for Saturday, the American grandmaster Reshevsky will not take part, citing religious reasons.

It seems it was at this moment that I learned for the first time that a Jew is the one who observes the Sabbath. What delights Papa in Reshevsky is that, at least somewhere on the globe, there is a person who dares to disclose his Jewishness publicly, even at the risk of disrupting the smooth course of such an important event as the World Chess Championship. Papa admires that Reshevsky, by taking a day off on Saturdays, seemingly says out loud, "Certainly, it's a big *kuved,* an honor, to become the World Chess champion. But even for the sake of that honor, I cannot break the precept of the Sabbath."

Reshevsky's behavior doesn't impress me. The American can kiss the championship title good-bye anyway. Whether or not he rests on Saturdays, it will hardly help him. He is no match for Botvinnik. Not only can nobody overtake our grandmaster, hardly anyone can even catch up with him. Botvinnik is way ahead of everybody else!

Altogether, Papa's division of people into Jews and non-Jews outrages me. What a backward notion! Doesn't he know that all peoples are equal in our country? It's even written in black and white in our country's constitution, Stalin's constitution. A Soviet citizen should root for all our Soviet grandmasters. Whether one of them is Jewish or not is no great matter.

My logic doesn't convince Papa. His hand cuts the air, as if he wishes to divide the world in two: there are Jews and there are non-Jews. And that's all there is to it! I don't argue about it with him. It's useless. Frequently, without a pretext, he declares, "Do you know that Yakov Sverdlov, the very first Soviet prime minister, was Jewish? Still under Lenin. Ah!"

I don't share Papa's admiration for that. What does Sverdlov's ethnicity have to do with it? His qualifications were right for this post, and that's why Vladimir Ilyich Lenin appointed him.

Papa sees that he hasn't convinced me with Sverdlov, so he hastens to add the names of other outstanding Jews who, in the past, occupied important government posts: "Volodarsky, Uritsky, Nakhimson . . ." I'm familiar with these names already. Some Odessan streets are named after them. I assume they deserve the honor.

Since these names don't seem to impress me too much either, Papa brings the heavy artillery into action. "And Trotsky?" Papa lowers his voice and looks back at the windows. "Do you know what his true name was? Lev Bronstein! *Lëvkele,* little Leo in Yiddish. Oh, in his time, he was the best speaker in the world. In his time, he was tops!" Papa lifts his finger toward the ceiling in admiration. "He was famous throughout the whole world."

Here I cannot stand it any longer and decide to draw a line of defense. To show that he can't brag about his Jews endlessly, I ask, "A better speaker than Lenin?"

"Better!" Papa nods without any hesitation. "Much better! No comparison whatsoever!" His hand cuts the air as if chopping off any possibility of comparison. "Lenin was far from it. He was unable to hold a candle to Trotsky."

I consider it best to shut up. I understand that Papa is biased on account of nationality. How could Trotsky be better in anything than Lenin himself? I don't dare to ask one more question that suggests itself to me: "What about Stalin?" Trotsky delights Papa so much that I'm afraid of his answer. I feel he might tell me that Trotsky was better than Stalin. Is such a thing even thinkable? Can anyone be better than Comrade Stalin in anything? I, for one, cannot even imagine such a thing.

True, I never heard our leader on the radio. He spoke to the nation on July 3, 1941, but I didn't hear his speech. He was about to begin talking, but the next moment an air attack started, and we ran with Mama to the basement of our building. But in the film *Kliatva (The Oath),* he delivers a speech at Lenin's coffin, and the whole country freezes while listening. Even the locomotives cease to let out steam: "When leaving us, Comrade Lenin scrupulously bequeathed to us the task of guarding the unity of the party and our working class like the apple of our eye." When I was watching the film, my skin got goose bumps. At that time, I still only vaguely understood the difference between feature movies involving our great leaders and documentaries. If they show it in the cinema, it means that that's the way it happened in real life.

It is clear that Papa can't have enough of Trotsky for the single reason that he's Jewish. But how is it possible to admire a traitor? From our fourth-grade history textbook, I learned that, shortly before storming the Winter Palace, together with Kamenev and Zinoviev, Trotsky leaked the plans of the Bolsheviks' revolt to Kerensky's provisional government. For a long time, it will remain a mystery to me why, in 1917, as soon as the Bolsheviks won power, all of these traitors weren't shot on the spot. Many years passed before the trials of Trotsky's and Zinoviev's followers were finally held. (When reading the textbook, I had more questions. But we pupils were not supposed to ask them. All that was required of us was to retell what we read, as closely to the text as possible. Not to mix up the years of Tsar Alexei Mikhailovich's reign, the date of the battle with the Tatars at the Kalka River, or the formation of the Novgorod princedom.)

Every year, *Pravda* publishes a list of distinguished people rewarded with the highest prize in the country—the Stalin Prize. Papa's sole interest in this event is the winners' names. Are there any Jews among them? As a rule, the names are Russian or Ukrainian. Frolov, Tkachev, Nechiporenko. At first, Papa's way of determining who is Jewish and who is not is fully a mystery to me.

"Petrovsky," I read aloud.

"No," Papa says. "Petrovsky is a goy."

"Sergeevsky."

"The same thing."

"Belotserkovsky."

"A *yid*," Papa comes to life. "It's quite possible that he's one of ours."

"Why is Petrovsky a Russian, and Belotserkovsky a Jew?" I ask with challenge in my voice. Papa's wish that at least some of the laureates turn out to be Jewish is too strong. "Both surnames end with *-sky*."

"Well," Papa says, "here is how it works. If a town's or a shtetl's name comes before *-sky*, it may mean that the man's Jewish. That's how the tsar assigned surnames for the Jews. For this particular engineer, Belotserkovsky, his father or grandfather is most likely a *yidlik*, a little Jew from Ukraine, from Belaya Tserkov town."

Papa stubbornly sorts out all the laureates' names. He does it to test by ear whether at least potentially some of them are Jewish.

"Melnikov? No, Melnikov's not a Jew. Melnik could be Jewish. But Melnikov? Not a chance. He's a goy."

I chuckle internally at this homespun reasoning. Melnikov or Melnik, what's the difference!

Though Jewish names come up from time to time in the list of Stalin's laureates, compared with the number of Russians and Ukrainians whose portraits are published, Jewish portraits appear only on rare occasions.

"Well, of course!" Papa waves his hand. "They have nothing better to do than to publish a picture of a Jew!"

Why does Papa feel that they should give the prize specifically to a Jew? To listen to him, they should do it only because the candidates for these prizes are Jewish. I read in a reference book that there are two and a half million Jews in the USSR. That is, just over one percent. If among ten winners, at least one Jew appears, that's already ten times more than there should be.

In response to my arguments, Papa does something that he rarely does—he loses his temper. "Why are you talking about percentages? Percentages! As if I don't know who is the real author of the project your Frolov or Petrov is awarded for. Well, of course, as though they would ever give a prize to a Jew!" he waves his hand. "You'll wait for that forever. You'll get *kadukhes* from them."

I already know what *kadukhes* is. In our home, my parents switch from Russian to Yiddish and back so often that the languages sometimes become entangled in my head. With difficulty, I find the Russian equivalent, *zhalkaia podachka*, a "pitiful handout." Papa's words anger me. Listening to him, you get the impression that all Jews are geniuses, and all Russians are imbeciles.

Once, in the list of winners, a certain Estrin comes up. "Estrin, Estrin,"

Papa mutters, as if trying to get his mouth around it. "In my city, in Minsk, there was one Jew whose surname was Estrin. Before the revolution, his father owned a fur shop on Kolodeznaya Street, not far from our house."

"What makes you think Estrin is a Jew?"

"Estrin," Papa says emphatically. "Ester (Esther) is a Jewish female name. Of course he's a Jew!"

I am glad that Estrin shamed Papa for his mistrust in the impartiality of the Stalin's Prize Committee judgment.

Once, a certain Richter appears in the list of laureates. It is not the famous pianist Svyatoslav Richter, whose concerts I listen to on the radio from time to time, but some other Richter.

"What's this Richter's first name?" Papa asks.

"They don't show it here in full. Just his initials—I. S. Some Isaac Solomonovich, I guess. What's the difference?"

"Big difference. Some Richters are Jews. But some are Germans. Is there a picture of the man?"

"Yes."

"Well, show it to me."

I roll my eyes toward the ceiling. Give me a break! To determine ethnicity on the basis of facial features! I'm only ten years old, but I already know that you cannot always tell a Jew from a Russian or a Ukrainian.

Papa puts on his glasses with their thick lenses, bends over the newspaper, and studies the laureate's face. "Well," he says, rustling the paper and turning it to the light. "It's difficult to tell. Though, in Minsk, before the war, two Richter brothers, Jews, lived in our building. This one resembles the younger one, Yoska, little Joseph."

"Aha!" I gloat. "Now you see for yourself. If a man deserves it, whether he is Jewish or not is irrelevant. They award him the prize."

"And what did they award this man for?" Papa is still curious.

"'For growing new sorts of apricots, cherry plums, figs, and olives,'" I read, pleased that I can shame Papa's nationalist feelings at last.

He interrupts me. "Oy!" he says, laughing in relief. "Wait a minute! Let me think. You say cherry plums and olives? Well, of course! It's crystal clear."

Papa grabs his knees and begins rubbing them, as he always does when he is about to impart something emphatic. In this way, he pumps himself up before expressing an impartial opinion, "It looks like this Richter of yours is not a Jew after all."

In his voice I hear strange pleasure, even triumph, of a man who saw the light.

"This Richter is as Jewish as I am Chinese. He's a German, that's what he is!" Papa blurts out.

"A German?" Papa's confident tone confuses me a bit. "Why? Where did you get that idea from?"

"Where from!" he says. "First, I have yet to meet a Jewish gardener. A Jew trading in apples—be my guest. But heaven forbid growing them yourself!"

In Papa's words, the echo of the anti-Semitic slurs, of which I have heard too many, makes me cringe: that the Jews are capable of trading only, that they shirk hard work. "A trader," "a shopkeeper" are some of the most insulting words in the Russian language of the time. Commercial activities are not thought of as requiring any effort. Big deal! He bought some stuff over there, and he has sold it here. The newspapers attack "speculators." They use that term to stigmatize people who get Czech boots or French bras at normal prices and, because these items are hard to get here, offer them at higher prices under the table. Police hunt down speculators. Everyone who is willing and has connections in a shoe shop or at a haberdashery warehouse engages in this business. But it is believed that speculators are exclusively the Jews.

"Why are there no Jewish gardeners?" I can't hide my ironic tone. "What? In our country, they permit tree-watering by ethnic attribute only?"

"Because it's not meant for the Jews. Even in tsarist times, land was never given to the Jews. The tsar didn't permit it. It's Russian land. Why give it to the kikes! Second, cherry plums, figs, and olives love warm weather. In our country, they grow in Central Asia only."

"What does Central Asia have to do with it?"

"Everything! When the war broke out, the authorities deported all Volga Germans and sent them there."

I listen with mistrust. I read nothing about these sorts of things in our history textbook. I'm going on my eleventh year, and I recognize my parents' authority in a rather limited sphere only. "Deported, yes?" I say maliciously. "So, they just took them and moved? One and all?"

Papa ignores my tone. "Yes!" he waves his hand as if it goes without saying. "In a single night! They sent out every single German—women, children, old men. Together with all their stuff. Their pots, their trunks. Onto a cargo train and on to Kazakhstan."

Papa moves his hand as if trying to throw women, children, and their pots as far as possible. "To Uzbekistan! To Tajikistan!"

"Why so suddenly?"

"By the order of the General Army Headquarters!" Papa says, pointing his index finger to the ceiling, his tone solemn and mocking at the same time. "To prevent espionage and sabotage in wartime! Well, at least they treated them humanely. They gave them land so that they wouldn't starve to death."

He is clearly holding something back. I feel that he doesn't want to burden me with excessive information; it seems to him that I am not able to digest it yet.

I myself also consider it best to stop my inquiries.

Then I forget about this conversation. I have more important concerns than to listen to tall tales from informal and unverified sources.

FIFTEEN

A Strange Orange

GRADUALLY, NOT QUITE conscious of it, I find myself following Papa's suit: I also begin dividing the world into who is Jewish and who is not Jewish. Apparently, trying to overcome my feeling of inferiority, I search for Jews whom I can be proud of. One day, in the course of our conversation, Papa reveals to me what isn't mentioned in my textbooks—that Karl Marx was Jewish and so is Albert Einstein. I mentally give credit to both of them as outstanding Jews. (Since books, newspapers, and radio usually mention Friedrich Engels and Karl Marx in the same breath, I want to add Engels to that list as well, but Papa stops me from going too far by informing me that Engels was Gentile.)

But both Marx and Einstein are too far from the world I live in on a daily basis. I feel like having as much proof as possible that here, where I live, there are Jews worthy of admiration. My relatives are ordinary people— housepainters, electricians, bookkeepers, and tailors. I need stronger stuff. After conversations with Papa, armed with the knowledge of how to tell Jewish surnames from non-Jewish, I scan newspaper articles devoted to leaders of industry, film actors, and other outstanding people. I go on searching for Jews whom I can be proud of.

Certainly, Botvinnik, as well as all other great chess players of Jewish nationality—Bronstein, Tal, Taimanov, and Geller—are my idols. But in the world of adolescents, the size of one's biceps matters more than the sharpness of one's intelligence. I still look for new evidence of the strength not so much of the Jewish intellect as of Jewish muscles. Accusations of Jewish cowardice during war, slanderous and undeserved, are still floating around and refuse to leave the anti-Semites' lips.

I still go to soccer games with Uncle Abrasha and his son, Boris. Despite his small height and puny figure, the right forward of our Pishchevik team, Matvei Cherkassky, manages to score, duping the opposite team's giant defenders. I admire him not only because the weak beats the strong but also because Matvei is Jewish.

I rejoice: the first Soviet world champion in weight lifting is a Jewish athlete, Grigory Novak. And when in *Pravda* they print a photo of the new Olympic champion in gymnastics, Mikhail Perelman, my happiness has no bounds. It seems to me that, without any effort on my part, my biceps grow, my shoulders develop, and my back straightens. I am unable even to pull myself up, but now I feel like jumping up on the parallel bars at once and, at a brisk pace, making a triple somersault. When another Jewish athlete, Boris Gurevich, becomes the Olympic champion in wrestling, I stick out my chest. If any of my offenders were to challenge me to a fight at this moment, I would twist them in a full nelson, a double headlock, in a jiffy. It seems that each muscle of my body shouts, "Get a load of us!"

"This is something! Who could think that it's possible?" Papa says, joyfully waving his hands.

Three days remain before the final round of the tournament for the World Chess Championship is over. Could it be that the impossible has happened? Papa's protégé, the American Reshevsky, has overtaken our Botvinnik? That can't be!

"This is really something!" Papa paces the room in excitement. "The United Nations itself voted. Ah! They didn't give much land, just a scrap. But still it's a separate and independent place."

I respond to Papa's excitement with a blank stare. I am an avid reader of newspapers. What important development has occurred in the world that I missed? In these years of communal everyday life for all, the word *separate* is a synonym for luxury and privilege; it means belonging to the elite. When you say that someone has a "separate apartment," you place this person in a special category of people toward whom you can feel nothing other than hopeless envy.

But Papa doesn't calm down, "After two thousand years! Ah, what good fellows! What a terrific thing! Our *yidlik*s are something!"

By Papa's quick glances at the windows, I guess that he is excited about something he has heard on his Grundig radio at night.

"The United Nations General Assembly's decided!" Papa especially stresses the word *general*. He keeps pacing the room and circling around the table where I sit doing my homework. "Gromyko himself, our permanent UN representative, has declared it, 'It's time to give the long-suffering people a place in the sun!' Gromyko himself!"

As always when he is excited, he raises his hand over his head. It seems that this time he himself votes at the special session of the United Nations: "And America supported it too! Oh, to get the recognition of America! Now that means something."

Papa cannot calm down for a long time. He repeats the same thing endlessly, and I can't understand why he is so overwhelmed with emotion. Yes, I recall a short note in the newspapers. Big deal, the tiny state of Israel has been formed. Why would we, the biggest country in the world, care about some mosquito of a state?

Since I do not react to the news in any way, Papa looks at me with sadness and waves his hand, as if giving up on me. Upset that his own son does not share his delight, he circles the table for a while. Then he sits down near Mama. Her breast covered with the collar of her dressing gown, she feeds my newborn brother.

Papa whispers something into Mama's ear for quite a long time. I suppose it's the same thing he's almost shouted circling around the room. Mama lulls my little brother, listens to Papa, and nods.

But Papa cannot wait until little Vova falls asleep. He keeps whispering into Mama's ear again and again. From time to time, out of excitement, his voice rises, and Mama motions in my direction, "Shush! *Der kleyner!*" That is, be careful when talking in the presence of the little one. How could she say such a thing? I am already going on eleven, and still the "little one"? Will there ever be an end to it?

Mama lays my sleepy baby brother down in his crib and says, "I don't know what to tell you, Abrasha. You'll see that it won't end with anything good for us."

Now Papa does not miss a night without pressing his ear against his Grundig speaker. He does it with oblivion, as if, instead of listening to the radio, he were in the midst of prayer.

The summer passes, and one day Papa gets excited again. "Ah, here is some woman!" he whispers to Mama over breakfast. "A heroine, not just some broad! Actually, her name isn't Golda Meir but Golda Meyerson. She is one of ours, a native of Kiev. She left for America as a young girl and then went to Palestine. And now she's the Special Ambassador to the USSR! Molotov himself met her at the airport. Ah! Who could ever think that such a thing could happen? Unbelievable!"

Aunt Clara brings a letter from her brother-in-law, Grisha, who lives in Moscow. She reads, nervously, "Here, on Rosh Hashanah, we have cause for great joy. Golda Meir visited our synagogue on Arkhipov Street. So many people gathered to see her that some almost jumped onto the shoulders of those in front of them to look at her. Even mounted police had trouble keeping them in line. A joke's circulating all over Moscow: They call Abramovich to the KGB headquarters. 'Comrade Abramovich, why did you deceive our authorities? To the question in your personal file whether you have any relatives abroad, you answered no. But we've learned that you have an uncle in Tel Aviv. What do you say to that?' 'I didn't deceive anyone,' Abramovich replies. 'It's not *he* who is abroad. It's *I* who am abroad!'"

"Where did you get it from?" Papa asks one day in excitement. He points to an orange in my hands. Failing to peel it with my nails, I'm about to bite through its skin.

"Where? Where?" I mutter. What a silly question! "Mama brought them from a store."

I nod toward a shopping bag filled with oranges.

"From a store?" Papa asks again. "What store? From *our* store?"

What's with him? In some northern Soviet cities like Voronezh or Orel, an orange is a novelty. But in Odessa, we have not only the regular fruits and vegetables that are raised from our rich black topsoil *(chernozem)* but exotic fruits like oranges, too. After all, Odessa is a seaport. Ships from all over the world visit us. Usually, they take the foodstuffs packed in boxes, barrels, and sacks from their holds and reload them onto freight trains rushing toward Moscow. And that's how it should be! Just imagine, foreigners coming to marvel at the successes of our Soviet country and finding no oranges. How could we let our capital be short of anything? Shame on us! Why give our ill-wishers reason to gloat?

But nature sometimes intervenes for us Odessans. From time to time, storms or fogs cause the cargo ships to linger at sea for too long. When they finally tie up in our port, a delegation from the State Commission goes aboard. They sniff the foodstuffs and examine them from all sides. If some fruits or vegetables clearly won't survive the long journey to Moscow, the commission makes the only sensible decision—to pass the stuff to the local trading network right away.

If the sea is calm for too long, riggers and crane operators do what they can to help the Odessans. By sheer accident, boxes with fruits slide off the hooks and smash on the asphalt pier. These overseas gifts sell to the Odessans, fond of gastronomic pleasures, faster than it takes a gust of wind to pass along Odessa's streets, straight as masts. As soon as a tarpaulin-covered truck with boxes of oranges rolls up to our neighborhood produce store, its manager, in a battery commander's tone before an enemy tank attack, shouts to one of his most efficient saleswomen, "Anastasia Grigorievna, get your tray out to the street!"

In the next minute, at the entrance door, her motley scarf covering her head and her gold-plated tooth sparkling in the sun, a stout woman pops up with her tray and scales with a full set of weights. The saleswoman is stern. It isn't easy to cope with the onslaught of buyers running up to her from all sides. Zhora, the store loader, doesn't even manage to open the first box of oranges before, in a flash, the public, until that moment carelessly sauntering along Deribas Street, suddenly turns into a centipede, a long line bristling with arms and legs. Those who wind up at the end of the line try to wrest their destiny from the hands of chance. Every time, I am amazed at how so many people whose relatives' bodies are dangerously low on vitamin C wind up in the very same line.

"Sell no more than a pound per customer!" one of them shouts. "I need it for my sick child!"

"My wife's just given birth!" another one yells.

Less than half an hour passes, and everything comes to an end—the line, the shouting, and the oranges. Lucky customers carry them all over the city, beaming with joy.

But Papa isn't excited by the mere fact that we have oranges. They don't look much different from those that Mama usually brings. The only difference is that their peel has a little chain of mysterious marks as if engraved with the tip of a soldering iron. While Papa examines these signs, I get another orange from the shopping bag. This one is inscribed in precisely the same way. The intricate curves of the letters, which resemble musical notes, seem somewhat familiar to me. For an instant, before my internal gaze, Yan's grandfather's face appears. Bowed over the book in black binding, he rocks in a prayer. Strange! Why are the letters on these oranges the same as those in that book?

"Here is something . . . in Hebrew," Papa says at last, excitedly.

"Hebrew? What's that?"

"It's in Hebrew," Papa's voice trembles. "Actually, I never learned the language. Only the alphabet. In a *kheyder*. Well, that's what they called a religious school. We learned Yiddish there. I was there . . . only a year," Papa says, faltering and waving his hand in a gesture of hopelessness. (Many years later, I learned from Uncle Misha why Papa felt self-conscious about *kheyder*. His family was in need, and Grandfather Uri took him to work as his apprentice quite early. There was no time for school.)

"I've forgotten a lot," Papa continues. He puts on his reading glasses and is about to approach the window, but then, though we live on the third floor and nobody could see him from the ground, he doesn't dare to examine the orange there for some reason. He takes it to the light bulb, hanging above the table. "Aha! I see . . . *Ches . . . Yud . . . Peh . . . Hei* . . . Haifa! Haifa! You don't say! What good fellows they are."

As always, when Papa gets agitated, his voice trembles a bit.

"To grow such oranges! And where? In a desert! To trade with the Soviet Union itself! What great fellows they are. What a feat of our little Jews."

He holds the orange in his palm carefully, as though it is the golden apple of Russian fairy tales, and he paces our room.

I still don't understand why so much fuss about a regular orange.

"What is Haifa?" I ask.

"What! Haven't they told you anything about Haifa in your geography class?"

I adore maps. At every opportunity, I move my finger all over all the continents. But I have never come across Haifa. Admittedly, even in our biggest bookstore, Two Elephants, on Richelieu Street, maps of the world are small. Only world capitals are printed on them.

"You don't know where Haifa is? How is that possible?" Papa is perplexed. "Haifa is the main port of the state of Israel!"

He pronounces the word *state* emphatically and with pleasure. The tone of his voice suggests that, if it were up to him, Papa would order that the name of this port I've never even heard of be printed on all maps of the world, in a font the same size as that for Moscow.

Finally, after gazing at the orange to his heart's content, careful not to tear off its skin in the inscribed place, he peels it and divides the fruit from the land of his forefathers (none of us thought of ever seeing it then!) into four parts. Many years will pass, when, already an American citizen, he will visit Israel. In response to my question regarding his impressions, Papa will say, surprised by his own words, "I felt as if I were there always." But for now, slowly, with delight, shaking his head in admiration at every bite, he consumes his share.

"M-m-m-m!" he murmurs. "How juicy and sweet! A *makhae!* Sheer pleasure! Something special. It's supreme. I think these oranges are the best in the world."

I shrug. I don't share Papa's delights. This orange is like any other orange. Perhaps, it is somewhat fresher than usual.

I never saw Papa's face so happy, either before or after that moment, as when he tasted his first orange from Israel. It seems that the taste of the fruit grown on the land of Palestine evoked something hidden deep inside him.

We eat all the Israeli oranges in a few days. However, Papa saves the peel of one of them. He hides it on our bookshelf, behind *Kniga o vkusnoi i zdorovoi pishche (The Book about Tasty and Healthy Food),* our Soviet best seller.

SIXTEEN

Who Are You?

EACH YEAR, IN THE LAST days of December, Papa brings home a spruce tree. To me, the tree has nothing to do with religion in any way. It is just a custom. As the New Year approaches, we put the spruce in a bucket with sand so that it won't fall over onto my bookshelf. Then we dress it up and place some gifts underneath it to open on New Year's morning.

On New Year's Eve, a few minutes before midnight, the radio suddenly stops broadcasting. You don't hear anything besides city noise. Interrupted only by the occasional car horn honking, this prolonged mysterious "silence" manages somehow to put you in a festive frame of mind.

I am still, waiting. When, at last, I hear the Kremlin chimes on the radio start ringing liltingly—*don, dee-don, dee-don, dee-don*—I get goose bumps. This minute, while small bells call to one another in a carefree manner, in the clearest way possible, Red Square appears in my mind's eye, strewn with snow—the granite chocolate bars of Lenin's Mausoleum, the fanciful crenellated edge of the Kremlin wall, the rook-shaped Spassky Tower. At the mausoleum, the sentries straighten their backs and raise their pointed chins. They stand motionless, not blinking even when snowflakes land on their eyelashes. Their crimson cheeks burn from frost. The bayonets sparkle coldly. As soon as the openwork hands merge on Spassky Tower's enormous clock face, the main bell strikes. The remaining strikes follow in even intervals: "two, three, four . . ." I count as my heart sinks.

"Happy New Year!" the radio announcer says at last. "Congratulations on your new happiness, dear comrades!"

It is the only time in the whole year that I feel any warmth in his voice. Usually, I cringe internally at the tone of the cold radio announcements, disallowing any doubts that follow the words: "Attention! Moscow speaks! All radio stations of the Soviet Union are at work!" He is about to make an announcement that will stir everyone around me. (Probably, this cowering was a reflex acquired in my early childhood. Each day, together with adults, I listened to the radio for the Soviet Information Bureau reports about military actions; those reports began with the same very words.)

Immediately after the congratulations, the deep opening chord of a giant orchestra resounds. After a pause, with the implacability of a storm wave, the voices of a boundless male chorus roll over me, submerge me in their sound. The chorus thunders, menacing and stern. It does not sing so much as inform the whole universe, at this midnight hour, hidden there, behind the windowpane of our apartment:

Great Russia has rallied forever
The indestructible union of free republics.
Long live the Soviet Union, unified and mighty,
Created by people's will.

The anthem crushes me with its might. The refrain rumbles in a thousand throats. The chorus voices merge into a roaring avalanche, sweeping away everything in its path:

Glory to our free Fatherland,
A reliable stronghold of people's friendship!
Our Soviet banner, banner of the people,
Is to lead us from victory to victory!

Now, on New Year's Eve, when everything pulsates with meaning, the anthem has a double impact on me. On the one hand, it lets me feel that I am protected by a world power. On the other hand—and I feel this especially acutely—the anthem shatters me. It penetrates every pore of my body. I am a tiny weight lobule, the little flat metal rectangle trembling on the edge of the tweezers that, during our classes in physics, we put on the chemist's scales. This powerful tide of voices raises me so high that, as happens when I swim in the sea, I lose my footing and anxiously move my legs to feel the bottom; but no matter how desperately I flounder, I am dragged beneath the tide.

On New Year's Eve, the majestic anthem renews in me the feeling that visits me on regular days as well: full dependence on somebody else's will that I don't stand a chance of controlling. I am a dwarf in the music box that my friend Kotya Liubarsky once showed to me when his parents weren't home, forbidding me to touch it. (Kotya's father had brought it from Germany when the war ended.) In that small box stood figurines in awkward poses in a semicircle: a midget blacksmith with a little hammer over his head; a tiny ballerina in her ethereal skirt, her leg frozen in air; a harlequin with a drumstick suspended over a tambourine. Only when Kotya wound up a miniature spring and released the key did music play, the figurines begin to move, and their ridiculous poses suddenly make sense. The midget blacksmith struck an anvil with his hammer. The ballerina spun and beat one leg against the other. The harlequin rapped on his tambourine and nodded in delight.

Awaiting the last, twelfth, strike of the Spassky Tower bell, I also freeze. "Moscow—All strings are set to stirring in Russian hearts by the sound of its name! How much it echoes in them!"—we learn these lines of Pushkin's *Eugene Onegin* by heart in class. The whole country heeds Moscow's voice.

"Happy New Year, dear comrades!"

"Happy New Year!" the adults around me sigh in relief that, finally, they can clink one another's glasses and kiss.

I try hard to reconcile the greater world of the newspapers and radio with the one that surrounds me, but it isn't easy. For example, I don't understand certain words that I come across in *Pravda*. Once I read an item titled "A Significant Progress in Autumn Plowing" and became flustered. Autumn plowing? It is clearly something agricultural. But what exactly? It's awful! *Pravda,* our chief newspaper, writes about it, but I don't know beans about it. *Pravda* is proud of how much progress they have made in it, and I . . .

I ask Mama.

"Ikh visn nisht," she says. "I don't know. Don't bother me with your nonsense."

Our reader *Native Speech* is full of stories, riddles, and verses involving nightingales, squirrels, and the great taiga forest. I live in a southern city of the steppes. I have never seen squirrels or heard nightingales. That faraway textbook world seems uniquely noble, mysterious, and beautiful. There, in the immense forests, pines, cedars, and spruces are not small, easily fitting into our low-ceilinged room, but enormous, the height of a three-story building. I know how a pine looks and what a cedar is only by looking at their pictures. Neither of them grows in Odessa. Here we have acacias, plane trees, and chestnuts. At the Arcadia beach, there are a few palm trees. Because all my textbooks are devoted to life up there, in the north, in Moscow, I naturally assume that life up there, rather than the one I live here, is the only one worth living. Our book for extracurricular reading points out quite clearly, "It is known that the Earth begins at the Kremlin." It is there, in Moscow, in the Column Hall of the House of the Unions, that each year they erect "the main Spruce of the country"—its photos are printed in all newspapers.

I hold up everything around me to the ideal of Moscow, to life in the North. Here in Odessa, as a rule, New Year is also not the way it should be. It is not frosty and snowy, but second-rate, a pale reflection of what winter is all about. It's warm outside, and only if we are fortunate will there be snow, which will melt quickly. We may even have a shower instead. There are no snowdrifts to speak of. To make up for this deficiency, when decorating my spruce, Mama and I use wisps of cotton wool and toys in the shape of twisted pieces of glass to simulate snow and icicles.

When we finish hanging the ornaments, Mama climbs up on a stool and sets up a stately star on the spruce's tip. Then, with sudden fervor in her eyes, she covers the tree in paper streamers. Now, our decorating finished, Mama hands me a giant cracker, which resembles a large, smartly wrapped cylinder of candy. I aim at the tree tip and turn my head away. She raises my elbow a bit higher still, so that I won't inadvertently hit our sideboard and break the dishes. I pull the cracker string with all my might. Bang! I squint. The pungent smell of burnt potassium-chlorate salt fills my nostrils. I make a face and sneeze loudly. When I open my eyes, I stand stock still in delight. My spruce may be small but, sprinkled with confetti, it becomes enchanting.

I have no idea that a spruce has anything to do with Christianity. They call it nothing but a "New Year spruce." And besides, in our home, hardly anything is strictly Jewish. Except food. I conclude that it is food that defines nationality. What we eat never appears on the table at the home of my Russian friend Zhenya. Neither ground beans (which Mama calls *tsimes mit fasoles*), nor *forshmak* (ground herring with nuts), nor chicken necks stuffed with the fried cream of wheat with cracklings, that is, bits of crisp, fatty chicken skin *(shkvarkes)*.

I distinguish Jewish holidays from regular holidays by the kind of pastry that appears in our house. In the beginning of December, Mama bakes a cake made of eggs, sugar, and flour. The cake is fluffy, sweet smelling, with cinnamon. She calls it *leykekh*. Why does she make things confusing? I am puzzled. A cake is a cake. Certainly, Mama's *leykekh* is different from the cakes sold at the confectionery store Zolotoi kliuchik (Little Golden Key), at the corner of Deribas Street and Greek Lane. Their cakes are stale and sometimes even smell of mold, while Mama's is fresh, tasty, and aromatic. It melts in my mouth as if intended not for eating but for drinking. Certainly, the way it tastes has nothing to do with what Mama names it—but everything to do with her baking skills.

As soon as Mama removes her *leykekh* from the oven, she begins kneading another chunk of dough and then rolls it on the kitchen table for a long time. The dough becomes so thin that, when she lifts it over the table, I can see through it the pinkish oval of her face, reddened from work.

Then Mama lays the dough flat and stuffs it with crushed walnuts, apple slices, and raisins while she rolls it up. This makes a long log that she then forms into a horseshoe and bakes in the oven. After some time, she pulls it out. It is nice and brown. Mama wipes her hands on her apron and announces with satisfaction, "*Strudel* is ready!"

There she goes again! Why does she insist on naming an apple roll something else?

Strudel marks the approach of Hanukkah. I have no objections to this holiday. I even look forward to it. Hanukkah gives me a chance to replenish my meager personal budget considerably. When Mama invites my cousins and treats them to strudel, nuts, and candies, their parents take me aside, saying, "Here's your Hanukkah *gelt*," and give me a ruble or sometimes even three. "*Zay gezunt und gliklekh!*" they add.

Still young, I remain indifferent to their wishes of health and good luck. I have enough health to spare. True, I have a sore throat sometimes, but that's in the nature of things; everyone gets sick from time to time. As to waiting for a lucky break, that's for superstitious people. Isn't "every person the blacksmith of his own happiness," as the Soviet slogan has it?

But Hanukkah *gelt* is something else again. Now I can afford to buy not the usual tin pistol that shoots pitiful paper percussion caps but a solid one, lead-cast, the one that uses heavy lead charges filled with a thundering mix. During the October Revolution and the First of May demonstrations, rural-looking men and women sell translucent pieces of hard candy in the shape of little greenish fish or red cockerels fixed onto smoothly planed little sticks (I remember even now the taste of wood saturated with sweetness.) There are also *kozinaki,* little briquettes of roasted sunflower seeds baked into hardened honey. I can also buy a pair of little clay balls covered with potassium-chlorate salt. Knocking them against each other produces remarkable crackling sounds and flying sparks. At school, I can buy a shiny ball-bearing from Vaska Fedotov, whose father is an auto mechanic. You can't do much with one of them, of course, but slipping it onto your finger, you can roll it down the handrail when descending from our apartment on the third floor to the courtyard. It makes the trip less boring. Lots of things in the world can please a boy's heart. No matter what you say, I approve of Hanukkah. I wish more holidays were like that!

When spring comes, Mama bakes triangular pastries filled with poppy seeds and jam. I know already that these pastries, by virtue of their name *(hamantashen)* and unusual shape, signify the approach of another Jewish holiday—Purim. As Mama explains, they symbolize the ears of a man named Haman, who, in ancient times, was a fanatical enemy of the Jews. I listen to Mama's explanation with mistrust. What a strange custom—to eat someone's ears! Though symbolic, it still smacks of cannibalism. But Mama's pies are extraordinarily tasty, and I eat up one *hamantash* after another, ignoring their symbolism.

September comes and Mama slices a few apples of the Antonovka variety (my favorite), arranges them on a platter, and says, "Dip them in honey and eat!"

"I don't like it too sweet," I say, making a face. "Antonovka apples are tasty enough as they are."

"Don't be a fool," Mama says. "You must eat them with honey so that you have a *zise ir,* a sweet year. That's the way it has to be done on Rosh Hashanah."

"Ro-sha-sha-na?"

"Well, of course. On the New Year."

"What New Year? The New Year is the first of January."

"For *them* the New Year is on the first of January. For us, it's now. This will be the five thousand seven hundred and ninth year."

I am confused. Forget about the New Year inexplicably moving to autumn; it has also jumped ahead almost four thousand years.

"Why five thousand seven hundred?"

"Because. It's the Jewish calendar."

Rosh Hashanah brings a larger company of people than ever to our home. It seems that Mama has invited every single relative, no matter how distant. There is hardly enough space for dishes on the table. Here you have aspic of meat and aspic of fish, liver pâté with fried onions and minced cooked eggs with cracklings, grated cooked beets with walnuts, stuffed peppers, the famous "caviar" Odessa style, called *sinen'kie,* "the little blue ones," a finely chopped spicy blend of baked eggplant, tomato, onion, and garlic, and many other things.

But dinner on Rosh Hashanah is not that different from similar meals in our home—on birthdays, anniversaries, and other special occasions. The only difference is that, crossing our threshold, the guests congratulate one another on the New Year and wish one another *gezunt* and *parnuse,* that is, health and income.

Hardly a week passes after Rosh Hashanah and, to my surprise, the terrible smell of singed fur spreads all over our apartment again. This unpleasant odor always accompanies Mama's preparation of ingredients for aspic of meat. Holding them over a kerosene stove, she burns cow shins along with the hoofs, then scalds them with boiling water, and, with the help of a little hammer, splits them into smaller sections. Again all the day long, she cooks and fries. But now, setting the table, instead of the usual blue cloth with white flowers, she spreads the starched white cloth she saves for special occasions. When all dishes with food are placed on the table, Mama covers it with a lacy fabric resembling a bridal veil. Then she fits a candle inside the single bronze candlestick.

"So, Milya," she says to me, looking over the table with satisfaction, "tomorrow's Yom Kippur. Papa doesn't work. We go to the synagogue. On Yom Kippur, no one must either eat or drink. But children are exempted. Here," she opens our refrigerator and, as if she's already afraid to touch the food, points her chin toward it, "this is for your breakfast. And this you'll take with you for lunch in school."

The next morning, Mama forces me to put on my best suit and a new shirt, as if I'm about to go not to school but to a relative's birthday party. In school, they stare at me. Out of curiosity, some of my classmates ask why I show off. I am silent. Naturally, I cannot tell them that my family observes religious holidays. I secretly sigh: what can be done? You don't choose your parents. And mine would hardly be reeducated in the spirit of atheism. I am consoled by the fact that, apparently, they are not unique in this respect. Other Jewish boys, Yurka Lerner and Vovka Braslavsky, have also showed up in their smart clothes.

I return home after school and wait for my parents a long time. They come late, toward the evening, their faces tired and drawn. I am hungry too. I glance at the table. I finished my sandwich in school hours ago, and here plenty of delicious food is buried under a cover of lace.

"Stay clear of the table," Mama says. "You won't die if you hold on a bit longer."

"How long do I have to wait?"

"Till the first star."

Time and again, I cast a sidelong glance at the windows, waiting for darkness. Can you believe such backwardness? Waiting for a star! What if the sky is cloudy? If you wait for the stars to show up, you might die of starvation. Isn't it easier to check the wall calendar for the sunset time?

Meanwhile, one by one, our relatives gather. Their conversations circle around the same question: "Have you fasted? We did, too. Did you go to work? I called in sick. Sometimes fasting is even good for your health." They talk half in jest, poking fun at themselves.

When at last it becomes dark blue beyond the windows, everyone sits down around the table. Mama lights the candle. She raises her wineglass filled with domestic cherry fruit liqueur. Apparently gathering her spirit—after all, Young Pioneers are at the table, and some are about to become Komsomol members—she pronounces in a solemn tone, "Let everyone be healthy, and may God forgive us for all our sins!"

This is the only time of year that Mama specifically refers to God, aside from casual statements, such as "My God, the milk's boiling over!"

"What does Yom Kippur mean?" I ask nonchalantly, reaching for a piece of meat aspic. I relate to the ceremonies of times long past without much interest.

"It's the Day of Judgment," Papa says.

I try to make a joke: "The Day of Judgment or the day of the loan?" (In Russian, the words *sud,* "judgment," and *ssuda,* "loan," sound almost the same.)

"This is the day," Mama says, turning a deaf ear to my wit, "when God judges how you've lived the whole year. Today it's necessary to ask forgiveness of everyone you've offended. And they should forgive you."

The concepts of sin and forgiveness in Mama's interpretation seem to me far from life, as strange as New Year in September. When two boys fight during school recess, the one who is defeated might force out, "Well, I apologize." But he does it only because the winner is jamming his nose with his fingers and demanding an apology. But has anyone ever apologized just like that, voluntarily? I do not remember such an occasion.

"And what if they won't forgive?" I say with a challenge in my voice. "Then what?"

"They'll forgive," Mama assures me. "They have to forgive. On Yom Kippur, everyone should forgive one another."

SEVENTEEN

One Passover in Odessa

IT IS THE SPRING OF 1951. Passover is approaching. All Mama's energy is spent on getting a carp at any cost. A carp for the Passover table becomes an obsession. I do not understand what is specifically Jewish about carp. This fish, I read in the *Bolshoi entsiklopedicheskii slovar'* (Unabridged Encyclopedic Dictionary), "is the domesticated form of wild carp. The main product of pond-fish breeding in most countries." That's it? Then everyone eats carp. Not only in the USSR, but also everywhere in the world. Why then is it specifically required for Passover?

Does eating a carp that Mama has stuffed really make you feel like a Jew? I have eaten it every year, and it has in no way affected my view of the world. I don't feel Jewish. It tastes good, but it's as simple as that. Why should one feel Jewish, anyway? You should feel like a citizen of the USSR. Like an internationalist.

But for Mama, you have to eat carp, and that's the final word. Now she can't live without it. How to get her hands on a carp—that's all she can think about. As the holiday approaches, she starts to run from store to store in our neighborhood. She intercepts deliverymen and shop clerks in dark corridors and storage rooms, waits at service entrances with a single goal in mind—to find out exactly when and where carp would be "thrown out." I am not a kid anymore and already know that certain words in conversation have meanings that are different from the ones given in the dictionary. To "throw out" doesn't mean that the carp has gone bad and is destined for the garbage. To "throw out" means to put on the market.

Finally, Mama succeeds in learning the secret of secrets—the best chance of buying carp is from the fish store in our own building. On the day of delivery to the store, I wake up earlier than usual because of a racket, the roar of a giant waterfall. Looking out the window, I find down in our courtyard a huge stirring python of a line coiled six times. (People are waiting at the back door instead of the front, because the long line would hold up traffic on the sidewalk.) I recognize Mama by her bright headscarf; she's the very first of the first dozen people separated from the rest of the line. This group jounces impatiently, waiting for the store to open. My mother's face bears the expression of someone who has survived risky surgery and is moving swiftly toward full recovery. The other lucky ones up front clasp the person just ahead of them by the waist, as if they are preparing, once the doors open, to throw themselves joyfully into a conga line. This is what I thought seeing scenes like this when I was little. Now, at the ripe age of thirteen, I already know that this has nothing at all to do with dancing. This is simply a safety measure, so that at the last minute some bully won't squeeze into the line that has already suffered an eternal wait.

In about fifteen minutes, Mama appears in the doorway of our apartment. She is pressing a squirming bundle to her breast, an enormous glittering carp. Mama is excited and happy. I had seen her in such a state only when she returned from the hospital with my newborn brother, Vova, in her arms.

"Come on and help me," Mama says breathlessly and instructs me with her eyes to take a smaller paper-wrapped bundle that she can barely keep under her arm. There, it turns out, is another fish, with a greenish back, brown stripes along its thin body, and a myopic, squinched-up face.

"Perch," Mama says in answer to my unspoken question: why is such a wimpy companion necessary when we have the giant carp? "You have to add perch to carp. It tastes better that way."

The perch is not showing any visible signs of life, apparently having come to terms with its fate. I have the flickering feeling that somehow this passive fish resembles many of my Jewish relatives.

But the carp is another story altogether! In this store, fish is sold not just fresh but alive. The customer points out a carp in a tank at the center of the store, and the sales clerk, using a long-handled sieve, scoops it out. Then he throws it onto the scales. With this unexpected change of environment, the carp is stunned for a moment and allows itself to be weighed. But then it regains its senses and tries to return to its beloved element. Now, when Mama lays it down on the oilcloth of our kitchen table, it immediately hurls itself to the floor with mighty flaps of its tail. It needs to be pacified with a spiked wooden hammer with which Mama usually pounds pork chops. (In our house "Kosher Jew" means someone holding on to vestiges of the past.) She entrusts this task to me. In the absence of my father, who is at work, I am the only capable man for the job. Mama ushers my four-year-old brother, Vova, out of the kitchen and shuts the door. Banished, he wails and bangs on the door with his foot. He wants to watch the live fish.

I pick the carp up from the floor, but for moral reasons I refuse to finish it off. To kill a defenseless creature is beyond me.

"What a softy!" Mama says. "But when it comes to eating it, you have no problem."

This kind of reproach shames me to tears.

"I won't eat it!"

"We'll see about that," Mama says.

While we are squabbling, the carp watches me with its silvery eye and continues to thrash the oilcloth with its tail. This gaze makes me feel dreary down to my very soul. A living creature is a living creature. This one opens its mouth a bit, and I see the rosy bellows of its gills.

"You're no help at all. I have to do everything all by myself!" Mama says.

She sighs deeply and gets down to business. I see that finishing off the fish isn't easy on her conscience either. She takes a long time to get up her courage, and then, turning her face away, she takes a swing and hits the carp on the head with the hammer. But the wooden hammer slides off its powerful jaw. Again, it winds up on the floor, where it begins to flap around in a war dance. I cautiously hoist the fish up onto the table, and Mama yells, raising the hammer up over her head, "Hold on tight!"

Covered with scales from head to foot, I hold the carp by the tail with both hands. But at the decisive moment it jerks, and Mama misses again. Finally, at the very moment that Mama is able to get really riled up and take an all-out swing, the carp, tired of fighting for its life, grows still on its own. Both of us breathe a sigh of relief.

Besides fish, Passover means the appearance of thin brittle squares of slightly browned, flavorless baked dough on the table. The name of this food, if I may so call it, is "matzo." I'm not surprised that it isn't sold in stores. Who wants to buy the bland stuff?

I already know what matzo is. During the Passover meal, when my aunts and uncles and their children gather around the table, one square of it is hidden, and the grown-ups encourage us to search for it throughout the entire apartment. While we search, they entertain themselves at our expense, because we run around madly trying to outrace one another. The person who finds the matzo is given one ruble, sometimes even three. For each of us, this is a fortune. Of course, we children like this kind of game. But the atmosphere of Passover lacks any kind of seriousness or significance. No rituals, except for the hiding of the matzo, are practiced. And even that is done lightly, like a joke, as if it were a mechanical imitation of a ritual in which the adults themselves do not believe. It is as though they do it out of some lingering custom, out of inertia. (As I will learn many years later, they have abandoned their Ukrainian and Byelorussian shtetlach for the larger world of big cities. I recall that only once Mama, hurried and off-handed, answered my question about where we acquired the custom of eating matzoth and why anyone would want to eat them in the first place. She said that those Jews who fled from Egypt thousands of years ago ate it. "Well," I thought, "I suppose in the desert there is no way around it. I guess there I would be forced to eat matzoth too.")

But Mama can't imagine how you could have Passover without matzoth. She is ready to get her hands on it, whatever it will take. One evening she announces that I am to go to bed early. I will have to get up very early the next morning.

"Why?"

"I need your help."

"What kind of help? Why help?" I begin to moan. I don't like to get up early. I'm a hopelessly heavy sleeper.

"You're going to Peresyp with me."

"Peresyp!" I whine. "That's all the way out in the boonies!"

"Boonies or no boonies, it makes no difference. We need to go there to get matzoth."

"Why do we have to go so far away?"

"Ask *them* that," Mama says, nodding her head in the direction of the window. "If *they* sold matzoth in the stores the way they did before the war, we wouldn't have to schlep all the way to the other side of the city."

I already know whom Mama has in mind. In her speech the pronoun *they* has two meanings, depending on the context. *They* are either Russians or the Soviet authorities. Often, it is hard for me to grasp the difference between them.

I keep quiet. It isn't so easy to argue with Mama or to change her mind.

Her point of reference is always "before the war," which I cannot take issue with. I don't remember what it was like before the war. Then I only had time to be born and to learn how to walk. Everything else in my life began after—when the war had already begun.

I sigh. There is nothing I can do. I have to go to bed.

Mama wakes me up at five in the morning, when the first streetcars start to run. Sleepy and bracing myself against the morning chill, I set out with Mama to some bakery all the way out in Peresyp, to the outskirts of the city, to get matzoth. We don't go empty handed but with two net bags, full of bags of flour. As it turns out, matzoth aren't simply sold; they are exchanged for flour. I don't understand this idiotic arrangement. Flour appears often in the stores. Why don't the people who bake the matzoth buy the flour themselves, instead of making us drag it across the entire city? (Years later I will learn that Jews are permitted to get matzoth baked from their own flour as a "community service" only in the Passover season and only at that one bakery.)

I wipe the foggy window with the sleeve of my jacket. In the faint blue of early dawn, my entire city slowly swims past, block by block, from beginning to end. Rabbit-eyed from lack of sleep, workers of the morning shift run up the streetcar steps wearing caps shiny from wear. Already we are passing single-story houses, sometimes we come upon whitewashed village huts, and still we keep going and going.

Finally we get off. Mama walks ahead. In her right hand is a bag with three packages of flour. She sticks out her left arm for balance. I drag along behind Mama, hauling another package of flour in a net bag. It keeps banging against the backs of my legs. My knees buckle.

Mama checks the address against a piece of paper. Finally we are pushing open a gate. I assumed that getting up so early we would be the first to arrive at the bakery. To my disappointment, in the back of the courtyard a small line made up of people like us, carrying bags of flour, has already assembled.

"Who's the last in line?" Mama asks the usual question.

For forty more minutes we shift from foot to foot in the courtyard outside a rundown shed. I shiver from the cold. I am still in a foul mood. I didn't get enough sleep, and I feel chilled to the bone. Anyone looking at me would know that I am not at this bakery of my own free will. If it were up to me, I would have slept to my heart's content, for at least three more hours.

Finally they let us in. Perhaps because I haven't had enough sleep, am chilled to the bone, and have bounced along on the streetcar, as soon as I set foot in the tiny dimly lit bakery and waves of warm air envelop me, I suddenly feel something I didn't expect to encounter here, in the far outskirts of the city swept by the steppe winds, fragrant with spring moisture—peace, quiet, and refuge. To my surprise, this tiny semidark bakery, lit by a single weak bulb sticking out from a bare, badly plastered wall, feels like home. It smells of warm flour, of dough, raw and baked. The flame of the oven flutters. I sense the particular domestic comfort that is felt only in close proximity to a hearth.

In a worn white coat, its sides flapping with his every movement, a young curly-haired baker with lively brown eyes is busy in front of a large oven. He is holding a wide, long-handled wooden paddle. Despite the early hour, he is wide awake, friendly, and even jolly. He tosses the paddle from one hand to the other, playing with it as if it were a pool cue, opens the oven door, and peers inside.

Finally throwing the oven door wide open, the baker begins to lift up the sheets of ready matzoth. In the oven's depths, by the far back wall, crimson-orange flames dance. The baker stores the ready matzoth in a carton once used for macaroni. With the same paddle, he snatches up from the tray the rectangles of thinly rolled dough—its dotted lines looking as though threads have been pulled out—and lines them up evenly, row by row, on the hearthstone. Then he shuts the oven door and nods cordially at Mama and me, wishing us a good holiday:

"*Gut Yontev!*"

"*Gut Yontev!*" Mama answers, brightening up instantly. "*Gut Yontev!*" she repeats and pulls at my jacket sleeve, motioning for me not to be rude and to respond to the greeting.

(On the surface, everything that happened after that wasn't at all remarkable, but much later my mind has returned to that moment again and again.)

His lively eyes shining, the baker picks up a still-warm sheet of matzo from the macaroni box, offers it to me, and says warmly and simply, "*Gut Yontev!*" At first I am frightened by the unexpected geniality, the special, familial closeness expressed by a total stranger.

(I couldn't guess then that the young baker—perhaps smiling at his own memories—easily read what was happening in my soul. He understood my stubborn and foolish refusal to accept the inevitable—my belonging to the Jewish people. I was too young to know that I did not have a choice.

The baker must have felt sympathy for the spiritual ignorance of the top student in class 5A, intermediate school number 43, who did not yet know the joy that he is not alone in a cold and lonely world, but with his people. Behind the metal door of the oven, on its brick floor, lay open the pages of the book of their destiny. The blazing tongues of flame at the far wall were the flames of history, in which they burned more than once—burned but remained alive. I was not yet capable of understanding that a holiday is the sensation of the warm hand of your people, with whom you already share a fate—if not a faith, the need for which you do not yet perceive because of your youth. It was as if the baker offering the piece of matzo said, "You and I are Jews, a single family.")

Still frowning, I take the matzo from the baker's hand. I do not yet realize the significance of this simple gesture. (Now, from the perspective of over thirty years of wandering in alien worlds and lands, I see that in my fingers the tiny flame-touched mounds in the matzo rise up like braille. Then I did not yet know that I was blind. I did not yet understand that what I held in my hands was the Bible for the illiterate, the history of the suffering of my people abridged for the uninitiated. I did not understand that by accepting the matzo from the hands of another Jew, I took the first step of my private Passover, my own exodus, my own private flight toward freedom. Did not know that this flight would last the same presaged forty years needed for the shameful habits of slavery to blow away in roaming through the desert. Nor did I know that to take the Passover vow to eat bland, crunchy, flat bread, to relinquish, if only for a time, thick, yeast-risen loaves, meant that I vowed to cast away my arrogance, to condemn with that act the sin of pride, of which, however short my life, I was already guilty. Secretly I considered myself smarter, better educated than my parents, who still obstinately clung to ancient traditions.)

"*Gut Yontev!*" says the baker.

I do not yet understand that at this moment I have approached my Rubicon. I cannot accept the matzo and say nothing. That would be truly rude. But to respond in what language? To answer in Yiddish would mean to admit my Jewishness, which I've resisted admitting for a long time. Even though we are meeting for the very first time, the baker addresses me as a family member, a close friend, an insider. How could I respond, "A good holiday to you too," in Russian? I do not yet understand but intuitively sense the incongruity of such a response, a response to a Jewish greeting spoken in the language of mockery and harassment.

If I were to switch over to Russian, by that very action I would reject the closeness and warmth held forth to me. I would push away the person offering me friendship. It would be the same as—no, worse than—hiding my hand behind my back or shoving it into my pocket if he extended his own hand to shake it.

I take the matzo from the baker's hand. My fingers are tense. The matzo breaks between them. I have yet to learn that other human values are equally brittle—freedom, trust, friendship, love, life itself. One awkward move can sometimes be enough to destroy them.

"Gut Yontev," overcoming myself, I finally say under my breath.

With two pillowcases filled with matzoth crumbling a bit under our touch, Mama and I leave the bakery. We walk toward the streetcar stop. Everything that I have lived through in the short stay in the bakery is soon left behind. Again, I press my forehead against the streetcar window, nodding off and thinking about what I have seen. A journey at the crack of dawn. The dark windowless bakery. There was no sign, no cash register as in a regular shop—Mama rolled up the money and shoved it into the baker's coat pocket. I guess that the bakery is a clandestine place. And *Gut Yontev* sounds like a password. I belong. I can be trusted. The thought flashes in my mind that, at the turn of the century, in such secret places underground, Bolsheviks printed their leaflets calling people to arms against the Russian autocracy.

PART THREE

EIGHTEEN

On Commissars, Cosmopolites, and Lightbulb Inventors

"HAVE YOU HEARD?" Uncle Misha asks in Yiddish. I prick up my ears. If adults in our house switch to Yiddish, it means something bad has happened. I have no clue why they do it. Though I don't speak Yiddish, I have understood it for a long time. If it's not from me they hide the content of their conversation, then from whom?

It's January 1949. It's Sunday, around noon. We've had our breakfast late. Mama is feeding farina to Vova, my one-year-old brother. In his high chair, he turns his head left and right and looks around with the dark gray buttons of his eyes, annoying her greatly. Beyond the window, the sky is gloomy. The wind chases the first snowflakes around the courtyard. It's cold. My courtyard peers are staying home. Only Kotya is running alone around the yard, kicking a half-pumped child's rubber ball, the size of a little melon. I have begun to think how I might get myself out of the house to chase the ball with him, when Uncle Misha, pale, his face troubled, enters the apartment, mumbles, "Good morning," and sits down. For a while he says nothing. He only moves his heavy black brows, scowling from under them.

"*Ekh, ekh, ekh,*" Papa sighs. In critical situations, as a rule, he prefers to say no more than that for as long as he can. You have to annoy him greatly to make him blow up and begin to talk.

"*Zoln zey ale farbrent vern,*" Mama says loudly also in Yiddish. "May they all be burned to ashes!"

"*Sha, sha, sha!*" Papa hurriedly interrupts her. "Shush! What are you, out of your mind? Be quiet."

But you can't stop Mama so easily when she's agitated.

"They do whatever they want," she says switching to a whisper and looking around at the window.

"Cosmopolites," Uncle Misha says scornfully. "Again they're having a go at us! They're looking for something to pick on. And our own, those little yids, they are also to be blamed. Theater critics! You want to be a critic, then you should know what's expected of you. You have to figure things out. Eh!" He waves his hand, letting us know what fools these critics are.

"*S'is gut paskudne.* It's real trouble," he says.

Listening to the grown-ups' conversations, I gradually begin to understand what's going on. But for the life of me I can't figure out why they are so upset. Yes, of course, it's too bad that new hidden enemies have appeared in our country. But why do my uncle and Mama and Papa react in such a way as if something were threatening them personally? What do they have to do with it?

Yes, I've heard the editorial in *Pravda* read on the radio. But in it there wasn't a single word spoken about the Jews. It concerned some cos-mo-po-lites. I already know something about them. In school, Galina Ivanovna already explained that these are foreign agents who try to diminish our achievements. She brought *Pravda* to our class and led a discussion with us on the article "The Superiority of Soviet Science and Technology." She explained to us what we'd already known for a long time—that our country was in the vanguard of all humanity. Not only because our political system was the most advanced, but because we were ahead in all spheres of life—science, technology, and culture.

"American bourgeois politicians do not hesitate to insolently appropriate for themselves somebody else's discoveries and priorities," Galina Ivanovna reads.

Cosmopolites claim that the British invented the steam engine, although everybody knows that, long before them, two Russian peasants from the Urals—the Cherepanovs, father and son—were the first to build one. But they were landlord Demidov's serfs, and the tsar didn't want to please them by making use of their invention. I'm offended for the Cherepanovs, both father and son. I already know quite well what injustice is done when people are judged by their origin.

But I am somewhat bewildered. Why didn't the tsar take advantage of this remarkable invention? If he was such a scoundrel, why wouldn't he give it the name of the landlord Demidov and order the engine multiplied? Of course, it was another of the injustices so common in tsarist times, but, after all, great industrial progress could have been made. Then I caught myself. Nothing in the story about the Cherepanovs was surprising. They had explained it to us in school many times: Russian tsars were not too bright (with the exception of Peter the Great and Ivan the Terrible). The tsarist system could only drag Russia backward.

"Who invented the lightbulb?" Galina Ivanovna asks.

I know that the true inventors of the lightbulb were the Russian genius of an engineer, Yablochkov, and his assistant Ladygin, not that smart aleck, the American Edison. He stole his bulb from them; it was that simple. I try to imagine for myself how this happened. This slippery character Edison arrived in Russia, disguised himself as Comrade Lenin, Vladimir Ilych, did, hiding from police, before the storming of the Winter Palace in the film *Lenin v Oktiabre (Lenin in October):* He put on somebody else's coat, a cap, a false mustache, and bandaged his cheek as if he had a gumboil. (For a minute, I lost myself in thought. Why would Edison need to mask himself if he hadn't invented anything and nobody knew his face anyway? But then I brushed aside this objection.)

Now, in the dead of night, through the first-floor window, this shady character Edison made his way to Yablochkov's laboratory, grabbed the bulb from the table, pushed it into his pocket, and rushed back to the border and then to his America. (Here again I paused to wonder why, while Yablochkov slept, his assistant Ladygin didn't guard their bulb. But then I figure that maybe he had a stomachache that night or a toothache or something else.) In fairness, the bulb should be named after Yablochkov.

I stand up with the answer to the teacher's question: "Yablochkov."

"Sit down, Draitser, excellent!" Galina Ivanovna says. "And now, children, who invented the radio and the telegraph?"

"Alexander Popov!" we shout in unison.

"R-r-right!" says Galina, proud of us. "Popov. But over there," she nods in the direction of the West, "they claim that it was their inventor—named something like Marconi or Macaroni."

We laugh readily. Macaroni. How about that! Such a funny name, and there he is again, trying to worm his way to fame.

"And the first airplane?"

"Mozhaisky!" we shout all together. And we put them in their place—all those Western inventors who have had the gall to challenge our supremacy.

Things are not always that simple, however. Sometimes I find it difficult to figure out the principle according to which our superiority is established. In the newspaper *Sovetskii sport,* I've read a headline, "Soviet Soccer School Is the Most Advanced in the World." I strain my memory, and no matter how hard I think, I can't remember when our national team won the world championship or Olympic gold. I'm an ardent soccer fan. I follow even the second-league games, among which the Odessa team plays often. It goes without saying that I read in papers the reports on our soccer games abroad. I know the voices of radio sports commentators, Vadim Sinyavsky and Nikolai Ozerov, as well as those of my relatives. How could I have missed such big news as our winning the world championship? In chess, both our grandmaster Botvinnik and the whole USSR team are the world champions. But in soccer? I'm lost and annoyed that I missed such important news. How come my friend Zhenya, who often listens to broadcasts with me, hasn't told me anything about it?

I reread the article. It turns out, "the most advanced school" does not mean primacy in either the number of victories or the overall score. Our soccer school is most advanced because Soviet soccer players are morally superior. If war were to break out, they would fight for their country as they fight on the field. The Western soccer players are all corrupted. They are bought and sold from one club to another. They don't play out of love for their motherland, but just out of love for money.

Surprises await me every day. Recently, Galina Ivanovna told us that, to stress our alleged backwardness, all those cosmopolites pollute our speech with words of foreign origin. After all, everyone knows that the Russian language is the richest, the best, and the most beautiful and melodious language in the world. We learned by heart a prose poem, "Russian Language," by Ivan Turgenev. I still remember it: "In the days of doubts, in the days of distressing thoughts about the fate of my native land, you alone are my support and help, oh great, mighty, truthful, and free Russian language!"

"Children," Galina Ivanovna says, "do you remember, we talked about the cosmopolites' attempts to ascribe our inventions to foreigners? Here's another example. To make believe that it was the Americans who made the first computing machine in the world, they sneaked into our day-to-day life their word *komp'iuter,* computer. That's terribly un-Russian, isn't it?

Therefore, we should call it by its right name—*elektronno-vychislitel'naia mashina'*, electronic counting machine. Well, it's a bit too long, but it's right."

I also notice the strange disappearance of some other words from print. After my baby brother, Vova, who just started walking, broke a few of Papa's beloved records, Papa went to the store on Deribas Street and replaced them. But they are subtitled differently now. A dance tune called "La Cumparsita" is no longer a tango, as was printed on the old record's label; now it's a "slow dance." Another one, "Tales from the Vienna Woods," isn't a waltz anymore but now a "ballroom dance." On the posters around town, I read announcements that our famous Odessan, Leonid Utesov, is coming to town with his orchestra. But the orchestra is no longer called a jazz orchestra; it's a "variety orchestra" now.

I conclude that getting all those *tango, waltz,* and *jazz* words into our vocabulary was another subversion by those cosmopolites, and they are taken care of now. (I ponder for a while whether the waltz is the only ballroom dance there is, but I don't know much about this adult entertainment, and I take it for granted—yes, waltz is the only one.)

Uncle Misha goes on talking. I take advantage of the grown-ups' preoccupation and slip out to the yard to play ball with Kotya. As always, Kotya scores more often than I do. But today my kicks are even worse than usual.

"Comrade Miss-them-all!" Kotya says and grabs the ball. "It's no fun playing with you. What is it, didn't you eat enough cereal this morning? Why do you miss the ball each time?"

I keep silent. Kotya puts the ball under his arm and heads home. As soon as he turns away, I run out of our courtyard and head toward Karl Marx Street. Over there, a dozen steps from the corner, is the *Pravda* newsstand. Gathered in front of it are an old man, a woman with a net shopping bag, and another boy, a bit older than I. I squeeze myself closer and find the article that Uncle Misha referred to. I have noticed that, for some reason, the front-page articles, unsigned, turn out to be the most important. Uncle Misha had said something about literary criticism. Here it is: "A group of rabid, malicious cosmopolites, people without kith or kin, hucksters and unscrupulous smooth operators in theater criticism . . ."

I strain my fourth-grader intellect to understand what the problem is with these people.

"Grown up on the rotten yeast of bourgeois cosmopolitanism, decadence, and formalism . . ."

I skip over words I don't understand.

"Like hooligans, they have disparaged, maliciously slandered everything new, advanced, all the best in Soviet literature and theater."

I still don't see why Uncle Misha is so distressed until I come upon a list of last names. From conversations with my father, I've already learned to distinguish Jewish surnames. I read: "Yuzovsky, Gurvich, Borshchagovsky, Al'tman, Varshavsky . . ." And further on I read about them: "Kowtowing to the cosmopolites' culture . . . They poisoned with their stench . . . People of rootless nationality . . . People without kith or kin, having no motherland, they are unable to appreciate the triumph of the Russian people, and of the Russian nature." I strain to understand what nature has to do with it. What does "triumph of nature" mean? Triumph over what?

I scan the article, trying to get its meaning. I stumble on two more surnames. Poets Eduard Bagritsky and Iosif Utkin. I haven't heard anything about Utkin, but Bagritsky's name is familiar to me. He's ours, an Odessan poet. I've even read somewhere about the pathos of his revolutionary poems. What awful thing has he done? As a patriotic Odessan, I feel embarrassed for him. How could an Odessan make a fool of himself? The article condemns the bourgeois-nationalistic approach in his poem "A Ballad about Opanas." I haven't read it.

Next day, I head for the library at the Young Pioneers Palace to change my books. There, as always, I stay near the shelves, and in the hope of finding something interesting, I scan the books' spines. But today all I can think of is Bagritsky. I want to know what kind of things he wrote in his "Ballad about Opanas." What made the press jump on him? I check the shelves three times, but I can't find any of his works.

At that very moment, Maria Vasilievna says to me, "Draitser, are you in much of a hurry? Could you sit for me? I'll be back in half an hour. All right?"

I've been coming to this library for three years. The librarian, Maria Vasilievna, the same woman whom I once spared the sight of a dead mouse, occasionally asks me to take over her desk while she goes on errands. Today she has asked me again.

I agree to stay. I like sitting at her desk. It's an important spot, but I don't have much to do. People return books. All I have to do is to pull out the reader's record and strike the title out. Then the book is checked in.

Maria Vasilievna leaves. I sit down and look around to find something to read. I pull out the lowest drawer of her desk. Right in front of my eyes, on top of some other books, lies a little blue volume of Bagritsky's poems. A book of that condemned Bagritsky! The tops of my ears begin to burn, as if one of my classmates has sneaked up on me from behind and focused the sun on them through a magnifying glass. I try to cool them off with my hand.

I push the drawer back right away. My ears keep burning. I look around. In the reading room, behind the table, two girls, Olya and Polya, are sitting. They wear brown school uniforms complete with white lace collars and black aprons. I've seen them here before. There's nobody else. The girls are looking at embroidery patterns in the magazine *Rabotnitsa (Working Woman)*.

I wait a few minutes and, constantly looking in the direction of the door, my heart pounding, I pick up the little blue volume. I place it on my knees so that nobody can see it. I open the book hurriedly. On the title page, the ink still wet, the stamped word *WITHDRAWN* jumps to my eyes.

I can hear my heart beating. My face is flushed, and I rush through the table of contents. I quickly find what I want. Here it is! "A Ballad about Opanas." Looking up toward the door every second, I skim through all five and a half pages of the poem. I don't understand anything and, to concentrate, I catch my breath and try to calm down. I read it again. Now the plot of the poem somehow becomes clearer in my head. But the main question still remains—why did *Pravda* pan Bagritsky?

I am about to read it for the third time, when I hear footsteps behind the door. I throw the book back into the drawer. Just in time! With a push of my foot, I manage to slide the drawer shut.

"Well, how did you make out, Draitser? All right?" she says with some suspicion, evidently noticing my flushed face.

"All right," I make myself say. And I clear out of her chair.

Looking upward to the gray sky, I hurry home; the harbor is on my left. The sky all the way to the horizon is covered with smooth dark gray wool. I run down Primorsky Boulevard past Pushkin's statue, past the Crimean War memorial (a cannon from a British frigate), past City Hall with its two maiden figures symbolizing night and day, past the colonnade of the archaeological museum. The wind is cooling my cheeks. Now I can try to think about what I have read. So what is the matter? Why is Bagritsky guilty of bourgeois nationalism? There's not a single bourgeois in the poem. There's the civil war going on. Opanas is a rich Ukrainian peasant, a kulak. As expected, he's the enemy of the people. During a battle, he takes a red commissar prisoner. But Opanas has a small weakness—it's difficult for him to shoot a prisoner in the face. He gives the prisoner a chance to run away.

This way he will have a reason for shooting—to prevent the prisoner's escape. Why then does *Pravda* attack Bagritsky? Because, in his poem, the kulak is not an inhuman bloodsucker, as he should be, but shows a little human weakness? Or because Bagritsky's commissar is not the kind of hero a red commissar should be? But in the poem, he behaves heroically. He proudly announces that he's ready to meet his death face to face.

But isn't that how the true communists should behave? I've read many stories and poems about them. I've seen them in the movies. All of them are big-time heroes, brave and fearless.

Why then, suddenly, does Bagritsky's commissar evoke the anger of the chief party paper? I keep thinking about it. I walk briskly, pushing my feet forward with my entire strength. I almost run. High fever seizes me, and I don't know whether it's because of the physical strain or because I not only guess but already know that the answer has nothing to do with anything other than the commissar's surname. In the ballad the commissar's name is Kogan.

And Kogan can't be a hero.

Logic has nothing to do with it. I already understand that it's somehow tied in with everything I read a few years ago at the Young Pioneers Palace. What I read in Pushkin, in Gogol. What I've heard many times standing in lines, riding the streetcars, walking the streets of my city. There are no Jewish heroes, so there can't be any with a name like Kogan. There can't be good, fearless Kogans. Even if they are communists. From conversations with my father, I already know there were many Jewish commissars during the civil war. Uritsky, Volodarsky, Nakhimson. My fourth-grade reader *Native Speech*, contains World War II stories about brave Uzbeks, fearless Tatars, courageous Bashkirs, but none about the Jews.

The essence of the *Pravda* article already pushes itself into my brain. I try to will it away. No, it shouldn't be that way! I almost shout it in my head, though I feel with the rest of me—the unthinking part of my being—that, though it shouldn't, it is.

NINETEEN

Them!

AUGUST 1949: I'M TWELVE. I don't feel like going home. Empty, devastated, I roam the streets making wider and wider circles. At first I go around our block. I go along Deribas Street, turn onto Gavan Street, then onto Lanzheron Street. I try not to raise my head. From the newsstands on my right and my left, the headlines of *Pravda, Izvestiya, Literaturnaia gazeta, Sovetskaia Ukraina* (Soviet Ukraine), and *Chernomors'ka komuna* shout at me: COSMOPOLITANISM'S IDEOLOGY OF IMPERIALIST BOURGEOISIE. LOVE OUR MOTHERLAND, HATE COSMOPOLITES. ROOTLESS COSMOPOLITANISM SERVES WARMONGERS. Sometimes I dare to look up. But I wince every time I see a Jewish name in the headlines: ANTI-PATRIOT BROVMAN, WITHOUT KITH OR KIN. ELDFEINBEIN'S SLANDEROUS WRITINGS. COSMOPOLITE KHOLTSMAN'S SABOTAGE.

It seems to me that I'm that miserable Tatar soldier in Leo Tolstoy's famous story "After the Ball," which we read in class. Caught in an attempt to run away from the backbreaking tsarist military service, he was made to run a gauntlet of steel spikes: BRING COSMOPOLITES-RENEGADES TO BOOK; CRUSH UNSCRUPULOUS ANTI-PATRIOTS.

Completing the circle, I reach our building at 18 Deribas Street, a typical Odessa building with a crumbling plaster facade, stray cats in the courtyard, and clusters of wild grapevines reaching above the first-floor windows.

I step under the arch but stop short at the last minute. Instead of going into the courtyard, I continue my walk till I reach the City Garden. I slowly cross it and, through a back alley, come to Preobrazhensky Street, where the streetcars run. I turn left and drag myself along beside the tracks, past the park on Sobor Square, until I get to Tiraspol Square. There, its brakes grinding and yellow-blue sparks crackling on the contact loop, a streetcar slowly circles the square for its return trip. I turn left onto Zhukovsky Street and move down toward Pushkin Street. Once I get under its plane trees, I head for Primorsky Boulevard so that I can set out again on the street leading to my home.

My steps make no sound. My head is empty, and my heart is smarting from humiliation and the premonition of trouble. I keep moving away from home and then going toward it. I have no place to go. There's no hope of escape. No matter where I run, I am branded. "Without kin," "Unscrupulous," "Rootless."

Wind sweeps along the sidewalk. Here and there, it twists the dry acacia leaves. The wind is like my fate: at one intersection, it pushes me from behind, at another it beats on my face. I walk and walk with no particular thought; oppressed by the loneliness of youth, not knowing my own future, I walk block after block, my vision unfocused, blurred, unable to take in the vastness of life.

What makes the situation even more ominous is that, though I have no doubt whom they have in mind, everyone around me stubbornly avoids the word *Jew*. In lines at the stores, people refer instead to "*them*" and "*that ethnicity.*" Newspapers also use substitutes of all kinds: "persons of nonnative ethnicity," "antipatriots," "Israeli stooges," "Zionists," "the fifth column," "bourgeois nationalists." And now they put new terms into circulation: "cosmopolites without kith or kin" and "those who hide under pseudonyms." That is, these aren't human beings but werewolves.

I'm not familiar with the word *pseudonym* yet. Under the influence of Lope de Vega's plays, staged at the Ivanov theater on Greek Street, I imagine a pseudonym as a lacy mantilla that, together with a large fan, the duenna uses to protect her young Donna from indecent gazes when she accompanies her to a secret rendezvous. One day, *Pravda* reports that the literary critic Kholodov is, in fact, none other than a certain Meerovich. "Kholodov" is his pseudonym, his mantilla. The literary critic Yakovlev is, in truth, Kholtsman. Another critic, Melnikov, is Melman, and Yasny is Finkelstein.

The papers place the true (that is, the Jewish) surnames of these literary critics in parentheses. They seem to me treacherous punctuation marks. A *Jew* means the one who's in parentheses. When Mama prepares ingredients for baking cakes and strudels, she makes me crack walnuts. Sometimes, the shells turn out to have nothing but a cobweb inside, rotten. These newspaper parentheses remind me of those defective shells. If they're placed around someone's surname, it implies that the person's rotten.

Since everyone avoids using the word *Jew*, the feeling that I belong to a strange, ill-defined ethnicity takes root in me and lasts for a long time. A gray shadow, a ghost, this ethnicity is there, and, at the very same time, it's also nonexistent. Just like when children play forfeits, when you must avoid saying "yes" or "no" or wearing black or white. It seems as though it's indecent to say the name out loud. A people like a curse. A people like a shameful nickname.

"*Your* people are used to a comfortable life!" the young female voice rings in my head. Her words smashed my fantasies of love and spelled the end of my childhood.

The fall of 1952. It rains more than usual. The situation on the home front is oppressive. From late August, rumors crawl all over the city—strange, absurd, troubling, and wild. Somewhere far away in the East, a war is raging in Korea. The newspapers are confident in the victory of the heroic North over the cowardly South, which is supported by the vile American militarists.

On my way back from a visit to my second cousin Yan's house, I'm sitting in a streetcar. On the bench next to me is an aged man. Gray whiskers, a prominent nose, and full lips. He reminds me a bit of my uncle Abram, only this man is a little shorter. On the front of his jacket—apparently once part of his formal suit, but now old, with soiled cuffs—is a bar of war veteran ribbons. From time to time, he fences himself off from me with his palm and bursts into a dry hacking cough. He holds on to the knob of a stick propped between his knees. His leg, stiff at the knee, is awkwardly turned out, and his foot sticks into the aisle. One leg of his pants is a bit pulled up. His sock, which hangs low on his ankle, reveals the head of a screw on a flat washer. A wooden prosthesis gleams under it.

The driver announces the stop on Mechnikov Street. A scarf around her neck, a trim twenty-year-old damsel appears in the aisle. A light braid wrapped around her head, her blue eyes and pretzel hairdo make my heart stop. I'm soon to be fifteen. Just being near a beautiful girl makes me blush. I don't dare look at her face. The only thing I venture to do is glance out of the corner of my eye at the binding on the thick volume under her arm. My gaze slips despicably onto her full breasts. I blush even more.

The spine of her book reads: *The History of Antique Art.* A humanities student! Well, of course! The university building is located right here, on Mechnikov Street. The girl is older than I am by at least five years. But, when it comes to love fantasies, age difference is no barrier. I dream of a career in humanities too, and my spirits immediately lift. It looks as if the beauty and I share the same interests.

As I'm busy imagining my professional as well as my personal future with her, the girl moves down the aisle past us and trips over the old man's outstretched leg.

"Oh!" she says, grabbing onto the railing. The art book falls out from under her arm.

"Pardon me," says the man. He bites his lip, trying to pull his offending foot under the seat.

But the girl shouts, "Look how he's sprawled himself out! *Your* people are used to a comfortable life!"

Silence fills the streetcar. You can hear only the chirping of the brakes as the streetcar turns. Some passengers stare out the window. Others gloat. Still others, barely turning their heads away, giggle.

My neighbor's face grows pale. Then blood rushes back to his cheeks. He squeezes the knob of his cane so hard that the skin around his knuckles whitens. His head nodding, he looks downward.

"Look what I've lived to see!" he whispers. "That's what you deserve, you old fool! That's what you deserve." I feel as though I've been doused with freezing water. My secret romantic fantasies have evaporated as if they never existed. The man next to me was insulted, not me. But I feel as though it's been done to me as well. The girl didn't clarify what ethnicity she was referring to. But I already know what ethnicity is not mentioned, only implied.

(It seemed that the very word *Jew* was repulsive to the authorities. How else could I explain its total disappearance from the public domain for such a long time? A few years later, in the cool reading room of the city's Gorky Library, looking over an old album of Rembrandt's paintings, I winced in surprise. The captions under the reproductions read: *Portrait of an Elderly Jew, The Head of a Jew, Portrait of an 80-Year-Old Jew.*

On the shelf next to that album, I found a newly published catalog of all the exhibits at the Hermitage Museum, in Leningrad, including reproductions of Rembrandt paintings already familiar to me. I leafed through it—and grew cold in the pit of my stomach. Under the very same pictures, the captions had been altered: *Portrait of an Old Man, Sketch of a Man's Head, Portrait of an Old Man in Red.* Look what had happened! There were Jews in Rembrandt's work, and now they were gone.

I rushed to the old album. I closely examined it and discovered that it was published twenty years before, in the 1930s. This album was part of that old, prewar time, a time whose disappearance my parents regretted not once.)

Sometimes, on Sundays, Papa reclines on the sofa, and we have a father-to-son talk. One day, apparently afraid to disturb my immature soul by touching on a delicate subject for which I'm not prepared (the way parents talk to adolescents about sex), Papa asks me with caution, "Have you read about Hershele Ostropoler already?"

(Now, half a century later, I understand his caution. In the climate of the time, how else could he speak to a Young Communist Leaguer about anything related to Jewish culture? In the same way that it's impossible for me to imagine a time when papers and journals in Yiddish were published in our country, Papa couldn't get used to the fact that, in the postwar era, such a thing was out of question. Though a down-to-earth working man, he was a secret dreamer. He accepted reality with an aching heart. He kept hoping that his dream was nearby—that it just hadn't been realized yet.)

"What Ostropoler?" I'm frowning, thinking that Papa is talking about another celebrated revolutionary he's proud of just because he's Jewish.

"Hershele Ostropoler! You haven't read stories about this remarkable man? He was terribly poor but survived by his wits." And Papa goes on to tell me how once this man tricked a greedy rich man.

This and other stories about Ostropoler are livelier and funnier than the Russian fairy tales about Ivan the Fool. In my youth, I can't understand for the life of me what there is to admire about Ivan. I am from a hard-working family. How can I care for that Ivan, a lazy bum who prospers only thanks to some pike's magic powers! Yet I have a hard time considering the very legitimacy of Jewish folklore. I don't let it even enter my mind that books of Jewish fairy tales have as much right to stand on the bookstore shelves as do not only Russian fairy tales but also Ukrainian, Moldavian, or Chuvashian.

One day, at my friend Zhenya's home, while he's running some errand, I approach one of his bookcases, one filled with the dark blue volumes of the newly released *Great Soviet Encyclopedia*. I pull out the *J* volume, looking for the entry on "Jewish literature." Of course Zhenya knows my ethnicity. My Jewishness has no effect on our friendship whatsoever. But still, leafing through the book, I listen for footsteps in the hallway, my heart racing, my ears buzzing. The secret curse of my belonging to Jewry isn't lessened by being in the house of a friend to whom it makes no difference whether I'm Jewish or not.

The *Great Soviet Encyclopedia* contains plenty of articles on Tatar, Georgian, and Uzbek literature, as well as the literature of many other ethnic groups who live in the USSR. But there's not a word on Jewish literature. Does this mean that I belong to an illiterate people? Who don't write books because no one could read them? That makes no sense: I've never met a single illiterate Jew, except for toddlers.

Tormented with this mystery of the adult world, willy-nilly I'm forced to turn to that source of knowledge that normally an adolescent cares not a whit about—I ask my father: "Why aren't Jews a nation?"

For a moment, Papa marvels at my uncharacteristically bringing up a hot topic myself. Then he says, "Stalin said that for a people to be considered a nation, it has to have three things." As always, my father raises his finger to the ceiling in a passionate gesture: "The would-be nation must have commonality of language, commonality of culture, and a territory with an outlet to the sea. The Jews don't have an outlet to the sea. This is why Jews are not a nation!"

I try not to get caught up in the tone of my father's voice when he says this. Mikhail Tsarev, Alexei Gribov, Igor Ilyinsky, and other superstars of Soviet theater and cinema would envy the complexity of his vocal orchestration when he speaks about our leaders. The tone of his voice becomes an intricate mixture of solemnity, awe, and mockery. He leaves it up to you how you wish to interpret his words.

(To this day, I don't understand why my father made up the part about the outlet to the sea. There's not a hint of it in Stalin's writings.) Now, in the 1950s, I'm at a loss. I pore over geographical maps. How could Comrade Stalin say such a thing? It's true that the Jewish Autonomous Oblast of Birobidzhan does not have an outlet to the sea. But, after all, Mongolia doesn't have one either. Yet, there's the Mongolian nation. And here, in Odessa, where many Jews live, the sea splashes at our shores.

That night I toss and turn for a long time. I have a hard time falling asleep.

And when this finally happens, I dream that Odessa is once again as she was in the nineteenth century, a *porto franco,* as my father once told me with delight. I will find out much later in my life that it meant only that the Odessan port was exempt from customs regulations. But every time Papa speaks of *porto franco* with such admiration, I take it that the whole city was a free and independent territory. And now, in my dream, the waves crashing against the coastal rocks produce the celebratory gun volley, a salute to a nation that has an outlet to the sea.

At the end of the 1950s, after the death of Stalin, on Pushkin Street, on the stage that belonged to the Odessa Philharmonic Society, some singers and storytellers, like Papa's friend Marshak, the remnants of Jewish theaters disbanded by the authorities after the war, perform from time to time. Nekhama Lifshits, Sidi Tal, Anna Guzik. My mother and father, when they return from the concert, become young again and excited. Mama has hardly removed her coat when she begins pacing around the room and throwing up her hands: "Ah, Anna Guzik! What a singer! What a voice!"

"Yes!" confirms my father, and in a sign of awe, he sticks out his lower lip.

"So many people were there!" my mother grabs her head with both hands. "A million!"

I listen condescendingly. Anna Guzik? I bet she's some amateur performer. A far cry from singers whose concerts are broadcast over the radio from Moscow. I especially love arias from the operas by Leonkavallo, Verdi, and Tchaikovsky. And here she is raving about some primitive ditties sung by some obscure singers. No match for the Bolshoi Theater stars—Obukhova, Kozlovsky, or Lemeshev. I've never heard any of these Guziks or Sidi Tals even mentioned on the radio. And I'm grateful that my parents don't take me along to these concerts. I'm already a college student and a Young Communist Leaguer. An interest in the culture of a politically unreliable ethnicity might complicate my life.

But my mother can't come to terms with her own son's far distance from what touches her heart. She is unable to keep her impressions of the concert to herself. As a way of justifying her desire to talk about the concert, she informs me that there were many goyim, Gentiles, at the concert: "They applauded so hard! So hard!"

For her, the presence of goyim at a Jewish singer's concert is the ultimate compliment. If even *they* applauded, then Anna Guzik must be worth something, that is, a great deal. "When Guzik sang one of her songs," my mother says, "the whole audience wept." And, in complete oblivion, Mama begins singing in Russian. She's still there, in the auditorium packed to capacity with people dying to hear a Jewish song:

> Friends, buy these cigarettes!
> Come closer, infantrymen and sailors,
> Come over and have pity on me.
> Warm me up, a poor orphan.
> Look at my feet, they're bare.

Overwhelmed with her feelings, Mama has to catch her breath. About to burst into tears, she finishes the song in haste.

"Sonya, Sonya!" my father admonishes her. "Please stop. Enough! Here she's taking up singing. You don't have a good voice."

It's not at all that he wants to upset Mama. He just has a hard time expressing his own feelings openly; he gets embarrassed. It's clear that the concert has affected him as well. Mama gets quiet. She looks hopelessly at me. Then she wipes her tears furtively. Apparently she is also embarrassed a bit by her own emotions. No matter how much time has passed, her heart's wound from the war still hasn't stopped bleeding.

"They begged her to sing the song in Yiddish," she tells me. "They begged her so much! But she . . ." Mama tightens her lips and, in pantomime, copies the moves that accompanied the singer's refusal; she nods apologetically, sighs, presses her palm to her heart, and bows. The singer's gestures mean she would have been very happy to grant the audience's request, but she cannot.

"And so, she didn't sing it," Mama says bitterly, and as she adds in an undertone, looking askance at me, "I don't blame her. *Oy vos far a melukhe mir khobn!* Some authorities we have!"

Then, over her shoulder she takes a quick look back at the windows and sings another stanza from the same song, only this time in Yiddish. It seems that the words of the song are coming from the very depth of her heart:

> *Koyft zhe, oh koyft zhe papirosn,*
> Buy, oh buy (my) cigarettes,
> *Mit blut und trern fargosn,*
> Wet from blood and tears,
> *Koyft zhe bilik benemones,*

Buy really cheaply,
Yidn, hot oyf mir rakhmones,
Jews, take pity on me,
Ikh bin a yosem fun der getto.
I'm an orphan from the ghetto.

"Ghetto, do you understand 'ghetto'?" Mama asks, blotting her tears away. "Do you know what a ghetto is?" She looks into my eyes. "During the war, they rounded up all the Jews, put them there, and murdered all of them, one by one."

Mama hopelessly waves her hand at me. She's bitter that I don't respond. I've heard the word *ghetto* at home before. But for me, the song is part of the past that my parents belong to. Already I don't remember the war very much. I was too small then, a baby. (As happens to many people, early childhood impressions will come to me in my mature years.)

During this recital, I notice that, in the Yiddish version, the orphan boy addresses the Jews *(yidn)*. But in the Russian translation of the song, *yidn* is replaced by the word *friends*. I already know that this is not an accident. That like every bit of text designed for publication, the authorities have censored the song to avoid "subversive ideological activity." By forbidding this song to be sung in Yiddish and by eliminating any mention of Jews in it, they have transformed a Jewish song about a Jewish orphan into a Russian song about a war orphan in general. Well, what of it? Wasn't the Great Patriotic War the misfortune of *all* people, a disaster for everyone? After all, did the bombs choose their victims according to ethnicity?

(When Mama sang the song, I still didn't know much about either the Holocaust in general or what the Nazi death squads, the Einsatz commandos, had done on Soviet territory in particular. Through the sobbing and lamentations of my grandma Sarah, I knew about my relatives murdered and tortured to death. When the war broke out, she and her fifteen-year-old son Samuil ran along the highways from Minsk to the East for weeks. In the end, they reached the Tatar Republic. Besides mourning her husband, my grandfather Uri, who went missing during the first days of the war (the details of his death became known much later), my grandma cried her eyes out recalling her oldest daughter, Judith, her husband, Yakov, and their three sons, Grandma Sarah's grandsons—sixteen-year-old Misha and the two-year-old twins Yakov and Yefim. She grieved for her small granddaughters, Dinah and Raya, the children of her daughters Asya and Tanya. Because the Nazis captured Minsk swiftly, not all of Grandma's family could escape in time. All the Jews who were trapped in the city were swept into "the Pit," as people nicknamed the ghetto in Minsk; few got out of it alive.

My mother also had her share of relatives who were victims of German atrocities—her father, my grandfather Wolf Bendersky, many of her male and female cousins. But she was able to hold herself together and suppress her tears. Grandma could not hold back her tears no matter how hard she tried to or how often she bit her lips. She tried to weep furtively. She turned away from me, covered her face with a handkerchief, and mumbled some prayer. Perhaps, from my early childhood, her suppressed sobbing contributed to my perception that, if you're a Jew, you have no right even to grieve openly for your kin. Once and for all, I came to accept as an axiom that to be persecuted is part of my gene pool, part of what it truly means to be Jewish.)

First as a Young Pioneer, then as a Young Communist Leaguer, I shy away from anything that identifies me as a Jew. I treat these family stories as isolated incidents; there's no need to generalize. Neither Soviet papers nor the radio of the time reports much about the Holocaust. In their attacks against the British and American warmongers, they do mention Hitler's death camps. But they always refer to the prisoners of those camps in no other way than as "anti-Fascists"—that is, implying with that term that those people, weapons in their hands, fought the Nazi regime. There is not a single word acknowledging that the Jews constituted the overwhelming share of Nazi victims among the civil population and that the only crime of the women, children, and elderly who perished was that they belonged to the wrong ethnicity. Released in 1949, *Padenie Berlina (The Battle of Berlin),* Stalin's feature film devoted to the events of the Great Patriotic War, which the Soviet propaganda machine dubbed the war with Hitler, shows Soviet troops freeing prisoners of a Nazi death camp. Among them are people of many nationalities: Russians, Ukrainians, Czechs, Serbians, Frenchmen, Americans. But not even one prisoner with a star of David.

The episode takes place on German territory. The newspapers also invariably refer to the camp sites located outside the USSR—Majdanek, Dachau, Auschwitz, Buchenwald, and Ravensbrück. I don't even suspect that over one-third of the monstrous number—six million starved, gassed, and shot—were Jews murdered in occupied Soviet territories.

This blocking of the truth about the Holocaust from the consciousness of Soviet youth turned out to be effective. It fully came to my consciousness, as well as to that of many others of my generation, in 1961, over fifteen years after the end of World War II, with the publication of Evtushenko's poem "Babii Yar." It had the effect not only of an emotional explosion but of an informational one as well. But the hushing up of the Holocaust continued for years to come, at least to some degree. Only recently, while doing research for this book, did I fully learn the depth and scope of the disaster that befell the Soviet Jews during the war.

Forty years after my mother tried singing for me, with tears in her throat—"Friends, buy some cigarettes"—I, by then an American citizen, stepped into the half-lit hall of the Yad Vashem Museum in Jerusalem and shuddered at the sight of the only exhibition in that hall—the multitude of candles behind the glass of the display cases. These candles symbolize the souls of Jewish children murdered by the Nazis. That day, the simple truth of my life penetrated my consciousness in all its horrific simplicity: only the blind luck of destiny crossed me off the list of those children whose names—all one and a half million of them, one after the other, day after day, year after year—are uttered slowly by a sad voice in the stillness of the dimly lit museum hall.

TWENTY

No Kith, No Kin

PEOPLE "WITHOUT KITH OR KIN," I repeat the newspaper words. I still don't fully understand their dark purpose. I get only their literal, bitter sense. The earth hasn't cooled down yet from the flames of the war. The bones of the slain haven't crumbled into dust yet, haven't vanished without a trace. My kin, my tribe, are nearby, under the very same soil I am treading, I am rubbing against, with the soles of my shoes.

To be without your kin, without roots, means knowing neither your grandfather nor your great-grandfather. If I belong to the "rootless," I am not of the native population. But my roots should be somewhere. Or am I a human tumbleweed? In the autumn I have seen how large prickly balls are swept by the wind across the naked fields. These gray freaks jump up on lumps of dry soil, turning over so quickly as they move that I can hardly see their crushed little roots.

Somewhere here in the Odessa earth lies my maternal grandfather, Wolf Bendersky. I am dragging myself along, assuming, in my naïveté, that "rootless" is not an intentional insult, not a sign of being blacklisted, not a signal for hounding—sic 'im, halloo!—but a simple statement of fact. I'm left without my kin. My tribe's scattered. I am a tumbleweed.

I share a long martyrology with many others of my generation. Only now, a half century after reading the disturbing newspaper remarks, do I attempt to glue together the image of my never-seen grandfather. Who was Wolf Bendersky? Where did he come from? Where did he go? What happened to him in between?

Then, in 1949, I didn't want to know anything about my Jewish ancestors. In front of me, in the haze of time, my future fluttered, full of my anxious, aggravated awareness of being an untouchable. I would be deprived of my people's language, history, and culture.

Without memory—culture—it's not surprising that one is not a human being any more, but a trifle, a sifting. This feeling of inadequacy has stayed with me for many years. Ultimately, it often forced me to act against my own interests and common sense. It's painful to admit it, but life is not a movie—you cannot stop it, rewind it to the original reel, and run it again at its old speed.

There was one more reason why I, a boy, didn't ask questions then. To dig into one's memory is a luxury of leisure, of relaxation, of at least some inner comfort. None of us had it then. Although the war was over, the danger was still there—in every knock on the door, in every hostile passerby, in the reek of every drunkard who could say, "Hitler started his work but didn't finish it."

Besieged on all sides by leaden words—"without kith or kin," "stranger," "rootless"—one's head goes down between one's shoulders, as mine had done in July and August 1941, in the basement of our building, when the German bombs burst above our heads.

Now, half a century later, I see myself as an unhappy boy, upset by malicious newspaper articles, wandering around my hometown. What did I know then about my roots, my grandfather, except that he hadn't been around for a long time and he'd never be back? Now I turn to the one whose absence in my life I truly feel only now—my grandfather. As a soldier longs for an amputated leg lost on the battlefield, I yearn for this cut-off root of my family.

Memory about the dead is memory about the past. "May I be cursed if I forget you, Jerusalem." Postulates of faith reflect deep understanding of human psychology, the essence of human existence. When one's ties with the past are lost, one's present is lost, too. The prayer for the dead is so important. So is the memory of them. As an ancient Scythian vase can be re-created by fitting together the shards, can I re-create the image of my grandfather from the fragments of somebody else's memory?

No photos are left; they all burned in the flames of war, but those who remember him recall a wide and graying beard. I try to picture him as having the features of his children. His older ones, my uncle Mitya (Morris) and my aunt Clara, resembled each other, even when older, in their noble beauty. Thick black eyebrows, dark eyes under long lashes, a dimpled chin, and the elegant oval of their faces.

I know that my grandfather perished in Odessa, during the German (and Romanian) occupation. Before finding out how he died, I wanted to know how he lived. What kind of person was he? Mama used to say that he was deeply religious and a scholar. He read a thick book. She showed with her hands how incredibly thick the book was. At that time *War and Peace* was the only thick book I knew. Only later did I guess that Mama had the Old Testament in mind. (I myself would read a Bible for the first time in a library in Rome at the end of 1974, in the first week after my arrival from my native land, which I had left forever.)

My grandfather was a native of Uman', Ukraine. From there, like bees from shattered hives, Jewish families, stirred up by the revolution, the Russian civil war, pogroms, and postrevolutionary tensions, scattered all over the world. Those who had relatives in America headed for New York or Baltimore. In the early 1930s, when the Soviet borders had already been shut down for good, other relatives settled closer. With his newlywed wife, Riva, the near-sighted daughter of a floor polisher, my grandfather's son Morris—we called him Uncle Mitya—left for Minsk in the north. Grandfather's son Avner and daughters Clara and Soybel (my mother)—set out for the South, lured by the warm, seething Black Sea, by Odessa, and a promise of a better life. Eventually Grandfather followed. Only the oldest daughter, the beautiful Esther, stayed behind in Uman'. She stayed behind—because her granite tombstone was too heavy for her to lift.

In this new millennium, I see in my mind's eye how Uman' lives its life in the green Ukraine. Its straw roofs are faded from the sun. Or a shower washes the dust off the cobblestones of its narrow streets. Sometimes a little snow falls. The town is known for everything the Ukrainian soil is famous for—its tomatoes, its cucumbers, its watermelons, and its country fairs.

The bloody year 1919 did not spare Uman'. It rolled over the town with its iron harrow of pogroms. My mother told me how her older sister, Esther, perished. The liberator Petliura wanted an independent Ukraine. And his Cossacks, their crotches stirred up by the pommels of their saddles, craved young girls' bodies.

In my mind's eye I see how one of these Cossacks, grunting with the foretaste of pleasure, threw off his belt with its bloodstained saber and its wooden holster with his pistol and set out after Esther. She ran up a green hill above the Umanka River, gasping for air, fleeing in horror from the stinking breath that was catching up with her.

I see how, at the very moment when, laughing loudly in her ear, he grabbed the thick strands of her braid, her heart stopped, as a horse in full gallop would respond to spurs pierced into its sides. Instead of living, re-sisting flesh, arousing lust, a limp body fell to the rapist's feet. The girl's lips didn't have time to finish whispering the words of appeal to the only rescuer who could save her innocent soul: *Barukh attah Adonai Eloheinu melekh ha-olam* (Blessed are you, Lord, our God, King of the universe).

The Cossacks left. Day and night, for a whole year, cantors' voices echoed around Uman' at the funeral services for the victims. Their heads in their hands, the survivors wailed, "How could this happen here?"

But you, Grandfather, would know how true were the words of Ecclesi-astes: "The thing that hath been, it is that which shall be; and that which is done is that which shall be done: and there is no new thing under the sun."

You would know, Grandfather, it had happened before. And more than once.

More than once Jewish blood had been spilled on the earth of Uman'. One hundred and seventy years before Petliura, the Haydamaks, bands of Ukrainian rebels, had pounced on Uman'. Casually, without dismounting, they cut off many Jewish heads with their swords, pierced women's breasts with their spears, set fire to the town.

Twice more, in twenty-year intervals, as if letting a new generation grow up, the Haydamaks returned. In 1768, as new unrest stirred in the land, not only its own Jewish population but Jews from the surrounding towns as well looked for protection in Uman', a garrison town by then. To the same green banks of the Umanka River, drunk with fury, Haydamaks came tear-ing along, waving their swords. They slashed to death all the Jews, both the locals and the refugees. Garrison or no garrison, the troops did nothing to protect them.

Twenty more years passed, and again Haydamak horses' hooves broke up the dry soil. The Cossack chieftain of the town's garrison, Ivan Gonta, met the leader of the rebels, Maxim Zheleznyak (the Ironman), at the town gates and proposed that Christian lives be spared in exchange for those of the "yids." So the Haydamaks burst into the town and, with their three-tailed lashes, rounded up the Jews on the town's square. The fierce Ironman was a great warrior, but, as if in mockery of his nickname, he had a little failing—he was born a bit softhearted. The Ironman gave the miserable infidels a chance to save their own lives. He ordered the erection of a huge wooden cross in the middle of the square and announced that he wouldn't touch those who, of their own will, would come under the protection of the only true God—Jesus Christ, whom they had murdered. Those who, in their stupidity, refused to appreciate the Ironman's mercy would have their throats cut at once.

Once again, the Ironman would regret his soft heart. Far from rushing to save their lives in exchange for an alien faith, the Jews began to say farewell to one another and chant *"Shema Yisra'el"* (Hear O Israel).

Maxim became annoyed. Instead of giving his Haydamaks the rest they deserved after many battles on the fields of Ukraine, he had to order them to work. To finish off twenty thousand unarmed people was hard labor too. They finished them all, sparing neither the crying children, nor the women, nor the old men bowing their heads under the curved sabers made of Damascus steel, shining in the light of the sun and the moon. They barely managed to complete the job in three days and three nights. Jewish blood forever soaked into the trampled dirt of the square. On June 18 (the fifth day of Tammuz), later generations of Jews would pray and fast in memory of this Uman' massacre.

To bring peace to the martyrs' souls thirty years after the massacre, Rabbi Nakhman, the famous *tsadek* (saintly man) from Breslau (now Wroclaw, Poland), his last hour approaching, came to Uman' to die in their cemetery. To this day, every year, on the holy day of Rosh Hashanah, Hasidic Jews clothed in white robes arrive from all over the world to prostrate themselves on his grave, to read the prescribed Psalms and have their sins forgiven.

You knew, Grandfather, what had happened before. You knew it would happen again.

On August 1, 1941, some twenty years after Petliura's raid, to confirm the bloody prediction of Ecclesiastes, German First Panzer Group tanks crossed the shallow Umanka River. Their caterpillar tracks clanking, smashing the cobblestones, they rolled onto the town's square. A month and a half passed, and on September 15, the German troops gathered all Uman' Jews and chased them from the town toward the airport. There, on the square in front of its terminal, trenches resembling pits for potato storage had been dug. From their trucks, with German precision, the troops put sacks of lime on the ground at regular intervals. From the sky, black-uniformed soldiers of the Einsatzkommandos SS came down in their transport planes, like angels of death.

One after another, undressing and neatly folding and setting down their clothes, as if before bathing, Uman' Jews lined up in front of machine gun muzzles. First, the Germans made the mothers watch how they smashed the children's heads as if they were coconuts, using the handles of their Parabellums, their pistols. "[G]rabbing the little legs, they threw the . . . children's bodies into the graves where both murdered and still breathing people lay together. Only after they inflicted on mothers this most horrifying pain, would they shoot them, freeing them from unbearable torture," wrote one German army officer, Über-Lieutenant Bingel, to his superiors.*

I read these lines in his report now and, once again, I wince realizing the power of chance over our fate, our impotence to control it. If, just a few years earlier, my mama hadn't left Uman', had stayed in her native town, the metallic spike of the Parabellum handle would easily have entered my still-soft skull as well.

For three years of occupation by the Wehrmacht troops, seventeen thousand sons and daughters of Israel in Uman' lay down under the bullets, filling the neighboring ravines and gullies with their bodies. Why did they calmly undress while the rifles were loaded? Why did they accept their death without murmur? Did they really come to realize the justice of Ecclesiastes' words: "As he came forth of his mother's womb, naked shall he return to go as he came"?

But all this was yet to happen. In the early 1930s, life for my grandfather, as well as for other Jews in Uman', became difficult. The ties of time came undone. The young scattered in all directions, attracted to the lights of big cities. Why survive the revolution, and the civil war pogroms, and hunger, and still stay in the same places prescribed by the tsar, the Pale of Settlement? Buoyant Soviet songs rang out over the radio: "We have no barriers on the sea and on the earth!" The new generation openly laughed at their

*Itzchak Arad, ed., *Unichtozhenie evreev SSSR v gody nemetskoi okkupatsii (1941–1944): Sbornik dokumentov i materialov* (Destruction of Soviet Jews in the years of German occupation: A collection of documents and materials) (Jerusalem: National Institute of the Memory of Victims of Nazism and Heroes of Resistance, 1991), 99.

ancestors' faith. Synagogues were turned into warehouses for turnips, potatoes, and beets. For the young, the old Jews dressed for prayer seemed
like scarecrows at a country fair.

Moscow was far away, in the North. You would need a lot of winter clothes
up there. Grandfather Wolf's own people—his sister-in-law with her husband and their children—headed from Rashkov, another small Ukrainian
town, down to the South, and to the Russian Paris, the warm Odessa. They
settled there. They became acclimated. The city was large. It would have
enough space for everyone; Odessa was a place of promise. Its openness to
the sea raised hopes that the winds of freedom blew down her streets, the
winds of opportunity for another life, not quite clear, but limitless to the
imagination. At their children's urging, Grandfather Wolf and his wife,
Khava, left Uman'.

What happened next? I question those who might remember him. Sub-
consciously, I expect to meet in these stories not a living man but a holy
one. Remoteness in time makes a figure pristine.

But what I hear catches me off guard. It makes me uncomfortable. Arriving in Odessa, my grandfather couldn't keep up with the "mighty step"
of the times. He lagged behind. He brought his Uman' with him. It kept
beating behind the pocket of his new city jacket. With its customary
rhythm, it made its presence felt.

"Do I remember your grandfather!" Uncle Misha says, his eyes wide open,
as if I had asked him a very stupid question. "Do I remember him? Ha! I
met him before you were born, when I came from Minsk to Odessa for
your parents' wedding."

My uncle would have been no more than ten then.

"Maybe you won't be pleased to hear it," he says. He averts his eyes and
raises his hand as if inviting someone from above to witness his love for
truth. "But I'll tell you the way it was. No bull. Your grandfather was lazy."

I am taken aback. "What do you mean?"

"Lazybones was his first name, and lazybones was his patronymic. He
didn't lift a finger!"

"How did he survive?"

"Your grandmother Khava worked like a horse. And he read his books!
He wasn't that old yet. He was—wait, let me count—he would have been
about fifty-seven, fifty-eight, no more."

"He read books? What kind of books?"

"What kind, what kind? It's clear what kind. His Bible. The Talmud. Well,
it was time for him to realize! He was in Odessa, not in his bedraggled Uman'.

I understand that over there he was considered a *sheyner yid,* an exemplary Jew. *Eydeler,* noble. *Erlekher*—honest and religious. A *khokhem,* a wise man, a great Talmud scholar. Three times a day he was off to his synagogue. Meeting him on the streets, everyone bowed. Reb Bendersky, my respect to you. In the synagogue he occupied the place of honor, by the Eastern wall, close to the Torah gates. They gave him the most important passages to read aloud. They baked matzoth for him first. They invited him to their homes and seated him at the head of the table, and he was the first to be served. They considered it a great honor when he held their children before bris, circumcision. They were all crazy about learning."

Uncle Misha shakes his head in disbelief: "OK, I understand, in Uman' he had great *yikhes,* status in the community based on his religious pedigree. I accept that; for a Jew with big *yikhes,* working with his hands would have been demeaning. He had to devote all his life to the study of the Torah. Well, tell me, what good was such learning? You can't even fry a potato with it. It would just burn. In Uman', it was your grandmother who toiled like a slave. Of course, over there, to take care of a *khokhem* of a husband brought her everybody's honor and respect. But she shouldn't have been so backward. *Yikhes-shmikhes* was left in Uman'. You're in Odessa now! Reb Bendersky, wake up! Come to your senses. Here you're *gornisht*—a nobody, a small fry who thinks he's a big fish. You should work—not read your books. But no! The same old story. Your grandma Khava's running to rich Jews' houses, cooking for birthdays, circumcisions, bar mitzvahs, and weddings. And your grandpa Wolf—may God forgive me for such blasphemy, of course—the same old story! It's raining or snowing—three times a day he's off to Pushkin Street, to the city synagogue. Ah! It was unheard of. A woman supports a man! Shame and disgrace."

I recall my cousin Eva's story. Soon after the war, on Yom Kippur, she entered the synagogue with her mother, and one of the old men stood up and offered his place to her mother. She was surprised—an old man yielding his place to a young woman. He explained that he did it in memory of her father, Wolf, "He was a *guter yid.*" A good Jew, that is. Those who sat next to him nodded respectfully.

A *guter yid. Yikhes.* While growing up, I heard these words more than once. But I never bothered to figure out exactly what they meant. Only now as an adult do I recall Mama's stories about my great-grandfather Morris, Wolf Bendersky's father. A legend about his being "a holy Jew" spread among Uman' Christians. He worked as a manager for a Polish sugar-plant owner, a descendant of the famous magnate Count Potocki, the very same Potocki who, in the eighteenth century, rebuilt the town after the Haydamaks had burned it, built the Sofievka estate, and laid out a remarkable park. Morris Bendersky ran the business so skillfully that he not only got the owner out of the red but also multiplied his wealth. The sugar-plant owner couldn't have been happier with his manager and generously rewarded him.

What did my great-grandfather do with his money? Before the Sabbath began, the tailor made him a new suit from the best English wool. When the first stars broke out in the Uman' sky, it was time to sit around the table, to break *khale* (challah), the braided bread sanctified with a prayer, and to pour wine into delicate goblets from the family set, splashing it over the edges a bit, as the ritual requires. Great-grandfather Morris, dressed in his brand new suit, walked down the crooked little streets of the town. There he looked for a pauper. He didn't have to look for long. He stopped a passerby and, smiling, led him back to his house. He sat him at the family table and treated him to good food and wine. When it was time for the guest to leave, he removed his brand new jacket—and if they were needed, his pants as well—and gave them to the stranger.

There wasn't anything eccentric about this. Great-grandfather simply tried to be a good Jew, that is, the kind that the Torah prescribes. He did his mitzvah indiscriminately—it wasn't important whether the man he met was a poor Jew, a hapless Ukrainian peasant, or a drunken Polish cobbler down on his luck. In 1919, when Petliura's whooping Cossacks poured into the streets of Uman' and the time for spilling Jewish blood came again, the town's Christians came to the defense of Morris Bendersky. They talked the Cossacks into sparing his life, for he was holy.

From all this I conclude that Grandfather Wolf's status in the town was of the highest order. He had double *yikhes*—his own, earned by his learning, and that which he inherited, in memory of his father.

Grandfather Wolf's further life in Odessa is a blank. What was on his mind during that time? One of the few known things is that in 1935 he lost his wife, my grandmother. She had a bad heart. It's also known that he stayed in the city when the war broke out. He perished during the occupation. Why didn't he try to evacuate, as many others did? Did his children leave him behind for certain death? It couldn't be! Then what happened?

I asked these questions of my second cousin Maya. In the prewar years, she was in her early teens. She could have remembered. Sipping her tea, she spoke somewhat timidly, it seemed. She thought she might hurt my feelings. She shrugged, "You see, for a year or a year and a half before the war, he became intimate with a woman. They lived together. She was ill and she couldn't leave. When the war started, his family got a steamship ticket for him. But he refused it. He stayed with her, with that woman."

She tried to make the story as vague as possible. Some kind of woman. Wolf Bendersky stayed with her. That was the whole explanation.

As our relative, she thought he should have been a one-woman man, devoted till the end to the memory of his deceased wife. What romantic rubbish! How unfair. And is it love, this self-sacrifice? Or maybe, more likely, love is a voluntary self-denial in favor of the new woman in his life—"live, love, be my light"?

Maya didn't know what I've learned only now. Because my grandfather had been single for about five years, for him, unlike for widowers of other faiths or for nonbelievers, it wasn't a question of choice whether to remarry or not. A religious Jew has to be married. The Torah instructs him that a Jew without a wife is only partly a Jew. Believing that his children, oblivious to Jewish traditions, disapproved, most likely he did marry that woman in a private ceremony, which explains my cousin's ignorance of it.

This woman with whom he spent the rest of his life is nameless for me. I know nothing about her. What was she—young or old, beautiful or ugly? Neither is very important. I know only one thing—for the sake of her, he consciously accepted death. Staying in Odessa, my grandfather knew what was in store for him. For years, till the secret Molotov-Ribbentrop Pact was signed in August 1939, Soviet antifascist propaganda had been in full swing. In the film *Professor Mamlok,* the Jewish protagonist's students beat him up and throw him out on the street. Other Soviet antifascist films also circulated—*Sem'ia Oppengeim (The Oppenheim Family), Bolotnye soldaty (The Swamp Soldiers; Concentration Camp).* The newspapers had already reported Kristal Nacht. With Hitler's invasion of Poland, Polish Jewish refugees who made it to Odessa brought with them horror stories about deportations and ghettos. The Molotov-Ribbentrop Pact could deceive only orthodox Communists—internationalists hooked on the idea of permanent world revolution. For them, Hitler's enemies at the time—France and England— were first of all bulwarks of working-class oppression.

The fact remains that Grandfather Wolf stayed in Odessa. He refused to leave behind a sick woman with whom he'd lived little more than a year. I feel that by forsaking his own life for the sake of another person, my grandfather made a sacrifice that, on the scales of fate, perhaps—no, for sure!— outweighs everything else. Grandfather stayed with the woman, stayed till the end of his days, to the last nail in his coffin, as the expression goes. It wasn't question of coffins, then. To know in which common grave your loved ones would lie was sheer luck.

Two versions of how Grandfather perished have come down to me—one more horrifying than the other. My cousin Eva heard that the Germans tortured our grandfather the same way that they tortured the captured Red Army general Karbyshev. Soviet newspapers often described the general's suffering. The fascists learned that he couldn't tolerate the cold. They took him out in severe frost, tied him to a tree, and poured cold water over him till he became one giant icicle.

No matter how honorable such a death would have been for my grandfather—he would be likened, at least in suffering, to the famed Russian general—I doubt this version. It's difficult to believe that the Nazis would have devoted so much attention to a pious, totally civilian old Jew. Why bother with so much to kill one "lousy yid"? From all that I know about how they finished off the Jews in Odessa, one bullet would have been enough. However, they rarely had to spend their ammunition on such a trifling business. People perished from hunger, from cold, from typhus, diarrhea, gangrene, pneumonia. With one strike of a rifle butt, the Germans finished off those who fell and couldn't get up.

Then there is Mama's story about how Grandfather Wolf met his last hour. It happened somewhere along the road to Liustdorf, the German colony near Odessa. The Romanian guards herded him, along with sixteen thousand other Jews, into an artillery warehouse and set it on fire. The machine gunners surrounded it and waited till the last wall collapsed, so that none of the women, children, and old men would be able to slip out.*

There are, however, many other possibilities. I read an eyewitness account of the fate of Odessa Jews by one David Starodinskii.† As a youth, he went through all the circles of this hell and by not one, but several, miracles managed to stay alive. Thanks to him, I can see clearly how my grandfather might have perished. Most likely, his fate was the fate of most Odessan Jews. Before the troops, mostly Romanian, took them to the death camp, they were rounded up in a ghetto created in Slobodka, on the city's outskirts. The death camp, one of several in the region, was organized northeast of the city, near the banks of the Southern Bug River, in the village of Domanevka.

In January 1942, the Nazis first took the Jews by train to Berezovka sta-

*Ibid., 154–55.
†D[avid] Starodinskii, *Odesskoe getto* (Odessa ghetto) (Odessa, 1991)

tion, forty miles away from Domanevka. From the station, they forced the prisoners to walk all the way to the camp. It was the harshest winter in the whole history of the region. When they inhaled, their nostrils froze shut. They were up to their knees in snow. A blizzard howled. According to survivor accounts, the German soldiers on the scene wanted to send some pictures to their wives and children, but they had trouble focusing their Leica cameras; they were roaring with laughter at the old men, women, and children crawling helplessly over snowdrifts, falling topsy-turvy. Who needs a circus?

Grandfather Wolf could have died on that road just from cold and exhaustion. After this point, the column of prisoners had to cross an area that had suddenly been flooded when a dam was blown up. The prisoners stopped, shifting their feet while avoiding the water, but the convoy forced them ahead. Grandfather could have collapsed after reaching Domanevka. Not even aiming at him, a Romanian guard could have finished him off. To kill a "Jude" with one shot was to do him a favor—to spare him the torments of slow death in the bone-chilling winds of the icy steppe. The guard wouldn't have bothered aiming, because he would have been busy with more urgent business. Looking for warmth that night and for pleasures of the flesh, his eyes would have searched the crowd to find a girl who hadn't reached the breaking point yet. But the women—wasted, haggard, gaunt— would only have enraged him. It was a degenerate race, no question about it. Skin and bones. Of the three thousand taken from Odessa only a few reached Domanevka. It's hard to imagine that Grandfather Wolf, my vanished root, was one of them.

As Starodinskii tells us, the road to the death camp was strewn with photos of the captives' loved ones, thrown away in the hope that someday someone would learn about the prisoners' fate. At that time, few could afford a camera. Soviet people took pictures for the most important document— the passport, as well as at weddings and other special occasions. It's possible that my grandfather had my first picture. In it, I'm six months old; I lie naked on a bearskin, sticking my plump leg up. I see how this picture, blown by the wind over the thin icy crust of the steppe, is rolling away from the shoulder of the last road along which, overcoming pain in his legs and whispering *Shema Yisra'el,* my grandfather Wolf walked.

TWENTY-ONE

Grandpa Uri

I DON'T HAVE TO GUESS how Uri, my paternal grandfather, left this world. Eyewitnesses reported: SS guards stabbed him to death with their bayonets. Four of them were needed to do the job. He was a sturdy man.

It's a pity I don't recall his face. I was only two years old when he visited us in Odessa. After that, World War II consumed all the material things related to his life. Not even a photo of him is left. Only separate episodes of his life have been saved in the memory of his children. Well, it isn't much. But for many people, even that much hasn't survived. It's as if the wind had blown into one window, picked up a sheet of paper from the floor, and sucked it out the other window. A life passed as if it had never happened. Memory—that's the most anyone can hope to leave behind. Memory in future generations is the afterlife. That's where he still lives.

"What did he look like?" I ask his daughter, my Aunt Asya (Esther), when she was in her eighties, living out her days in Boca Raton, Florida.

"Like a count! Handsome. With a proud look," she says, her eyes shining.

Judging by her stories, Grandfather Uri didn't resemble those Jews I grew up with in Odessa. He wasn't short, didn't pull his head into his shoulders. Over six feet tall. Wide-shouldered. Fair curly hair, which, in the style of the time he parted in the middle. A long mustache, its ends twirled dashingly. In one move, he could grab a cavalry horse across its mane and wrestle it to the ground. In the army, he served as a dragoon in a privileged tsarist platoon.

Many years later, after his discharge, Grandfather would show his youngest son his military bearing. "Well, little Moulya," standing up straight to his full height, he would bark, "repeat after me! Atten-tion! Keep your eye on your officer! 'Who are you, lads?' 'We're the Seventh-Dragoon-Novorossiisk-His-Imperial-Highness-Grand-Duke-Nikolai-Nikolaevich's-Platoon.' 'At ease!'"

Hot-tempered, Grandfather couldn't stand an insult—a response that was a luxury for a Jew, especially when serving in the tsarist army. One Sunday, absent without leave (he had sneaked out from the barracks to the city dance hall), he returned late at night. He was straightening his back after pulling off a spurred boot when the field sergeant appeared in the barracks doorway. "Hey you, kike's mug!" he screamed. "Where the hell have you been? Get up! Why are you lounging as if you were at your uncle Isaac's birthday party? Well, you motherf—."

One boot off, Grandfather slowly rose to all his six feet. With a full sweep of his arm, holding his huge size 15 boot, he struck the field sergeant's face. Others pulled Grandfather away from the field sergeant with great difficulty. They put him in a guardroom first. Then, on the field sergeant's charges, they court-martialed him. They gave him three years of disciplinary service—the army equivalent of hard labor. Grandfather served two full years of this sentence. Then, on the birth of Tsarevich Alexei—the very same royal hemophiliac for whose sake the half-mad monk named Rasputin was brought to the high court—they knocked a year off my grandfather's sentence.

Discharged from the army, he took to his family trade—housepainting and wallpaper hanging. Among workmen, weddings happened quickly. Grandfather liked drinking. He never became gloomy; on the contrary, after a shot of vodka, he felt an irresistible lust for life. He liked all that was good in life, couldn't stand everyday dreariness. One day, he found himself married to little Sura-Rivka, a young lady with mischievous eyes. She worked at home, making cigarettes.

First he was bewildered. How could such an event have occurred unnoticed? Then he recalled some especially boisterous revelry that had taken place the week before and reconciled himself right away to being a married man. Besides, his bride wasn't a total stranger. They had met at the town dance hall. Picking her up in a hansom cab, Grandfather had appeared on her doorstep in his full dragoon's grandeur: his mustache waxed, he wore a luxurious knee-length overcoat trimmed with lambskin. His tall hat was also of lambskin.

Sura-Rivka's head hardly reached her suitor's chest.

"Why did you marry such a shorty?" his daughter Esther would ask him when she was in her teens.

"Well, she could dance," he would respond, winking.

On learning that he was married, Grandfather didn't get upset about losing his freedom; he began reaping the sweetest fruits of matrimony. He did it with such energy and joy that soon enough, one after another, two noisy children appeared on this earth, and the third one was awaiting her turn.

During the long Byelorussian winters, there wasn't much painting or papering work. Grandfather was forced to make ends meet by bookbinding. It was a dreary business—sitting all day long in his little house on the outskirts of Minsk and keeping busy with his hands alone. Without a shot of vodka, one could just fade away. Sura-Rivka began doing what her mother and grandmother had done for as long she remembered—nagging a husband. He looked down at her, smiled at his own thoughts, and remained calm. A big chunk of life was still left to live. Why spoil it? Why get upset? He took unhappiness as nothing but a shortening of life, as death on an installment plan. He didn't fight back. He just chuckled to himself over her shortsightedness. In vodka, she saw nothing but a threat to the family budget. If she smashed his bottle with a hammer in anger, Grandfather calmly pulled on his boots and went to buy another one.

One winter day, when his wife's tirades were especially fierce, Grandfather lay on the couch, stretched his long legs, and announced that he was sick. His wife jumped up and down around him, accusing him of feigning. No illness, she said, would get him down. But Grandfather insisted on having his own way. He said that he was truly sick. His doctor had advised that he adjust his alcohol consumption once and for all. And that this was necessary to do right away. Groaning, as if overcoming his infirmity, Grandfather got up from his bed. Dumbfounded, Grandmother watched his every move with disbelief.

With an expression of unbearable suffering on his face, Grandfather bent over and shuffled out of the house. Half an hour later, he returned in somewhat better spirits, under his arm a half gallon of some transparent liquid. Grandmother was about to assail him again, when Grandfather suddenly said, "I've got my medicine. It should be enough for a long while. It's my doctor's prescription."

Not trusting her eyes, his wife read the prescription label attached to the bottle again: "Uri Draitser: Take one shot three times a day till the day of your demise. Shake before use. Refill as needed. Keep in a cool place."

Grandma didn't let the joke go. She began cursing her good-for-nothing husband up and down again. But gradually she calmed down. She accepted her fate.

Meanwhile, Grandfather turned melancholy. Day after day, he'd look at the skies in the evenings, at the carmine of the sunset. He even began drinking less.

In the twilight of a windy and snowy March day in 1910, he threw on his short sheepskin coat and went out to the street to close their window shutters from the outside. It was their evening routine. He pushed the long bolt through the frame and yelled to his wife to fasten the bolt end with the latch.

"Got it?" he barked from the outside.

"Got it," his wife responded and headed for the stove to heat up some water for their evening tea.

But Grandfather didn't come back from the street. The water began to boil, and he was still missing. Grandmother looked out the door. There was no one around. What was he doing this late, the rascal? Again on his way to the tavern?

Cursing, she walked to the street corner. The wind swept the ground and swung the streetlight on the only lamppost on their block. A blizzard was coming. The icy walls of the little houses gleamed under the streetlights. Grandfather wasn't in the tavern. Nobody had seen him there that evening.

Grandma went home, bundling herself in her little coat. She remembered that her teapot was still on the stove. It might burn itself out.

Grandfather was absent all night. He didn't appear the next day either. Grandma went to his friends—the carpenter Iossel and the wheelwright Nyumka. She sobbed: What's with him? Did he go nuts? How could he leave her and the children on their own? How should they survive? His friends swore they hadn't seen him that day.

Grandma went to Vassily, the local police officer. He tried to calm her; her husband would turn up soon. He had no place to hide, anyway. Well, if it were summertime, then it would be possible—just in case—to drag the Svisloch River with a grappling iron, for catching corpses. But it was still cold, and the river was frozen. To poke holes in the ice in search of a body was most likely futile.

On the sixth day, a telegram came from Calais, France. Grandfather asked his wife to forgive him for leaving without saying good-bye. He thought it would be better that way.

What made Grandfather take off to a faraway land?

One of the fringe benefits of his wallpaper hanging trade was to learn about things he otherwise might have been ignorant of. One of them was the advice given to the tsar by Konstantin Pobedonostsev, his closest adviser and the chief procurator of the Holy Synod, on how to solve the Jewish problem in Russia. In his enlightened opinion, the solution was a matter of simple arithmetic: one-third of the Jews should be baptized, another third should starve to death, and the rest should emigrate.

Grandfather was well aware of one more option for himself, which the tsar's adviser hadn't mentioned in that conversation—to wait till the 1903–1905 wave of pogroms in the southern cities of Kishinev, Odessa, and Kiev, which left hundreds of Jews dead and injured, reached Minsk. And the trouble was in the making already. Less than four years before, a big pogrom had taken place much closer to home—in Bialostok. Eight hundred Jews fell victim to it. The local Russian army garrison helped in looting Jewish homes and shops. Even the State Duma, the Russian parliament, accused the tsar of inciting violence against the Jews. They found that the bloody Bialostok pogrom had been organized by local officials. The military commander praised his troops for "glorious actions" during the massacre. A few days after these events, another fifty Jews were murdered even closer to home, in a small Byelorussian town near Grodno. Should Uri Draitser, a family man, sit out and wait till the mob takes care of all his problems once and for all here, in Minsk?

Listening to the heated discussions in the Jewish homes he was fixing, Grandfather also learned about the efforts of the German philanthropist Baron Maurice de Hirsch to help Russian Jews to emigrate from the country. The baron did not decide on that course of action right away. First, he had a word with the Russian tsar. "Your Highness," the baron reportedly said to the Master of the Whole of Russia, as the tsar's full title had it, "I'm in no position to tell you how you should treat your Jews. You deny them rights to own any land? Fine. After all, it's your land. You forbid them to enter government service at any rank? You're the boss. They can't even live outside the Pale of Settlement, all those little towns in the western part of Byelorussia, Ukraine, and Crimea? I'm not telling you that such a policy is backward and unbecoming of a civilized nation. To think of it, your Jews should be thankful that you don't deport them to Siberia.

"But you have to draw a line somewhere. Among other civil rights, you deny them education. May I dare to say, Your Highness, that is the worst thing you can do to a Jew. Don't you know that we Jews are education freaks? You may give no bread to a Jew, but give him a book.

"Oh yes, you consider the ten percent quota that you set for Jewish students, even in schools within the Pale of Settlement, to be generous. And for schools outside it, the quota only half of that meager percentage. In your heart, you have even found it possible to allow the whopping three percent quota for those Jewish kids who dare to apply to the best Russian schools, those in St. Petersburg and Moscow. But, strictly between you and me, I'll tell what these quotas mean for my fellow Jews. They mean one thing only, which can be expressed by one word—*Gevald!* That is, help, whoever can! I'm telling you, these education quotas are a regular torture.

"But, luckily, there's a happy solution for getting your Jews out of this predicament. I'll make you an offer you can't refuse. Here are two million British pounds, and let the Jews set up schools in the Pale of Settlement so that they can teach their children to their little hearts' content. What do you say?"

The tsar said, "Phooey!" Which meant that, though he liked the money, he couldn't stand for some foreigner, never mind a Jew, to meddle in his domestic affairs. The Jews were Russia's sore spot, and he would take care of them the way he saw fit.

It was at that very moment that Baron Hirsch realized that nothing good awaited his fellow coreligionists in the land governed with such an attitude. He used the money to set up a fund that would help Russian Jews to seek better fortune outside Russia.

Many of them went to Europe; even more set their sights on America. But, as romantic at heart as he was, Grandfather got it into his head that he wanted to see a land even more exotic than America—the country of Argentina. Why Argentina? You wouldn't ask this question if you too, for days in a row, had heard your customer's teenage daughter playing records with those blood-boiling tunes—the tango. Grandfather couldn't wait to set his foot in that faraway country where, as all tango lyrics had it, people die for the sake of love alone.

Grandfather decided that first he would go to the new land on a reconnaissance mission. If things worked out for him, he would bring over the family. To have company along the way, he took along his brother Motka, a blacksmith. With their boat tickets taken care of by the baron's money, the brothers managed to earn extra cash by getting hired as stokers on a merchant ship leaving for Buenos Aires, whence they would let their families know their whereabouts.

Grandfather lived in Once, the first Jewish quarters of Buenos Aires, for over four years. For those who knew him, it wasn't hard to imagine his days and nights in a foreign city, speaking a foreign language. At first, he found a job at a warehouse. There he hauled bales of coffee beans and boxes of black pepper and cinnamon. Sometimes, the mixture of smells made him dizzy.

Though he wasn't overly religious, every Friday evening he dressed in clean clothes and went to a temple for *shabes*. There he glanced from time to time at the parishioners. He took note of who prayed with belief and who did it just for appearances or at best to seek forgiveness for their sins. There were many more of the latter, thus confirming Grandpa's guess that the world had not been set up by God. Otherwise why would He flood it with nonbelievers? He himself tried to pray sincerely. If for nothing else, he prayed out of the fullness of his heart—for being alive and healthy, for still, like a boy, rejoicing at the sight of the sun every morning.

Having mastered as much Spanish as needed, he bought brushes and buckets and began doing painting jobs all over Buenos Aires, the City of Fresh Air indeed. In his spare time, he offered merry-go-round rides to children on the streets, by twirling them around his huge body. The little ones screeched with delight. But Grandfather missed his own offspring. He sent everything he could save to his family, and his parcels to Minsk became more and more frequent. He guessed at what his children looked like now. He knew it wasn't good to stay apart from his family for too long. It was time to take them all out of Russia. Especially now that the Beilis affair, a blood libel campaign waged against Jews in Russia, was over. It had lasted two years and horrified Jews around the world, including those in Buenos Aires. The Russian anti-Semites had accused one Menahem Beilis, a Kievan Jew, not even an overly observant one, and the father of five children, of a ritual killing of a young Ukrainian boy. They arrested the man, kept him in prison for two years while the Russian press waged such a vicious anti-Jewish campaign that the whole world talked about it. Every Russian Jew trembled, expecting the worst if Beilis was convicted.

Gathering on every street corner in Once, the Buenos Aires Jews asked one another, "Are they out of their minds?" and shook their heads. "Don't they know that spilling human blood is against all that Judaism is about? Even a drop of chicken blood makes the meal unkosher. It takes a *shoykhet,* a specially trained butcher, to see to it that the law of Moses isn't broken. Ah!"

Thank God for the great Russian writers Maxim Gorky, Vladimir Korolenko, and some others, the best of the Russian intelligentsia; may they all be blessed and live to their hundred twenty years. They rushed to Beilis's defense, and finally he was acquitted. But who was to guarantee that, the next time charges were trumped up, enough righteous Russians would close ranks in defense of a single Jew?

Now, having spent several years in Argentina, Grandfather was fully convinced that Russia was a poor place to live. It was a damp, sluggish, dull place in which one felt bored and listless. He put aside enough money for tickets for his whole bunch. To save on his trip back to Europe, as he'd done on his way to Buenos Aires, he got himself a job as stoker on a merchant ship.

He had left for Argentina sporting his bushy blond mustache, but he returned home with just a little brush under his nose. Many years later he'd entrust his youngest son, Moulka, who became his assistant, with his male secret—how he'd lost his proud hair. It was all because of the tango, he explained with a wink. Among the many young women in Once was one gentle girl who was easily moved to laughter. She eyed him, El Ruso, the giant from Russia, for a long time. One hot night, on a dance floor, he felt a tremendous urge to do a few "La Cumparsita" steps with her. "First, shave off your mustache," she said tauntingly. He resisted the temptation for a long time. But finally he couldn't hold it off.

The news about the exciting voyage to an exotic country was not destined to stir his household's imagination for long. Grandfather returned to his little house in Minsk on the evening of August 13, 1914. The very next morning, newsboys ran through the streets shouting, "War! War!" At the tavern, where Grandfather went to see Iossel, Nyumka, and other old friends, nobody knew what had happened in the world. Nobody understood why life was suddenly tilting. A neighbor's son, a high school student, reported that somebody had assassinated some archduke. And that "arch" was important as a symbol. And if you kill a symbol, then the only way out is war.

The draft came after Grandfather the next day. He shook his head in displeasure, hugged his children one after another, and left for action. He thought they'd send him to the cavalry for old times' sake. But no! He was assigned to the infantry, which was acutely short on troops. They ordered him to clean his rifle, gave him a too-short overcoat, but allotted him one and a half times the regular soldier's ration. At least they got one thing right: A hungry fighter would be of little use.

The war was blazing somewhere in Europe. Since Grandfather had worked with horses in his dragoon days, he was appointed as a forager in the transport attachment. It was good that he was with horses again, but he was bored. After a few weeks, he'd had enough of it. He asked to be transferred to the front line. There, he hoped at least to have a glimpse of the Germans—to see for himself how much they differed from the Argentineans. Not too many were volunteering to hear bullets whistling over their heads, so the military honored the former dragoon's request.

Once on the front line, they ordered him, for starters, to dig trenches, which were dug shallow. Perhaps they were about right for undersized Russian peasants. But moving in those trenches under fire was a torture to Grandfather. He was forced to bend very low.

In the very first battle, an enormous dragonfly with fanciful crosses on its wings appeared in the sky. It flew over their heads along and across the front line. From time to time, the pilot waved his hand in greetings and threw down some round thing, the size of an orange. It blew up on the ground. One of those oranges landed next to Grandfather. It showered him with dirt and pummeled his chest mightily. He fell in total silence. He managed only to think—here's the end of me.

He woke up in a coffin. Its pine boards smelled of wood alcohol and pitch. Somewhere nearby, men swore in what sounded like strange Yiddish. That surprised Grandfather a great deal. He didn't quite believe in life after death, but when he did occasionally consider it, he didn't imagine it populated by cursing people. A moment later, when he regained his full consciousness, he realized the men were Germans.

He also understood that he was the one they cursed. Their funeral party scolded him for all he was worth for not fitting into a standard coffin. They had to knock together a new one. Grandfather opened one eye slightly. Against the background of low and gloomy skies, the mustached face of a little soldier slowly emerged. The man's eyes popped out in disbelief. He thrust his rifle with a fixed bayonet in the direction of the "deceased," whose eyes had begun blinking. This German happened to be utterly uninteresting—with a little wrinkled face and scanty hair sticking out from under his spiked helmet. Grandfather felt upset that he had risked his life to look at such a nothing.

The Germans held him in an infirmary for half a year. Then they sent him to a camp near Leipzig. From there, he was ordered to work. First, he rolled logs in a sawmill. Then he milked cows on a farm. In the evenings, he played a harmonica and waited until this swinishness called war ended at last.

He returned home at the end of 1918, after having labored in Germany all four years of the war. Nobody saw much difference in him. Only a scar, the shape of a half moon, appeared on his right cheek, under his ear. How it got there, he didn't want to say.

In 1918, straight from the world war, he entered a smaller war, but one no less vicious—the civil one, in which Jewish pogroms were occurring all over Great Russia, wherever, of course, some Jews could at least be found.

After somehow surviving that one, his bad luck hit him again. In the beginning of the 1920s, he became jobless. There was hunger no matter where you looked. To free the family of an extra mouth, his older son, Abram, my father—then a boy of twelve—left for Moscow. There, he dyed clothes, working as an assistant in a shop where people brought their shirts and dresses, hoping to expand their wardrobes despite shortages in the stores. The shop was run by a man who had moved from Minsk to Moscow, seeking better fortune in the capital. His helper, my father, also ran back and forth along busy Neglinka Street selling newspapers and bagels.

Soon Lenin introduced the New Economic Policy. The new power of workers and peasants surprised everybody, allowing some private enterprises in a time when the Russian economy, severely damaged by civil war, was failing. Grandfather returned to his trade. Again his blood began rushing through his veins. It did so in such an unruly manner that while a grandchild was already appearing on the horizon (his oldest daughter Judith had married), he himself was fathering his own newborns—two sons. In 1924, Lazar; in 1926, Samuil, nicknamed Moulka.

In the 1930s, Grandfather was so busy that he lost track of time. Could Lazar be a schoolboy already? The only trouble was that Lazar was interested not in wallpapering but in writing verse. For a working family, this was a loss. Luckily, the youngest son, Moulka, my uncle Misha, didn't mind continuing in the family trade—housepainting. During the summer, when school was closed, under his father's watchful eye, he rolled out wallpaper rolls on the tables and spread them with glue, squatting to look for missing spots, which could earn him a blow to the back of his head; his father couldn't stand sloppy work.

Then Grandpa's oldest son, Abram, my father, married Soybel, my mother, and moved to Odessa. Coming for the wedding, Grandfather took along his son Moulka. The bride's sister and her husband, together with the groom, made space for the newlyweds by building a partition in the middle of the room they occupied on Lenin Street.

Then more grandchildren began to appear. First I came along, an infant in that half room. Then, in Minsk, Grandfather's daughter Judith added twins to her son Mishka.

Thus, time rolled on to that fateful summer of 1941. When the first bombs began exploding all over Minsk, everybody was confused. They rushed away from the city, wherever one could think of going.

Grandfather remembered that it was his payday. "Well, Moulka, write me a bill," Grandfather ordered his younger son, who, already an eighth grader, served as his personal accountant and secretary. "Write it down— 'To the Zhdanovichi Region Office of Communal Housing . . .'"

"What bill, Uri?" his wife shouted, grabbing now a frying pan, now a pillow. "What's with you? Are you out of your mind? Who needs Soviet money now? We have to run!"

"You run," Grandfather kept saying. "I'll catch up with you. It's not right to leave your hard-earned dough behind. We're not bourgeois, you know. Don't worry, I'm long-legged; I'll move fast. I'll catch up with you in no time. I'll just make a quick run to that Zhdanovichi office."

That last day of his life, Grandfather covered twenty miles on his own two feet. Near the town of Zhdanovichi, German paratroopers took him. They'd already rounded up a few thousand men caught on the roads. They put them in a camp hurriedly organized near Drozdy, a settlement five miles from the city.

As eyewitnesses recalled, Grandfather perished in the very first hours of detention. In the German he had learned during his World War I captivity, he began to pester the guards. He told them to stop making fools of themselves and to let him go. He was already getting on in years; he'd passed his sixty-year mark already. He argued that he was a civilian. And he was taking his pay to his family. He had too many children and grandchildren to take care of.

Alas, Grandfather wasn't endowed with foresight. He hadn't had it when he beat up the tsarist field sergeant, or when he returned for his family on the very eve of World War I, or now, inside the rows of barbed wire in

Drozdy. How could my grandfather imagine that a hardworking, meticulous, order-loving people, amid whom he'd lived for four years—those very same people who believed in going to bed early, sleeping with windows flung open whatever the weather, and getting up with the sunrise, the very same people whom he found perhaps a bit boring but, in all other ways, not much different from any other people—would willingly annihilate women, children, and old folks whose only fault was being Jewish?

It's conceivable that the story his wife had told him on his return from German captivity might also have contributed to his misconception. When, in the course of World War I, German troops had entered Minsk, they roamed the courtyards with rifles under their arms but touched not a single civilian. Once, on a cold day in February 1918, as the evening sun was about to set, a German soldier, tall and rosy-cheeked, his mustache twirled up à la Emperor Wilhelm, his backpack slapping his shoulders, wandered into their courtyard. A baby was crying.

He asked my grandmother, "Is that your baby crying at the top of its lungs, frau?"

"Who else do you think it could be?" Never at a loss for words, Grandma cut him off. "She's crying because she's hungry. I fed the little rascal some soup in the morning. Now she's howling again. She wants bread. I'm asking you: does she have any *saikhel,* that is, brain? Where would I get bread when the war's all around?"

The German shook his head disapprovingly, removed his huge backpack from his shoulders, and took a loaf of bread out of it. Then, from its sheath on his belt, he pulled out his army knife and cut a hefty chunk, as wide and thick as his palm. Next to the knife, a flask filled with honey turned up. The German trickled honey all over the bread and extended it to Grandma saying, "Give it to your baby girl, frau. It's not her fault that she cries. War or no war, a baby's hungry anyway." He left the courtyard, leaving the rest of the loaf behind.

How could my grandfather know that, although this time the Germans came along the same road, they were totally different now? They came as if bewitched by some ancient horrific curse that made hearts frozen, stony, merciless. When Grandfather began pestering one of the guards, three others came running up to take care of the troublemaker. They pierced him through at once with their fixed bayonets.

I can only guess why Grandfather behaved so recklessly. Knowing his hot-tempered nature, recalling how, back in his army days, he had beaten the plump field sergeant's face with his boot, I assume they most likely killed him for no particular reason. Or, rather, for a universal reason—for interfering with authorities.

But the sorrowful fact was that Grandfather's move was, though ruinous, the right one. He put up his final fight while it was still possible. As eyewitnesses recall, there, in Drozdy camp, shortly after the incident the Nazis began to check the nationality of the detainees. They let the Byelorussian, Russian, and Polish men go. Then they brought all the Jewish ones to the far end of the camp and, silently, without any explanations or formalities, as if doing some unpleasant but necessary domestic chore, like washing dishes after a big party or disposing of garbage, shot them.

It wasn't an easy job—to shoot and bury so many men. It was the early stage of the Reich's final solution to the Jewish question. The industrial, conveyer-like murder machine had not been set up yet. They hadn't used the deadly chemical Cyclone B on humans yet. And they were still to build ovens large enough to burn human bodies. Finding a way to dispose of a large number of human lives required ingenuity and shrewdness. On August 1, 1941, shortly after Grandfather perished, Reichsführer SS Heinrich Himmler ordered his Second Cavalry Platoon in Byelorussia to drive Jewish women and children into swamps. To Himmler's chagrin, his clever idea didn't work. Byelorussian swamps were marshy enough, all right, but they turned out not to be as ruinous as the Reichsführer had hoped. They were only three feet deep. A mother could lift her child out of the muck and both would survive for a time.*

Grandfather's asking for trouble turned out to be not so much foolhardy courage as unrealized wisdom in choosing his fate. If German bayonets hadn't pierced him in Drozdy, he would have shared the fate of his fellows in Minsk. In the course of the following three years of German occupation of the city, some hundred thousand Jews were first gathered into a ghetto, "the Pit," and then finished off by all means available—starvation, disease, and shooting.

Even if Grandfather had been of a cooler temperament and, by some miracle, had gotten out of Drozdy alive, as a craftsman he might have lived only a few more months. At least for a while, the Third Reich still needed Jewish artisans. On December 2, 1941, one Loze, Reichscommissar of Ost-

*Arad, ed., *Unichtozhenie evreev SSSR*, 90–91.

land, appealed to the commissar general in Minsk: "I urge you to stop the liquidation of Jews who are used as a skilled work force at our military enterprises and the repair shops and whom it's so far impossible to replace with local inhabitants."*

But, alas, my grandfather probably would not have benefited even from this flimsy opportunity. He had the wrong skills in his hands. If he had been a locksmith, a lathe operator, a riveter, he might have lived a little longer. But a housepainter or paperhanger was needed in peacetime. It was wartime. Who cared about fixing up rooms?

*Ibid., 170.

TWENTY-TWO

Missing Mikhoels

ONCE LATE AT NIGHT, after listening to his Grundig, Papa whispers, "They're on our case again!" He rubs his knees over and over, as he always does when anxiety takes hold of him.

November 1952. The green napping cat's eye of the radio tuner is blinking again. There's a lonely whistling on the radio. Suddenly, a trumpet roulade resounds. It repeats several times before an energetic male voice, quite unlike that of the Muscovite newscaster, who's never in a hurry, pronounces, *"Kol Yisra'el. Kol Tzion la-Golah"* (Voice of Israel. Voice of Zion to the Diaspora).

And then in pure Russian: "This is Israeli Radio in Tel Aviv. Here's the breaking news. Prague . . ." The newscaster's voice fades away, and Papa moves even closer to the radio.

"Prague," I think, trying to fall asleep. "What could possibly be of interest there?" When I read the newspapers, I usually skip reports under the heading "In the Countries of People's Democracy." Whatever they have to say about life there usually isn't much different from what they say about events in our country: "Romania: College Student Population Is Rising." "East Germany: Socialist Labor Competition Is Widening." "Polish People's Republic: The Party and the Working Class Ties Are Strengthening." Et cetera, et cetera. I have nothing against that rising, that widening, and that strengthening. But I'm embarrassed to admit to myself that I'm bored to death with these reports.

"Yesterday," the Israeli newscaster's voice returns, "here in Prague, the high-profile trial of a group of prominent figures of the Czechoslovakian Communist Party, headed by its former secretary general, Rudolf Slánský, took place."

The tuner's green light makes Papa's face seem paler than usual. He's holding his breath. Once again, I try to fall asleep, but Papa's tension passes on to me. I sit up in bed. This news is unusual indeed. Say what you want, but the secretary general of a brotherly Communist Party isn't tried in court every day. What has this Slánský character done?

"Sleep, sleep!" Papa whispers and motions to me to lie down.

I do what he says, but of course I keep listening. The newscaster's voice fades away again. Then it comes back, only to be jammed by a sound resembling a motor buzzing. I know now where this buzzing comes from. To prevent their spreading lies about our country, our government jams foreign broadcasts. But why would they jam this news? What's wrong with it? It rings true. Why lie about something like that? After all, it only proves that Czechoslovakian Communists are vigilant when it comes to protecting the people's interest.

The jamming comes and goes. I'm able to make out the titles of the accused: "Together with Rudolf Slánský, thirteen other high officials have been brought to trial. Among them are the former vice minister of defense . . . the former minister of foreign affairs . . . the former editor of the Czech Communist Party newspaper *Rude Pravo . . .*"

A political analyst replaces the announcer. It turns out that, of the fourteen accused, eleven are Jews. Slánský and ten others have been executed; seven of these men are Jewish. Slánský in particular was held accountable for "serving the interests of a Zionist, bourgeois-nationalist group."

Before that night, I didn't know much about Slánský. In fact, I knew only his name. Six months earlier, near the end of the school year, in order to prepare for the interview that is part of the procedure of joining the Communist Youth League (Komsomol), I had to learn by heart the names of the secretaries general of all brotherly Communist parties. Todor Zhivkov of Bulgaria, Imre Nagy of Hungary, Maurice Thorez of France, Palmiro Togliatti of Italy. Learning these names turned out to be a waste of time. The examiners didn't ask me about them at all. They simply accepted me, as well as all my classmates, in a hurry, wholesale. They brought us into the local Komsomol office in droves and, without asking a thing, shoved the thin, passportlike booklets with burgundy covers into our hands, along with a tiny pin in the shape of a red flag with the acronym *VLKSM* (All-Union Lenin Communist Youth League) on it. They also took a ruble twenty as first-year membership dues and glued a puny stamp into the booklet. My life didn't change in any way. Joining the league made me, a Jewish boy, perhaps a tad more politically reliable in the eyes of the authorities than I had been before going through that silly ritual.

The day after the news about the Prague trial, Papa, Mama, and Uncle Misha sit around the table, their faces grim.

"They're back on our case," Papa says.

"Well, of course," Mama adds, "they shot them because they're Jews."

"I don't understand you," says Uncle Misha, his eyes full of feigned amazement. "This is news to you? Don't they always do to us whatever they feel like doing?"

As a freshly minted Communist Youth Leaguer, I resent this kind of talk. Of course, since the episode with Bagritsky's poem, I already know that being Jewish means being unjustly accused. But it's one thing to blame someone; it's quite another to shoot him. In response to the recent events in Prague, my family's obviously gone overboard. It looks to me as if they are just suffering from a persecution complex based on their ethnicity.

At the same time, the news from Prague makes me feel uncomfortable as well. Questions that I don't know how to answer begin crawling around in my head. How could the head of the Communist Party be a hidden bourgeois nationalist? Surely before he was appointed to such a high position, his candidacy had been thoroughly discussed at the highest level—at a meeting of experienced and responsible Politburo members. Is it possible that they had no inkling that Slánský was Jewish? But if they did know this, how could they elect him to such an important post in the first place? Of course, we also have a Jew in the top echelon of our government, Lazar Moiseyevich Kaganovich. He is one of several deputies of Comrade Stalin. But would he ever have been considered for the post of the secretary general? It's unthinkable.

The newspapers state that Zionism, of which Slánský is accused, is a threat to world peace and democracy, and I suddenly realize that I don't really understand what this Zionism thing is all about. To sort it out for myself once and for all, I hurry to the reading room on Preobrazhensky Street, on the corner opposite the entrance to the City Garden. I ask the librarian for recent issues of *Bloknot agitatora (Propagandist's Notepad)*. The newspaper phraseology is too complex for me, and I choose *Notepad* because it is designed to spell out all political issues of the day in the simplest possible terms.

A stack of the booklets under my arm, I sit down next to other readers at a long table. Just in case, I cast a sidelong glance to the left and right of me. After all, I'm Jewish, and a stranger might misconstrue my interest in Zionism. I find the relevant entry and use my forearm to hide from the man next to me what I am reading about: "Zionism (from the name Mt. Zion, in Jerusalem) is a reactionary ideology concerned with the rebirth of Jewish self-consciousness through the encouragement of immigration of Jews to Palestine and the creation of a Jewish state on that territory."

I read it again. I don't understand a thing! What on earth is so terrible about the Zionists? If all they want is to encourage Jews to move to Israel, then let them keep trying to their hearts' content. What harm can it do? I think of the strange people with long beards and side curls that I saw rocking in prayer in a synagogue Papa brought me to once a few years earlier. He took me there for Yom Kippur. If those backward individuals in that synagogue want to go to Palestine, good riddance! Wouldn't it then benefit the Soviet authorities if these religious fanatics would no longer constitute a nuisance to youth?

"They're back on our case," Papa said about the events in Prague. Why "*our* case"? What do *we* have to do with it? Czechoslovakia's far away. Neither my parents nor I personally have anything to do with Zionism. What would I do in Israel? I'm not religious. I don't know how to read or write either Hebrew or Yiddish. Except for Sholom Aleichem, I don't know any Jewish writers. The writers I do know far better are American—Jack London, Howard Fast, Upton Sinclair; their novels are published here in large quantities. There is even one American writer with almost the same last name as mine—Theodore Dreiser. I read his *American Tragedy;* it's about the evil of money and its ability to destroy human feelings: in order to marry a girl from a wealthy family, a young American drowns his pregnant girlfriend, who belongs to a lower social class.

I fidget in my reading-room chair. Well, I've finally read about Zionism, but I still can't figure out what all the fuss is about. This difficulty gets on my nerves. It makes my face itch.

I leave the reading room, still trying to unravel the web of logic in this situation. In lines at the stores or in packed streetcars, as soon as anyone who looks Jewish expresses any displeasure with the way things are going in our country, quite often somebody yells, "If you don't like it here, clear out to your Palestine!" If Israel is a place of exile and living there is a form of punishment, then what kind of threat does Zionism pose? Who would want to be banished into exile? I don't understand anything!

The confusion caused by the Slánský trial heightens my anxiety. Bad premonitions have been taking hold of me for some time. Since the end of the summer, the papers have begun to publish satirical columns with increased frequency. I usually look for them; they are the liveliest part of any Soviet paper. But now, reading these columns makes me gloomy. Once funny and entertaining, these columns have turned sullen and malicious. Time and again, they report the discovery of a great number of crooks, scalpers, scoundrels, and embezzlers, all of whom have only one thing in common— they all have Jewish names. In *Pravda Ukrainy* (Ukraine's Truth), they assail the officials of some regional consumer exchange union, a certain Leynson, Schwartz, Beylinson, and Pollinger. In *Pravda,* they attack a certain Bukhman, Rakhman, and Schlessinger, and in *Izvestiya,* a certain Spektor. No matter what bastard they talk about, his surname indicates that his ethnicity is always the same.

One day, I read a satirical column about the schemes of an economist, Matvei Razmanov. His surname ends in -*ov;* that is, it doesn't look outright Jewish. There's a similar Uzbek surname, Rakhmanov. Maybe Razmanov is just a variation? But I read another paragraph and learn that the schemer's patronymic is Moiseyevich, that is, he is unmistakably Jewish. And I have the feeling that the journalist resorted to the patronymic to dispel any doubt of the crook's ethnicity.

As winter approaches, the satires grow more and more sinister. In *Pravda Ukrainy,* a column appears under the headline "A Gang of Economic Saboteurs." It tells the story of a Khain, a Yaroshetsky, and a Gerzon, whose crimes had brought them before a military tribunal. I'm taken aback: a military tribunal during a time of peace? I reread the satirical piece again and again. Maybe these three men tried to poison the city drinking water? Derailed a train packed with passengers? Blew up a military base? No, nothing of the sort is mentioned. These men aren't enemy paratroopers or spies; they're employees of a consumer-goods warehouse. And they face a military tribunal for "counterrevolutionary sabotage in commerce and commodity turnover."

This means that they took some goods that are in short supply from the warehouses under their management and sold them on the side. I despise speculators. Our working-class family considers this means of making money dishonorable. But still, it's hard for me to understand why this haberdashery monkey-business is considered "counterrevolutionary." Being brought in front of a military tribunal is not quite the same as being fired from a job and given a long-term prison sentence. It spells death. And indeed, a few days later, the papers report that all three men were sentenced to capital punishment and shot. I imagine a bullet flying toward my chest and go rigid in fright.

"Where're you off to?" Papa asks me one day.

"To the Gorky Revival Movie Theater. They're screening *Circus*."

November 1952. Sunday. It's muddy in the courtyard. The bad weather makes melancholy sink even deeper into me. It has captured my mood for several months now and won't let me go. So to cheer myself up, I've decided to go see a comedy.

"*Circus*?" Papa asks. For some reason, he is surprised; there's even a note of disbelief in the tone of his voice.

"Why not?" I say, pulling on my windbreaker. "It's a classic."

I want to see this movie for the umpteenth time not only because it's a comedy classic. The star of *Circus* is Lyubov Orlova, with whom I'm secretly in love. In this movie, she plays an American circus performer who comes to Moscow because she's persecuted at home for having a black child.

"*Circus* is playing?" Papa asks again. "Are you sure?"

Now it's my turn to be surprised. Papa usually trusts my ability to find information in the newspaper. I show him the last page of *Bolshevitskoe znamia* (Bolshevik's Banner) where they print the repertoire of Odessa movie theaters.

"You know what?" Papa suddenly says, getting up from the sofa. "Let's go together. Do you mind?"

As a rule, Papa goes to the movies with Mama, and I go there with my friends, Kotya Liubarsky or Zhenya Henriksen. But I don't mind going to the movies in Papa's company once in a while. When it happens, afterward he usually takes me to an ice cream parlor on Deribas Street and treats me to the best ice cream in Odessa. He also shells out a few rubles, often three, sometimes even five, as my pocket money. He keeps this a secret from Mama, who's convinced that money spoils children.

Generally speaking, Papa can't stand Soviet-made films. He prefers foreign ones, especially the Hollywood films taken as a trophy from German warehouses at the end of the war. He likes only a handful of Soviet pre–World War II entertainment flicks, of which *Circus* is his favorite. He's seen it many times. And not because Lyubov Orlova is the star. She doesn't enthrall him. Yes, she's pretty. Yes, she sings and dances well. But to him, that's about it. For a long time, I was puzzled as to what has driven Papa to watch *Circus* so many times, if not the desire to see our most adorable movie star.

In time, it dawns on me: he does it for the sake of seeing the last episode in the film one more time. In this episode, people of different ethnicities sing a lullaby to the heroine's black baby. First they do it in Russian. Then they sing it in Ukrainian; then in the Buryat language and in Georgian. Finally the boy winds up in the arms of a man with a large, slightly flat nose and big lips. He sings the lullaby in Yiddish. And that's what attracts my father—to hear a few words in Yiddish sung by a Jewish actor.

I haven't seen this actor in other films. The first time I saw *Circus,* I was too small. It was soon after the end of World War II, and I saw it with my parents. During the screening of the film, Papa leaned toward me and whispered excitedly into my ear, "You know who that man is? It's Solomon Mikhoels, the one and only!"

For a long time after the movie was over, Papa still talked about Mikhoels and what a great actor he was. His part in *Circus* is small, but he was the artistic director of the State Jewish Theater in Moscow. ("State!" Papa raised his finger to emphasize the importance of the state's sponsorship of the Jewish theater.) Before the war, Mikhoels had staged *King Lear* in his theater and played the lead part so well that, though the play was performed in Yiddish, even the theatergoers who knew not a word in that language flocked to his performance. Papa also said that during the war, as it had been reported in the newspapers, Mikhoels went to America and raised millions of dollars for tanks and other weaponry for the Red Army.

I already know that this actor is no longer alive. He died in a car accident in January 1948. Everyone at home said that it wasn't an accident at all and the authorities have something to do with it, but I dismissed these wild claims. After all, they gave Mikhoels a state funeral in Moscow, and a book about him was published the same year. My parents always overdramatize whatever happens around them. To me, an accident is just an accident. Bad things can happen to anyone. I was convinced that my parents spoke like this only because they imagine persecution aimed at the Jews coming from all sides.

Recently, Mikhoels's name has resurfaced in our family conversations. The broadcast from Tel Aviv reported that twenty-four Jewish poets and writers were sentenced to death and shot in the basement of the KGB headquarters at Lubyanka Square in Moscow. Among them were David Bergelson, Peretz Markish, and Itzik Fefer. All of them had been members of the Jewish Anti-Fascist Committee, set up on Stalin's orders when the war with Germany broke out. Mikhoels himself had been elected chairman of that committee.

"Where are you off to?" Mama asks sternly when Papa and I are already at the door. She wants to know about everything that's going on at home.

"We have to go out." Papa cuts his answer short, putting on his coat.

"What do you mean 'have to'?" Mama says. "May I know where you're going?"

"To the movies," Papa replies, heading toward the door.

"To the movies? Since when do you start going to the movies without your wife?" she asks.

"Oy, Sonya, stop it," Papa loses his temper. "Can't I go to the movies with just my son once in a while? Or do you just *have* to be in between?"

Seeing that Papa's upset on some account, Mama steps aside.

We head off toward Sobor Square. The Gorky Revival Movie Theater is nearby, at the corner of Preobrazhensky and Greek streets. The show starts on time, and everything in the film takes its normal course. Then the last scene begins, the one that involves singing a lullaby to the black boy who's passed from one adult's arms to another. From a Russian woman to a Ukrainian one. Then to a young Buryat sailor. Then to a Georgian man. In the dark, Papa lightly clicks his tongue, as he always does when he's tense. He can't wait for his beloved Mikhoels to show up on the screen.

But right before that moment, the image on the screen jerks, the music skips a few notes, and the boy suddenly appears not in Mikhoels's arms, where he's supposed to be, but in the arms of the person who usually follows Mikhoels—a young black man. And that man's already singing to the child about his own happy life in the Soviet Union, assuring the little one that "a hundred roads and a hundred paths" await him here, in our country.

His mouth agape, Papa stares at the screen. First, he nudges me with his elbow. Then he turns and looks at me. His bewildered face expresses the unspoken question: "WHERE'S MY MAN? WHERE'S MIKHOELS?"

I shrug: *How am I supposed to know?*

Once again, Papa fixes his gaze on the screen. He even rises a bit in his seat, as if still waiting for Mikhoels to turn up in the movie, even if in the wrong place.

But the film's quickly coming to its end. Lyubov Orlova's already singing the famous song, "I don't know another country like this one, a country where a person breathes as easily." Yet the puzzled look is still frozen on Papa's face.

The last frames of the movie's May First Parade are fading in, the letters *T, H, E* and *E, N, D* are already descending, each on its own little parachute, and the closing credits are rolling, but Papa still can't come to his senses. He's pale, his mouth's open.

The lights slowly come up in the theater. The seats bang up as they fold into place, but Papa's sitting still as if he's suddenly gotten a cramp in his neck. Motionless, he darts his eyes left and right.

Finally, the theater's almost empty. He gets up, whispering under his breath in Yiddish: "*Dos is dos*"—"This is how it is."

He grabs my hand and squeezes it in his palm, wide, rough, cracked from working with paint.

Surprised, I feel like yanking my hand away: what am I, a first grader or something, holding Daddy by the hand? I'm almost fifteen!

I carefully free my hand. What's with him? Apparently, something out of the ordinary is happening to him. I can hardly remember the last time Papa let me know how strong he was. In fact, he did it only once during my entire life, when he spanked me with his belt. I was no more than eight years old at that time, and I deserved it. In my parents' absence, carrying the only key to our apartment in my pocket, I set off to the outskirts of the city, together with my friend Kotya, to the Otrada Beach. Worried to death about what might have happened, my parents ran all over our neighborhood looking for me. When we finally came back late in the evening, Papa spanked me not so much of his own volition but because Mama urged him to. She felt I should be taught a lesson.

But now, after watching *Circus,* something has come over him. He grabs my hand again and squeezes it in his fist with all his might, as if he's afraid something is going to happen to me the very next minute. Geez! Could it really be just because his Mikhoels wasn't in the movie? Of course, I understand that Papa would have liked to admire his beloved actor one more time. But where's the tragedy here? Big deal! The film's old. It's possible that it's deteriorated to such an extent that they had to cut a piece of it out.

I free my hand again. He lets it go but urges me to hurry up. We go back toward our home on Deribas Street. Papa's silent and tense. Now he takes his glasses off, now he puts them on. Again, just as he did in the movie theater, without turning his head, he looks warily from side to side.

We get closer to the gates of our building's courtyard. But instead of passing it and proceeding to the ice cream parlor, only some fifty yards down the street, Papa grabs my hand again and pulls me toward our house.

I resist, "What about ice cream?"

"There will be no ice cream today," Papa says quickly, his voice muffled, but his tone unexpectedly uncompromising. "We're going home!"

He almost drags me to the gates.

I balk. I don't feel like going home. It's too early to go to bed. The lights in the first-floor window of Kotya's apartment are on. I want to stop by his place. To chat with him. Or to play a game of chess. Why sit at home, doing nothing?

But Papa harps on the same string, "We're going home immediately!"

"But why?"

"Don't ask silly questions!"

We walk through the front door of our wing's main hall.

"What's going on?" I say. "You've got yourself all worked up just because of Mikhoels? Is that what it is? But what do *I* have to do with it?"

"Shut up!" Papa almost yells at me.

Somehow his state of mind passes on to me. I stop talking and follow him up the stairs.

He stops on the second-floor landing, and, to assure himself that no one is following us, he looks back down the flight. Then, although there's no one who could possibly eavesdrop on his words, he whispers, his throat half-choking in fear, "Go home. Do your homework, read. And never talk to anyone about Mikhoels. Understood? If he isn't in the movie anymore, then that's how it ought to be."

"Why? Who would want it that way?"

"Whoever wants it, knows it," Papa says, his lips dry.

That evening, he and Mama whisper to each other for a long time. Even though we live on the third floor, for some reason they close the shutters especially tight that night.

TWENTY-THREE

Black on White

"MILYA," MY MOTHER'S VOICE reaches me for the third time. "Get up!
You'll be late to school."

Early morning January 13, 1953. It's cold. Gusty winds howl outside. They
thrash window frames, as if whipping them with giant sheets. Wind whistles mournfully through the telegraph wires above the roofs. There's no snow.
It was raining last week. Now ice covers the puddles. I don't feel like getting up this morning, but I have to go to school. It's a regular weekday,
Tuesday. My couch is in the corner of our one-room apartment.

Finally, I manage to sit up, eyes closed. I want to finish my dream about
my ethnic Russian neighbor, Liza Lyaskovsky, the blue-eyed beauty, tall and
fair-haired, the girl of my secret longing, whom I try to forget but can't.

"Milya, get up!" Mama says. After a short pause, again: "How many times
do I have to tell you? Get up!"

She's sitting on a stool next to the window, combing her long, luxurious,
light-brown hair. She has a few hairpins, big and small, in her mouth for
arranging the braid around the top of her head.

"M-m-m-m."

Finally, I open my eye enough to see my way to the wash basin in the
corridor. To wake up for good, I splash cold water onto my face. Then I sit
down at the table and eat my sandwich with Krakow kielbasa and drink a
glass of sweet tea. Only now do I see that my papa is still in bed. He lies

on his side, propping himself up on his elbow in order to stare out the window. His tongue's lightly clicking "ks, ks, ks."

I have no idea what troubles him. I'm fifteen, and my parents' problems are the last thing on my mind. I have enough of my own. I'm in eighth grade, and my marks aren't too bad. That is, they are solid A's. But, in my family, having straight A's is no great shakes. It's considered normal. Last week, I "caught" a B in algebra. The expression's from Mama's vocabulary, like "catching cold."

"What do you think of yourself?" she asked as if she really wanted to know my answer to her rhetorical question. "Who told you that you have a moral right to have B's?"

A long dramatic pause followed. For a moment, it seemed Mama was indeed waiting to find out who had fed me such grossly false information. "If anybody told you this, you should know that you've been fooled. If you were a goy, that would be another matter altogether. In that case, you could even bring home a C!"

For Mama, my getting a C would be the lowest possible moral downfall. As to a D or an F, she never mentions them. After all, you don't take earthquakes into account in the everyday flow of life.

"Don't ever forget that you're Jewish," she says. "You have no right to get a B in this country. No such luck here for you. This is not America, I have to remind you."

In this way, America came early into my life as a legendary place where a Jewish schoolboy could have the luxury of getting a B once in a while.

I finish my breakfast. From time to time, Papa sighs deeply. This winter he and Uncle Misha are finding even fewer apartment-repair jobs than usual. Since the beginning of September, soon after my papa heard over the Voice of America the news about the secret trial of Jewish writers and poets, rumors have spread all over the city. I pay little attention to them. From time to time, the newspapers mention the rumors, invariably attacking their pessimism as narrow-minded and malicious. That's true. Rumors are usually negative. I have never heard even once people whispering, "They say the good life will begin soon." I deem as rumors everything whispered around me that the newspapers are silent about. I write these off as backward, moss-covered, and antisocial.

Rumors have a negative impact on Papa's work. Apartment repair is the last thing on people's minds when there's so much uncertainty about tomorrow.

I wrap my coat with its dyed-black rabbit collar around myself more tightly, grab my fur cap with earflaps, pass through the corridor, and push the exit door, almost knocking my incoming uncle Misha off his feet. Something in his face is strange. His usual early-morning vigor isn't there. A former master sergeant of a tank regiment in his army service, he keeps himself in shape by doing fifty push-ups and fifty sit-ups every day. He still jogs for forty minutes and then, crouching, his knees spread, works out with his forty-pound barbell. He usually comes to us after taking a cold shower and rubbing himself down with a towel—excited, heated, as if he were not about to paint ceilings and hang wallpaper all day long but about to fight a rival in the jujitsu style he learned in the army. His face then expresses an urge immediately to throw the imaginary rival over his shoulder and top off the throw with a bump of his knee to the rival's ass. Sometimes, I have been a victim of my uncle's morning enthusiasm. He mocks me for not developing any serious biceps and finds a pretext to use one of his beloved jujitsu moves on me. I end up on the floor feeling sorry for his former soldiers.

This time, he's out of his usual humor. We collide with each other in the doorway of our apartment; I'm leaving, and he's coming in. As we struggle with each other at the front door, I can't help wondering: There isn't any work for him and Papa. So what has brought him over so early in the morning? His face is tense and pale.

"Where are you going?" he says.

"What do you mean, where? To school."

"To school?" Uncle Misha says absentmindedly and slaps me on the shoulder. "Ah, yes, yes. Press on. Just be careful, understand? Keep your eyes open."

Before I close the door behind me, I hear Uncle's voice talking to my papa as he enters our room.

"Have you heard?" Uncle Misha asks in Yiddish. "It's quite bad! Abram, can you switch on your *grager,* your noisemaker? What do they say over there?"

In my uncle's language, the noisemaker is our Grundig, the German-made radio receiver. I feel in Uncle's high-pitched voice that something extraordinary has happened. But what?

I leave our building gates. I turn right, heading for school, and immediately spot a small crowd standing at the *Pravda* newsstand next to the stationery store. I squeeze through it and, over somebody's shoulder, try to read what the others are reading—an article on the front page. It's not an editorial, which is usually printed on the left-hand side of the page, but an article, the same size as an editorial but placed on the right. The bold-faced headline reads: DESPICABLE SPIES AND MURDERERS MASKED AS DOCTORS.

The article isn't signed. It's eerie. I've long noticed that if a threatening article is signed, it somehow feels less ominous. Anonymity makes it horrific. It means that the article is not one person's opinion but that it comes from somewhere very high up, from the final level of authority. Therefore, it's not subject to any discussions. The only thing left is to carry out its orders.

I jump from line to line. A band of doctor-saboteurs has been arrested. They "ruined the lives of Zhdanov and Shcherbakov, leading rulers of the Soviet state, as well as those of military leaders—Marshals Vasilevsky, Govorov, Konev, Army General Shtimenko, Admiral Levchenko. . . . Monsters of the human race in white coats . . . by purposely using the wrong medical treatment, they killed the great Russian writer Maxim Gorky, along with outstanding public figures of the Soviet state Kuibyshev and Menzhinsky."

Who are these saboteurs? Because of the adults' heads in front of me, no matter how high I jump, I can't read the piece to the end. I run out of time. My classes start soon. I recall that another newsstand is next to my school, on Gogol Street. It's a side street; fewer people should be there. However, the stand is next to the Central Post Office, which is often quite busy. In doubt that I'd manage to learn the names of the supersaboteurs before school starts, I rush along the streets dragging my heavy briefcase. Suddenly, my uncle's pale face flashes in front of me, a premonition producing a sucking feeling in my stomach. I have that feeling whenever I'm not well enough prepared for class. Then I always hide my eyes, lower my head, and hold my breath while our teacher, trying to decide whom to call to the blackboard, scans the class list mumbling, "Well, well, well."

I run along the left side of Gavan Street. I pass the painted black wrought-iron fence of the City Garden, the Voennyi Slope, and Bania Alley. I'm on Gogol Street already. Under my fur hat, my head is sweating. My heart thumps against my chest.

I approach the newsstand. To my relief, next to it is only a little old man in a patched-up quilted jacket. Smoking a rolled-up cigarette, the old man moves a bit to the side, inviting me to share his amusement. He mumbles in good humor and sighs, "Oh Lord, it's a weird world out there! And I thought I'd heard and seen everything!" For a moment, his voice calms me. The old man reads this mind-boggling news as if it were about some archaeological find—some ichthyosaur remains discovered in Antarctica. It's a curiosity, but no more than that.

The clock above the main post office entrance shows five to eight. The school bell's about to ring. I fix my eyes on the article. Aha, here are the saboteurs' names. A moment before I read the list, I already know deep in my stomach what kind they are. My worst fears are justified. Most of them are Jewish. M. B. Kogan, B. B. Kogan, Egorov, Feldman, Ettinger, Greenstein. I'm just a bit surprised that a few of the names don't sound outright Jewish to me: Maiorov, Vinogradov, Vovsi.

I read the Jewish surnames, one after another, with difficulty, as if swallowing razor blades. I feel a bitter taste on my tongue, the kind I get when I have strep throat, which I've had often. Now my back gets wet as well. My heart pounds loudly as if it has moved to my ears. *Do-doom, do-doom, do-doom.*

A sharp buzzing. It's my school bell. I tear myself away. It's time to go. I am about to dash across the street. Just when I place my foot on the cobblestones, brakes screech next to me. The heat of a radiator reaches my cheek. A pale sprawling face leans out of the cab of a truck that has appeared from nowhere. The driver shouts, "Motherfu—."

I don't wait for him to finish. Headlong, I charge to the school doors. Thank God, they aren't locked yet. In one move, I fly up to the third floor, to our eight-grade "A" auditorium.

I'm a minute late, but they haven't started the roll call yet. Out literature teacher, Vera Vasilievna, has just opened the class list. She looks at me as if seeing me for the first time. I've never been late before. It seems to me that everybody else is looking at me too. Some even smirk. No matter what you say, it's a pleasure when a straight-A student, as I am, is like everybody else—late to school.

"May I sit down, Vera Vasilievna?" I utter, panting.

"Well, you may."

I pull my coat off and hang it in the corner, on a nail in the wall. I open our reader. In case the teacher calls on me first, I'm scanning our homework again, Nekrasov's nineteenth-century poem "Who's Happy in Russia?" But I have a hard time concentrating. For some reason, one surname in the article on the doctor-saboteurs gets stuck in my brain. Vovsi. I've never heard this name before. Is Vovsi Jewish or not? I chase these thoughts away. I try to concentrate again. I don't want to get a bad mark today. That would be too many unpleasant things happening to me in one day.

I feel as if I'm running a fever. My cheeks glow. I'm not too surprised that most of the names in the *Pravda* article are Jewish. After all, for about half a year, "evil" Jews have already been appearing in almost every newspaper column. But so far, those columns have mostly been printed in Odessa and Kiev newspapers. Having a list of those names as saboteurs on the front page of the most important paper, *Pravda,* is much more sinister than if it appeared in any satirical column. My stomach contracts. Once again my Jewishness turns out to be a lousy fate.

Doctors have poisoned marshals. I have a hard time believing it. It's too bizarre even for me, who have read through every single issue of the series of the Library of War Adventures. This series has described enemies of every conceivable kind, none of them men of medicine. But *Pravda* is our major newspaper! Its editors wouldn't print anything there without first thoroughly checking the facts.

I try keeping my head down. I look surreptitiously at Vera Vasilievna. Is she mad at me? Not for being late, of course. When she hasn't even begun roll call yet, you're not considered late. But maybe she thinks that somehow I am guilty of the reported crimes. I understand that it's stupid of me to think that way, but I can't brush it off, no matter how hard I try. I push the thought back into the same convolutions of my brain from which it crawls out without asking my permission.

I struggle with it for a while. When it seems I begin to control it, to my horror, a voice resounds in my head—not even my own voice, which has already begun changing, at times turning to droning, but somebody else's voice, the squeaky voice of a Young Pioneer, perhaps, even that of a young Oktyabrenok.*

"Vera Vasilievna! You have my word of honor. I've nothing to do with that horrible crime. I don't even know about all its victims. I know of Kuibyshev and Menzhinsky only what our fourth-grade history textbook says of them. The Trotskyites and Bukharinites murdered them in 1935. That year, I wasn't born yet. I was born two years later. And those marshals! Konev. Vasilevsky. Govorov. Vera Vasilievna, how could I even think of harming them? They were my wartime idols! When I was a first grader, my first public assignment as a Young Pioneer was to make a poster, 'They Fought for Our Motherland.' I collected postcards with all our marshals' portraits. Sasha, my second-floor neighbor, is a draftsman. He gave me a large sheet of Whatman paper. I drew the headline in beautiful block letters with a poster pen. I took great care—no

---

*Literally: a child of October (as in the October Revolution). Usually a six- or seven-year-old who is preparing himself for entry into the Young Pioneer League.

inkblots. Galina Ivanovna, our first-grade teacher, even shed tears on seeing my work. She even kissed me in front of everybody."

I try to shut up the squeaking in my head. I'm ashamed. An obscene feeling of guilt crawls into my soul, makes me wince out of disgust for my very self. I'm staring into the reader. I begin murmuring lines from Nekrasov's poem. But I can't focus my attention on it no matter how hard I try. Who is happy in Russia? I can't find the answer. At the moment, it certainly isn't me. The same squeaking voice comes on in my head again:

"And Gorky! I couldn't possibly hurt him. He's my beloved writer. I read much more of his work than our school program calls for. I read his My Childhood *and* In the World *and* My Universities. *And his "Chelkash" story. And about the young hero, Danko, who tore out his heart from his chest to give light to his people. I even read his novel* Mother—*all of it, though it wasn't easy; I was quite bored. But all the same, Gorky's close to me. He also comes from a working family. He also had a hard childhood. He defended all the weak and the deprived of the world. I even got an A for reciting one of his prose poems, "Song of a Storm Petrel," by heart. I did it without stumbling even once, though it wasn't easy to memorize: "Over the gray plain of the sea, the wind drives the clouds together. Between the clouds and the sea, proudly, like black lightning, a storm petrel soars. The storm, the storm will break out soon!"*

(The time will come when Gorky will grow in my eyes apart from his artistic achievements. After all, he will turn out to be one of the few Russian writers who held anti-Semitism in contempt and fought it in his works. "Once upon a time," he writes in his *Russian Fairy Tales,* "in some tsardom, in some state, there were Jews, simple Jews—for pogroms, for slander, and for other state needs.")

Comes the big school recess. Looking back, to see if anyone is watching me, I run across the street, back to the newsstand. My doubts about Vovsi seem to be resolved: "Most of the terrorist group (Vovsi, Kogan, Feldman, Ettinger, Greenstein) were connected with the international Jewish bourgeois-nationalistic organization 'The Joint [Jewish Appeal],' created by the American intelligence service allegedly for giving material aid to the Jews worldwide." And then: "Through Doctor Shemilovich and the well-known bourgeois nationalist Mikhoels, they [the saboteurs] received the Joint's directives for spying and terrorist and other subversive activities." I read the article to the very end. There are no more names. The article ends with calls to be more vigilant in exposing warmongers and their agents.

As I run back to my classroom, an even bigger conflict starts in my head.

The unclear becomes clear, and the clear turns misty. Who's that Shemilovich? I've never heard this name before. But Mikhoels! A well-known bourgeois nationalist? How come? Is he called that because, in that famous movie *Circus,* he sings a lullaby in Yiddish? But it must have been in the script. Can an actor sing whatever he feels like?

As always, holding his pale fist as high as possible, our hunchback physics teacher, Fedor Ivanovich, is scribbling formulas on the blackboard. He presses the chalk with all his might, but it refuses to leave any marks. It just scratches the board. Our pranksters have done it again. They've waxed the blackboard. I make a wry face at the grinding. But, no matter how hard I try, I can't think of anything but the *Pravda* article.

"Joint, Joint." In front of my eyes, a big yellow can. It's open and spreads the smell of corn beef around me. When we escaped from the war zone to Tashkent, Mama would open a can of Spam or condensed milk or a package with egg powder. When this happened, we had a true holiday. Mama said, "That's what the Joint sent us."

"What's that—Joint?" I asked, sinking my teeth into a piece of rye bread with Spam spread on it or licking a teaspoon after the last drop of milk dripped down into my glass of tea.

"That's from America," Mama said and sighed. "The American Jews are helping us." Of course, she was glad that we could get hold of such tasty stuff, but her pride suffered. She didn't like handouts.

And back in Odessa, right after the end of the war, parcels from America would arrive, with all kinds of clothes—jackets, pullovers, sweaters, raincoats, suits, and dresses. They impressed us not only with the quality of the material but also with the fine finishing touches. Even the buttonholes seemed overstitched for the sake of appearance. Mama gleefully ran her hand over the surface of the cuffs, peeked under the jacket arms, turned the coats inside out, felt their silky lining. The clothes had been worn, of course, she said, but only slightly so. She shook her head in admiration. I went with her when she took the things to our flea market on the outskirts of the city—to sell, to exchange for food. Every time I thought we wouldn't stay there for long. They'd snatch such beauties from our hands at once, and we'd go home soon. But the market swarmed with people like us— loaded with American goods. From that time on they called that flea market Amerikanka.

America! On the other side of the planet was a great, sun-lit, and generous country populated with careless rich people who could afford to give away such remarkable things to total strangers. Now, reading about the Joint in *Pravda*, I have a hard time seeing that sending those parcels was not an act of goodwill but one of sabotage.

The school day finally draws to its end. I glance from time to time at other Jewish boys in my class—at the fatty Vovka Braslavsky, at the skinny, always agile Yura Lerner, at our tallest pupil, Edik Barmash. I see their bent backs. Not by chance, I feel, are we sitting without raising our heads from our desks. They too pretend to be busy. For the first time, I think that they must feel as I do.

Finally, the bell rings. The covers of our desks drop, sounding like cap pistols being fired. Books and notebooks crammed into briefcase. Often I go home together with Vovka Braslavsky. He lives across the street—at the corner of Krasny Alley and Deribas Street. He's a good boy; he's kind. Sometimes we visit each other's apartments. On the way home, we usually chatter, but today we keep silent.

Soon after we leave our school, he looks around for some reason and stops suddenly. "My shoelace," he mutters without looking at me. "You go ahead. I'll catch up." Instead of giving his briefcase to me, he sets it on the ground, gets down on his left knee, and begins tying his shoelace.

I walk alone for a while. Vovka's still behind me. What's the matter with him? How long should it take to tie a shoelace? I feel it's not by chance that he's dawdling over it for such a long time. He wants to fall behind me, to go home alone. For a second, I feel offended. Some friend! But suddenly I feel relieved. He's right—today it's better to walk separately. In the papers, Jewish names are always brought together. The papers hint that Jews cover up for one another, for whatever bad things they have done. In lines at the stores, Jews are also accused of making room for other Jews. Maybe, that's why Vovka tries keeping some distance between us. It's the survival instinct.

After a while, I turn around. Vovka's still bending over his shoelace. I catch him glancing in my direction. As he meets my look, he lowers his head, works with the shoelace again. I hurry home—now alone.

There, for some reason, the first thing I do is ask Papa about something that has already been clear to me, "M-m, Papa, what do you say? Is Vovsi a Jewish name?"

Papa is sitting at the table, *Pravda* in his hands. From time to time, he sighs deeply. On hearing my question, he fidgets in his chair for a while. "Yes," he finally says as calmly as he can and shakes his head in frustration. "Back in Minsk, I knew a Jew with that name."

TWENTY-FOUR

Time Like Glass

"THIS IS THE BBC. The latest anti-Semitic campaign has begun in the Soviet Union, a campaign that may have far-reaching consequences."

Later in the evening, Papa moves closer to our Grundig radio. The station's commentator speaks calmly, in a measured tone, as if letting you know that no matter how sensational the events are, you won't confuse him. He sounds encouraging, "It is hard to believe that Soviet generals and admirals, who rarely have health problems more severe than a light head cold, could fall victims of false diagnoses of the Kremlin doctors."

The broadcast comes to an end. A short time passes, and the calming effect of the radio commentary evaporates, like Novocain, administered before a tooth extraction, treacherously abandons your gums, and the pain that you hoped to have parted with forever resumes its pulsing. I am seized with anxiety again. Tonight, I fall asleep not as usual, that is, the instant my head touches a pillow, but with difficulty, tossing and turning for a long time.

I wake up way too early. Beyond the window, the skies are still ink blue. I cannot wait till dawn. To give myself time to read the newspapers, I leave for school earlier than usual. As frequently happens in Odessa, a short thaw suddenly arrives in the middle of winter. Garlands of icicles tumble to the ground from the roofs, producing thunder and scattering crust under the feet of passersby. Either because of the gusts of wind or the tension that I am under, I feel the cold more than usual. I wrap my throat with a woolen scarf. The wool bites. In search of *Pravda,* I hurry to a newspaper stand, and I feverishly reread the headlines. And I am relieved: nothing about the doctor-murderers.

But the next morning, bang!—*Pravda* publishes its editorial: "DOWN WITH EXTREME CARELESSNESS IN OUR RANKS." This is the very same phrase that ended the article about the "murderers in white robes."

I rivet my eyes on the text. I jump from line to line. Already familiar phrases about the intrigues of enemies, about extreme absent-mindedness, about the loss of vigilance. Now some example should follow, as is customary in a *Pravda* editorial. Aha, here it is. An incident in the Ministry of Non-ferrous Metallurgy. In that institution, they discovered two employees lacking vigilance—Korshun and Suleimenov. The surnames don't look Jewish. Thank God!

Three more days pass. In *Pravda,* nothing else connected to the murderous doctors appears. But in *Pravda Ukrainy,* in an editorial about swindlers in the state trade network, all the surnames are unmistakably Jewish. It's even worse than that; these surnames are used in the plural, that is, as generic surnames denoting entire nationalities: "All these Cohens and Goldbergs, Greensteins and Kaplans evoke the deep hatred of people." The purpose of this stylistic device is clear; people with such and similar surnames are one and the same.

Again, I become ill at ease. But I console myself with the thought that *Pravda Ukrainy* is just a provincial, not a national, paper. The main thing is what *Pravda* says.

"Well, you Komsomol member!" says Uncle Misha again, running into me at the door of our apartment the next morning. "Komsomol's a reliable assistant to the party, ah?" He likes teasing me by repeating ubiquitous propaganda slogans. "And, as everyone knows, the party's our helmsman. Do you already know that this bitch has been awarded the Order of Lenin?"

Though Uncle Misha and Papa still do not have work, he keeps coming to our place each morning; he wants to find out what news the foreign stations broadcast over our Grundig the night before.

I screw up my face at the word *bitch.* I am brought up on the great classics of Russian literature, works that know nothing of street language. But I already know to whom Uncle is referring. The night before, they announced over the government radio that, for her help in exposing murderous doctors, Doctor Lydia Timashuk has been awarded the Order of Lenin.

Papa condemns her right away: *"A farbisene khazeyrine!"* that is, "a furious pig." To my surprise, neither *Pravda* nor *Izvestiya* has published Timashuk's picture. Hmm, shouldn't the country know its heroes? But I am still able to picture her physiognomy, distorted from spite, her lips pursed. I have seen such facial expressions more than once—when looking at the anti-Semites shouting in the streetcars. (Many years will pass before I find out the truth about Dr. Timashuk; without her knowledge, the officials made her the central figure in the vile provocation, first awarding, then defaming her.)

Two more alarming weeks pass. Everyone expects something to happen at any moment. And true to their expectations, suddenly, in all the papers news appears about a bomb exploding on the territory of the Soviet Mission in Tel Aviv and the severing of diplomatic relations with Israel. Papa loiters around our apartment, pale, searching in vain for something to distract him from his agitation, bustling about from corner to corner. Mama launches into a general housecleaning mission. She wants to wash the whole stock of our bed linens. This is her way of overcoming her anxiety.

Nobody really knows exactly what happened in Israel, why the bomb was thrown and who threw it, but the gossips, smoldering since autumn, instantly blaze up in the city. According to them, a war with America will begin any time now, and, if not today, then tomorrow, you won't find any salt, soap, or matches in the stores. Everywhere extraordinarily long lines of prospective buyers begin growing.

In the big grocery store at the corner of Deribas and Preobrazhensky streets, there's no air to breathe. The stuffy air reeks of stale herring, the store workers' rubber boots, and the sawdust scattered all over the floor tiles. The buyers press themselves close against the store walls, clasping knit shopping bags and cardboard boxes to their chests. The line gushes out the store and extends to the end of the block.

With a white robe thrown around his shoulders, a bald undersized manager trips along the line. His military riding breeches show from under his robe. It looks like he is a retired quartermaster colonel. The manager's face has turned pink in agitation. Certainly, with such a crowd of buyers, he can have his monthly plan fulfilled in a few days, thus obtaining the award of the Challenge Red Banner and an increased bonus from the city authorities. But the sudden confluence of multitudes of people on the territory he is responsible for makes him nervous. Unable to decide whether to be pleased with the increased consumer demand or saddened by it, he trots along the line, anxiously peering into the shoppers' faces. Time and again, he cries out, his thin voice turned hoarse from strain, "No more than two bars of soap and ten boxes of matches per customer! No more!"

"What about salt?" someone asks.

"One pack per person, comrades. Only one! They called from the warehouse. They're short of trucks there."

Mama pulls me with her to the lines again. As always, I resist.

"You don't want to stay in the lines?" Mama says. "Maybe you don't want to wash yourself too? Or you're clean already as you are? Have you washed yourself once and for all?"

Each day I cling again and again to the glass of newspaper stands with the thoughtless frenzy of nails digging into a wound that is about to heal over. I read every word of the *Pravda* headlines. A review of the film *Maksimka (Maximka),* or Little Maxim. I saw this movie a month ago. It is a story about a group of Russian seamen who rescue a black boy from the hands of slave traders. One of the sailors becomes so attached to the boy that he adopts him. He gives him a Russian name—Maxim. I liked the movie very much. I even secretly envied the boy. If that Maxim were not a black boy but a Jewish one, would they fuss about him that much? Even in a wild flight of imagination, I cannot picture a movie with such a plot. And what would they call such a picture? *Abramka,* Little Abram?

"Oh! A guest!" Mama says, smiling when she sees her old girlfriend Tanya ("Aunt Tanya," as I call her) standing at the entrance to our apartment. "What is it?" Mama darts a glance at our old wall clock, its two pig-iron weights shaped as pine cones. "Is today your day off?"

"Yes," looking down, Aunt Tanya says after a pause. "Day off." Then she begins nodding, "Tomorrow's also a day off. And the day after tomorrow. I have ma-a-any days off now. Make merry as much as you want. What great luck has come my way!" However, she utters this without much enthusiasm, in a muted tone. She speaks quietly as if afraid to strain her aching throat. (I also talk that way when my throat is sore.)

Mama immediately seats the guest down at our table and then offers her tea.

The last days of February. I have just come from school. The sun is shining, and, probably in contrast with it, I notice at once that Tanya's face is unusually motionless and gloomy.

She starts blinking intensely, as if a gnat got stuck in her eye. From her purse, she pulls out a lace handkerchief and a plastic powder box. Her lips are unusually pale. The color is drained from her cheeks as well. Her eyebrows are also not penciled, as they usual are.

Aunt Tanya opens her powder box, looks in the pocket mirror, and blots the corners of her reddened eyes with the edges of her handkerchief. She tries to examine the harmful gnat closely. I have no time to ponder about where gnats come from in the middle of winter, before a muffled groan resounds from the chest of our guest. Dropping her powder box, Aunt Tanya presses her head into the crook of her arm resting on the table. Her hair spreads in disarray over her shoulders and back as she cries silently.

I jump up from my seat at the table out of surprise.

"Little Tanya, my dear!" Mama rushes to her girlfriend and grabs her shoulders. "Calm down! What's with you?"

Our guest cannot utter a word for a long time.

"Get out of here!" Mama tells me. "Put on the teapot!"

I am still dazed.

"Quickly! Who am I talking to!"

I am already fifteen, and I don't like being ordered around. But our guest's strange behavior frightens me, and I go into the corridor. Apparently, something truly extraordinary has happened. While I fill the teapot with water, I glance through the crack of the door and try to catch what they talk about at the table.

"Tanya, get hold of yourself," Mama sits down next to her girlfriend and hugs her. "Calm down. *Zoln zey ale geyn in drerd.* May they all go to hell!"

"I . . . I . . ."

"Calm down, calm down," Mama gives Tanya a glass of water. "Here, drink. Do you want some valerian drops?" She rushes to our first-aid kit. "You'll get a job at the ambulance station," Mama says confidently. "They're always short of doctors there."

"Well, all right," Aunt Tanya says at last, her voice constrained, "the bosses could dismiss me from work. I can understand that, if they are ordered to do so by the regional Health Management Office. They could cite my political unreliability. But mothers!" she catches her breath. "That's impossible to understand. Why? The very same mothers." Aunt Tanya waves her handkerchief in a short farewell gesture. "The very same mothers. Just recently they brought me flowers. Boxes of chocolate. Perfume on my birthday. I always tell them, 'You shouldn't do that.' After all, they're all poor people. No, they insist. I take their presents so as not to offend them. The very same mothers! Sonya, I always have lines of patients during my working hours at the clinic. I'm forced to linger at work almost every day. Sasha always pesters me, 'You have a child and me, your husband. You have a family. After all, you can't give everything to your work!' This morning, I come to the clinic and ask my nurse, a Russian woman, 'Zina, how many patients made an appointment for today?' And she says to me, her face red, ashamed, 'Tatyana Borisovna, no one.'"

Aunt Tanya swallows convulsively. Mama hastily brings a glass of water to her lips again, almost forcing her to drink.

"They're afraid!" the guest utters, gulping water mixed with her tears. "Do you understand? They're afraid to entrust their children to me. To me! Yesterday, I tell one mother, Stepanenko, 'Your little Polina has pneumonia. She's running a high fever. We have to hospitalize her at once.' And she says to me . . . She says to me . . ." Aunt Tanya sips some water from the glass before she continues, her voice hoarse: "And she replies to me, 'I'd rather let her die at home than in your hospital from poison.' It'd be better if she had driven a knife straight into my heart!" Aunt Tanya begins sobbing.

"Spit on them!" Mama says. "Phooey on their heads! Spit on them and forget about it."

"I don't understand," the guest continues. "After all, they know that I love their children. For me, somebody else's sick child is the same as my own child, as my Senya. Well, what should I do now? What? How can I live without them? How?"

"To hell with them!" Mama says. "You'll find another place for yourself. I have connections in the ambulance station. Nadezhda Viktorovna, the head physician there. She's a decent woman. I met her mother when we were both in line to buy Polish bras. I'll go to her right away," Mama says resolutely and looks at the clock. "I can still find her at work." Mama grabs her handbag and begins applying her lipstick.

"Sonya, what are you talking about?" Aunt Tanya says. "What ambulance? Who will take me there? In the City Hospital, they suspended the surgeon Dr. Feinblat from performing operations. Just like that. Without giving any reason. My acquaintance, Doctor Shamis—last year, we were together at advanced training courses in Kiev. An excellent gynecologist! An honored doctor. From year to year, he gets awards from the Ministry of Public Health for outstanding service. Yesterday, he submitted his resignation. One woman's husband—I don't know whether he was drunk or sober—told the doctor, 'If the child is stillborn or with any defect, you can only blame yourself. I know your people. Don't think that we're illiterate.

We read newspapers.' What's that supposed to mean, I'd like to know! How could his tongue move, saying such things? After all, we're doctors. How can they say such things? Yesterday, I passed by a line of people at our bread store. A neighbor from the second floor of our house was standing there. She knows me well. And she says to another lady, loudly enough for me to hear, 'Have you heard what *they* do? In the hospitals, they infect Russian babies with cancer. Under the guise of injections, they infect them with cancer bacillus.' What's that supposed to mean, I'd like to know! What savagery! How could they utter such nonsense?"

Aunt Tanya stays with us till evening; then she gets ready to go home. Mama sees her off to the streetcar. Already on her way out of our apartment, Mama suddenly turns around and tells me in a peremptory voice, "Milya, you stay put in my absence!"

"Why?"

"Because I say so."

Aunt Tanya's visit convinces Mama that her grounding me is justified. Since the day they published the article about the "murderers in white robes," she doesn't let me go anywhere, except to school. The moment I put on my windbreaker jacket she immediately asks me, "Where are you going?"

"To the library."

Mama nods in the direction of my bookshelf: "What about all these ones? Have you read them all already?"

"Yes."

"Read them once again. To remember them better."

"What for?" I am getting irritated. "It's not a homework assignment."

Realizing that she doesn't have enough reasons to keep me locked up, Mama casts aside any attempts to camouflage her prohibition. "No trips anywhere! After school, you must come straight home."

"But I—"

"No 'buts'! Haven't you heard what's going on in the city?"

"What's going on?" I mutter discontentedly.

"What, what? They expect pogroms any day now in Moldavanka."

Moldavanka is an area on the outskirts of the city. I rarely go there. The area exists for me mainly in the realm of folklore. Rough and uncouth people live in Moldavanka. When Mama condemns someone's lack of culture, she says contemptuously, "That Dvoira, though she lives on Theater Lane, she's totally Moldavanka. Phooey!"

"But that's Moldavanka," I say. "After all, we live on Deribas Street. In the very center of town!"

"As if *they* would be ashamed to do it downtown."

In a few days, I somehow manage to persuade Mama to let me go see my second cousin Yan, to play chess. I promise to come back home at the slightest sign of street disorder.

Yan and I sit at a dinner table in his little front room. They have no chess sets in the stores, so we play with small wooden checkers on which we drew chess characters in ink.

Suddenly, the front door flies open. Yan's mother, whom I call Aunt Dunya, bursts into the apartment. Her face is white. At first, I assume that it is because of the cold. Then I recall the thaw outside. There is slush in the streets.

Aunt Dunya goes straight to a bookshelf near the table. Not paying any attention to us, without a word, she begins convulsively pulling out books and throwing them onto the floor. I recognize the books. They are all in black jackets and written in Hebrew. They belong to Yan's grandpa.

Then Aunt Dunya rushes to the stove. She feels over all its nooks in search of matches. At last, she finds a box. She strikes matches, but they break in her shaking fingers. The matches that she manages to light die away on the spot.

Yan and I stare at each other in perplexity.

"What is it, Mom?" Yan says imperturbably, although with eyes wide open. (Coolness is one of his character traits I admire.) "What's happened?"

"What's happened?" my aunt Dunya asks as she keeps rushing now to the bookshelf, now to the stove, where the fire still refuses to catch. "What's happened? Trouble, that's what! *Vey iz mir-r-r! Vey iz mir-r-r!* Oy, what gr-r-r-ief!"

She has difficulty pronouncing the letter *R* when she is worried.

Yan's grandfather runs out of the adjacent room. As always, he wears a black skullcap and slippers. His white beard is all tangled up. He is taken aback as he stares at his daughter. His face shows bewilderment to such an extent that his eyes become very round, revealing the pink underside of his eyelids.

"*Oy, meyn Got!*" he shouts, throwing his milk-white hands, knotted with dark veins, up in the air. "What are you doing!"

"Because of you they'll ship all of us to Siberia!" Aunt Dunya shouts. "In freight cars. Like cattle! That's what you want? Yes? Tell me! That's what?

It's all because of you. Because of your books. You only think about them. You don't think of what would happen to all of us. To hell with us!"

Aunt Dunya snatches out the next book from the shelf and throws it into the stove.

"*Vey iz mir!*" Yan's grandfather cries out in an uncharacteristically loud and piercing voice, as if someone had thrust a knife into his heart. "What are you doing?" He lowers himself in front of the stove, squatting, and tries to pull out a book, which has flamed up in the fire. At last, he succeeds in retrieving it. Pages of Hebrew script flash by.

In the meantime, Aunt Dunya sets about grabbing another book from the shelf. Like a hockey goalkeeper desperately trying to catch a puck, Yan's grandfather kneels and waves his hands in the air, trying to rescue the book: "You want to kill me? Then kill me! I've already lived for a long time. But don't touch the books. Let me die in peace. These books mustn't die. God doesn't want it."

"God!" Aunt Dunya exclaims, tossing back her fluffed-up hair. "Where is he, your God, now? What, you don't know what's happening? For all of us—at the Odessa Tovar-r-naya Station—f-r-r-reight ca-r-rs are waiting. The whole city's already talking about it. You speak to God? Well, then ask him, What for? Ask! It's inter-r-r-resting what he'll tell you. One and all, just like cattle. To Siberia! Kazakhstan! Chukotka!"

Taking advantage of the commotion, I slip out into the streets and come back home so that Mama doesn't get disturbed by my long absence. Otherwise, she will ground me again.

True, such rumors have been circulating in the city since August of last year. Adolescents, we haven't been afraid that they will deport us to Siberia. It is just the adults' imagination. Certainly, there are anti-Semites, even a large number of them. It is not hard to become convinced of that after taking just one ride on a city streetcar. But suddenly, for no reason, to take our homes away from us just because we belong to the wrong nationality? This is completely crazy. On this score, the adults have obviously gone too far.

As if in response to this reasoning, Papa says to Mama once while sitting at the table, "You think for *them* it is such a big deal? Over one night, they moved the Crimean Tatars, the Kalmyks, the Chechens, the Ingush, the Greeks, and many others. Why not the Jews as well? What makes us any different?"

I regard his words with mistrust. I knew about the existence of most of the nationalities Papa mentioned only through books. I never read anything about their deportation. But the mention of the Greeks does disturb me.

A few years earlier—I was a fifth grader then—a tall and handsome man lived right under our room, in the second-floor apartment. He had dark long hair, with streaks of gray, reaching almost down to his shoulders, which was unusual in that immediate postwar, spartan time. I called him "Uncle Sasha." His surname was unusual. It was neither Russian, nor Ukrainian, nor Jewish; it was Kostanakis. Papa once explained it me: he was Greek.

Uncle Sasha was always dressed neatly and thoroughly shaved. His swarthy, olive face expressed a dignity, rather rare in those days; I always envied this quality in others and tried to cultivate it in myself. But my consciousness of belonging to the Jewish people interfered with it.

Uncle Sasha made a living as a draftsman. However, in his free time, he was an enthusiastic stamp collector. At that time, I was also fond of philately. Uncle Sasha helped me to put together my first collection. Extremely neat himself, he was irritated with the sloppiness of my little albums. I created these albums by cutting chubby accounting notebooks into halves, notebooks produced of poor-quality, brownish paper, the only suitable material for posting stamps I could find in our stores. Uncle Sasha patiently showed me how to handle stamps. The moment I touched them in his presence he screamed, turning away his head in disgust, "With your hands! Touching stamps with hands? Tweezers, only with tweezers!"

For Uncle Sasha, stamps were no less fragile and fancy creatures than African butterflies. He taught me to remove stamps from envelopes the right away: not by digging them up with my nail, which, to his horror, I did, but by preliminarily soaking them in warm water, as Mama did with mustard plasters before sticking them on my chest. After that, he removed the stamps carefully and placed them inside thick books until they dried.

My mentor's stamps were in ideal condition. Before giving me one of them, he planned for a long time which corner of the stamp to bring his tweezers to. His albums were of solid, prewar vintage, with sheets of tissue paper, behind which his chosen stamps were arranged, just like a bride under her veil. Unlike my primarily postwar, rather boring stamps, Uncle Sasha's were strikingly designed and brightly colored. His stamps were from the 1920s and early 1930s. (Many years passed before I found out that those stamps had been created by Russian avant-garde artists, at that time not all of them imprisoned yet or exiled.)

So, one day, as usual, on a Sunday afternoon, I took my little album to

Uncle Sasha. Sometime earlier, on my way to school, still a half a block from it, a middle-aged man with albums of stamps had appeared. Sitting on the iron hand-rail around some basement apartments, he sold his stamps to us schoolboys. I bought from him a few items that I needed to have a full set of one of the series. Then I hurried to see Uncle Sasha to brag about my lucky purchase.

An old lady opened the door, her face blurred from sleeping. Her unwashed nightshirt was barely covered by her dressing gown. Had I knocked on the wrong door?

"What do you want?" she said in irritation.

"Is Uncle Sasha home?" I was dumbstruck. I had never seen this old lady before. Maybe she was some relative visiting with him? But she was so strikingly untidy, so much unlike my friend, always groomed and always washed.

"There's no Uncle Sasha of any kind here," she slammed the door in front of my nose.

Perplexed, I returned home.

"It's entirely your own fault," Mama reproached me. "You're so secretive. Why didn't you tell me that you go to visit that man? I would have warned you. Him—well, last night your uncle Sasha left Odessa forever. He won't be coming back."

I didn't pay attention to my mother's slip of the tongue at the time. I didn't understand the terrible implications of "him."

"Why won't he be coming back?" I mumbled, having a hard time comprehending Uncle Sasha's sudden disappearance. "Where has he gone?"

Blood rushed to my face. How could Uncle Sasha have left forever, without saying good-bye? After all, we were friends.

"He's gone home," Mama abruptly told me. "To Greece. Don't ask anyone about him anymore. Understood?"

I felt deserted. I wasn't sociable. I didn't have many friends. Besides my relatives and my parents' friends, Uncle Sasha was my only adult friend. And suddenly, overnight, he disappeared. (A decade later, I learned that, to spare my feelings, Mama didn't tell me the whole truth—that, on Stalin's orders, over one night, they came for Uncle Sasha and other Odessan Greeks and sent them not to their homeland but to the Kazakh steppes.)

Rumors about the forthcoming deportation of all Jews to Siberia become more and more persistent. Mama's energetic nature cannot stand passivity. She goes to consult with her girlfriend Anna Ivanovna. Worried, Anna

Ivanovna takes Mama to Pirogov Street, where her mother, Katerina Ilyinichna, lives. She is nearly seventy years old. There is a mark of quiet northern nobleness on her face. Though she does not come from nobility—she is a daughter of a rural priest and, maybe, precisely because of that—Katerina Ilyinichna has a rare instinct for justice that serves as her compass in all life's storms.

"Here's what it is, Sofia Vladimirovna," she says. "Don't worry. We won't let them offend you. If this misfortune strikes, we'll hide you at our place. Then, we'll send you to our relatives, to the village. They live near Serpukhov, south of Moscow."

Katerina Ilyinichna's words rouse Mama even more. The prospect of travel into these faraway regions is real to her. She already considers what else, in addition to warm clothes, is necessary to take along. She repeats again and again that she would not swap Anna Ivanovna for any Jewish girlfriend.

"Take a leytyshe kristlekhe," she says. "She's truly a decent Christian. There are scoundrel Jews and there are decent Russians. I have to admit that."

A few more tense days pass. Time and again, Mama approaches the window of our apartment and, under the pretext of airing out our room, she now opens the small hinged pane, now tightly closes it. Taking care of things around the house, she heeds any sound coming from our courtyard. Once, catching the sound of some loud blows, she rushes to the window again. Then, with some relief, she moves away from it. Right after her, I look down, into our courtyard. Despite the frost, Filipenko, one of our neighbors from the ground floor, is chopping fire wood with no jacket on.

My parents' faces are sleepy in the mornings. Apparently, they sleep poorly at night. Sometimes, in the afternoon Mama cannot last; she lies down on a couch and covers her ears with a pillow.

Staying home is torturous for me. Once, so as not to arouse suspicion, I slip out of our apartment without putting my windbreaker jacket on, instead carrying it under my arm. I come out from the front door of our building. Pashka is standing to the left of me, in his usual place, leaning against a little fence. He smokes, clamping a cigarette between his fingers. For some time, he stares at me with his little eyes, cold and gray, like nail heads.

"So, big-nose," he spits through his teeth in my direction, "is it true that in drugstores they sell poisoned cotton padding to women? What will the poor things be corking themselves up with, ah?"

Pashka is like me, hardly more than fifteen; we are at the age at which female anatomy both excites and horrifies. It is the age when, for mean-natured males, a woman becomes a contemptible and horrifying though desirable creature at the very same time. Bookish young men, like me, run in the opposite direction: We push the female body away so that it soars above the earth for a long time; we are afraid to accept women for what they are—not angels, but also not devils.

I clench my fists inside my jacket pockets. I want to throw myself onto the bastard and bring all my hatred, now seemingly reaching its apogee, down on him. Everything in him disgusts me: his adolescent misogyny, his blunt anti-Semitism, his habit of spitting through the crevice of his teeth, far and with gusto. The vulgarity of all of his gestures, of everything low in people that I try not to notice, grates on me. Pashka probably senses my revulsion and tries, by teasing me, to provoke me into a fight.

Though I despise myself for my cowardice, I still can't bring myself to attack him. I lower my head onto my chest. There is a heavy frost. Trying to inhale superficially, not to chill my throat, I zip up my jacket and I leave the courtyard. I don't stop to choose which way to go. It is unimportant where I head, as long as I move as far away as possible from the cruel, dull, and vulgar world that surrounds me.

No breeze. The cold air seems like glass. And the time seems like glass as well: hardened but fragile at the same time, at any moment ready to scatter splinters, threatening everything living around.

TWENTY-FIVE

The Death of Stalin

"LOOK AT HIM," UNCLE MISHA says in Yiddish, appearing in the doorway of our one-room apartment. "What a time for you to fall sick. Along with Stalin!"

March 4, 1953. I'm in bed. I didn't protect my throat from the cold. I have difficulty swallowing. My fever is one hundred degrees—a good enough excuse for skipping school.

My uncle always teases me. Isn't he joking now? Some joke!

This news of Stalin's illness catches me off guard. In my consciousness, the words *sick* and *Stalin* don't belong together. For me, he's a bodiless being. If there's no body, what can be ailing? Our leader has rarely appeared in public, speaking only on special occasions. (At my age, I didn't yet know that he had avoided being photographed. Apparently, he felt self-conscious about his Georgian accent, his short stature, and his pockmarked face.)

On July 3, 1941, two weeks after Germany had attacked us, Stalin appealed to the nation over the radio. Since I was only three years old then, I haven't kept his voice in my memory. During wartime and a few years afterward, whenever I heard important government news read in the baritone voice of the Moscow radio announcer, it gave me the creeps. I was convinced that it was Stalin speaking. It didn't matter on whose behalf that solemn and measured voice spoke—the Soviet Information Bureau, the Politburo, the government, the Central Committee of the Communist

Party, or the Supreme Soviet. (I couldn't figure out the hierarchy of all those organs for a long time. All of them seemed synonyms for the highest, unconditional power over our lives. These reports seemed to come from the ultimate authority, subject to no discussion.)

The rareness of Stalin's public appearances has enhanced his mythology. He has been an unreal reality, like the heroes of Russian *byliny* and fairy tales—Ilya Muromets, Nightingale the Robber, or Kashchey the Immortal. Somehow Stalin has combined all three of them, evoking admiration, veneration, and trepidation at the same time. Now and then, Stalin's face has flashed in newsreels, his smile frozen, his hand raised in greeting, when he has been honored with parades on Red Square. Because of his mustache, it is hard to know whether he is smiling warmly or grinning mockingly. In portraits everywhere, he wears the modest khaki shirt of a Communist Party worker or the uniform of the generalissimo in full regalia.

Not much is known about him as a person—just that he wears comfortable Georgian boots and smokes his famous pipe and "Gertsogovina Flor" cigarettes, the most expensive in Russia. And female Young Pioneers present him with flowers during demonstrations on Red Square. Every time I come across a girl in a white blouse, with a red Pioneer tie on her chest and a big bow in her hair, I see her as a celebrity.

Three years earlier, I saw the film *Padenie Berlina (The Battle of Berlin)*. It shook me up, because the director had managed to reflect in it my own attitude toward Stalin. The movie's protagonist is Alexei Ivanov, a young Stakhanovite, a steelworker. The Communist Party secretary of his plant informs him that he has been invited to Moscow for a talk with Comrade Stalin.

Alexei turns pale. He's dumbfounded. When he regains his speech, he refuses to accept the invitation. "I won't go! I can't even imagine. I'm not cut out for it! What could I say?"

"What could you say?" the party secretary laughs. "He'll do the talking. And you only listen and absorb. You lucky dog! Such happiness befalls him, and he resists it!"

Listening to the party secretary's words, I couldn't figure out why Alexei has to go to Moscow. If all that Comrade Stalin wants him to do is to listen, can't he tell Alexei whatever he has to tell him over the phone? But Alexei is on his way. I was not prepared for what came next. I'd seen Stalin in other films—*Tretii udar (The Third Blow)*, *Stalingradskaia bitva (The Battle of Stalingrad)*, *Kliatva (The Oath)*. In all of them, he's in his official capacity. He speaks from a rostrum or bends over a military map and gives instructions to his marshals. Their mouths agape, they absorb his every word and venture to exclaim from time to time, "Remarkable!" "Excellent!" or something of that sort.

There are many such scenes in *The Battle of Berlin,* but another scene caught me off guard. I froze. For the first time, I saw the genius of all mankind without his usual regalia, as an ordinary citizen, resting in his dacha. The sleeves of his light jacket rolled up, Iosif Vissarionovich is standing in his garden. An ordinary shovel in his hands, he's tending to some little fruit trees. The sun is shining. Somewhere in the branches, birds burst into careless song. Stalin stops working, raises his face and smiles, listening to the birds. Off screen, female voices sing as if they were a chorus of angels.

Fear seized me. I slipped halfway down in my seat and covered my face with my hand. I just moved a finger so as not to miss what was coming on the screen.

On seeing Stalin, Alexei steps back. He tries to run away. He almost steps on his escort's feet and then nearly tramples down some rose bushes. Stalin, great and almighty—that's understandable. But for Stalin to be a simple mortal—that's too much for him.

"Hello, Vissarion Ivanovich!" Alexei finally utters in fright.

"That was my papa's name: Vissarion Ivanovich," Stalin corrects him softly. "And my name's Iosif Vissarionovich."

"Ah, I'll be damned!" Alexei says to himself. "I know, I know."

(Only many years later would I realize why the filmmakers—or, more to the point, Stalin himself—wanted Alexei to make such an implausible slip. Could any Soviet citizen ever forget the first and patronymic names of the "beloved leader and teacher"? This clumsy maneuver had one aim only— to let the masses know that, though Stalin, a Georgian, wasn't a son of the Great Russian people, he was their grandson at the very least, tied to them by blood. That was a deception. Stalin's grandfather's name wasn't Ivan, but Vano, a Georgian name that was Russianized in documents by the tsarist authorities, who forced Georgians to use the Russian language as their official state language—policies that Stalin reinforced on his own watch. Equally deceptive was Stalin's warm reference to his father—"my papa." Years later, I would learn that, in fact, he hated his drunkard father, who beat the living daylights out of him and his mother. It came to be generally accepted that much of Stalin's cruelty was caused by his displaced hatred of his father.)

In the film, noticing Alexei's shyness, Stalin chuckles. He begins talking to him as a father would talk to his son. He pats him on the shoulder. And

Alexei opens up to him as if confessing. He tells Stalin more than he would tell his own father—that he loves a girl and has trouble bringing himself to declare his love to her. And he gets Stalin's advice on his problem.

"Love her, and she'll love you in return," the leader says. "And if she doesn't, then write to me about it."

When I watched this movie, I was thirteen. Girls seemed to me touch-me-nots. And I envied Alexei. It would be good for me to have such an adviser on my side. As I understood Iosif Vissarionovich's words, it was in his power to make any woman take a strong liking to a man.

And now, March 4, sick with a sore throat, I'm lying in my bed. Uncle Misha leaves, and I switch on the radio. I hear the announcer's strange words: "hemorrhage taking over the brain area, the most important for life functions . . . paralysis of the right hand and leg . . . speech loss . . . disruption of heart and lung activity."

The name Stalin, uttered in this bulletin only once, seems to be included in this list of medical terms by sheer accident. Stalin and hemorrhage?

I listen carefully to each phrase: "up to 36 breaths per minute." Hm, is it too many or too few? Tucking my blanket under me, a compress on my throat—a towel moistened with vinegar—I sit up in bed. I try checking my own breaths. Lacking a stopwatch, I lose count. Then I come to my senses. What am I doing? Stalin and I! What has my breathing to do with Stalin's?

Every detail is confusing; "bloodletting by leeches has been administered." Can it be that they're curing Stalin in such an archaic way?

Perhaps because I'm running a fever, phrases of songs from my childhood are stuck in my head. In them, Stalin figures either by himself or in the company of his comrades-in-arms. "Comrade Voroshilov prepares us for the battles to come. . . . We'll meet our enemy as Stalin does."

(Many years later, when it became known how Stalin really met our enemy, these lines mocked us. Though warned many times by his own agents about German intentions, when he was told about Hitler's attack and lightning-fast capture of huge Soviet territories, of thousands and thousands of prisoners, our beloved leader fell into shock. Upset when Hitler attacked him without declaring war, he secluded himself in his office for about two weeks.)

"Er is fartik!" Uncle Misha says. "He's ready. Done. He's a 100 percent candidate."

What nonsense: Stalin is a candidate for the other world?

The news from Moscow stirs up not only Uncle Misha but all our other relatives and our friends as well. None of them has a telephone at home. First one, then another appears in our apartment under various pretexts. We live a stone's throw away, at the center of Odessa, in the middle of Deribas Street.

Aunt Clara and Uncle Abram are the first to come over. My aunt's eyes shine in alarm and yet a vague hope. Some twenty years ago, Uncle Abram studied at a veterinary school. He is supposed to have a good idea about brain and heart functions. What's his reading of the bulletin? Of course, Comrade Stalin and a calf are not one and the same, he says, but physically, like other mammals, they are ruled by the same laws of nature.

Uncle's words horrify me. How is it possible to relate the leader and teacher of all progressive mankind to the category of mammals! As always, my uncle speaks a bit aggressively, as if beforehand attacking those who disagree with him. But nobody is in the mood to argue. Everyone's silent.

"One thing's clear," my uncle says, "*es's nisht gut*. Things aren't OK."

Mama's friend Tanya, the pediatrician, comes in next, dark circles under her eyes, her face drawn. They haven't fired her, as they had some other doctors, after the case of the Jewish doctors, "the murderers in white coats," was made public seven weeks ago. But she doesn't do much at work. People still don't bring their children to her for fear she might poison them. She spends her days in an empty office, weeping and rewriting one old case history after another. Asked now about Stalin's health problems, she responds silently, with a wave of her hand—that is, his demise is just a matter of time.

Another night passes. In my consciousness, Stalin's image turns a bit human. I can manage the thought that Iosif Vissarionovich has been somewhat overworked. The morning broadcast announces, "Specific gravity of urine remaining normal, albumen and red blood cells discovered in it."

Another wave of doubt comes over me. Stalin and urine? Back in the second grade, we learned by heart these lines from one of the poems about Stalin in our reader:

Over the Soviet land,
The light won't be replaced by darkness:
Stalin the Sun shines above us.

What urine can the sun possibly have?

I've been convinced for a long time that Stalin is not a regular person but a giant whose head is of extraordinary capacity, like that of the huge pot that Zaporozhian Cossacks kept on the open fire—the kind they used to cook kasha for their whole fraternity. This belief began one day when, stopping for stamps at our post office on the corner of Lanzheron and Karl Marx streets, I saw a slogan stretched over the whole wall: "NO MATTER HOW BUSY I AM, EVERY DAY I MANAGE TO SCAN AT LEAST 500 PAGES." J. STALIN.

I realized my intellectual handicaps, and I shrank inside myself. And I'd considered myself a bookworm! "To be like Stalin is impossible," I'd read in one book, "but to learn from him, with each act bringing oneself in line with Stalin's teaching—that's the goal toward which one should aspire."

On the morning of March 6, I switch on the radio. The low note of a French horn. Chopin's funeral march. I hold my breath. It seems there's no end to the music pulling at my heart.

Finally, a radio announcer. Constantly stopping in order to swallow and take in air, his throat dried out from nervousness, he slowly rolls the words into the airwaves: "On March 5th, at 9:20 P.M., without regaining consciousness, our dear and beloved leader passed away." *Resigned before resumption of play*—a set phrase from chess championship reports flashes in my mind. "Pathological and anatomical studies confirmed the diagnosis by medical authorities who had examined Stalin."

(Many years would pass before I'd understand why it was necessary to confirm the initial diagnosis. Seven weeks before Stalin's death, they had reported the arrest of "the murderers in white coats." If the authorities hadn't assured people then, when Stalin died, that no sabotage was involved in his case, that he had expired naturally, the news of his death could have fired up unrest in the country.)

And so, Stalin the Sun has suddenly stopped shining. I look out the window and am not surprised that the sky is covered with clouds, heavy, unpleasant, the color of milk turned sour, frozen in place.

The next day, all the theater billboards nearby are pasted over with rolls of blank paper. And that's understandable: what kind of entertainment can there be when the great leader is dead? Small worried groups gather on the street corners. Often Odessans start up conversations without much reason, just to share their excitement about life. But now very little is spoken. The usual Odessan humor gives way to anxiety. If conversations do start, they're as haphazard as the clacking of pool balls by a rookie player. Before crossing the street, waiting for the green light, strangers exchange impressions of the day.

"It doesn't look good," some say. "With him, we at least knew what to expect. And what's going to happen now?"

"God willing," others say, "things will turn out all right. We've survived somehow so far. We might just be surprised and fare no worse in the future."

At the corner of Gavan and Deribas streets, leaning against the wall in utter exhaustion, his dirty shirt torn on his chest, some drunk shouts, "The damned kikes have poisoned Stalin! They've ruined our father!"

Nobody's stopping near him. Nobody feels like spending much time in the streets. Everyone hurries home, where everything's familiar. The same wallpaper with small flowery patterns, the same old dresser and wardrobe, the sagging couch, the bookshelf. The whir of the little primus stove and the whistle of the teapot are calming. Off, off the streets right now.

In the evening, we too sit silently around our dinner table and sip tea. Again, Uncle Abram and Aunt Clara come over. They bring with them their daughter, Eva, tears in her eyes. A big girl already, a seventh grader, she clings to her mama, who says that when the teachers told their classes about Stalin's death, all the girls began weeping. With a guilty smile, my aunt adds that Eva had joined them in thinking that war with America would start soon and that everyone would die of hunger.

Excited, his eyes rolling, my uncle Misha bursts into our apartment. He sits down at the table. Mama pours him tea, but he moves his glass, takes a half liter of vodka from his pocket, and bangs it down on the table.

"God himself has ordered us to wash down this news with alcohol. Let's have a shot. What do you say?" he asks my father. Then he turns to my mother, "Sonya, do you have any snacks left?"

What's with him? We've already had our dinner. In our house, vodka's drunk only on big holidays. As if answering my thoughts, my uncle looks straight into my eyes and explodes, "Today *is* a holiday. Yes! If you want to know, the greatest holiday you can imagine!"

"Shush, shush," Mama leaps up from her chair to make sure the windows are closed. She waves her hands in the air. As if goldfinches or canaries have somehow escaped from their cages, Mama is trying to keep my uncle's words from breaking loose beyond our apartment. "What's with you? Are you out of your mind? Why do you have to shout? Do you want to get us jailed? That's what you want?"

"What are you afraid of, Sonya? What? Haven't we been scared for too long? To drink to the dead is a custom. Let them think that we drink to the repose of his rotten soul!"

And then, without waiting for a shot glass, or snacks, or Papa's company, my uncle empties his tea glass, pours the vodka from the bottle, and, bottoms up, tips it into his throat. Then he bangs the table again with an empty glass and yells, "That damned Yoska! Let him lie there on a bed of needles! It serves him right!"

His words take my breath away.

"Yes, yes!" my uncle turns toward me. "They brainwash you in school. How many people has he killed for no reason! For that bastard, death isn't enough!"

I move away from the table into a corner. I have never heard such monstrous sacrilege. From my Komsomol viewpoint, my uncle is totally out of his mind. But so much sincere hatred and bitterness are in his voice that I hear truth in the ring of his words. This truth is frightening.

On March 7, the day after Stalin's death was announced, there is a knock on our door. It's Yuri, a district police officer.

"What's the matter, Yuri?" Mama asks the young man.

She's on friendly terms with him; he likes Mama. He is disarmed by her charm, though distrusting people is his professional duty. He often turns to Mama, who serves as our neighborhood representative. She volunteered for this work to channel her excess energy, to become an active member of society, not just a housewife. (As I realized years later, her desire to be in contact with the agencies of Soviet power also served her as a means of learning what they had in mind and, if possible, of preventing any blows to our family.)

"Well, Soybel Wolfovna," Yuri says. "You have a birthday coming up in your family, don't you?"

The way Yuri addresses Mama tells me that the officer is about to tell her something important. Usually, when he expects Mama's cooperation, he calls her by the name all our neighbors use—Sofia Vladimirovna, that is, by the Russian variant of her first and patronymic names. Addressing her according to the Jewish name in her ID papers, Yuri seems to underscore the strictly official character of his visit.

Mama is not used to responding right away to representatives of Soviet power. She waits for a few seconds. "W-well, let's assume it's true that tomorrow my younger son's going to be five."

"There must be no celebrating. The leader has died. Is that clear?"

I'm taken aback. Is it possible that Mama has become such close buddies with this police officer that she tells him about all our family events? I still have no idea that he is not actually questioning her about my brother's birthday, that his question is merely a ploy to deliver his warning. (A district police officer along with an apartment house caretaker, or *dvornik*, were the strongholds of the totalitarian regime. Everything about everybody was made known to the authorities. Our residence permits in the building register recorded our birthdays. Whether Yuri had received a directive from a local authority or orders had come from Moscow, or he himself decided that, when the leader died, the country should stand at attention—this would remain a mystery for me.)

"*Kushn mir in tokhes,*" Mama says as soon as the door closes behind Yuri. "Kiss my ass. This little twerp is going to tell me what I should do in my own home? Light the stove," she tells me. And right away she starts kneading dough for her celebrated napoleon birthday pastry.

On Monday, March 9, as soon as I get to school, they announce that all classes are canceled for the day. But we can't go home. Light trucks with collapsible benches inside arrive at the school entrance, and all high school seniors are ordered to board them.

They take us across the city to Kulik Field, a vast space beyond the railroad station. It's unpleasant there, empty, windy. Usually, before the First of May and the October holidays, they build temporary grandstands here so that local party bosses can receive parades of garrison troops and the demonstrations of city workers. People never come here on their own. Anyone winding up nearby walks past, just as experienced hikers avoid marshy places.

The field turns blue with police raincoats. We jump off the trucks. I land quietly because I'm wearing the pride of my fatherland's production—galoshes with red fleecy linings from the Moscow factory *Krasnyi treugol'nik* (the Red Triangle). According to our newspapers, these galoshes are the best in the world. It seems that, before the first Sputnik appeared, they were the only Soviet product that set world standards. But I hate galoshes in general. I see them as meant for old men. The day has promised to be wet, and Mama has insisted that I wear them. Usually, to avoid conflict with her, I put them on but remove them at school and shove them under my desk. Today I couldn't get rid of them in the usual way.

Their noses red from the cold, the police line us up—all the Odessan high school seniors—opposite the grandstands, where there is a huge picture of Stalin, almost two stories tall, framed with branches of spruce and black ribbon. The grandstands are still empty; the party bosses are late. But the aluminum faces of the huge loudspeakers are aimed at us; they will broadcast the ceremony from Red Square.

The funeral march lowers our morale, which isn't great to begin with.

The nasty weather of the early Odessan spring is depressing. It's cold and damp. A penetrating wind whistles in our ears and tears off the policemen's caps. We stand, our eyes downcast. This seems proper not only at a funeral (even a virtual funeral) but also because we don't dare raise our eyes to meet Stalin's all-penetrating gaze. It seems that even his portrait is an X-ray machine capable of seeing through us. What if he decides that the sorrow in our souls is not what it should be—that is, not total, not overwhelming, not altogether unbearable?

We are starting to get chilled when, finally, sparkling with the radiators' silver grills, black limousines roll up to the grandstands. The Odessan party bosses in their durable black coats alternate with the generals in their tall hats of gray lambskin topped with red. They line up in the stands. They look not at us but somewhere up there, at the sky covered with damp clouds.

The first voice heard from Red Square is Malenkov's. I've seen his picture at the *Pravda* newsstand near my school. I haven't yet formed an opinion of him, haven't noticed anything special about him, except that he looks young. Fighting the boredom that has already taken hold, I try to tune in to his speech. But I soon give up. No matter how I try, my brain begins to spin over the surface of worn-out words: "Deep sorrow in our hearts . . . The gravest, unrecoverable loss . . . The greatest genius of mankind . . . His name will live in the ages . . . Our sacred duty."

When, after Malenkov, Beria begins to drone on and on, I'm really tired and chilled to the bone. And when it's Molotov's turn to talk, I switch off altogether. The speeches seem endless. "He forged friendship among peoples . . . As a result of his tireless efforts . . . To develop an indissoluble tie with the people . . . To guard his legacies as the apple of one's eye . . . In the spirit of infinite devoted service to our people . . . Let's close ranks even tighter around the Central Committee of the Communist Party and the beloved Soviet government."

No matter how I stamp my feet, I'm freezing. I've just been home with a sore throat. Could I be sick again?

Yes, I could. When I go home, I'm running a temperature. Mama sends me to bed right away. She starts to concoct *gogol'-mogol'*, her favorite homemade remedy of hot milk, butter, egg yolk, and sugar. I hope Mama won't add baking soda, as she usually does. Then her *gogol'-mogol'* becomes unbearable for me.

But everything works out fine. Maybe on the occasion of the death of the leader of all progressive mankind Mama takes pity on me. Maybe she is confused. Anyway, she forgets about the baking soda. Her concoction turns out to be tolerable. And, in a mysterious way, it even calms me down.

A few days later, I learn from the BBC that I wasn't the only victim of those long funeral speeches. Klement Gottwald, the leader of the Czechoslovakian Communists, has just died as a result of his exposure to the cold. Of course, now I can only guess what happened. He forced himself to endure the cold while standing for two hours, through the whole funeral. Moscow on the day of the funeral was even colder than Odessa. (Years later, I figured out that Gottwald had probably recalled the recent execution of his predecessor, Rudolf Slánský, accused of treason for no apparent reason. Suffering from his chill, Gottwald may not have dared to leave the funeral before its end. Such a move could have been read as a kind of dissent.) On his return to Prague, he fell ill, and in a few days he died. A source of consolation for him would have been the appearance of his picture on *Pravda*'s front page, where he was called "a faithful follower of Stalin." Faithful indeed. Unto death.

But from the same broadcast, I also learn that many Russians died that day, but one would look in vain for their obituaries in *Pravda*. On the day of Stalin's funeral, thousands of weeping Muscovites—men, women, and children—rushed to Red Square to say the last good-bye to their leader. The crowd grew uncontrollable. Hundreds were trampled to death.

In Odessa, I get off with a sore throat.

Epilogue

"*NISHT GEKHERT GEVORN*," Uncle Misha says. "That's unheard of. That those bastards would ever apologize? It's a miracle!"

After Stalin's death, the anti-Semitic articles in the papers disappear, and in a month, on April 4, those doctors implicated in the "heinous crimes against our leaders" are fully rehabilitated.

As soon as she hears the news, Anna Ivanovna comes to us with a big Kiev cake that she bought after standing in line for almost half a day. She rejoices enthusiastically, as if not only our family but her own as well had been in danger of being exiled to Siberia. Proud of her Russian girlfriend, Mama tells our relatives about this visit for a long time and repeats that she would never trade Anna Ivanovna for any Jewish girlfriend.

Uncle Misha appears with a newspaper in his hands. He sits down at the table and reads aloud the report of the Ministry of Internal Affairs one more time. He reads it solemnly, as if it were an ode by the great eighteenth-century Russian poet Gavriil Derzhavin.

"Those bastards!" he bursts out, hardly finishing his reading. "They've ruined one of them, after all!"

"How do you know that?" I ask.

"How, how? See for yourself, if you don't believe me. Here it is, in black and white!"

I reread the report. Uncle Misha always invents things! Whom have they ruined? There is nothing like that in the paper.

"Give it to me, *shlimazl*," Uncle Misha takes the paper back. "What a clod! What the heck do they teach you in your school? Do you see the names of the released?"

"Yes."

"Haven't you noticed anything?"

"What should I have noticed?"

"Some honor student! You should have noticed a lot. First, don't you see that those sluts—." My uncle sees me blushing, and he corrects himself, "Pardon, those bitches. Don't you see that those bitches are still pulling the wool over your eyes? That they don't admit the doctors were arrested on the basis of their nationality alone? They are washing their hands after the fact. Look here! In January, they said that they had jailed nine people: judging by surnames six Jews and three Russians. And now they've released fourteen: five Jews and nine Russians, that is, more Russians than Jews. Correct? Naturally, the first question that comes to mind is this: How has it turned out that more doctors are released than were originally jailed? How does it go in the textbook for the first graders? 'They poured nine buckets of water into a barrel and they've poured out fourteen buckets.' Nonsense! So, how could such a thing possibly happen? Only if the barrel wasn't empty to begin with. Therefore, it's one of two things. Either they arrested more Russians than Jews but announced that there were more Jews among the 'murderers.' What for? Oh, it's not much mystery here: to let everyone know what to do. As the slogan of the Black Hundred, that group of prerevolutionary Russian anti-Semites who incited the pogroms, goes, 'Beat the kikes to save Mother Russia!' Or, to put up a bold front, they lie now about initially arresting more Russians than Jews. That is, the Jewish doctors weren't the main target; they were arrested incidentally. Now do you understand?"

I still have difficulty getting his point, and my uncle sticks *Pravda* under my nose again, "Do you see here? Except for Vinogradov, Maiorov, and Egorov, they've released six more people with Russian-sounding names: Vasilenko, Zelenin, Preobrazhensky, Zakusov, Popov, and Shershevsky. Where did they come from? The papers never informed us that they had been arrested in the first place. Perhaps, they were jailed later and for another reason. Or, maybe these doctors don't even exist at all! Wait till they tell you the whole truth and nothing but the truth. One thing's clear; now these swine are trying to cover up their tracks. They kicked up the whole world's heels, and now they want to assure us that they cooked up the 'Doc-

tors' Plot' not the least bit to kindle hatred toward the Jews. Therefore, now they're trying to make everyone believe that the majority of the prisoners related to this case were ethnic Russians. They are protecting their uncle Joe, their godfather, posthumously. And themselves at the same time. His corpse stinks already in the mausoleum, under the glass, and they still . . ."

I imagine Stalin as a stinking corpse and recoil.

My uncle adds with fervor, "Yes, yes! What do you think? They threw his innards to the dogs at the garbage pit, and they stuffed his repulsive skin with chemicals. The old bastard is no more than memories, and they're still afraid of him. All of them, all of his gang." Uncle Misha motions upward, to the ceiling, "They're no better than he was. How many people have they ruined? And now they're forced to admit that they tortured to death one of the Jewish doctors."

"What doctor?" I utter mistrustfully, once again scanning the article. "Where do you see it?"

"Some honor student!" My uncle brings the newspaper almost to my nose. "Your head doesn't cook well at all. Look here! There are two Kogans on the list of the arrested, one B. B. Kogan and another M. B. Kogan. But, in the list of the released, there's only one of them—B. B. And where is the second Kogan? Where is M. B. Kogan, I ask you? Even a baby would get it. They haven't let him out because there is no M. B. Kogan anymore. They tortured that man to death. Don't you see it? They themselves admit it: 'The wrong means of interrogation were used on these prisoners.' Do you know what that means?"

I'm silent. I don't fully understand what the article implies.

"It means," my uncle says in a mockingly ordinary voice, as if talking about brushing his teeth and washing up in the morning, "they drove needles under their nails. They gripped their fingers in a vise. They banged on their kidneys. They gave them electroshock. Eh-eh-eh, you're still too young to know all these things. The conclusion's clear: M. B. Kogan couldn't endure it. That's why there's no mention of him in the last report. After all, they tortured professors, as a rule, elderly and decrepit people. Even robust young men cannot last in their hands for too long, and here you have fragile intellectuals. Eh, eh, eh. And all of you got so softhearted here, 'Thank God, thank God!' Mark my words. They still will show themselves, all these dogs of the Stalin pack."

Soon after this conversation, I again run into Pashka in our courtyard. He sits on the handrail of the little pig-iron fence near the front door of his entrance hall and smokes a cigarette clasped in his fist.

"Well, it looks like you Yids have tricked your way out of it this time," Pashka shouts, spotting me. "But your American Joint Jewish Appeal is still out there, isn't it? It's still scheming!"

Blood rushes to my face. My fists clench by themselves. I lower my head and dash toward him. Apparently, Pashka never anticipated that I would be capable of such a thing. I ram his belly with my head. Out of surprise, he screams, "Ouch!" and nearly falls from the handrail onto the grating of the basement window well. I am about to attack him again, but, at the last minute, he dodges me and runs up the stairs of his entrance hall.

I dash after him. I hear nothing around me except my own feverish breathing and quickened heartbeat. The rage and offense overflow me. I don't want anything else in the whole wide world besides catching up with Pashka and punishing him. Not only for today's prank, but for everything, for everything.

Already at the door of his apartment on the third floor, he presses hard on the push button of the bell. I catch up with him finally and begin banging my fists all over his back first. When he tries to stop my thrashing and turns around, I box his face. The whites of Pashka's eyes rush in front of me in fear. He defends himself, putting his hands in front of himself and trying to push me away.

"Seryoga!" he shouts, calling his older brother, a college student, for help. "Seryoga!"

As soon as the door opens slightly, Pashka manages to scamper inside. His brother comes out wearing a T-shirt. Boulders of muscles move under his freckled skin. I recall that Pashka once bragged that his brother was a weightlifting champion of his Polytechnical Institute.

"What's this noise without a fight?" he says, but I already roll down the stairs.

Only after I catch my breath and come to my senses do I figure that Pashka could easily have beaten me up. He is head and shoulders above me, and his muscles are bigger than mine. That day, for the first time, I understand that, to win, more strength is not necessary, only more rage and hatred for the enemy.

On Sundays, Papa still listens to his prewar recordings of Yiddish songs, one after another. Gradually, I begin to understand the lyrics. These unpretentious ditties touch me with their warmth. One of them is about a young man by the name of Izzy. This name still irks me; in the streets, they use this name to taunt Jewish boys. But, listening to this song, I smile involuntarily:

Di mame meg shoyn visn,
Mom can be told already,
Der tate meg shoyn visn,
And Daddy can be told already,
Az Itsikl hot khasene gehat.
That Izzy already has gotten married.
Oy, Itsikl hot khasene gehat.
Oy, Izzy already has gotten married.
Oy, Itsikl hot khasene gehat.
Oy, Izzy already has gotten married.

In another song, a pensive girl's voice inquires with hopeless sadness, "Where am I to get flour for my dumplings *(varnechkes)*?" (Mama notices that I heed these words and remarks, shaking her head in sympathy, "Poor folks lived in those shtetlach.")

In the second stanza, the singer complains that she has trouble getting butter for her dumplings. Then, when she solves this problem too, she asks around for some salt and pepper. At last, the singer manages to find all the ingredients for her dumplings. And they've come out marvelously. But the maiden's voice is still sad, "Yes, my dumplings are all right. You can lick your fingers. But where, where should I find . . . a guy to eat my dumplings?" It turns out that the song is not so much about a poor girl's culinary woes as about her longing for love.

I like this song. From time to time, I already secretly crave love for myself. I listen to the Yiddish songs with ever-growing eagerness and pleasure without realizing yet that through them I'm gradually filling myself with the spirit of my people.

"Have you heard this one?" Marshak asks, his olive eyes sparkling. Everyone grows quiet, anticipating the pleasure of hearing some new joke. "Shortly after Yoska died, *eyn alter yidlik,* one little old Jew, small, half stooped, big bearded, approaches Spassky Tower on Red Square and addresses the sentry at the entrance to the Kremlin." Marshak raises his shoulder, crooks his mouth, closes one eye, and instantly turns into a stooped old Jew.

It is June 4, 1953, Mama's birthday. At the same time, it is also a housewarming party. With some extra cash paid to the previous owner, Papa managed to exchange our old one-room apartment for a new, more spacious one, located at 21 Lanzheron Street, just around the corner, some two blocks from our former residence. We are pleased with the exchange. True, it is a ground-floor apartment and, because it used to serve as the building's laundry, it's damp. But, instead of one room for all of us, we now have two rooms. One room is bright, thanks to two big windows opening into the courtyard. If you don't want to be examined like fish in an aquarium, you have to keep your curtains lowered during the day and close the shutters at dusk. Another room, which serves as a passage to the other, is dark. My five-year-old brother and I sleep on little couches there, fencing ourselves off with tall bookcases. Our parents' sofa is located in the bright room, which, at the same time, serves as both our dining room and our living room. That's why their sofa is a foldout. Also, we have a kitchen with a single little window, which Papa has cut through the wall. (We can fling open that window only when a piece of rag in the kitchen catches fire; on the other side of the wall is a passage to the courtyard restroom.)

As always on Mama's birthday, the apartment is packed to capacity; everybody comes—all our relatives, Papa's and Mama's friends and a few of our neighbors. There aren't enough chairs. On the far sides of the expanded table, we position stools and place planed boards between them. We save these boards for such occasions and keep them in our tiny shed in the back of our building.

Everyone's mood is better than it was during the winter. At Aunt Tanya's office, lines of patients have stretched out again; mothers have begun bringing their children to her again. She is glad, but a bitter crease has forever lodged around her mouth.

At the table, all they talk about is the "Doctors' Plot" and Stalin's death. Did he die by himself, or did somebody help him? Aunt Dunya reports that her father, Yan's grandpa, is convinced that it was not by chance that Stalin died on Purim, the ancient holiday of deliverance of the Jews from their planned doom. The Russian tsar Nicholas the First, who forced Jews to serve in the Russian army from early childhood, to renounce their faith and eat pork, also died on Purim. I'm skeptical about this reasoning. If Purim has the power to destroy the enemies of Jewish people, why then did the most furious enemy of the Jews, Adolf Hitler, enjoy immunity against him? He died on the last day of April, two full months after the Jewish holiday that year.

"And so," Marshak continues, wrinkling his flattened nose in a funny way, "a little old Jew comes to the Kremlin and he says to the sentry, 'Please, may I have a word with Comrade Stalin?' 'What are you, from another planet?' the sentry replies."

Marshak makes a dull face, portraying the sentry. " 'Don't you know that Comrade Stalin is dead?' 'Excuse me please,' says the old Jew and leaves.

"In about twenty minutes, he comes back: 'Excuse me again a thousand times, but I do have very urgent business to discuss with Comrade Stalin.' 'Are you making fun of me? Is that what it is?' the sentry shouts. 'I've told you already: Comrade Stalin has died.'

" 'Oy, pardon me, please pardon me, comrade sentry.' *Der yidlik* again leaves. Then he comes back again, 'I beg your pardon many, many times, very fine comrade sentry, but I have very, very, very pressing business to discuss with Comrade Stalin.' 'Ah, you kike's mug! You're driving me crazy! I'm telling you for the umpteenth time: Comrade Stalin is dead, dead, dead!' 'Oy, may you live to a hundred twenty years, comrade sentry! I'm so grateful to you. You can't even imagine how much I'm grateful to you! I just can't hear this news enough!'"

The room explodes in raucous laughter. It seems that the joke expresses everybody's feelings about Stalin's demise.

Dinner is finished. We carry the boards out of the room and move the table against the wall. The dances begin. First, Papa puts an old record of *Freylekhs,* a Jewish wedding score, on the player. Then comes a jolly dance tune called "Seven-Forty," or as Mama calls this cheerful melody, "From the Bridge to the Slaughterhouse." Then "Tum-balalaika." The spirit of dancing music, free, even somewhat unceremonious, infects me as well. Despite my patronizing attitude toward this shtetl, that is, backward, music, no match for the refined quadrilles and mazurkas of classical ballets I hear on the radio, my feet begin beating in time to the music. Its tempo increases, first slowly, then faster and faster. It's tough to stay seated:

Tum-bala, tum-bala, tum-balalaika!
Tum-bala, tum-bala, tum-balalaika!

I can hardly keep myself from breaking into a dance. The music's happy mood disarms me. The serious learned person with eight years of education in the Soviet school system, the most progressive in the world, abandons me. A wedding melody rumbles. The uncontrollable merriment of people

that, even at the moment of a wedding, cannot keep from laughing at themselves, takes me along:

> *Svad'ba veselo idet*
> The wedding cheerfully goes on,
> *Zhenikh sidit, kak idiot,*
> The groom sits like an idiot,
> *A rodichi zhenikha*
> And the relatives of the groom
> *Pliashut—gop-kha-kha!*
> Dance—hop-ha-ha!
> Hop-ha-ha!

Glancing from time to time at the windows (though the shutters are closed
to stave off unwanted gazes, the curious people can always bring their ears
close to them), Marshak stops acting and begins singing. He moves his eyebrows and claps, inviting everyone to join in:

> *Lomir ale in eynem, in eynem,*
> Let's all together, together,
> *Lomir ale in eynem, in eynem,*
> Let's all together, together,
> *Trinken a bisele ve-e-yn.*
> Drink a tiny bit of wine.

First timidly, also looking back at the shutters, then louder and louder, everybody around the table begins singing along. The wrinkles on their faces
straighten out, their lips stretch into smiles, and their eyes grow dim recalling the former, prewar era of their native lands left behind forever:

> *Lomir ale in eynem, in eynem,*
> *Lomir ale in eynem, in eynem,*
> *Trinken a bisele ve-e-yn.*

I catch myself smiling too. I am still far from being one with my people. I
still distance myself from things Jewish, though I feel that my internal alien-
ation from them is both futile and ridiculous. Sitting at the table with the
rest of the guests, hearing how a tune of hope and an appeal to brother-
hood breaks loose from the depth of the souls of those who are singing, I
cannot control myself. My palms begin clapping by themselves in time to

the song. Many ordeals and bitter insights are still in store for me. More than once, life's sorrows will come back to haunt me. More than once, the sense of hopelessness will visit me, hopelessness that, eventually, will force me to leave forever the country in which I was born and grew up.

But all this is still ahead of me. For now, without asking my permission, my feet start moving by themselves in time with the music. And when once again "The wedding cheerfully goes on!" resounds from the record player and the guests, one after another, form a circle on the floor, I can't stand it any longer. I tear open someone's linked hands and interlock them with my own. The music rattles, and, forgetting my body, I dash off in a dance. I suddenly discover that my feet produce all the needed dance steps by themselves. I place my hands on my hips, and I put my fingers in the armholes of an imagined vest, and I clap my hands, and I twirl my hand above my head in the triumph of delight. In the synchronized stomping of feet, I rush about in a circle and, as long as the dance lasts, I am happy. Oh, if only it were possible to live without stopping the dance, there would be no sorrow in the world! I'm convinced that this idea arises in my head. But it turns out that these are the words from the song composed by the people from whose centripetal whirling I cannot escape. At this moment, I don't even think of trying.

I'm dancing, and everything that has been my life in those distant years rushes past me in a whirlwind: a brush in his hand, Papa on top of his ladder; Uncle Misha with a sprayer; Mama with bed sheets beating in the wind; Uncle Abram with cupping glasses; Yan with a chessboard; his grandpa with the Bible pressed against his chest. Zhenya rushes by, holding a model of a steam engine. Liza, her light ringlets curling in the wind—Liza, with whom I will never speak again.

An invisible wind picks all of them up. They come off the ground and fly into space, higher and higher. They squint at the sun, drink tea, and read newspapers. They argue with one another; they hug one another, they laugh and cry. And, together with them, my youth, my painful entry into the world, the torturous sting, my desperate desire to understand who I am—all of these rush by me, leaving me staring into the distance, alone with my memories.

Marshak is singing, and, still covering my mouth with my hand, so that others don't see, for the first time I join in singing together with everybody:

Lomir ale in eynem, in eynem,
Lomir ale in eynem, in eynem,
Trinken a bisele ve-e-yn.

my genealogical tree

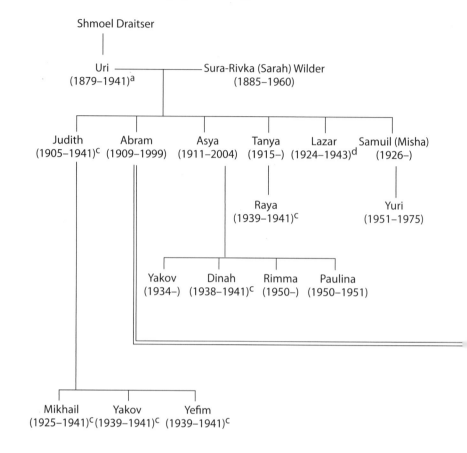

Shmoel Draitser

Uri ——————————— Sura-Rivka (Sarah) Wilder
(1879–1941)[a]   (1885–1960)

Judith   Abram   Asya   Tanya   Lazar   Samuil (Misha)
(1905–1941)[c] (1909–1999) (1911–2004) (1915–) (1924–1943)[d]   (1926–)

Raya   Yuri
(1939–1941)[c]   (1951–1975)

Yakov   Dinah   Rimma   Paulina
(1934–)   (1938–1941)[c] (1950–)   (1950–1951)

Mikhail   Yakov   Yefim
(1925–1941)[c] (1939–1941)[c] (1939–1941)[c]

[a]Stabbed to death by German troops in Minsk.
[b]Perished in the Odessa ghetto.
[c]Perished in the Minsk ghetto.
[d]Killed during the Battle of Kursk.
[e]Died during the Petliura pogrom in Uman'.

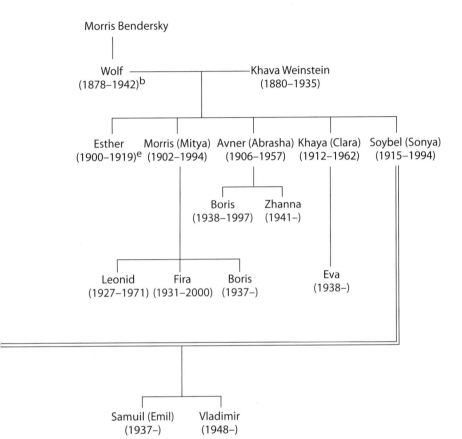